GET THE LED OUT

{ HOW LED ZEPPELIN BECAME THE BIGGEST BAND IN THE WORLD }

{ Based on the Hit Radio Show }

{ DENNY SOMACH }

{ FOREWORD BY CAROL MILLER }

STERLING
New York

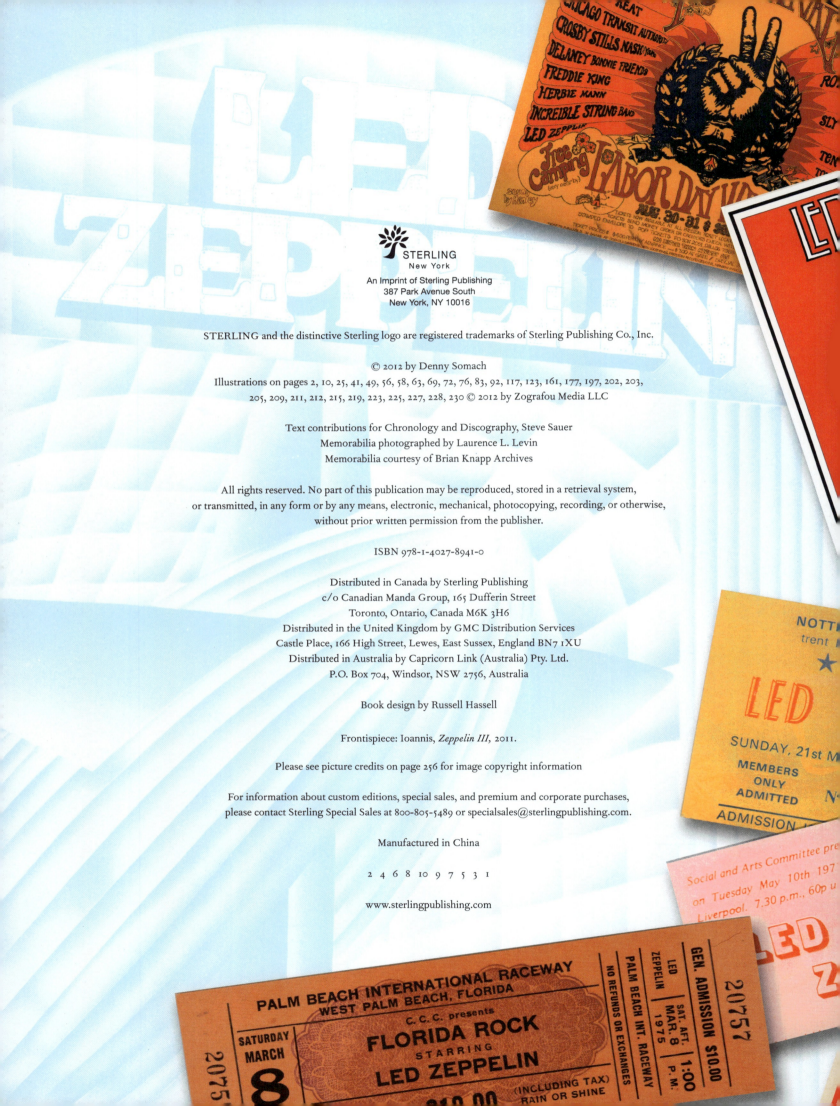

STERLING
New York

An Imprint of Sterling Publishing
387 Park Avenue South
New York, NY 10016

Text contributions for Chronology and Discography, Steve Sauer
Memorabilia photographed by Laurence L. Levin
Memorabilia courtesy of Brian Knapp Archives

ISBN 978-1-4027-8941-0

Distributed in Canada by Sterling Publishing
c/o Canadian Manda Group, 165 Dufferin Street
Toronto, Ontario, Canada M6K 3H6
Distributed in the United Kingdom by GMC Distribution Services
Castle Place, 166 High Street, Lewes, East Sussex, England BN7 1XU
Distributed in Australia by Capricorn Link (Australia) Pty. Ltd.
P.O. Box 704, Windsor, NSW 2756, Australia

Book design by Russell Hassell

Frontispiece: Ioannis, *Zeppelin III*, 2011.

Please see picture credits on page 256 for image copyright information

For information about custom editions, special sales, and premium and corporate purchases, please contact Sterling Special Sales at 800-805-5489 or specialsales@sterlingpublishing.com.

Manufactured in China

2 4 6 8 10 9 7 5 3 1

www.sterlingpublishing.com

CONTENTS

❦ *FOREWORD* ❦

As a Yardbirds fan, I had been waiting to hear Jimmy Page's new project. "It's here!" said my college buddy Glenn, as he raced into the lobby of the girls' dorm holding a bag from Jerry's Records in Philadelphia. The grayish white cover, the photo of the doomed Hindenburg—this was going to be heavy.

From the first sonic assault, as the needle hit side one, cut one, I had never heard anything of this intensity before. The thunderous chords, and the otherworldly voice: "In the days of my youth, I was told what it means to be a man . . ." Another cut, with an ominously descending scale, as the voice sang, "Been dazed and confused for so long it's not true; wanted a woman—never bargained for you!"

It didn't matter that I was a girl, and I wasn't exactly sure what these guys meant. Led Zeppelin was conveying something way bigger and more cataclysmic than their lyrics. The whole was greater than the sum of its parts. The band was a massive, dangerous, and thrilling force, and I'd probably be afraid to meet them. But I would become a lifelong fan. Just like you.

I started my professional career on FM rock radio at WMMR in Philadelphia at the end of 1971, and Led Zeppelin was there with me from my very first show. *Zeppelin IV* had just come out, and I had the privilege of premiering all the band's subsequent releases on WPLJ and WNEW-FM in New York.

In the early eighties, as the radio landscape was changing, it became more obvious than ever that Led Zeppelin defined the rock format. I began doing a feature called *Get the Led Out*, playing a long set of Zeppelin every weeknight, and while I can't claim to be the first with this phenomenon, I'll betcha I've been doing it the longest—nearly thirty years. During this time, I joined Sirius/XM Satellite Radio, and met and interviewed Jones, Page, and, more frequently, Plant, who has often been on the air promoting a solo project. (The guys didn't scare me anymore.)

When I moved to Q104.3/New York's Classic Rock in 2004, so did my new and improved *Get the Led Out*. Now I wrote and narrated a minute of Zeppelin history, which was aired along with the music, and *GTLO* began running twice a day.

Enter Denny Somach, a noted radio producer, syndicator, and archivist, who called to suggest that he add the great exclusive musical sound bites and interview elements from his extensive library, and that we take the show national. I suggested that we add Zep historian Steve Sauer and technical producer Joe Cristiano to our team, and, thanks to Andy Denemark of the United Stations Radio Networks and your listenership, we're heard all across the country.

With all his archival audio, text, and photography, the next natural step was for Denny to put it together in book form, to present the big picture on the total Zeppelin story. He hasn't missed a thing. And he's got stuff here you've never seen before. Enjoy!

Thanks for reading, listening, and, as always, Gettin' the Led Out!

—Carol Miller

Robert Plant and Carol Miller at the WNEW-FM station in New York, 1993.

❦ *PREFACE* ❦

NO SURPRISE THAT MORE THAN THIRTY YEARS after declaring, "We wish it to be known that the loss of our dear friend, and the deep sense of undivided harmony felt by ourselves and our manager, have led us to decide that we could not continue as we were," Led Zeppelin is still one of the biggest and most influential bands in the world.

They started life in 1968 out of the ashes of the Yardbirds, and in fact began under the moniker of the New Yardbirds.

Today, after more than seven hundred concerts and two hundred million records sold, after having been inducted into the Rock and Roll Hall of Fame and having recorded the most requested rock song of all time, we revere them and share their music with the next generation. Led Zeppelin neither "burned out" nor "faded away."

BELOW: A detail of a poster from the canceled concert at the L.A. Forum, 1968.

FOLLOWING PAGES: A view of the crowd and the stage as Led Zeppelin performs at the Alameda County Coliseum in Oakland, California, on July 23, 1977.

PAGE 10: Ioannis, Immigrant Song, 2011.

Led Zeppelin T-shirt he was wearing, a replica of the 1977 World Tour shirt.

I knew then and there that the band's influence on music, style, and personal expression had crossed the generational divide—that Led Zeppelin's appeal is not only contemporary and global but multigenerational as well. The sheer number of today's top recording artists who cite Led Zeppelin as a key influence on their music (several of whom were interviewed for this book) testifies to the band's enduring importance.

And the radio show? Now in its fourth year of syndication, *Get the Led Out* has become one of the most popular syndicated rock programs of all time.

I went through a little bit of anxiety when the idea first came up about doing a *Get the Led Out* book. Literally hundreds of Led Zeppelin books have been written over the years, some good and some not so good. What was left to say? On the other hand, most of the books were written by people who never actually met the band; in fact, several were written by people who never even saw them play or weren't even born when they disbanded, let alone when they formed. What's more, there still hasn't been an authorized version of the band's story.

I thought: What will make this book different? How can it add something to the Zeppelin legacy? I didn't want to tell yet another version of the band's story. I wanted to relate the tale as told by the members of the band themselves—in rare, unguarded interviews—and by the individuals who witnessed it all. I wanted facts, not myths; eyewitness accounts, not critiques. I wanted information from credible sources, not gossip from the usual suspects.

I tried to include something for the casual fan as well as the hard-core devotee. I hope you will enjoy reading it as much as I have enjoyed assembling it.

—DENNY SOMACH

But I wasn't always so sure. When we started the *Get the Led Out* syndicated radio show, I wondered in the back of my mind how long we could keep it fresh and entertaining. After all, there are only nine official Led Zeppelin studio albums and maybe twenty songs that get regularly played on the radio. How long could we keep it going?

Whatever reservations I had were shattered when I arrived at the offices of our distributor. I was in the lobby when out came a seventeen-year-old intern to let me know that the executive vice president of programming was finishing up a phone call and would be right with me. He asked if I wanted some coffee, water, or soda. But what he actually offered me was a confirmation that this radio show would not only be a hit but that it would be on the air for a long time. How did I know? By the black

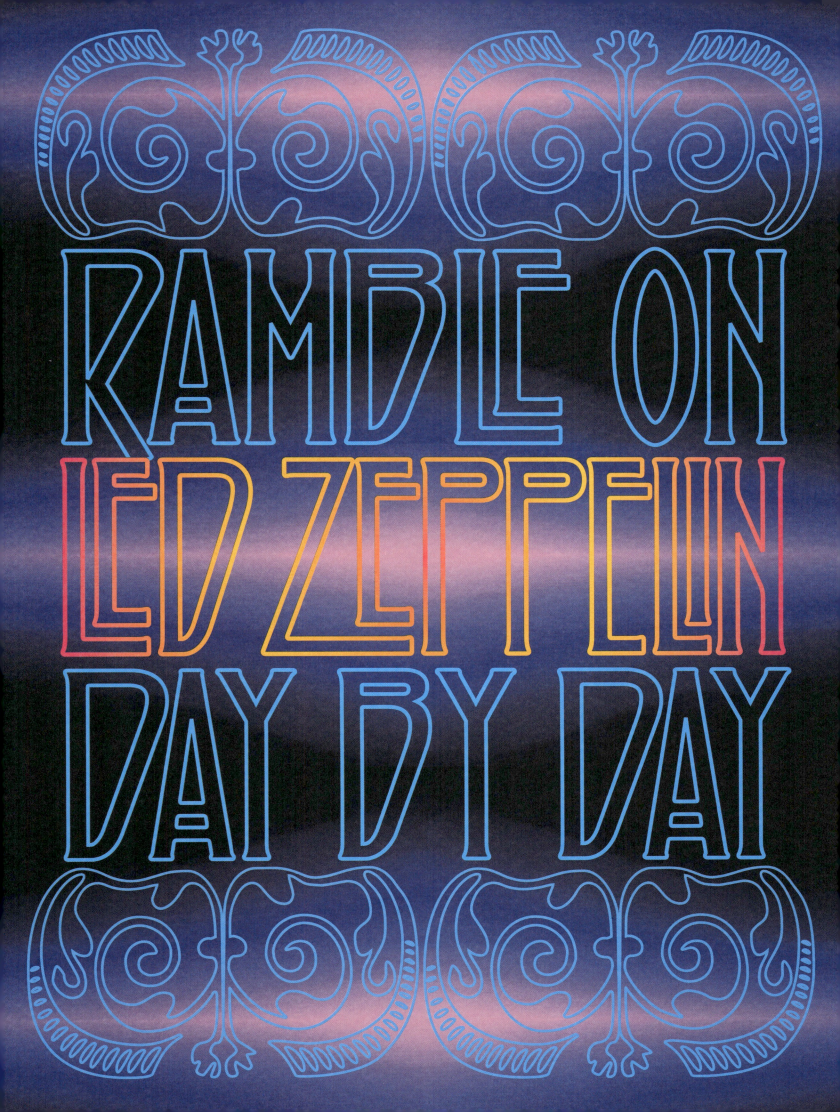

1968

JUNE Jimmy Page, who had been with the Yardbirds for just over two years, wanted to expand the group's hard rock leanings. Two of the three remaining original members preferred to opt out, having been with the group for five years. Singer Keith Relf and drummer Jim McCarty preferred playing softer music in the style of Simon & Garfunkel and the Turtles.

Page, however, sought to assemble a new lineup of the Yardbirds and develop a new sound. At one point, he told *Go* magazine he envisioned having a member of his band play a keyboard instrument called the mellotron because it was capable of sounding like flutes, strings, or trumpets. "The mellotron will be there to give added interest, but the guitar will still be featured," said Page. "The whole idea is to get a new sort of collage of sound that is not the sound normally associated with a rock 'n' roll group. But it will still have a beat backing."

With bassist Chris Dreja and manager Peter Grant, Page began auditioning musicians at his boathouse in Pangbourne, England. Grant had booked a tour of Scandinavia to take place in September, and it would be Page's new lineup playing on it.

LEFT: Jimmy Page takes a bow to his Fender Telecaster at a Yardbirds concert during their January 1967 Australasia tour.

OPPOSITE PAGE: The Band of Joy poses for a portrait in Kensington, London, 1968. From left to right: drummer John Bonham, organist Chris Brown, guitarist Kevyn Gammond, lead singer Robert Plant, and bassist Paul Lockey.

JULY 7 The Yardbirds' lineup of Keith Relf, Jimmy Page, Chris Dreja, and Jim McCarty played their final show. It took place at Luton Technical College in England.

MID-JULY Page asked rock vocalist Terry Reid to join the new band, but he was unavailable; former Yardbirds manager Mickie Most had booked him in a U.S. tour with Cream. Instead, Reid suggested Page look up a Midlands-area singer named Robert Plant, who had sung for the Band of Joy.

JULY 20 Peter Grant took Jimmy Page and Chris Dreja by car to Wolverhampton, England, to hear the band Obs-Tweedle. Page went backstage before the show and spotted a muscular kid he assumed to be a roadie and proceeded to ask him if he could meet Robert Plant. The kid said that's who he was. When Page watched Plant perform and heard him sing, he wondered why Plant hadn't made it big already. Page thought maybe Plant had some kind of personality problem that had prevented him from becoming a star.

JULY 31 Grant took Page and Dreja to the Hampstead Country Club in London, where singer Tim Rose was performing. On drums that night was John Bonham, who'd been recommended to them by Plant. "John Bonham was an absolute must-have," Dreja recalls from the conversation on the return trip from the venue. "A little iffy about Robert."

EARLY AUGUST As the lineup for Jimmy Page's new band was coming together, there was one change on bass. Chris Dreja, who'd been the Yardbirds' rhythm guitarist since their formation in 1963 but then switched to bass shortly after Page joined in 1966, decided to drop out of music to go into photography.

This suited Page, who landed a bassist in John Paul Jones, a fellow veteran of London studio session work. Jones, tired of working in that profession, took the advice of his wife and responded to Page's ad in the magazine *Disc*. For Jones, joining Page's band and getting on the road would be a welcome change of pace.

Manager Peter Grant sent telegrams to both Robert Plant and John Bonham. Reaching Plant was easy, and he accepted an offer to visit Page at his Pangbourne boathouse to discuss the musical direction Page had in mind. However, reaching Bonham proved more difficult. Grant had to send several telegrams to Bonham, who was skeptical of the call to join their group. For one thing, his concert tour with Tim Rose the previous month had been his first big break, even though it had occurred several years into his drumming career. He was hesitant to believe that an offer to join the Yardbirds could be lucrative.

Plant boarded a train to visit Page. There, the two listened to records and discussed music. They quickly found that they shared some of the same interests in the folk- and blues-music niches, particularly in records that had to be imported into England or purchased secondhand from collectors.

Following his meeting with Page, Plant returned to the Midlands raving about the possibilities. He tried to coax Bonham into coming along next time, but John's wife, Pat, was hearing none of it. Several times in the past, Plant had shared his enthusiasm for bands he thought would be perfect for Bonham's drums, but that had amounted to little but frustration. Pat assumed this was just another example of a band that would go nowhere. Despite her objections, John Bonham agreed to give Page's band a shot.

AUGUST 12 Jimmy Page again welcomed Robert Plant to his boathouse, this time along with the two others potentially recruited, John Paul Jones and John Bonham. Jones was a complete stranger to both Bonham and Plant, who, after hearing Jones was a session bassist, pictured him as some type of older chap smoking a pipe. Jones did not fit this description; he was only two years older than Bonham and Plant and two years younger than Page.

The four met at Page's house to talk before packing themselves and their musical instruments and amplifiers into a small room in London's Chinatown district. That was the make-or-break moment, when they played all together for the first time. (Page and Jones had played with each other, and Plant and Bonham had played with each other, but the four of them hadn't yet played as an ensemble.)

First, what should they play? They compared notes on something all four of them might know. Page suggested a tune called "Train Kept A-Rollin'," a regular concert staple for the Yardbirds. The tune was a cover, originally a 1951 single by Tiny Bradshaw that was coproduced by Ahmet Ertegun and Jerry Wexler and made into a rock 'n' roll number in 1956 by Johnny Burnette and the Rock and Roll Trio.

October 18, 1968, at the Marquee Club in London—two days before the New Yardbirds officially became Led Zeppelin.

Page showed the riff to the others, and it was a pattern they'd all recognize. Page and Jones pumped out that riff together. Bonham pounded away, following Page's lead. Plant wailed away on vocals. Within only minutes, they knew they'd created a special musical bond, something they'd have to be careful to protect against losing.

LATE AUGUST John Paul Jones had a studio session for which it was his duty to book a band, so he booked Jimmy Page on guitar, John Bonham on drums, and Robert Plant on harmonica. The session resulted in the medley track "Jim's Blues/George Wallace Is Rollin' in This Morning" on P. J. Proby's album *Three Week Hero*, released the following April.

With the Yardbirds' lineup now firmly in place for the Scandinavian tour the following month, the group rehearsed. It became quite obvious the band would be something entirely different from the Yardbirds and a new name would be required.

EARLY SEPTEMBER As the band prepared for their Scandinavian tour as the Yardbirds, manager Peter Grant began to seek out a deal from a record label, doing so only on the basis of his own reputation and that of Jimmy Page, rather than with the aid of any recordings. This would be the only concert tour of Led Zeppelin's that Grant would miss.

SEPTEMBER 7 Led Zeppelin's first and second concerts took place in Denmark, where the group was billed as the Yardbirds. Without there having been any advance promotion of the changes to the Yardbirds' lineup, those in attendance might very well have been surprised to see Keith Relf replaced by an eighteen-year-old hippie with golden hair. That was the case at the Gladsaxe Teen Club for sixteen-year-old house photographer Jørgen Angel, who didn't realize until years later that he'd actually shot Led Zeppelin's first-ever concert.

For both shows that day, including the second, at the Brøndby Pop Club, the Yardbirds headlined over other bands.

SEPTEMBER 8 The group continued for a second day of touring in Denmark, performing another pair of shows that billed them as the Yardbirds. At both of these shows, the headlining band on the bill was a topless female act called the Ladybirds.

SEPTEMBER 12–18 The band's Scandinavian tour as the Yardbirds continued with a string of shows in Sweden. The group is believed to have played two shows in Stockholm on September 12 and 13. Ahead of an appearance on September 14 at Ängby Park in Knivsta, Uppsala's daily newspaper ran a photo and blurb introducing the new members of the Yardbirds, recruited by Jimmy Page.

John Paul Jones was introduced as having played bass on Donovan's last three records. John Bonham was noted for having drummed for the American singer Tim Rose. Singer Robert Plant, it was said, was popular in England's blues circles.

SEPTEMBER 27 The band recorded at least three tracks at Olympic Sound Studios in Barnes, London. Raw tapes have surfaced of unreleased studio versions of "You Shook Me" and "Babe I'm Gonna Leave You"—two covers from outside the rock universe—plus a third, "Baby Come On Home," a song very much in the soul tradition. Written on the tape's blank label as the title of this song is the designation "Tribute to Bert Berns," although its regular title would not be revealed until another version of the song was officially released in 1993 on a Led Zeppelin box set. Recording sessions continued over the next few days.

EARLY OCTOBER After thirty hours of studio time, costing Jimmy Page £1,782, the nine songs on Led Zeppelin's first album had been completely recorded.

OCTOBER 4 Led Zeppelin's first concert in England took place on this Friday night at Mayfair Ballroom in Newcastle, albeit under the name the Yardbirds. Terry Reid's own band, Fantasia, also performed, featuring the singer who'd turned down the opportunity to front Led Zeppelin but had recommended Robert Plant. Confusingly, advertising and the concert tickets themselves state that the Yardbirds had returned to England from a "successful" and "amazing" tour of the United States.

OCTOBER 18–19 Led Zeppelin played two concerts over the weekend: a Friday booking at London's Marquee Club and a Saturday booking at Liverpool University. For both appearances, the group was billed for the last time as the Yardbirds. At the Marquee Club, the band was called both the Yardbirds and the New Yardbirds. The date was publicized at the time as the group's British debut (although the October 4 date in Newcastle clearly preceded it). The Liverpool date was publicized as the group's final appearance as the Yardbirds, after which they would permanently be known as Led Zeppelin. The October 19 editions of both *Melody Maker* and *New Musical Express* carried stories to this effect.

OCTOBER 20 According to *Melody Maker*, it was on this date, a Sunday, that Jimmy Page's band officially became known as Led Zeppelin. To this point, the band had yet to play any concerts under that name. Jimmy Page said in subsequent years there had been pressure for the band to be booked in England under the familiar name of the Yardbirds; Led Zeppelin was an unfamiliar name.

LATE OCTOBER Manager Peter Grant flew to New York, where he met both cofounders of Atlantic Records, Jerry Wexler and Ahmet Ertegun, and proposed a deal that would make Led Zeppelin one of Atlantic's recording artists. Purportedly, Wexler signed them on a handshake because that was the way Peter Grant did business. Following the verbal agreement, precise details were hashed out later, including a reported cash advance for the group that may have been about forty-six times the amount Page had spent recording the band at Olympic Sound Studios earlier in the month. One revolutionary

marquee
90 Wardour Street   London. W.1

KISN GOOD GUYS present
VANILLA FUDGE
Produced by CONCERTS WEST
DEC'BR 29 1968
SUN. EVE. — 7:30 P.M.
CIVIC AUDITORIUM
222 S.W. CLAY
PORTLAND, OREGON
ADMIT ONE $5.00
NO REFUNDS - NO EXCHANGES

ABOVE LEFT: An ad for the December 1968 lineup at the Marquee Club proclaims that "LED ZEPPELIN (Nee THE YARDBIRDS)" will perform on December 10.

ABOVE RIGHT: This ticket from the Vanilla Fudge and Led Zeppelin concert of December 29, 1968, at the Civic Auditorium in Portland, Oregon, does not include the name of the opening act—Led Zeppelin.

detail was that the deal granted Led Zeppelin complete artistic control over their image and all releases.

No official announcement about Led Zeppelin's contract with Atlantic was made right away, although it was rumored in the music press that Atlantic would be the group's outlet in America. The official announcement would come in the form of an Atlantic Records press release the following month.

OCTOBER 25 Led Zeppelin's Friday concert at Surrey University was the first one performed anywhere under their new name. Even despite this fact, and despite all the publicity surrounding the name change, a poster drawn up for this occasion still bears the legend "New Yardbirds featuring Jimmy Page."

NOVEMBER 9 Robert Plant married his girlfriend, Maureen Wilson, but then had to join Led Zeppelin for an overnight performance at the Roundhouse in London. One positive aspect of the performance was that the band shared the bill with American bluesman John Lee Hooker. On the negative side, the venue had placed an ad in *Melody Maker* listing the band as "Yardbirds now known as Led Zeppelin."

NOVEMBER 16 Led Zeppelin performed a Saturday night concert at the Institute of Science and Technology in Manchester, although there exists no known signage or advertising to determine whether Led Zeppelin succeeded in shedding the "Yardbirds" name in any of the billing.

NOVEMBER 23 On the same day Led Zeppelin performed at Sheffield University, Atlantic Records issued a press release stating that the band had been signed to their label in a long-term deal. The exact terms of the contract were not released, although the music press speculated that Led Zeppelin had received a $200,000 cash advance.

The label felt it sufficient to say, "It is one of the most substantial deals Atlantic has ever made."

NOVEMBER 29 The Crawdaddy Club in Richmond, which had served as the Yardbirds' regular concert venue in 1963, hosted Led Zeppelin for a performance. An ad placed in the November 23 edition of *Melody Maker* referred to the group as "Led Zeppelin (formerly Yardbirds)."

DECEMBER 10 The band performed at the Marquee Club for a second time, this time billed as Led Zeppelin, although the club listed the band's name in preshow advertising and a concert program as "Led Zeppelin (nee The Yardbirds)."

DECEMBER 13 Led Zeppelin performed at the Bridge Place Country Club near Canterbury, with their name listed as Yardbirds in an advertisement.

DECEMBER 16 Led Zeppelin performed a Monday-night showcase at the Bath Pavilion with another act called Yellow Brick Road. Promoter Freddy Bannister had originally booked the Jeff Beck Group to headline, but Beck backed out of the commitment. Peter Grant, who was managing the Jeff Beck Group in addition to Led Zeppelin, arranged for Led Zeppelin to serve as the replacement act.

DECEMBER 20 Led Zeppelin's performance at the Fishmongers Arms in London, with the bands Closed Cell Sponge and Explosive Spectrum, is the last known UK appearance by the band before they departed for their first American tour. An ad in *Melody Maker* pronounced the group "Led Zeppelin (formerly Yardbirds)."

DECEMBER 24 The members of Led Zeppelin boarded a plane and set off for North America to play a U.S. tour,

several dates of which had been vacated by the Jeff Beck Group. Led Zeppelin's tour manager going forward was Richard Cole.

DECEMBER 25 The members of Led Zeppelin spent Christmas in the United States. After landing in the New York area, John Paul Jones remained there for the day and joined singer Madeline Bell and her family for what he called a "soul Christmas." The other members of Led Zeppelin went on from New York to Los Angeles.

DECEMBER 26 All four members of Led Zeppelin met up in Denver, Colorado, where their first show on American soil was to take place. They were opening for the bands Spirit and Vanilla Fudge. Led Zeppelin was not even listed on the bill for this show.

DECEMBER 27 Despite a blizzard dropping eight inches of snow on the city of Seattle, a decent crowd attended the Vanilla Fudge concert at the Seattle Center Arena, for which Led Zeppelin was the opening act.

DECEMBER 28 An audience reported to be 3,708 in number attended the Vanilla Fudge concert at the Pacific Coliseum in Vancouver, British Columbia, Canada, with Led Zeppelin second on the bill, performing after a band called the Trials of Jayson Hoover.

DECEMBER 29 Vanilla Fudge and Led Zeppelin returned to the United States for their concert at the Civic Auditorium in Portland, Oregon. A few transposed vowels resulted in the opening act being listed in an advertisement as "Led Zeppilen featuring Jimmy Page."

DECEMBER 30 A concert with Vanilla Fudge and Led Zeppelin took place at Gonzaga University in Spokane, Washington, where another unfortunate spelling error resulted in the band being listed in an ad as "Len Zefflin."

An audience tape of Led Zeppelin's performance from that show—the earliest audience tape of a Led Zeppelin show in circulation among bootleg collectors—reveals that John Paul Jones had already begun playing the bass line that Spirit's Mark Andes played during the song "Fresh Garbage." The two groups had shared the bill in Denver four days earlier. Jones was using it in part of a heavy rock medley Led Zeppelin extended on a near-nightly basis over the following months.

The medley showed the breadth of Led Zeppelin's musical influences, as it centered around the song "As Long As I Have You," popularized by Philadelphia soul singer Garnet Mimms, and often incorporated bits of lyrics by Eddie Cochran, Traffic, and Bo Diddley, along with music by Miles Davis and Cream. This medley is one of the finest examples of how the early Led Zeppelin jammed on cover tunes while contributing a unique sound of their own.

It was Led Zeppelin's last concert of the year.

Led Zeppelin in London, December 1968.

1969

After the final four months of 1968, in which Led Zeppelin developed from a mere concept into a confident, cohesive, and capable unit, the year 1969 marked another watershed period in the group's history. It is the only year in which the band released four album sides comprising newly recorded material, and it is the year with the largest number of concerts. Only toward the end of the year did Led Zeppelin rest up from some of its most bombastic performances. It was during 1969 that the band created the memories that would compel them to continue their association for longer than a decade.

JANUARY The year started ambitiously, with the band continuing a tour of North America that had begun in the final week of December 1968. The only difference was that now, instead of being left off of concert posters, the name "Led Zeppelin" was more often present than not. And whereas at the beginning of January, the band was being booked as an opening act, by the end of the month even that would change. This was due to the huge surprise their concert act represented for American audiences. The scene was just right for the group to take the United States by storm, city by city. The band's first three major victories all took place by month's end, in San Francisco, Boston, and, finally, New York. These were the locations where Peter Grant had sent the Yardbirds on their first tours of the United States. Luckily for him, that band had established Jimmy Page as a memorable star guitarist in America. This factor, combined with early airplay of the first Led Zeppelin album on FM radio stations in the United States and Canada, led to welcome receptions in these parts. The band was quickly enjoying its first taste of sweet success.

JANUARY 1 After Led Zeppelin and crew fought their way by motor vehicles through a historic snowstorm in Washington and Oregon, they arrived in Los Angeles. Fortuitously, they did not have to play a New Year's Day concert, as had previously been scheduled, in Salem, Oregon. There exists a refund check from General Artists Corporation in New York made out to RAK Management

The Heavy Sounds On Atlantic-Atco Records

IRON BUTTERFLY
BALL

IRON BUTTERFLY
BALL   Atco SD 33-280

LED ZEPPELIN
Atlantic SD 8216

Send for FREE catalogue: ATLANTIC RECORDS, 1841 Broadway, New York, N.Y. 10023

LEFT: *A 1969 Atlantic Records advertisement for Iron Butterfly's* Ball *along with the first Led Zeppelin album.*

in the amount of $150, providing evidence that Zep was once supposed to make an appearance at the Salem Armory Auditorium.

JANUARY 2–5 When Alice Cooper arrived at the Whisky a Go Go to play alongside Led Zeppelin, it was his first time hearing the band's name. He figured it was the name of some local band but was surprised to learn that Led Zeppelin included Jimmy Page, formerly of the Yardbirds. He was, of course, a fan of the Yardbirds. (The band was billed as "Led Zeppelin Featuring: Jimmy

Page, formerly of the Yard Birds." Led Zeppelin is known to have played a unique adaptation of the Yardbirds' "For Your Love" at least once during the stint at the Whisky.)

Unfortunately, both Robert Plant and Jimmy Page were in poor health after their experience in the Pacific Northwest, forcing them to drop at least one of Led Zeppelin's scheduled eight sets between Thursday and Sunday. They were scheduled to play two sets each night over the four consecutive nights. By 1976, Plant's recollections of this time were hazy. In an interview for *Circus* magazine, he said, "We came back here to the Whisky, where Jimmy and I were both chronically ill and only played one gig out of three we were supposed to have played."

Having three days off before Led Zeppelin's San Francisco debut was crucial for the sick members' recovery.

JANUARY 9–11 In warm San Francisco, Led Zeppelin played their first shows promoted by the legendary Bill Graham. Headlining these four shows at the Fillmore West was the folksy jam band Country Joe and the Fish, a San Francisco mainstay. It was a three-night stint, with the first show falling on a Thursday night. Bluesman Taj Mahal, then twenty-six years old, played the opening set each night.

JANUARY 12 Led Zeppelin's first album was released in the United States.

JANUARY 15 Hawkeyes should be proud that the University of Iowa was the location for Led Zeppelin's first concert after the release of their debut album. The university's Central Party Committee sponsored the concert in the Memorial Union. The local rock ensemble Mother Blues also performed. Led Zeppelin took the place of jazz bandleader Count Basie, who was originally scheduled but had canceled. The show received a fair amount of publicity ahead of time, with multiple newspapers running a blurb that referred to Led Zeppelin as "one of the most exciting groups performing in Britain." A photo of opening act Mother Blues performing against a Led Zeppelin backdrop was included in the 1969 Hawkeye yearbook.

JANUARY 16 Led Zeppelin may have made their concert debut in New Orleans, Louisiana, although details of a show there are nonexistent.

JANUARY 17–19 Three weekend concerts at the Grande Ballroom in Detroit, Michigan, featured headliner "Led Zeptlin." They were joined on Friday night by the groups Linn County and Lawrence Blues Band; on Saturday night by the group Target; and on Sunday night by the group Wind.

JANUARY 20–22 Led Zeppelin may have performed their debut concert in the Washington, D.C., area on January 20, 1969. In 2009, filmmaker Jeff Krulik hosted an event to which he invited anybody with recollections of attending a Led Zeppelin performance that was

LED ZEPPELIN THE RAVEN
JANUARY 23, 24, 25
THE BOSTON TEA PARTY
53 BERKELEY ST.   338-7026   LIGHTS BY THE ROAD

Tickets: Krackerjacks, Headquarters East, Bottega 2 George's Folly

RIGHT: *The Boston Tea Party club was one of the most popular venues in New England in the 1960s. This poster advertised the legendary series of shows Led Zeppelin played there from January 23 to 25, 1969.*

thought to have taken place in front of a crowd of fifty-five people at the Wheaton Youth Center in Wheaton, Maryland. The *Washington Post* took an interest in the debate over the existence of this Wheaton show and left it up to readers to evaluate the conflicting accounts and fading memories of the concert and the lack of concrete evidence that it even took place at all.

Details are also shaky regarding other alleged concerts on January 21 in Pittsburgh, Pennsylvania, and on January 22 in Cleveland, Ohio.

JANUARY 23–26 Led Zeppelin played four consecutive nights at a music club in Boston's South End called the Boston Tea Party. The club was once a synagogue; when it was transformed in the '60s to become one of the most popular venues on the Boston music scene, the pews stayed intact but the walls were lined with psychedelic images. It was to this backdrop that Led Zeppelin gave some of its most legendary performances back in 1969, something John Paul Jones often cites as one of his fondest memories of playing with the group.

Says Jones: "The early Boston Tea Party concerts was the biggie, really, for us, and we really knew it was working. In fact, it was the longest concert we ever did. We played four and a quarter hours, I think, which, with an hour-and-a-half act, is some going, I can tell you. We played four nights at the Boston Tea Party, and the last night we did the act twice, and then we did everybody else's act. We did the Beatles songs and Stones songs and

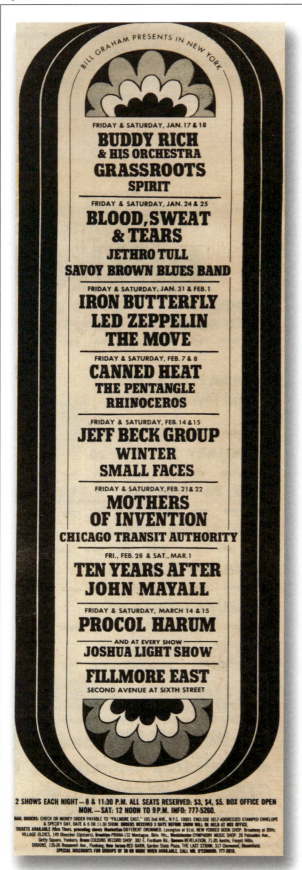

BILL GRAHAM PRESENTS IN NEW YORK

FRIDAY & SATURDAY, JAN. 17 & 18

BUDDY RICH
& HIS ORCHESTRA
GRASSROOTS
SPIRIT

FRIDAY & SATURDAY, JAN. 24 & 25

BLOOD, SWEAT
& TEARS
JETHRO TULL
SAVOY BROWN BLUES BAND

FRIDAY & SATURDAY, JAN. 31 & FEB. 1

IRON BUTTERFLY
LED ZEPPELIN
THE MOVE

FRIDAY & SATURDAY, FEB. 7 & 8

CANNED HEAT
THE PENTANGLE
RHINOCEROS

FRIDAY & SATURDAY, FEB. 14 & 15

JEFF BECK GROUP
WINTER
SMALL FACES

FRIDAY & SATURDAY, FEB. 21 & 22

MOTHERS
OF INVENTION
CHICAGO TRANSIT AUTHORITY

FRI., FEB. 28 & SAT., MAR. 1

TEN YEARS AFTER
JOHN MAYALL

FRIDAY & SATURDAY, MARCH 14 & 15

PROCOL HARUM

AND AT EVERY SHOW

JOSHUA LIGHT SHOW

FILLMORE EAST
SECOND AVENUE AT SIXTH STREET

2 SHOWS EACH NIGHT—8 & 11:30 P.M. ALL SEATS RESERVED: $3, $4, $5. BOX OFFICE OPEN
MON.—SAT: 12 NOON TO 9 P.M. INFO: 777-5260.

MAIL ORDERS: CHECK OR MONEY ORDER PAYABLE TO "FILLMORE EAST," 105 2nd AVE., N.Y.C. 10003. ENCLOSE SELF ADDRESSED STAMPED ENVELOPE
& SPECIFY DAY, DATE & 8 OR 11:30 SHOW. ORDERS RECEIVED 3 DAYS BEFORE SHOW WILL BE HELD AT BOX OFFICE.
TICKETS AVAILABLE (thru Thurs. preceding show): Manhattan-DIFFERENT DRUMMER, Lexington at 61st; NEW YORKER BOOK SHOP, Broadway at 89th;
VILLAGE OLDIES, 149 Bleecker (Upstairs); Brooklyn-PRANA-132 Montague, Hts. Hts., Westchester-SYMPHONY MUSIC SHOP, 29 Palisades Ave.,
Getty Square, Yonkers; Bronx-COUSINS RECORD SHOP, 382 E. Fordham Rd.; Queens-REVELATION, 71-20 Austin, Forest Hills,
DISKINS, 135-25 Roosevelt Ave., Flushing; New Jersey-RED BARN, Garden State Plaza; THE LAST STRAW, 317 Glenwood, Bloomfield,
SPECIAL DISCOUNTS FOR GROUPS OF 30 OR MORE WHEN AVAILABLE. CALL MR. O'CONNOR, 777-3916.

Who songs and everything. It was really good, and it was really steaming."

Even before the release of Led Zeppelin's first album on January 12, WBCN listeners were hearing Led Zeppelin songs being played on the air. J. J. Jackson, one of the radio station's DJs at the time (and destined for national fame on MTV much later), played an advance test pressing of the album throughout the month of January, helping to promote Led Zeppelin's album and the appearance at the Boston Tea Party. That's something the band realized when they arrived in town and met J. J. Jackson. As he told author Frank Reddon in 1999, "It really hit home when Page and the rest of the group expressed their gratitude to me. I was delighted but thought it was only right that they receive as much promotion as possible. They were unbelievable and I was very happy to tell everybody that."

In that same interview, Jackson also talked about the perception that Led Zeppelin's manager, Peter Grant, was like another member of the group. "Every word of that is true," said J. J. "In the middle of the week at the Tea Party that first time in Boston, I looked over to the side of Bonzo, who was flailing away at his drum kit near the end of one of their numbers. Peter's face was beaming as he watched Bonzo wind things up with a 'I knew you could do it all the time' type of look. As the song ended, the place exploded and Peter couldn't have been any prouder of them. What a sight that was! Zeppelin as a whole felt it, too, and they were delighted to be playing in such a receptive venue with their manager and mentor looking on."

John Paul Jones says he remembers Peter Grant giving the entire band a giant bear hug as they came off the stage after their four-hour show at the Boston Tea Party. Jones once said, "Peter called all of us out, and I think he lifted all four of us off the ground."

JANUARY 27 Another Led Zeppelin show is rumored to have taken place, this time at the Municipal Auditorium in Springfield, Massachusetts. (Led Zeppelin is known to have performed at this venue later in the year, on Halloween, for the venue's music festival.)

JANUARY 31–FEBRUARY 1 In the closing days of January 1969, Led Zeppelin arrived in New York for a four-show weekend schedule of two Friday shows and two Saturday shows. The location was the Fillmore East, which was Bill Graham's response on the East Coast to the success of his venue in San Francisco.

In New York, Led Zeppelin was booked to open for Iron Butterfly, the group that was still riding high at the time with a hit from the previous year, "In-A-Gadda-Da-Vida." But members of Iron Butterfly were afraid that if Led Zeppelin opened for them, there was a chance they would be blown off the stage by their opening act.

Led Zeppelin surely amazed the hip New York audiences that weekend. At the four shows, the band played material from their first album, including the blues song "I Can't Quit You Baby," showcasing Jimmy Page's guitar. Page's solo instrumental "White Summer" kicked off one of the Saturday sets. John Bonham played a drum solo called "Pat's Delight."

LEFT: *Led Zeppelin played two nights at Bill Graham's famed Fillmore East in the winter of 1969—January 31 and February 1—when they opened for Iron Butterfly.*

After the last note of "How Many More Times" on the second night, the band even got a little help from the house light show—provided by Joshua White's Joshua Light Show—when the word "More" appeared in bright blue letters on the screen. The audience responded by chanting, "More!" Their calls went on for several minutes straight, even long after Robert Plant apologized and said the band had to go. They were, after all, an opening act for Iron Butterfly. But finally, because the audience wouldn't stop requesting it, the group returned for more than one encore. As a result of the Fillmore East shows, Fred Kirby wrote in *Billboard* magazine that Led Zeppelin "showed it could develop into the next big supergroup." And a blurb in *New Musical Express* told its British readers that in New York, Led Zeppelin played "90 minutes of absolutely incredible musicianship." Iron Butterfly didn't give the reporters as much to write about, and one audience member at Led Zeppelin's first Saturday set was even yelling, "To hell with the Butterfly!"

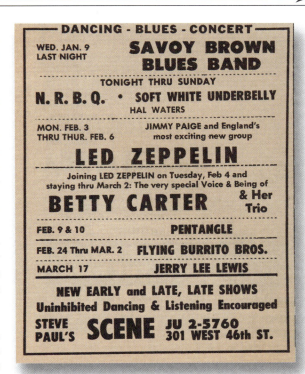

FEBRUARY Led Zeppelin's welcome receptions in North America continued in Toronto, Chicago, and Miami, where they were the new headliners. News of these successes were reaching England, where the group had been all but ignored before its first visit to the United States. Still, Led Zeppelin's return trip to England saw only one British concert appearance in February: a single show in Robert Plant's neck of the woods.

FEBRUARY 2 Led Zeppelin traveled north from New York into Ontario, Canada, and played at a rock music club in Toronto called the Rockpile. One of the primary sources of information about the group's appearance there is Ritchie Yorke, a Toronto-based journalist who was writing for the *Globe and Mail*. Impressed with the group, he did his part to talk up the band to the locals, with a positive review of the LP. And his efforts must have paid off. Between 1,200 and 1,500 people showed up to hear Led Zeppelin that Sunday evening. It was a lot more than the Rockpile was used to having; the line of people waiting to get into the club was several blocks long.

At the concert, Yorke went onstage to introduce Led Zeppelin. He was wrong when he said it was Led Zeppelin's first Canadian appearance, but he might not have known that the band had played in Vancouver back in December, when they were opening for Vanilla Fudge. But this was February, and a lot had changed in the past few weeks. Now their first album was out and was selling in hot spots where they had just played, like New York, Boston, San Francisco, and Los Angeles. And now the band could even get away with headlining shows.

After Led Zeppelin left Toronto, a concert review by Yorke was published in the *Globe and Mail*. He didn't come off as entirely blown away by the band and was even confused as to which of the two members named John was on bass and which was on drums. But Yorke was full of comparisons to the group Cream, whose breakup a few months earlier had sent the rock music world into a tailspin. Yorke said Led Zeppelin wasn't about to replace the vacancy left by Cream, but they were on their way.

He did, however, have some great things to say about one particular musician at the Rockpile concert. "One visual image stood out," he recalled. "It was the sight of Led Zeppelin's hero-worshipped lead guitarist Jimmy Page—resplendent in an avocado velvet suit, bent over as if in agony to the audience, his fingers working like a typist's touch, his foot thumping like a kangaroo's tail, the sounds as clear and as piercing as a bedside phone in the stillness of 3 a.m."

Five years later, Yorke authored *The Definitive Biography of Led Zeppelin*.

FEBRUARY 3–6 John Bonham left the United States temporarily to return home to England and tend to his son, Jason, age two and a half, who had an illness. This forced the cancellation of Led Zeppelin's scheduled Monday-through-Thursday appearances at the New York club Steve Paul's Scene at 301 West 46 Street.

FEBRUARY 7–8 Vanilla Fudge once again joined Led Zeppelin, this time as Zep supported them in Chicago. The venue was Aaron Russo's psychedelic club at 4812 North Clark Street, the Kinetic Playground. The shows were a triple billing with, for the first time, fellow British band Jethro Tull. A column in the *Chicago Tribune*, "The Sound," previewed Led Zeppelin in advance of the concert, making note of the radio play Led Zeppelin had been receiving thanks to local underground DJs Spoke and Psyche.

After the concert, columnist Robb Baker mentioned Robert Plant's affinity for "pepper[ing] his deliveries with lines and phrases from other songs." Baker noticed Spirit's "Fresh Garbage," Buffalo Springfield's "For What It's Worth," the *Porgy and Bess* show tune "Summertime," and "By the Time I Get to Phoenix," popularized by Glen

Campbell. Baker said Psyche also spotted "Green Door," which in 1956 had been a number one hit in the U.S. for Jim Lowe (and, also that year, a number two hit in the UK for Frankie Vaughan).

Baker also noted that John Paul Jones, who was touring at the time without the benefit of an organ to call his own, was able to sneak in a solo on one song using Mark Stein's organ. This was probably for the blues number "You Shook Me," which Led Zeppelin ordinarily played live without bothering to replicate the organ solo heard on their album.

FEBRUARY 10 Led Zeppelin's first concert in Memphis, Tennessee, may have taken place on this date at Memphis State University.

FEBRUARY 14–15 Led Zeppelin arrived in Miami, Florida, several days ahead of their Friday and Saturday sets at the famous Thee Image club at 183 Street and Collins Avenue. Onstage, Robert Plant said they'd been in town for four days and were happy to be playing music again. Before introducing "Dazed and Confused," he mentioned it was from Led Zeppelin's album, which he noted was "currently doing pretty well, apparently."

FEBRUARY 24 Led Zeppelin's first proper UK tour kicked off in Wolverhampton, England, at Club Lafayette. Progressive rock band Galliard was also on the bill. John Bonham threw a birthday party for his wife, Pat.

MARCH It was during this month that Led Zeppelin began to take off in England, thanks to the UK release of the first Led Zeppelin album. The month kicked off with a string of concert dates in small British venues the group disliked. However, March also saw Led Zeppelin reach out to mass-market media, recording interviews and songs especially for radio and TV stations at home and abroad. This included one movie that would be released by year's end and also one media appearance in Denmark. To ensure success, the band reached out in a media-friendly manner they would never quite repeat.

Also, some highly positive critical reception of Led Zeppelin in England was beginning to emerge. For one, Tony Palmer, a music critic for the *Observer*, reviewed the band's first album and found them to be the successor to Cream, which had just broken up. Palmer would remain one of Led Zeppelin's most high-profile supporters, even drawing up a supportive feature about the group in 1975, at a time when their popularity was waning.

Felix Dennis, editor of the London-based radical underground magazine *Oz*, made an early public remark that Led Zeppelin's record was "so obviously a turning point in rock music that only time proves capable of shifting it into eventual perspective." This was accompanied by a prediction that England would lose Led Zeppelin to the United States. Dennis also interviewed Jimmy Page in the following issue of *Oz*.

MARCH 1–2 Led Zeppelin's UK tour continued with a Saturday night show at the Van Dike Club in Plymouth, England, and a Sunday night show at the Fishmongers Arms in London.

MARCH 3 Led Zeppelin recorded their first-ever radio session for John Peel's BBC program *Top Gear*. Jimmy Page wasted no time airing his harsh feelings about BBC Radio in general but thanked Peel for offering just about the only show on the British airwaves that could possibly showcase Led Zeppelin.

The freedom Peel allowed Led Zeppelin was evident from the broadcast. Led Zeppelin's session at the Playhouse Theatre included a couple of four- and five-minute blues numbers, including one with an alternate verse taken from Muddy Waters. Their version of "Communication Breakdown" barely exceeded the three-minute mark, but the band sounded amused when John Peel encouraged them to perform something longer. Their version of "Dazed and Confused" lasted longer than six and a half minutes.

MARCH 5 Led Zeppelin's first UK date outside of England took place. It was in Cardiff, Wales, at the Locarno.

MARCH 7 Led Zeppelin's string of UK dates continued with a London appearance, this one at the Hornsey Wood Tavern.

MARCH 10 With Led Zeppelin touring the United Kingdom, their first U.S. single was issued: "Good Times Bad Times," backed with "Communication Breakdown."

MARCH 13 Led Zeppelin offered one further live date in England before leaving for a string of dates in Sweden and Denmark. This last British show was called the Pyjama Dance, held at Leicester University's De Montfort Hall. Led Zeppelin played that Wednesday alongside the acts Ferris Wheel and Decoys.

MARCH 14 Led Zeppelin played two shows in Sweden, sharing the bill at both with Country Joe and the Fish. (They'd first played together in San Francisco back in January.) The first show was in Stockholm's Konserthuset, and the second was at nearby Uppsala University.

During Led Zeppelin's first song of the day, "Train Kept A-Rollin'," Jimmy Page broke one of his guitar strings. He finished out the song but, instead of his normal segue directly into "I Can't Quit You Baby," chose to pause for a change of string. Meanwhile, the three other members of the band carried on without him, improvising their way through a song called "I Gotta Move." Like "I Can't Quit You Baby," it was popularized by Otis Rush. Robert Plant carried the song with his harmonica and whatever lyrics he could recall or improvise, and Page was ready by the end of the song to join in for the final chord.

MARCH 15 Led Zeppelin's itinerary in Denmark on this Saturday was a repeat of the band's first-ever day of touring, as they moved from the Gladsaxe Teen Club to the

TOP TO BOTTOM:
Ioannis, Led Zeppelin
1973 *(details)*, 2011.

Brøndby Pop Club. A lot had happened in the intervening six months, but the biggest bragging point was their brand-new album.

At the Gladsaxe Teen Club, their set was delayed by about forty minutes. The Ox had played before them, and Uffe Sylvesters Badekar had opened the show. Led Zeppelin's set kicked off with half an hour's worth of cover material, and then it was time for their final song. For that, they chose the original "Communication Breakdown."

MARCH 16 Country Joe and the Fish met up again with Led Zeppelin, this time in Copenhagen, Denmark. This concert, at the Tivolis Koncertsal, was billed under the title "Super Session." Third on the bill was the Keef Hartley Blues Band. Each band played two sets.

MARCH 17 Led Zeppelin's first-ever television appearance took place at a studio in Denmark, where a small audience of teenagers seated themselves on the floor in a circle enveloping the band and their equipment for a special performance of four songs from the Zeppelin album. The music lasted for just over half an hour and included "Communication Breakdown," "Dazed and Confused," "Babe I'm Gonna Leave You," and "How Many More Times." Black-and-white footage of this TV spot has survived over the years, and it was included on the two-DVD set the band released in 2003.

MARCH 19 Back in England for the rest of their UK tour dates, Led Zeppelin appeared on an AM radio program hosted by Alexis Korner that featured rhythm and blues tracks of the day. Aside from typical renditions of "I Can't Quit You Baby" and "You Shook Me," Zeppelin played something called "Sunshine Woman."

It was an up-tempo blues-rock number featuring John Paul Jones on piano and Robert Plant quoting some blues lyrics. It's the only time the group is known to have performed this number, and unfortunately the master tapes appear to have been erased.

Only a poor-quality and incomplete recording of the broadcast remains as evidence of this one-time appearance.

MARCH 21 No recording is known to exist of a forgotten Zeppelin session on a BBC TV show called *How Late It Is*. The band was booked, so the story goes, as a last-minute replacement for the Flying Burrito Brothers. They shared an unusual bill with jazz musician Rahsaan Roland Kirk. Host Michael Wale allowed Led Zeppelin to perform "Communication Breakdown" on the show.

One home viewer who was left impressed with the group managed to get his letter printed in a British newspaper. "The BBC flattened their knockers with their new *How Late It Is* series," wrote Mark Robertson of Rhu, Dunbartonshire. "The musical content was first class, multi-instrumentalist Roland Kirk was superb, and Led Zeppelin showed they are going to be a top attraction. What a marvelous change from the incessant commerciality of *Top of the Pops*."

MARCH 22–23 Led Zeppelin performed Saturday night at the Mothers Club in Birmingham, England, with support from Blodwyn Pig. One story holds that John Bonham could not complete Led Zeppelin's encore due to illness and that Blodwyn Pig drummer Ron Berg filled in for him temporarily. On Sunday, Led Zeppelin were joined at the Argus Butterfly by the group Middle Earth.

MARCH 25 On March 25, 1969, Led Zeppelin were in a British studio, recording a version of "Dazed and Confused" for a movie called *Supershow*. Jimmy Page couldn't remember certain details about *Supershow* when Led Zeppelin's official DVD was coming out with that performance on it in 2003. For instance, he wasn't sure if *Supershow* was a movie or TV show, and he didn't know the director's name (John Crome). But Page was able to recall that "Dazed and Confused" surely was the only song Led Zeppelin performed that day. The director was hurrying along, rushing to capture footage of all the other performers, including Eric Clapton, Stephen Stills, Buddy Miles, and Buddy Guy, among others.

MARCH 27 Led Zeppelin made a rare TV appearance, this time filming a song for the program *Beat Club* on their first trip to West Germany. In the Radio Bremen TV studio, they lip-synched to the studio cuts of the songs "You Shook Me" and "Babe I'm Gonna Leave You." In the footage that has been seen, John Bonham looked particularly irked to be told to mime playing his instrument.

MARCH 28 The UK release of Led Zeppelin's first album had been delayed from January to coincide with Led Zeppelin's British tour and national media appearances. One key concert was their third show at the Marquee Club in London's Soho district. This time, the Marquee Club date was accompanied by an Atlantic Records press release that proudly proclaimed Led Zeppelin "the most talked about and raved about British group of the moment." The press release continued: "All eyes are on Led Zeppelin following the fantastic success of their first album, which in a matter of weeks in America climbed rapidly into the upper limits of *Billboard*, *Cashbox*, and *Record World* charts. This album, entitled simply *Led Zeppelin* . . . seems destined for similar success."

MARCH 29–31 Led Zeppelin's UK tour continued with a Saturday night gig at the Bromley College of Technology in England. Support came from the group the Maddening Crowd. On Sunday, Smokey Rice opened for Led Zeppelin at the Farx Club in Southall. The month closed out with a Monday appearance at the Cooks Ferry Inn in Edmonton, although that spring tour of the UK was just getting started.

APRIL March included some record promotion in England, Denmark, and West Germany. The small amount of filming Led Zeppelin did gave the band some temporary frustration but, at the same time, proved quite effective in spreading the buzz. Entering April, the group had club dates booked almost every night for the first half of the month. But not all was positive at home; some of the small club scenes were tiresome, and press coverage wasn't overwhelmingly supportive at all times. After their UK tour, they were returning to the United States for a second go-round.

APRIL 1 Led Zeppelin's month kicked off with a sixth consecutive day of performance, this time at Klook's Kleek in Hempstead, England, with Pale Green Limousine and the End.

APRIL 2 The UK tour returned to Cardiff, Wales, for "Progressive Blues Night" at the Top Rank Suite Club. Led Zeppelin headlined over Kimla Taz and Eyes of Blue.

APRIL 5 Led Zeppelin headlined a performance at the Roundhouse in Dagenham, England.

APRIL 6 Led Zeppelin headlined a performance at the Boat Club in Nottingham, England.

APRIL 8 Led Zeppelin headlined at the brand-new "Bluesville '69 Club's the Cherry Tree" in Welwyn Garden City. At the venue's grand opening one week earlier, Led Zeppelin became the second group to headline there. The first was the Taste, with Rory Gallagher on guitar.

APRIL 13 Led Zeppelin appeared at Kimbell's Blues Club in Portsmouth, England, following a published newspaper article touting their appearance and featuring an early interview with John Paul Jones. The bassist said, "We do not like being dubbed the new Cream; however, we would like to fill the space that the group left." He also dispelled the idea that Led Zeppelin's music ought to bear a message, saying, "I do not think it is true to suggest there are underlying notions behind these songs; we just want to be accepted for music's sake."

APRIL 15 Led Zeppelin appeared at the Place in Stoke-on-Trent, England.

APRIL 16 Led Zeppelin made a Wednesday night appearance at the Tolby Jug in Tolworth, England.

APRIL 17 Led Zeppelin's first proper UK tour finished off exactly where it began: at Club Lafayette in Wolverhampton, England. This gig was played in favor of a canceled appearance at the Bay Hotel in Sunderland.

APRIL 18 One strenuous touring itinerary would have had Led Zeppelin flying from London to New York immediately after the last UK show and getting ready to play the very next day at New York University's Jazz Festival. However, this plan was scrapped, and instead Led Zeppelin had close to a week off before beginning their second U.S. tour on the West Coast.

Led Zeppelin performs in a studio for their first television performance, in Copenhagen, on March 17, 1969, in front of a small group of teens.

ONE SHOW ONLY — 7:30 P.M.
SUNDAY, MAY 11

INCREDIBLE STRING BAND

FRIDAY & SATURDAY, MAY 16 & 17

THE WHO
SWEETWATER
IT'S A BEAUTIFUL DAY

FRIDAY & SATURDAY, MAY 23 & 24

SLY AND THE FAMILY STONE
CLARENCE CARTER
ROTARY CONNECTION

FRIDAY & SATURDAY, MAY 30 & 31

LED ZEPPELIN
WOODY HERMAN & HIS ORCHESTRA
DELANEY & BONNIE & FRIENDS

FRIDAY & SATURDAY, JUNE 6 & 7

CHUCK BERRY
ALBERT KING

FRIDAY & SATURDAY, JUNE 13 & 14

BOOKER T. AND THE MG'S
YOUNGBLOODS
CHICAGO

FRIDAY & SATURDAY, JUNE 20 & 21

GRATEFUL DEAD
BUDDY MILES EXPRESS

FRIDAY & SATURDAY, JUNE 27 & 28
(TO BE ANNOUNCED)

FRIDAY & SATURDAY, JULY 11 & 12

JOHN MAYALL
PRESERVATION HALL JAZZ BAND

FRIDAY & SATURDAY, JULY 18 & 19

CREEDENCE CLEARWATER REVIVAL
RAVEN

FRIDAY & SATURDAY, JULY 25 & 26

IRON BUTTERFLY

FRIDAY & SATURDAY, AUGUST 1 & 2

CANNED HEAT
LITTLE RICHARD

FRIDAY & SATURDAY, AUGUST 8 & 9

JEFFERSON AIRPLANE
AND AT EVERY SHOW
JOSHUA LIGHT SHOW

FILLMORE EAST
SECOND AVENUE AT SIXTH STREET

2 SHOWS EACH NIGHT — 8 & 11:30 P.M. ALL SEATS RESERVED: $3, $4, $5. BOX OFFICE OPEN MON.-THURS: NOON TO 9 P.M.
FRI.-SAT: NOON TO MIDNIGHT/ INFO: 777-5260.
MAIL ORDERS: CHECK OR MONEY ORDER PAYABLE TO "FILLMORE EAST," 105 2nd AVE., N.Y.C. 10003. ENCLOSE SELF-ADDRESSED STAMPED ENVELOPE
& SPECIFY DAY, DATE & (8 OR 11:30 SHOW). ORDERS RECEIVED 3 DAYS BEFORE SHOW WILL BE HELD AT BOX OFFICE.
TICKETS ALSO AVAILABLE (thru Thurs. preceding show): Manhattan-BOOKMASTERS, 3rd Ave. at 59th St., NEW YORKER BOOK SHOP, Broadway at 89th;
VILLAGE OLDIES, 149 Bleecker (Upstairs); Brooklyn-PRANA-132 Montague, Bkln. Hts.; Westchester-SYMPHONY MUSIC SHOP, 28 Palisades Ave.,
Getty Square, Yonkers; Bronx-COUSINS RECORD SHOP, 382 E. Fordham Rd.; Queens-REVELATION, 71-20 Austin, Forest Hills;
DISKINS. 135-26 Roosevelt Ave., Flushing; New Jersey-RED BARN, Garden State Plaza, Paramus; THE LAST STRAW, 317 Glenwood Ave., Bloomfield.
SPECIAL DISCOUNTS FOR GROUPS OF 30 OR MORE WHEN AVAILABLE. CALL CRAZY DIANA: 777-3910.

The Fillmore welcomes its new ticket outlet on Manhattan's East Side at BOOKMASTERS, Third Avenue & 59th Street.

the who
SUNDAY
MAY 25
8:00 PM
Led Zeppelin

ADVANCE TICKETS $3.75
mail orders payable: L. G. PRODUCTIONS
3344 M St. NW
enclose self ADDRESSED stamped envelope
Available at Giant Music Joint Possession Soul Shack & Empire Music Waxie Maxie

MERRIWEATHER POST PAVILION OF MUSIC
COLUMBIA, MARYLAND

A LESTER GROSSMAN PRODUCTION

OPPOSITE PAGE: Led Zeppelin returned to the Fillmore East on May 30 and 31, 1969. This ad lists the rest of the lineup—the jazz bandleader Woody Herman and his orchestra and the husband-and-wife duo Delaney and Bonnie Bramlett, whose performing "friends" often included George Harrison and Eric Clapton, among others.

ABOVE: Led Zeppelin and the Who were only on the same bill once: May 25, 1969, at the Merriweather Post Pavilion, an outdoor venue in Columbia, Maryland.

RIGHT: Led Zeppelin played the Bath Festival of Blues at the Pavilion Recreational Ground on June 28, 1969; the twelve-hour show was organized by Freddy Bannister.

APRIL 24–27 Led Zeppelin's second trip to San Francisco was for four more concert dates promoted by Bill Graham. The last time Led Zeppelin had played one of Graham's establishments, the New York crowd fervently cheered them on through multiple encores, much to the chagrin of headlining band Iron Butterfly. This time, Led Zeppelin was allowed to top the bill.

This left artist Randy Tuten in charge of designing the first Fillmore handbill to feature Led Zeppelin as a headlining act. Many Led Zeppelin promotions at the time used the imagery of a crashing Hindenburg airship, as seen on the cover of the first album. Tuten's decision to feature an avocado with eyes on the Fillmore handbill stood in stark contrast to that.

The two other acts on the bill, repeated over the four nights, were the Colwell-Winfield Blues Band and Julie Driscoll, Brian Auger & the Trinity. The first show was on a Thursday, again at the Fillmore West. However, the Friday and Saturday shows would be at another venue in town, the Winterland Ballroom, which Graham often rented for larger shows. For Sunday night, Led Zeppelin was back at the Fillmore West again.

For these concerts, Led Zeppelin reprised and expanded their "As Long As I Have You" medley, having learned first-hand from Vanilla Fudge how to explore musical territories outside their comfort zone. In addition, Led Zeppelin were now latching onto Howlin' Wolf's blues song "Killing Floor" in the live setting. These would be Led Zeppelin's final concerts of April 1969.

MAY Because Led Zeppelin had been so successful in several of the larger musical markets, it was now time to test the waters elsewhere in the vast United States. Several destinations on Led Zeppelin's second North American tour were in secondary markets across California, in Canada, and in other U.S. locations. The end of the month included return trips to Chicago, Boston, and New York, in the psychedelic clubs Led Zeppelin had already conquered.

Pressure from the record label was building to deliver a second album. The band even had their own reasons to record again. Because their music was changing and expanding, they believed their first album no longer represented what the band was capable of. It was, as members of the band pointed out, recorded only a few weeks into the band's existence. Led Zeppelin had more to prove, and so booking studio time was becoming as much a priority as performing live. The two priorities coexisted, and the recording process became almost routine, with Jimmy Page extending his task as the band's producer.

JUNE 28 Led Zeppelin played at the Bath Festival of Blues, one of the earliest rock festivals in Britain.

JULY 22 Atlantic Records threw a party for Led Zeppelin at the Plaza Hotel in New York, where company vice president Jerry Wexler presented the band with gold record awards. Of Atlantic's various executives, Wexler had the earliest and most profound impact on Led Zeppelin. That dynamic would soon change.

BATH FESTIVAL OF BLUES
RECREATION GROUND—PULTENEY STREET ENTRANCE

Saturday, June 28th

FEATURING

John Mayall - Fleetwood Mac
Led Zeppelin - 10 Years After
Nice
Chicken Shack
John Hiseman's Colosseum
Mick Abraham's Blodwyn Pig
Keef Hartley
Group Therapy
Liverpool Scene
Taste - Savoy Brown's Blues band
Champion Jack Dupre
Clouds - Babylon
Principal Edward's Magic Theatre
Deep Blues band - Just Before Dawn

Compére JOHN PEEL

REFRESHMENTS AND HOT SNACKS WILL BE AVAILABLE ALL DAY

In case of bad weather there will be a substantial amount of under cover accomodation.
12 NOON—10.30 p.m.

IN ADVANCE
All day 18/6. Eve only 14/6
ON DAY
All day 22/6. Eve only 16/6

TICKETS ARE AVAILABLE FROM:
BATH FESTIVAL BOX OFFICE or COLSTON HALL BOX OFFICE
Abbey Chambers BRISTOL 1.
Abbey Church Yard, BATH

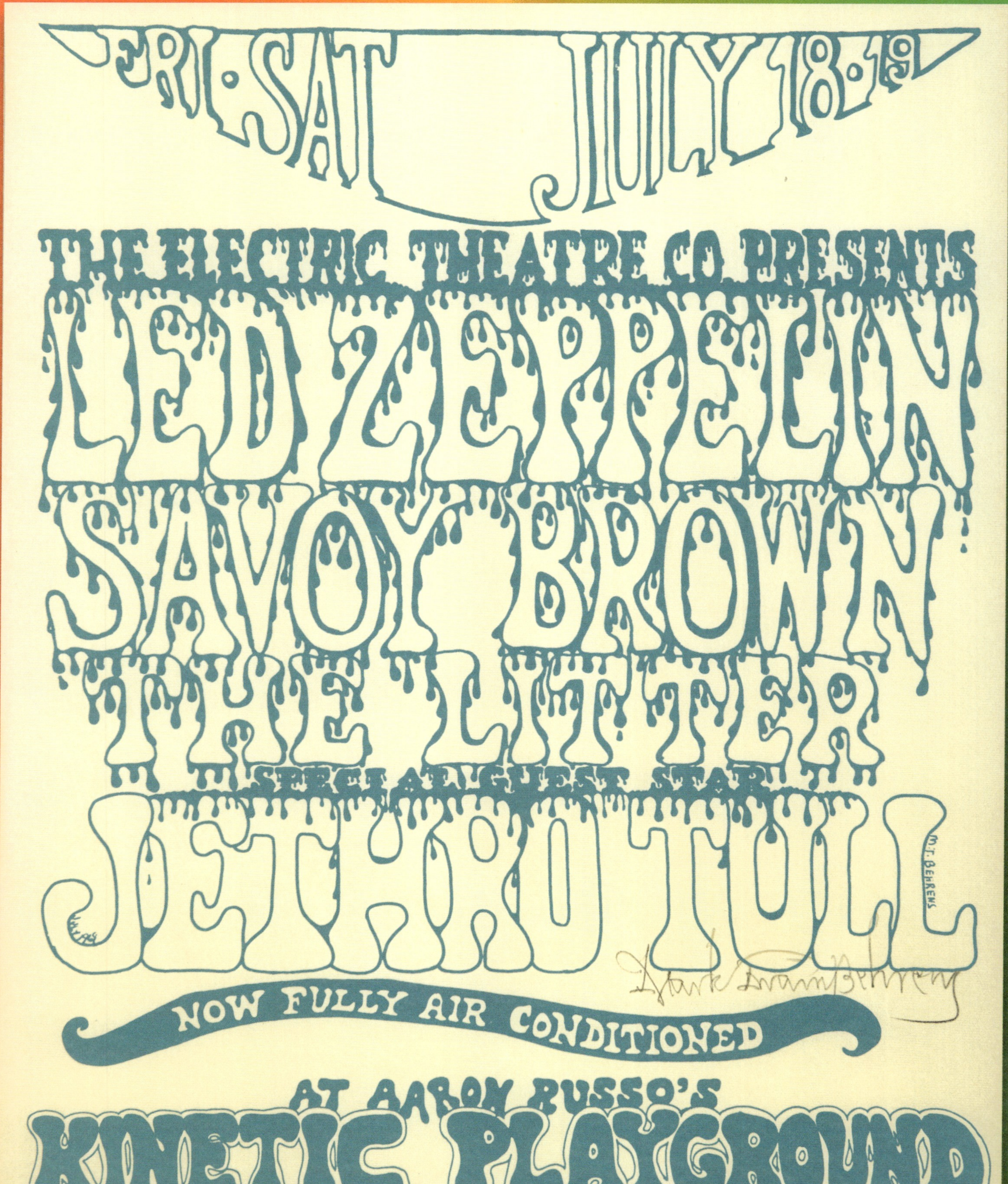
FRI-SAT JULY 18-19
THE ELECTRIC THEATRE CO. PRESENTS
LED ZEPPELIN
SAVOY BROWN
THE LITTER
SPECIAL GUEST STAR
JETHRO TULL
M.T. BEHRENS
NOW FULLY AIR CONDITIONED
AT AARON RUSSO'S
KINETIC PLAYGROUND
4812 NO. CLARK
784-1700

The band members sported great moods during this presentation. Jimmy Page told *New Musical Express*, "We didn't tell Bonzo. He thought we were going to get one [award] between us and we'd have to split it up, each of us getting it for three months at a time. I think he's speechless."

AUGUST 9 Jimmy Page and Robert Plant were in Los Angeles when they met up with two of their fellow British musicians. One of the two was Spencer Davis, founder of the band that first featured sixteen-year-old Steve Winwood and had hits with "Gimme Some Lovin'" and "I'm a Man."

The other musician Page and Plant ran into was Screaming Lord Sutch, a recording artist who'd made a name in England by twice running for Parliament. But now he was on tour in the United States, driving his Rolls-Royce around with a Union Jack flag on the roof.

Spencer Davis, Screaming Lord Sutch, Page, and Plant jammed together at L.A.'s Experience Club that night. And Lord Sutch invited Page and John Bonham to perform on the album he was recording. That album was released the following year with the title *Lord Sutch and Heavy Friends*.

AUGUST 10 Led Zeppelin topped the bill at the San Diego Sports Arena over Jethro Tull. Frontman Ian Anderson, with his famous one-leg-in-the-air stance while playing the flute, was already an iconic figure. But today he'll admit that he's always been jealous of Robert Plant.

AUGUST 31 Led Zeppelin headlined the second night of the Texas International Pop Festival, outside of Dallas. Zeppelin had already played six other U.S. music festivals in the summer of '69: Atlanta; Newport, Rhode Island; Laurel, Maryland; Philadelphia; Milwaukee; and Seattle. This festival date in the Dallas area was the last show on Zeppelin's tour before they were to fly home to England. It was not, however, a date that had been planned on at the beginning of the tour.

SEPTEMBER Led Zeppelin enjoyed a month off from touring activity for the first time in the band's history.

OCTOBER 3–5 Led Zeppelin toured Holland for the very first time, playing shows on three consecutive nights in Scheveningen, Rotterdam, and Amsterdam. A fourth concert in the Netherlands may have taken place on October 9 in Haarlem.

OCTOBER 10 Led Zeppelin played a concert in Paris that was professionally recorded for a French radio broadcast. Memories of this broadcast faded away almost completely until the concert was aired again in 2007.

One person who brought a camera to the show, Gilles Chateau, recalls that a planned light show was scrapped at the concert when the equipment began to malfunction. However, crew members in the rafters above the stage were able to project spotlights on Jimmy Page and Robert Plant. Jimmy selected one overhead photograph of Plant and himself in the spotlights in Paris to appear in his pictorial autobiography, published in 2010.

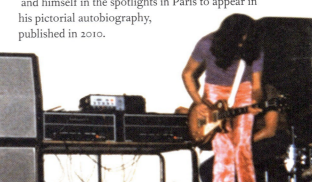

OCTOBER 12 Led Zeppelin's final European tour date before returning to America took place in London—a headlining performance at the 21,000-seat Lyceum Ballroom with support from the bands Audience and Frosty Noses.

OCTOBER 17 As two shows at New York's Carnegie Hall opened Led Zeppelin's fourth American tour, John Bonham reminded his bandmates in the wings that they were following in the footsteps of numerous greats who'd all played at the prestigious Manhattan venue, among them revered jazz drummers Buddy Rich and Gene Krupa.

OCTOBER 18–25 Led Zeppelin's American tour continued to Detroit for one show, Chicago for two, Cleveland for one, and Boston for one.

OCTOBER 29 Jimmy Page and Robert Plant jammed onstage with a future member of the Eagles. The setting was a local nightspot called J.B.'s in Kent, Ohio, within about an hour's drive of Cleveland, which is where the band the James Gang hails from. And less than a year into the group's existence, Joe Walsh joined the group on guitar. And he of course would later join the Eagles.

Joe Walsh jammed with Page and Plant at J.B.'s, and within a month he was in the studio with the James Gang to record their second album, *James Gang Rides Again*. One of the songs on that album, "The Bomber," includes a passage from the classical piece by Maurice Ravel popularly known as "Ravel's Bolero." This was a favorite of Jimmy Page's, and in fact inspired Jeff Beck's own single "Beck's Bolero," which features Jimmy on guitar, and the "Bolero" section of Led Zeppelin's "How Many More Times."

OCTOBER 30–NOVEMBER 1 Led Zeppelin's tour continued through the Northeast to Buffalo, New York; Springfield, Massachusetts; and Syracuse, New York.

NOVEMBER 2 Led Zeppelin played at the O'Keefe Center in Toronto, Ontario. Two thousand people attended the show, and usually the place could pack in more than that. But unfortunately, ticket prices were considered too high for rock fans who'd already spent their concert money a week earlier seeing Iron Butterfly.

John Bonham was under the weather, so much so that he didn't play his drum solo, a regular part of the set. Also, there was some technological trouble midway through the

BELOW: *A poster from the Texas International Pop Festival, held on Labor Day weekend of 1969 at a park at the Dallas International Motor Speedway in Lewisville, Texas. Led Zeppelin played on August 31 along with eight other bands and musicians, including Chicago Transit Authority, Herbie Mann, and Santana.*

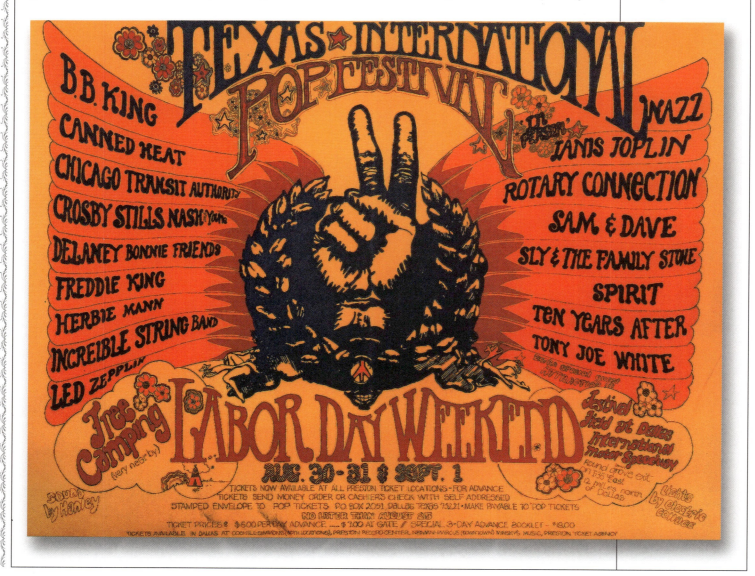

ANNOUNCING TWO NEW RECORD STORES:
CS9737
999 THIRD AVE. (bet. 59th & 60th Sts.)
60 EAST 8TH ST. (near B'way)
NOW AVAILABLE!

LED ZEPPELIN II
in stereo
on Atlantic Records

Bookmasters
RECORDS 999 THIRD AVE. 60 EAST 8TH ST. RECORDS

ABOVE: *Bookmasters, a record store in New York, announced the new* Led Zeppelin II *album in a newspaper ad in the fall of 1969.*

RIGHT: *An ad for the October 17, 1969, Led Zeppelin appearance at New York's Carnegie Hall.*

Howard Stein presents

LED ZEPPELIN AT CARNEGIE HALL

NEXT FRIDAY NIGHT (THE 17TH) AT 8:30 AND MIDNIGHT
Standing Room Only
57th Street and 7th Avenue. CI 7-7459

set, when Jimmy Page's amplifier blew out. Despite all the concert's shortcomings, the small audience remained loyal through the whole thing. Jimmy Page said afterward, "They were a very good audience. I mean, they were really with it at the end. You could see that."

NOVEMBER 4–8 Led Zeppelin's tour continued with one more Canadian date in Ontario, this one at the Memorial Auditorium in Kitchener, before moving to the midwestern U.S. on the following day with two shows in Kansas City, Missouri. The band then immediately went to California for three dates in San Francisco at Bill Graham's Winterland Ballroom.

Coinciding with the second Winterland date, on November 7, Atlantic Records released Zeppelin's second

U.S. single, "Whole Lotta Love," backed with "Living Loving Maid (She's Just a Woman)." Two versions of the single were produced, one at the full length of 5:33 and one edited down to 3:10 to be more consistent with radio stations' customary time constraints.

DECEMBER 6 Led Zeppelin played their final concert of the year. It was a multiple billing at a venue near Paris, France, with Zeppelin headlining above four other groups. One of those groups was the Pretty Things, which several years later would become one of the recording artists signed to Zeppelin's own Swan Song label. But this early on, Zeppelin was still with Atlantic Records, and in fact the band was finding some of its earliest chart successes in the United States.

1970

The year started as a continuation of what was begun late in 1969; Led Zeppelin busily toured on the strength of their second album as the headliner in university towns at home and arenas abroad. By the summer, a third album was being prepared and was soon released, signaling a new direction for the band. By the end of the year, a fourth album was already being prepared.

JANUARY Led Zeppelin spent the first month of 1970 on tour in the United Kingdom, shortly after which *Led Zeppelin II* would advance to the top of the charts in that country. At the same time, the U.S. single "Whole Lotta Love" was achieving its peak position on the *Billboard* chart at number four.

An issue of the British music magazine *Disc* contains an interview with John Paul Jones. Normally, Jimmy Page and Robert Plant were the ones being interviewed, because they were much more high-profile onstage. Jones said in that interview that he didn't want to be out front playing, as Jimmy was. He said, "I believe you should do what you have to, and if I'm bass, rather than try to lead on bass and push myself, I prefer to put down a good solid bass line."

Jones ended up being the member of Led Zeppelin with the lowest profile, which he says had its advantages. He would be able to change his hairstyles throughout the 1970s, enabling him to avoid public recognition. Since that was the case, he could get away with wild and crazy behavior that would have been reported in magazines and newspapers if he had had the visibility of Page, Plant, or John Bonham.

JANUARY 3 John Paul Jones turned twenty-four years old during his last weekend off before touring.

JANUARY 7 Led Zeppelin's winter tour of the UK began at Town Hall in Birmingham, England. Around this time, they began adding a slow blues tune entitled "Since I've Been Loving You" into the set list. For this song and one other, John Paul Jones was playing the organ onstage regularly, expanding his typical role beyond that of a mere bassist for the first time. "Since I've Been Loving You" was a constant in the set list months before Led Zeppelin recorded it for *Led Zeppelin III* in the spring.

JANUARY 8 The second show of Led Zeppelin's tour took place at Colston Hall in Bristol, England.

JANUARY 9 Jimmy Page's twenty-sixth birthday fell on the date of Led Zeppelin's filmed return performance at the Royal Albert Hall in London. It was said at the time that a documentary would be produced using the footage of the concert. However, it was not used in any official capacity until the 2003 release of the *Led Zeppelin DVD*.

JANUARY 13 Led Zeppelin performed at the Guild Hall in Portsmouth, England.

JANUARY 15 Led Zeppelin performed at City Hall in Newcastle, England.

JANUARY 16 Led Zeppelin performed at City Hall in Sheffield, England.

JANUARY 24 Led Zeppelin performed at Leeds University's Refectory Hall in Leeds, England.

FEBRUARY Early in the month, *Led Zeppelin II* was hitting the top of the charts in England and had already sold two million copies since its October 1969 release. Led Zeppelin still resisted the temptation to release any singles in its home country.

FEBRUARY 6 Robert Plant was injured in a minor car accident near his home. The car crash took place when Robert was on his way back from seeing Spirit in concert. He suffered cuts to his face and damage to his teeth. He was taken to the hospital and released following examination.

FEBRUARY 7 Led Zeppelin postponed their show at Usher Hall in Edinburgh, Scotland, due to Robert Plant's condition.

FEBRUARY 17 Led Zeppelin's postponed Edinburgh show took place. It was their final UK date.

FEBRUARY 23 Led Zeppelin entered Finland for the very first time, for a concert at Kulttuuritalo in Helsinki.

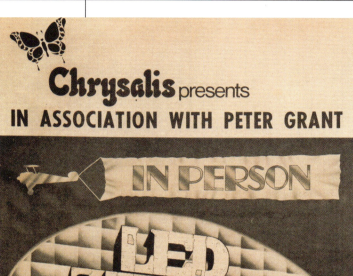

A newspaper ad for Led Zeppelin's English tour in January 1970.

Onstage, Robert Plant introduced Jimmy Page's guitar solo "White Summer" as "White Caulk."

FEBRUARY 25 Led Zeppelin returned to Sweden for a show at the Konserthuset in Göteborg.

FEBRUARY 26 Sales in Sweden of both Led Zeppelin albums earned the band a gold record award. Only the Beatles had earned Sweden's gold record award prior to this.

Led Zeppelin's second concert in Sweden during this tour took place at the Konserthuset in Stockholm. A journalist claimed in a write-up of this show that Jimmy Page spat on an audience member. The reviewer defended Page's action, saying the "fan" insisted on playing harmonica throughout the one-man guitar instrumental "White Summer."

FEBRUARY 27 Led Zeppelin is said to have played at the Concertgebouw in Amsterdam, the Netherlands.

FEBRUARY 28 By the time Led Zeppelin arrived in Denmark, the band had another unexpected turn of events, this time in the form of a legal threat from Countess Eva von Zeppelin, the granddaughter of the late German inventor of the zeppelin dirigible airship.

Jimmy Page recalled years later that at first the countess had been thrilled to learn there was a British band using the family name; however, she changed her mind after seeing the image on the band's first album, the crash of the Hindenburg, which was a zeppelin! The countess said if the band were to use the name in her country again, she would sue.

Rather than take a chance, on the occasion of the group's February 28, 1970, concert in Copenhagen, Denmark, Led Zeppelin reportedly changed its name for one night only to the Nobs, British slang for "male genitals."

This story has been passed down for ages. It is undocumented, however, and no one knows how exactly this storied name change took place. After all, the name Led Zeppelin does appear on concert posters and tickets.

MARCH 7 Led Zeppelin headlined at the Casino, a popular venue in Montreux, Switzerland. It was Zeppelin's only concert there in 1970, and they would play there twice more in 1971 before—as Deep Purple's song "Smoke on the Water" recounts—it burned to the ground.

MARCH 8 Led Zeppelin's first tour of West Germany opened in Munich at Circus Krone Bau. Prior to this, the band had not played in West Germany except to tape a lip-synched film sequence for television.

MARCH 10 What would have been Led Zeppelin's second West German concert was to take place in Frankfurt at the Jahrhunderthalle, the two-thousand-seat venue where ticketless fans rioted outside a Jethro Tull concert in February. When Led Zeppelin's concert was canceled, it was explained that the venue was too small to hold a Led Zeppelin concert without risking a repeat of the February riots. The promoters ended up finding an outdoor fairgrounds venue in Frankfurt where Led Zeppelin would play over the summer.

So instead of Frankfurt, Led Zeppelin spent March 10 in Hamburg, where they played the first of two consecutive nights at the Musikhalle. Following the performance of "Heartbreaker," Robert Plant mockingly referenced the opening lyrics of the song that followed it on *Led Zeppelin II*: "With a purple umbrella." When he stopped there, the audience laughed and applauded.

MARCH 11 Led Zeppelin performed a second night at the Musikhalle in Hamburg, West Germany.

MARCH 12 Led Zeppelin's European tour concluded at the Rheinhalle in Düsseldorf, West Germany.

MARCH 21 Led Zeppelin began a historic fifth North American tour that would put them on the road for a solid month without more than about four nights off.

And each Zeppelin show would be close to two hours long. Led Zeppelin was setting a new precedent. The standard had been to have multiple acts; the presence of the opening act reduced the length of the headlining act's performance. The concept of not having an opening act was unheard of at the time.

One of the more outspoken voices within the band was John Bonham. Zeppelin's drummer normally didn't have much contact with the press, but he did grant an interview to talk about what the band was doing on tour. Bonham said, "Say we had a couple of supporting acts. The kids don't really want to see them. They want to see us. Other groups that have backup acts are just backing it so they don't have to play so long. Most don't have to do two hours like we do. There is a lot of money involved. If the kids pay four dollars for a ticket, it is better to give them value than have them see two acts they never heard of before us and see us [for] forty-five minutes."

The first concert on this tour was in Vancouver, British Columbia, Canada, where they broke the Beatles' attendance record. An audience recording of this night was the first one ever to be released as a bootleg.

MARCH 22 Seattle, Washington, became the first U.S. city to host Led Zeppelin on their fifth North American tour. The concert was held at the Seattle Center Arena.

MARCH 23 Led Zeppelin's tour continued south within the Pacific Northwest, to the Memorial Coliseum in Portland, Oregon. The concert was sponsored by KISN Radio.

MARCH 25 Led Zeppelin performed at the Denver Coliseum in Colorado. It was their first time back in Denver since their first U.S. concert in 1968, a fact that Robert Plant did not let pass without mention.

MARCH 26 Led Zeppelin performed at the Salt Palace Arena in Salt Lake City, Utah. Previously, in 1969, they had opened for Vanilla Fudge at the Terrace Ballroom in town.

MARCH 27 Led Zeppelin returned to the Los Angeles area for their first concert at the L.A. Forum, which would be their almost exclusive area concert venue for their remaining years. It is located in Inglewood, California, just outside Los Angeles.

MARCH 28 Led Zeppelin performed in Dallas, Texas, at the Memorial Auditorium.

MARCH 29 Led Zeppelin performed in Houston, Texas, at the University of Houston's Hofheinz Pavilion.

MARCH 30 Led Zeppelin performed at the Civic Arena in Pittsburgh, Pennsylvania.

MARCH 31 Led Zeppelin performed at the Spectrum in Philadelphia, Pennsylvania.

APRIL 1 Led Zeppelin is rumored to have performed at the Boston Garden in Boston, Massachusetts.

APRIL 2 Led Zeppelin played their one and only show in the state of West Virginia: at the Civic Center Arena in Charleston. This was the first of several concerts in the South during the month of April. There, Led Zeppelin traveled with extra security in response to dirty looks and the occasional death threat.

APRIL 3 Led Zeppelin played at the Macon Coliseum in Macon, Georgia.

APRIL 4 Led Zeppelin played at the Indiana State Fair Coliseum in Indianapolis, Indiana. It was the group's first time performing in the state, and they would be back within two weeks.

APRIL 5 As Led Zeppelin performed at the Civic Center in Baltimore, Maryland, equipment trouble plagued the band. During the opening song, Robert Plant's microphone shut off, which was the first of several times it would malfunction during the concert.

APRIL 6 Led Zeppelin may have performed in Atlanta, Georgia.

APRIL 7 Led Zeppelin performed at the Charlotte Coliseum in Charlotte, North Carolina.

APRIL 8 Led Zeppelin performed at the J. S. Dorton Arena on the North Carolina State Fairgrounds in Raleigh.

APRIL 9 Led Zeppelin played at the Curtis Hixon Hall in Tampa, Florida.

APRIL 10 Led Zeppelin played at the Miami Beach Convention Hall in Miami, Florida.

APRIL 11 Led Zeppelin played at the Kiel Auditorium in Saint Louis, Missouri. It was their first concert at the venue. (A scheduled concert on June 1, 1969, was to feature the Who and Led Zeppelin billed over Joe Cocker, but the show was canceled.)

APRIL 12 Led Zeppelin played at the Metropolitan Sports Center in Bloomington, Minnesota.

APRIL 13 Led Zeppelin returned to Canada to perform at the Forum in Montreal, Quebec. As was also the case on Led Zeppelin's previous Canadian date, the Montreal show saw the band break an attendance record previously set by the Beatles.

APRIL 14 Led Zeppelin's third Canadian appearance of the North American tour took place at the Civic Centre Arena in Lansdowne Park in Ottawa, Ontario.

APRIL 15 Led Zeppelin may have played a fourth Canadian date in Winnipeg, Manitoba.

APRIL 16 Led Zeppelin returned to the United States for a show at Roberts Stadium in Evansville, Indiana.

Led Zeppelin rocks out at the Musikhalle in Hamburg, Germany, on March 11, 1970.

APRIL 17 Led Zeppelin received the keys to the city of Memphis and, later in the day, performed at the Mid-South Coliseum in Memphis, Tennessee. Legend holds it was at this concert that Led Zeppelin manager Peter Grant was held at gunpoint and told to remove his band from the stage.

APRIL 18 Robert Plant's voice was hoarse as Led Zeppelin performed at the Arizona Coliseum in Phoenix, Arizona. An audience tape of what is believed to be the complete concert includes fewer than ninety minutes of music, or about half an hour shorter than the typical Led Zeppelin concert of the era. It ends shortly after Jimmy Page explained to the audience, "I don't know whether you know, but Robert's been very ill tonight, and as he came off, he's just collapsed and we just called for a doctor and everything. We'd really like to do more, but obviously, this makes it impossible. But thanks. You've been a great audience."

APRIL 19 One final Led Zeppelin concert of the fifth North American tour was to take place at the Las Vegas Convention Center in Nevada. However, the concert was canceled due to Robert Plant's condition.

APRIL 26 Jimmy Page made a rare television appearance, appearing by himself on Julie Felix's BBC program to perform his solo instrumental "White Summer."

MAY Robert Plant was under doctor's orders not to sing, so he retreated with his family to the mountainside cottage called Bron-Yr-Aur, in Wales. He invited Jimmy Page to join him, and they began writing acoustic material together that would influence the sound of Led Zeppelin's next album. Page has said it was during this time that he and Plant really got to know each other well, and their musical partnership was vastly improved.

The same month, Led Zeppelin began recording sessions for their third album, first recording on location

BELOW: *The second Bath Festival took place in the small English town of Shepton Mallet on the weekend of June 27–28, 1970. Pictured here are a flyer for the event and a ticket for the second day, when Led Zeppelin performed. Melody Maker reported that by 8:00 p.m., before Led Zeppelin came on, "it was estimated that a quarter of a million people—roughly the population of the city of Leeds—were champing at the bit awaiting Led Zeppelin."*

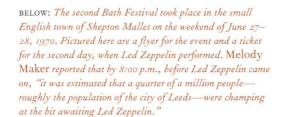

inside the mansion Headley Grange in Hampshire, England, with the aid of a mobile recording studio. Further *Led Zeppelin III* recording sessions took place at Olympic Sound Studios in London throughout May and possibly into June.

JUNE 22 Led Zeppelin's next concert date could very easily have not taken place. With certain workers on strike in Iceland, the construction of a stage necessary to host the Led Zeppelin concert in Reykjavik would have been nearly impossible were it not for volunteer students from a local university. These students preferred that their first chance to see Led Zeppelin perform in their home country not be taken away, so they constructed the stage themselves.

Led Zeppelin performed in Iceland as part of a cultural exchange between that country and England.

JUNE 27 Led Zeppelin was originally scheduled to perform two shows at Madison Square Garden in New York on this date. However, the shows were rescheduled for September so that they could instead accept an offer to perform at the Bath Festival for a second year in a row.

JUNE 28 Led Zeppelin headlined at the Bath Festival of Blues and Progressive Music. It was a new name for the festival, previously called the Bath Festival of Blues. It was also held in a new and larger location this year, at the Royal Bath & West Showground in Shepton Mallet, England. Years later, promoter Freddy Bannister wrote about his experiences promoting Led Zeppelin several times between 1969 and 1979.

Onstage, Robert Plant commented: "We've been playing in America a lot recently and we really thought that coming back here we might have a bit of a dodgy time, but we're starting to get a bit, uh . . . There's a lot of things going wrong in America at the moment, that are getting a bit sticky and whatnot, and it's really nice to come to an open-air festival where there's no really bad thing happening, and everything has carried on peacefully. It's really nice."

The concert includes the first known performances of two songs from *Led Zeppelin III*. The band opened with "Immigrant Song," the Viking lyrics of which reflected Led Zeppelin's fresh conquest of Iceland. Prior to the addition of "Immigrant Song," the opening song at Led Zeppelin concerts all year long had been "We're Gonna Groove," which was not heard on any Led Zeppelin album until *Coda* in 1982.

Also at this show, the members of Led Zeppelin sang four-part harmony on what may be the first acoustic song to be played at one of their concerts, "That's the Way."

Led Zeppelin's performance was filmed against the backdrop of the setting sun, but the footage was subsequently deemed unusable and shelved for this reason. The footage has never even leaked into circulation as a bootleg.

JULY 16 Led Zeppelin kicked off the year's second tour of mainland Europe with a date at the Sporthalle in Cologne, West Germany.

JULY 17 Led Zeppelin's tour continued with a performance at the Gruga-Halle in Essen, West Germany.

JULY 18 Led Zeppelin performed at the Festhalle on the Frankfurt Fairgrounds in West Germany.

JULY 19 Led Zeppelin performed for the first time in West Germany's capital city of West Berlin. Held at the Deutschlandhalle, the show marked the final date of the European tour, and Led Zeppelin was headed back to North America within a few weeks.

AUGUST Two concert festivals where Led Zeppelin were originally scheduled to appear during the month of August were canceled for separate reasons.

The Strawberry Fields Festival was scheduled to take place in Moncton, New Brunswick, Canada, with a Led Zeppelin appearance scheduled for August 8. However, in July, the local government in Moncton decided against approving an amusement tax license and also revoked a previously issued traveling license. Organizers were unable to move the festival to another location, so they canceled it altogether.

Meanwhile, Led Zeppelin was also scheduled to headline Boston College's one-day Eagle Rock Festival on Friday, August 14. However, the week of the concert, the event was pulled due to pressure from a local association whose members largely opposed it.

The cancellations were a blow to the Led Zeppelin organization, but there was another good reason why some other concert dates from this period went to the chopping block. In England, John Paul Jones's father, Joe Baldwin, was gravely ill. While Jones remained in England at his father's side, the tour dates changed.

Some shows were able to be rescheduled for later in the month or for September. Such was the case in Detroit, Michigan; Cleveland, Ohio; Oakland, California; Boston, Massachusetts; and Hampton, Virginia. Others were not able to be rescheduled. These included Cincinnati, Ohio; Pittsburgh, Pennsylvania; Charlotte, North Carolina; Jacksonville, Florida; and Tallahassee, Florida.

In the meantime, Jimmy Page assisted with the mixing of *Led Zeppelin III* at Ardent Studios in Memphis, Tennessee.

AUGUST 15 Led Zeppelin's delayed summer tour of North America finally began with a date at Yale University's Yale Bowl in New Haven, Connecticut.

AUGUST 17 At Led Zeppelin's second concert of the summer tour, they brought their acoustic set for the first time to the United States. The fifth song of the set was "That's the Way," which had just been recorded for *Led Zeppelin III* and would be released the following month. This show also saw the first known live performance of a new Jimmy Page guitar instrumental entitled "Bron-Yr-Aur." The studio version of that track was already completed but wouldn't be released until 1975.

AUGUST 20–21 Led Zeppelin's first two concerts in the state of Oklahoma took place in Oklahoma City on

BELOW: *A ticket from the July 18, 1970, Led Zeppelin concert in Frankfurt, Germany, at the Festhalle. Apparently, almost half of the crowd was made up of personnel from the many U.S. military bases located in Frankfurt at the time.*

BOTTOM: *An ad for Led Zeppelin's August 15, 1970, performance at the Yale Bowl, a football stadium in New Haven, Connecticut. The small print under the name Led Zeppelin notes that the concert is sponsored by Silly Putty.*

OPPOSITE PAGE: *Ioannis, John Bonham: Moby Dick, 2011.*

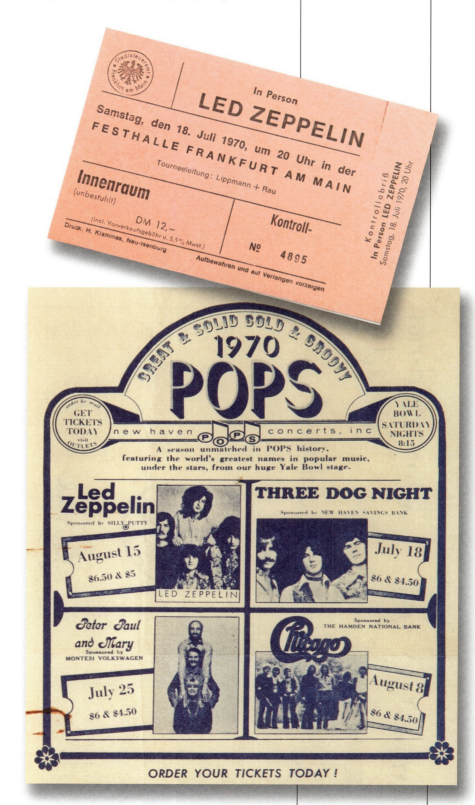

Concerts West
Presents

AN EVENING OF

LED ZEPPELIN

AUGUST 20th—OKLAHOMA CITY FAIRGROUNDS COLISEUM

TICKETS — PICATAPE
STEREO CITY
LITTLE JACKS
(STILLWATER)

August 20 and in Tulsa on August 21. Robert Plant told the Tulsa audience to expect the concert to warm them up: "Be prepared to take off your ties." Just as the acoustic set was about to begin, Plant spotted people he thought appeared to be sleeping.

AUGUST 26 The time of Led Zeppelin's concert at the Public Hall in Cleveland, Ohio, was shifted from 8:30 p.m. to 5:30 p.m. This was because John Paul Jones's father, Joe Baldwin, had just died. Ticket refunds were offered to those who were inconvenienced by the change of time. A local newspaper reported that Jones had left the concert early and that an unidentified girl wearing a T-shirt bearing the name of the concert promoter, Belkin Productions, filled in on bass for an encore.

AUGUST 27 Due to the funeral of Joe Baldwin, Led Zeppelin's scheduled concert in Milwaukee, Wisconsin, at the Milwaukee Arena, was postponed for four days and made up on August 31.

AUGUST 29 Led Zeppelin's performance at the Manitoba Centennial Pop Festival was in jeopardy because of rain and thunderstorms in the afternoon.

Some of the equipment outside at Winnipeg Stadium was ruined, and organizers rushed to move the festival to Winnipeg Arena. A call went out on the radio for local musicians to bring any type of equipment—instruments, microphones, cables—to the venue. As the arena opened its doors, it let people in regardless of whether they had tickets or not. When it was filled to capacity, the doors were closed and many people with tickets remained outside. Led Zeppelin finally went onstage around 3:00 a.m., using whatever equipment was available to them.

SEPTEMBER 1–9 As the month began, Led Zeppelin were beginning the West Coast dates of their tour. These included a return to the Seattle Center Coliseum on September 1 and the L.A. Forum on September 4, with shows in Oakland and San Diego on the two days in between. The tour continued on September 6 with two Sunday shows at the International Center Arena in Honolulu, Hawaii. An afternoon show on September 9 at the Boston Garden was canceled, but an evening show on the same day did take place.

SEPTEMBER 16 As the *Melody Maker* Poll Awards ceremony took place in London, Led Zeppelin became the

ABOVE: *A British flag adorns the flyer for the Led Zeppelin concert at the State Fairgrounds Arena in Oklahoma City, August 20, 1970.*

first band to end the Beatles' eight-year streak as the most popular group chosen annually by *Melody Maker* readers. In addition, Robert Plant was named the best male vocalist. In conjunction with the news, both John Bonham and Robert Plant were interviewed on the set of the BBC news program *Nationwide*.

SEPTEMBER 18 Led Zeppelin returned to North America for the conclusion of their tour. A day ahead of the last two shows at Madison Square Garden, the good news of Led Zeppelin having replaced the Beatles as Britain's most popular group prompted a press conference attended by New York media. This press conference can be viewed among the bonus features of *Led Zeppelin DVD*, released in 2003.

Meanwhile, back in London, Jimi Hendrix died on September 18. The precise circumstances of the twenty-seven-year-old's death have never been fully explained, and in the first twenty-four hours all sorts of stories were being passed around. Everybody was confused and shattered and just wanted the reports of his death to be untrue.

SEPTEMBER 19 Led Zeppelin played two shows at Madison Square Garden. The venue was a step up from the smaller shows they'd played the previous year at the Fillmore East, Central Park, and Carnegie Hall.

The band was supposed to be in a good mood, but Hendrix's death contributed to the less-than-stellar atmosphere. At the first show, the crowd was very loud when Led Zeppelin was trying to play a set of acoustic material previously unheard in New York. When certain members of the audience contributed to the rowdiness by being loud and pushing their way toward the stage, it didn't help things, either.

Amid all this tension, Led Zeppelin's set at both shows included their song "Thank You," which opens and closes with the lyrics, "If the sun refused to shine, I would still be loving you. When mountains crumble to the sea, there would still be you and me." These words may have actually been derived from the Jimi Hendrix Experience tune "If 6 Was 9," released on *Axis: Bold as Love* in 1967. That song opens with the lyrics: "If the sun refused to shine, I don't mind, I don't mind. If the mountains fell in the sea, let it be, it ain't me."

It was right after Led Zeppelin played "Thank You" at the first Madison Square Garden show that Robert Plant finally addressed the elephant in the room: "They've asked me to say something about something that's quite a delicate point, but yesterday something happened that really wasn't the best-timed thing ever. Jimi Hendrix died, and we were all

really sorry because he contributed a lot to the current music thing, and we'd like to just hope that everyone thinks that it was a brutal shame." The audience responded with applause.

The crowd at the second show that night was, at times, even louder. Plant took another opportunity to comment on Hendrix's passing, and this time he did so earlier in the concert. During the third break between songs, he at first had to plead twice with the audience to be quiet. When they did, he addressed the situation more eloquently than before, saying: "Yesterday, a rather uncomfortable thing happened for everybody. A great loss came about for the whole of the music world. And we would like to think that you, as well as us, are very sorry that—that Jimi Hendrix went. I spoke to a close friend of his about half an hour ago, and he said that he would probably prefer that everybody get together and have a really good time, rather than talk about it. So we'd like to get on and try to make everybody happy, right?"

Since the audience seemed agreeable, Plant then immediately introduced the next song, which was the one that featured John Paul Jones on mandolin, called "That's the Way." The second concert lasted over two hours in all and included an improvised encore medley of songs by Little Richard, Chuck Berry, and Eddie Cochran.

This was Led Zeppelin's final concert of the year.

OCTOBER 5 *Led Zeppelin III* was released in the United States.

OCTOBER 16 Led Zeppelin received a pair of gold record awards in London for exported Led Zeppelin recordings. The band, minus John Bonham, attended to receive the awards for sales of the U.S. single "Whole Lotta Love" and for sales of *Led Zeppelin II* in Europe.

OCTOBER 23 *Led Zeppelin III* was released in the United Kingdom.

OCTOBER 31 *Led Zeppelin III* reached number one on the *Billboard* album chart.

NOVEMBER 5 Led Zeppelin released their third U.S. single, featuring "Immigrant Song" on the A side and, for the first and only time, a nonalbum track on the B side, "Hey Hey What Can I Do."

NOVEMBER 7 *Led Zeppelin III* reached the number one position on the UK album chart, where it remained for three weeks.

DECEMBER With Led Zeppelin very much aware of the success of their third album, they entered the studio for further recording sessions. They returned to the mansion Headley Grange in Hampshire, England, for recording sessions there using a mobile recording studio. They also recorded for the first time at Island Studios in London.

DECEMBER 12 *Led Zeppelin III* reached number one on the UK album chart for a second time.

BELOW: *An ad for Led Zeppelin's first performance at Madison Square Garden in New York, on September 19, 1970. They did two shows, at 2:00 and 8:00 p.m.; tickets for the best seats were $7.50. Led Zeppelin performed fourteen shows at the Garden in total between 1970 and 1977.*

1971

The end of 1970 saw Led Zeppelin being so productive as to begin work on a fourth Led Zeppelin album just as the third was picking up steam. Their high level of productivity at the beginning of the year would pay off immeasurably—but only after a frustrating delay.

JANUARY Led Zeppelin continued recording their fourth album, mostly on location at the mansion Headley Grange in Hampshire, England, but also at Olympic Sound Studios and Island Studios, both in London.

FEBRUARY Led Zeppelin announced a new tour, dubbed Back to the Clubs, as the band would find themselves playing small clubs again. Band manager Peter Grant told *Melody Maker*: "A lot of the small clubs have disappeared because groups have charged too much in the past. We want to prove the biggest of groups can go out and play there."

John Bonham said in the same article: "It'll be great because the atmosphere is always much better than a big place like the Albert Hall. We wanted to do a tour where the greatest number possible could come and see us, at the places that made us when we started out."

Jimmy Page told *Record Mirror*: "The audiences were becoming bigger and bigger," but also this month, Led Zeppelin faced rumors they were breaking up after their UK tour, with reports suggesting the band members were interested in pursuing solo projects. Led Zeppelin members, manager Peter Grant, and spokesman Bill Harry all denied the breakup rumors.

Robert Plant told *Disc* and *Music Echo*: "To go into the clubs to play and make nothing at all seems to be the only way we can go without being crucified. The being-recognized thing isn't nearly so bad today, but I see now that the Beatles must have been the most pestered people in the world."

FEBRUARY 14 *Disc* and *Music Echo* announced Led Zeppelin was the top group in the world, as chosen by readers' votes (and also, somehow, the number four group in the United Kingdom). *Led Zeppelin III* was voted the number three album. Jimmy Page was voted the number three musician. Robert Plant was voted the number three singer.

MARCH 5–25 Led Zeppelin performed live again for the first time since September 1970, this time debuting new songs on March 5 at Ulster Hall in Belfast, Northern Ireland. During the concert, Robert Plant asked the crowd in the war-torn city, "Now, you see, if everybody was like this every single day, there'd be no hang-ups, right? No problems." The following night also saw Led Zeppelin's first (and only) concert in Dublin, Ireland.

From the very first night, the set list throughout the Back to the Clubs tour benefited from some of the new material that had just been recorded, including "Rock and Roll," "Black Dog," and "Stairway to Heaven."

The Back to the Clubs tour did see Led Zeppelin planning their return to five of the same venues that had hosted them in 1968 and 1969. These were Leeds University's Refectory Hall (where they'd played once in January 1970); the Bath Pavilion (where they'd played in December 1968); the Mayfair Ballroom in Newcastle (where they'd played a date as "the Yardbirds featuring Jimmy Page" with four other bands in October 1968); Liverpool University's Mountford Hall (where they'd played their final concert billed as the Yardbirds in October 1968); and the Marquee Club in London (where they'd played three times in their first six months of touring the UK).

Led Zeppelin also reached out to other small venues in towns they'd visited in earlier times, and even some venues in previously unexplored British towns. Such concerts took place in Canterbury, at the University of Kent; in Stoke-on-Trent; in Manchester, at Manchester University; in Sutton Coldfield; in Nottingham; and in Southampton, at Southampton University's Old Union Refectory.

The scheduled return to Liverpool University's Mountford Hall on March 16 was canceled due to Plant's vocal problems. It was rescheduled for May 10, during a European tour. Vocal problems again plagued Plant later

OPPOSITE PAGE, TOP LEFT: *Led Zeppelin played at the Nottingham Boat Club in Nottingham, England, on the Trent River, on March 21, 1971, as part of their Back to the Clubs tour. The venue was a boathouse belonging to a historic rowing club (now part of the Nottingham Rowing Club), where numerous concerts were held. The ticket shown here specifies that only members of the club could gain admittance to the concert.*

OPPOSITE PAGE, BOTTOM LEFT: *On May 10, 1971, Led Zeppelin played at Liverpool University, another intimate venue, to a crowd of less than two thousand. This simple ticket from the concert lists a price of 60 pence, approximately $1.40 at the time.*

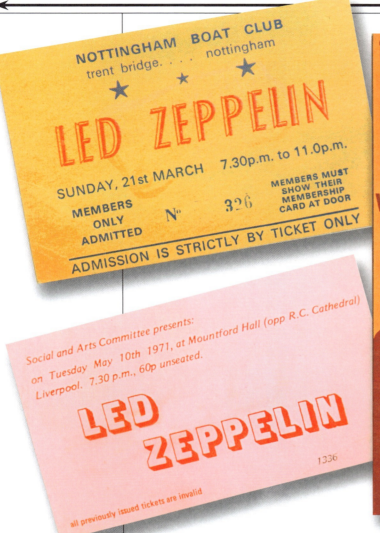

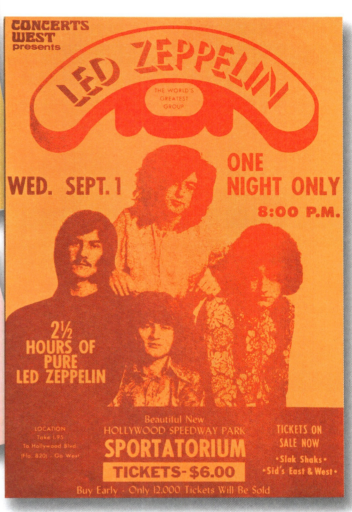

TOP RIGHT: *A handbill for the Led Zeppelin show at the Hollywood Sportatorium arena in Hollywood, Florida, September 1, 1971.*

in March, and a March 25 performance at the Paris Theatre in London, to be recorded by the BBC, was rescheduled for one week later, on April 1.

APRIL 1 Led Zeppelin performed the Paris Theatre concert, recorded by BBC Radio for John Peel's *In Concert* program.

MAY 3–10 Led Zeppelin performed at least one show in Denmark, at K.B. Hallen in Copenhagen on May 3. A performance the following day at Fyens Forum in Odense had not been confirmed. The band returned to England to make up their canceled date from March at Liverpool University's Mountford Hall in England. Further songs added to the set list at this time include the then-unreleased "Misty Mountain Hop" and the *Led Zeppelin III* track "Four Sticks."

JULY 5 As Led Zeppelin headlined an Italian music festival in Milan, Italy, their performance was interrupted by riots after police teargassed the crowds. Led Zeppelin fled the stage while roadies scurried to salvage their equipment before the stage was destroyed.

AUGUST 7–8 Led Zeppelin performed a pair of concerts at the Casino in Montreux, Switzerland, their second

and third appearances there—and their last before the December fire that claimed the casino. These shows were essentially warm-up dates for the North American tour, which would begin later in the month.

AUGUST 19 Led Zeppelin's North American tour began in Vancouver, British Columbia, Canada. At the Pacific Coliseum, the show was overcrowded, causing part of the stage to collapse and some fans to be injured. With the Milan debacle from July fresh in his mind, Robert Plant granted an interview to Rick McGrath of the local underground newspaper *Georgia Straight* after the concert. Plant impressed the interviewer with his knowledge of past events in Vancouver, including community activism, protests, and clashes with police. During the interview, Plant recognized it was after midnight and so it was now his twenty-third birthday.

AUGUST 20–SEPTEMBER 17 Led Zeppelin's North American tour comprised at least twenty-one additional concerts, including two at the L.A. Forum, four throughout Texas, one at New York's Madison Square Garden, two in upstate New York locations, two in Berkeley, California, and two final shows in Honolulu, Hawaii.

While in Los Angeles, Led Zeppelin set up at Sunset Sound for the mixing of their fourth album.

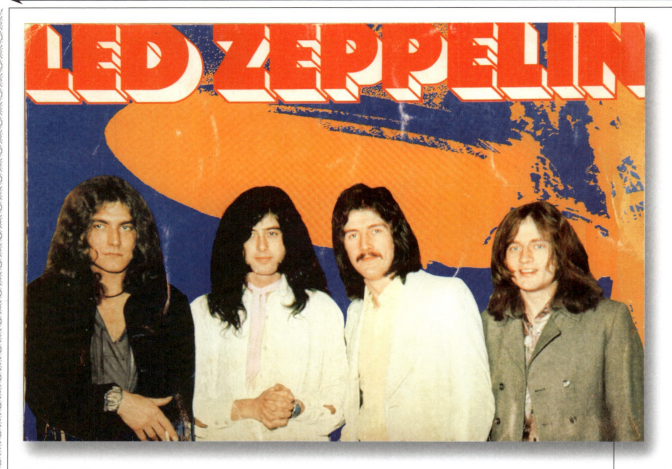

SEPTEMBER 23–29 Immediately after the Hawaiian shows, Led Zeppelin toured Japan for the first time. Their "Immigrant Song" single was number one in Japan. They opened with two nights at Tokyo's Budokan arena, closed with two nights in Osaka, and performed one concert in Hiroshima in between. On the day of the Hiroshima concert, Led Zeppelin received peace medals and the city's Civil Charter.

OCTOBER John Paul Jones and John Bonham returned home to England, while Jimmy Page and Robert Plant continued touring the Far East. Their destinations included Hong Kong, Thailand, and India.

Meanwhile, back home, word arrived that the band's fourth album was soon to be released—and that it would not bear a title or have any writing whatsoever on the cover. In London, Jimmy Page helped Glyn Johns mix the album. Word was released at the end of the month that Led Zeppelin would return for their first UK tour since the Back to the Clubs tour in March.

NOVEMBER 8 Led Zeppelin's untitled fourth album was released in time for the UK tour.

NOVEMBER 11–DECEMBER 21 Led Zeppelin's UK tour kicked off on November 11 with a concert at City Hall in Newcastle, England. The band had played at that venue before, in January of 1969 and in January of 1970. Following the tour opener, Led Zeppelin played at least sixteen additional concerts through the end of the year.

The highlight of the tour was the pair of shows on November 20 and 21 at the Empire Pool (currently Wembley Arena) in London, dubbed Electric Magic. The shows included other musical acts and all manner of circus acts, including plate spinners, trapeze acts, and performing animals. "I expected a bit more from the pigs, didn't you?" joked Robert Plant onstage during the shows. "I could have brought some goats."

Led Zeppelin's untitled fourth album made its way up the UK charts in November. By the first week of December, it had reached the number one spot on *Record Mirror*'s album chart. It remained in the top spot for two weeks. In the United States, the album reached number two.

Led Zeppelin also released "Black Dog" as a single in the United Sates, backed with "Misty Mountain Hop." It would reach number fifteen in the U.S. The single was also released in Australia, where it fared slightly better, charting at number eleven. Led Zeppelin announced late in the year that their next tour would take place in Australia.

ABOVE: *The front of the concert program booklet for Led Zeppelin's Japan tour, September 23–29, 1971.*

BELOW: *A ticket from the first show of the 1971 Japan tour: September 23 at the Budokan in Tokyo, the famed rock arena where many live rock albums were recorded over the years.*

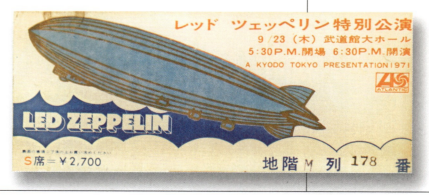

As was the case the previous year, Led Zeppelin found themselves entering January with a new studio album having been released and catching on. More notably, they once again had some time off before the next tour dates on the horizon. Jimmy Page took advantage of the break to attempt some recording at his home studio early in the year. There would be further recording opportunities elsewhere in England and even in India over the next few months.

Before long, Led Zeppelin had written enough music for yet another album. However, 1972 would be the first year in Led Zeppelin's history that a new album would not be released. Despite this setback, the band remained active throughout the year, touring four continents, and engaging in some friendly competition with the Rolling Stones to see who would be the top live act in the United States.

JANUARY Jimmy Page hosted Led Zeppelin at his home studio for rehearsals. Led Zeppelin also returned to Olympic Sound Studios in London, where parts of every Led Zeppelin album to date had been recorded.

FEBRUARY 12 In the United States, the "Black Dog" single reached its peak on the *Billboard* chart at number fifteen.

FEBRUARY 14 A planned Led Zeppelin concert appearance in Singapore was scrapped because the Singapore government was struggling to keep Western influences from seeping into the culture. In short, the band would not be allowed in Singapore due to their long hair. They continued on to Australia for a full-fledged tour of the country.

FEBRUARY 16 Led Zeppelin's first and only tour of Australia opened with a concert in Perth, Western Australia. Fans without tickets were forcing their way inside the venue, and fans were pushing their way onto the stage. More than one hundred police officers were called in to control the madness, but fans were still able to mob the group after the show was over, ripping Robert Plant's shirt.

FEBRUARY 17 Led Zeppelin woke up in their Adelaide hotel rooms to a raid by a drug squad. The police were unable to find anything illegal. Police said they were acting on a tip they had received, but Jimmy Page commented in an interview that it smelled more like retaliation to him.

FEBRUARY 18 As was the case with most of the shows on the Australian tour, their show in Adelaide was to be held at an open-air stadium. But it rained all day in Adelaide. The show was postponed to the following afternoon.

Jimmy Page and Robert Plant followed a recommendation to go see a Sydney-based blues-rock band called Fraternity playing at the Largs Pier Hotel. Between sets, Page approached the singer and offered to sit in with the group. The singer didn't recognize Page and Plant and told them to get lost. So they left. But once a roadie pointed out those two Englishmen were in Led Zeppelin, the Fraternity vocalist ran after them but couldn't find them. That singer who snubbed Page and Plant became somebody famous two years later as the original singer for AC/DC; his name was Bon Scott.

FEBRUARY 19 The postponed concert at Memorial Drive Park in Adelaide, South Australia, took place in the afternoon.

FEBRUARY 20 Rain interrupted Led Zeppelin's concert at Kooyong Stadium in Melbourne, Victoria. After a run-through of "Rock and Roll," Robert Plant told the audience, "I tell you what, we're in terrible danger up here, so cool it. And as soon as it stops pissing, we'll come back." He kept to his word, and they went back on, performing "Whole Lotta Love" and a medley of rock numbers, after which he said, "Thank you very much, and we've got to go. And you've got to go, too. Otherwise, we'll all blow up. We can't do it because the electricity and water just don't get together at all."

In an interview afterward, Plant explained, "It started raining at different points, and everybody knew that if we stood there too long, we'd get electrocuted, you know. And yet, when we said we can't do anymore, they said, 'Awww, awww.' We had to stop for about ten minutes and put tarp all around the stage and come back on, and when we came back on, there was about a forty-mile-an-hour wind blowing. The tarp holding over the PA system was falling down all over the guy who was controlling the PA. One minute he'd be there, and the next minute he's immersed in this big tent."

FEBRUARY 21 Gliding on the momentum of the "Black Dog" single, Atlantic Records released "Rock and Roll" as a single in the United States. It was the first time two separate U.S. singles emerged from any Led Zeppelin album.

FEBRUARY 25–29 Led Zeppelin played a show at Western Springs Stadium in Auckland, New Zealand, on February 25, and then returned to Australia for two more shows: on February 27 at the Showground in Sydney, New South Wales, and at Festival Hall in Brisbane, Queensland. During the Auckland show, a brief instrumental portion of the forthcoming album track "The Song Remains the Same" was inserted into a live version of "Dazed and Confused."

MARCH After the Australian tour ended, Jimmy Page and Robert Plant continued touring the world, just as they had following their tour of Japan the previous year. Their destinations again included India, where they arranged to rehearse some music with members of the Bombay Symphony Orchestra. Their rehearsals were recorded, showing that they attempted two Led Zeppelin songs: "Friends" from *Led Zeppelin III* and "Four Sticks" from the untitled fourth album.

APRIL 15 In the United States, Led Zeppelin scored a second hit single for the year with "Rock and Roll." It reached *Billboard*'s number forty-seven.

APRIL–MAY During this time, Robert Plant's wife, Maureen, gave birth to a son, Karac Pendragon Plant. The band convened at Mick Jagger's estate, Stargroves, in Berkshire, England, for some on-location recording sessions using the Rolling Stones' recording studio, engineered by Eddie Kramer. Further recording sessions took place at Island Studios and Olympic Sound Studios, both in London. Led Zeppelin was quickly back in action with two warm-up dates in Holland and Belgium on May 27 and 28, preceding a North American tour. Two of the new pieces recorded during those sessions, "The Crunge" and "Walter's Walk," were being inserted into instrumental portions of the live "Dazed and Confused" beginning around this time.

WELCOME BACK

LED ZEPPELIN ON TOUR:
6 June—Cobo Hall, Detroit
7 June—Montreal Forum, Montreal
9 June—Coliseum, Charlotte
10 June—Memorial Auditorium, Buffalo
11 June—Civic Center, Baltimore
14–15 June—Nassau County Coliseum, Hempstead, N.Y.
17 June—Memorial Coliseum, Portland, Oregon
18 June—Coliseum, Vancouver
19 June—Coliseum, Seattle
21 June—Coliseum, Denver
22 June—Swing Auditorium, San Bernardino, California
23 June—Sports Arena, San Diego, California
25 June—L.A. Forum, Los Angeles
27 June—Arena, Long Beach, California
28 June—Community Center, Tucson

Use the Power VOTE

JUNE 6–28 Led Zeppelin's North American tour comprised seventeen concerts. The tour hit many of the usual venues in places like Seattle, Portland, Denver, Charlotte, Baltimore, and Philadelphia. Notably, New York's Madison Square Garden was omitted this time, apparently due to high booking fees, but two shows at Nassau Veterans Memorial Coliseum on Long Island were booked instead.

After the tour, John Bonham expressed his dissatisfaction that the UK papers had almost completely ignored Led Zeppelin's overseas touring—at least compared to their coverage of the Rolling Stones, with whom the band shared a friendly rivalry. Zeppelin's drummer complained to *New Musical Express*: "We've just toured the States and done as well if not better than the Stones, but there was hardly anything about it in the British press. All we read was the Stones this and the Stones that, and it pissed us off, made us feel, 'What the hell.' Here we are flogging

ABOVE: *An ad welcoming Led Zeppelin back to the United States for their 1972 tour, which started in Detroit and ended in Tucson.*

OPPOSITE PAGE: *Ioannis,* Jimmy Page 1972, *2011.*

our guts out and for all the notice that's being given to us we might as well be playing in bloody Ceylon, because the kids in England didn't even know we were touring the States. It comes across as though we're neglecting the kids when we're not."

JUNE 14–15 While in New York, Led Zeppelin mixed their fifth album at Electric Lady Studios under the direction of Eddie Kramer.

JUNE 16 In London, a bill passed the House of Commons that increased fines for the manufacture or sale of bootlegs from $125 to $1,000. Punishment for a second offense could include two years' jail time. For years, Led Zeppelin manager Peter Grant had been rather vocal about the fact that he despised the practice of bootlegging because it ripped off artists and their fans alike.

JUNE 18–19 In Vancouver, British Columbia, fans rioting at a Rolling Stones concert vandalized the venue. This prompted officials to cancel the Led Zeppelin show, which had been scheduled for June 18. The Canadian concert was replaced on Led Zeppelin's itinerary by an extra U.S. show in Seattle, and ticket holders from Vancouver were encouraged to cross the border and attend.

Led Zeppelin did not miss the opportunity to play some of their newly recorded material in concert early on. The group's show in Seattle on June 19 witnessed the very first live versions of four songs: "The Ocean," "Over the Hills and Far Away," "Black Country Woman," and "Dancing Days." ("Black Country Woman" had been recorded during those recent sessions but would not be included on the next album. It was held back until *Physical Graffiti* in 1975.)

In fact, "Dancing Days" came up not once but twice during the second Seattle concert. Introducing it for the second time, as an encore, Robert Plant said, "This is one that you might have heard about two hours ago. This is called 'Dancing Days.' We like it so much, we're gonna do it again."

JUNE 25–27 Two of the last three concerts—specifically, those at the L.A. Forum on June 25 and at the Long Beach Arena on June 27—were recorded and ultimately edited together for the 2003 live release *How the West Was Won*.

AUGUST John Bonham gave an interview to *New Musical Express* in which he said: "You get all these letters in the music papers saying that Led Zeppelin aren't playing and recording anymore because they're too busy buying country mansions and Rolls-Royces, you know.

The scene at Rodney Bingenheimer's English Disco in Los Angeles, June 1972—Robert Plant (second from left), John Bonham (second from right), Jimmy Page (seated in background behind Plant), and John Paul Jones (standing in background behind the standing woman), along with a few female friends, including legendary rock groupies Sable Starr (far left) and Lori Maddox (far right).

LED ZEPPELIN

A UDO ARTISTS. INC. PRESENTATION 1972

特別

¥2,900

OPPOSITE PAGE: *Led Zeppelin headed back to tour Japan in 1972 from October 2–10; the cover to the tour program booklet is shown here.*

BELOW: *Tickets from the 1972 Japan tour, from left to right: the October 4 show in Osaka (blue), the October 9 shows in Osaka (green and yellow), and the October 3 shows in Tokyo (orange and red).*

"For a start, there ain't one person in this band who owns a Rolls. It must all stem from false information people have read in articles written by people who assume that's what we're doing. I'm still living in the same bloody house as I was when we first started. So's Robert. Nobody's changed that much.

"What most people don't understand is that we're always working, even if we don't choose to spread it all over the place. Everyone thinks we're just laying around relaxing, when in fact we are constantly rehearsing and recording. So that puts paid to all that crap, doesn't it?"

OCTOBER Led Zeppelin returned to Japan for a second tour, from October 2 to 10. It would be their last tour of Japan. Following the Japanese tour, the band returned to England to rehearse with their touring rig in London at the Rainbow Theatre. The month closed with two consecutive days' concerts at the new Pavillion venue in Montreux, Switzerland.

NOVEMBER In another sign that Led Zeppelin's feud with the Rolling Stones over publicity in England was not so serious, Jimmy Page and the Stones jammed in Jamaica.

NOVEMBER 10 Tickets for Led Zeppelin's upcoming tour of the United Kingdom went on sale. Within four hours, all 110,000 tickets were sold out.

NOVEMBER 30–DECEMBER 23 Led Zeppelin performed pairs of concerts in five cities in England, Scotland, and Wales as part of the first leg of a lengthy UK tour. These shows took place in Newcastle, Glasgow, Manchester, Cardiff, Birmingham, and London (at the 8,250-seat Alexandra Palace). They also played a single date in Brighton.

1973

JANUARY 2–30 Extending their UK tour from the previous month, Led Zeppelin played a further twelve dates in England, Scotland, and Wales, making this their longest and most extensive UK tour to date.

Early in the month, Robert Plant had the flu, causing a temporary setback for the band. The January 2 opening concert in Sheffield went ahead as planned, but the following two dates—January 3 in Preston and January 4 in Bradford—were made up later in the month. However, Plant's voice was permanently changed around this time

MARCH 2–APRIL 2 On the heels of their most extensive UK tour to date, Led Zeppelin embarked on their most extensive European tour to date. The tour opened with a single Danish date in Copenhagen, followed by at least two shows in Sweden. A planned date in Norway was scrapped. Several concerts in West Germany and France followed, with a single date in Austria also in the mix. Tapes of the band during many of these concerts reveal them to be at some of their most adventurous in terms of improvisation.

MARCH 28 Led Zeppelin's fifth album, *Houses of the Holy*, was released at long last. The album went straight to number one in the United Kingdom, the first time any Led Zeppelin album had done that. It also topped the charts in the United States.

APRIL 4 Atlantic Records announced that *Houses of the Holy* automatically qualified as a gold album due to the number of preorders made by retailers. The label's vice president of marketing stated, "The demand for Zeppelin's new album has been absolutely fantastic. Every one of their LPs has been a gold record, and this one is already number five."

APRIL 23–30 Led Zeppelin was implementing improvements to their stage show in time for their North American tour. Zeppelin prepared for the U.S. dates by rehearsing at Shepperton Studios in London with their high-tech, costly lighting and sound systems, on loan from Showco, a company based in Dallas, Texas.

MAY 4 Led Zeppelin began their ninth U.S. tour at Atlanta Stadium in Atlanta, Georgia. That outdoor show set a local attendance record of 50,000 people and made the front page of the *Atlanta Constitution*. Led Zeppelin manager Peter Grant wanted news of a big success like this to leak over to England, so he got their publicist, Danny Goldberg, to do the job. Goldberg wrote a statement saying that Led Zeppelin was the biggest thing to hit Atlanta since *Gone with the Wind* and attributed it to the city's mayor, Sam Massell. New York music reporter Lisa Robinson used Goldberg's invented quotation in a piece published in *Disc* and *Music Echo*.

MAY 5 For Led Zeppelin's second show of the tour, held at Tampa Stadium in Tampa, Florida, publicist Danny Goldberg was able to create further excitement by saying to the press that Led Zeppelin was officially "bigger than the Beatles." The notion came from the fact that Led Zeppelin sold more seats at Tampa Stadium than the Beatles had at their famous Shea Stadium concert in 1965. A local TV news report that ran with the "bigger than the Beatles" statement was included on Led Zeppelin's 2007 DVD rerelease of the film *The Song Remains the Same*, and Zeppelin also showed the TV film clip onstage to kick off their London reunion concert in December 2007.

MAY 7–JUNE 3 Following the opening pair of concerts, the first leg of Led Zeppelin's ninth North American tour comprised another sixteen shows, including one held at the L.A. Forum on John Bonham's twenty-fifth birthday.

During that tour, much of Led Zeppelin's time in California was spent in Los Angeles. The band flew in a rented commuter jet for gigs in other cities, such as an outdoor afternoon show on June 2 in San Francisco. After that show, Led Zeppelin experienced a frighteningly bumpy ride back to Los Angeles. The heavy turbulence on that flight gave Zeppelin a good reason to want to improve their air transportation for the next part of the

BELOW: A tour button from Led Zeppelin's 1972–73 British tour.

OPPOSITE PAGE, TOP: A ticket from Led Zeppelin's May 4, 1973, show at Atlanta Stadium (now called Atlanta-Fulton County Stadium); a record-breaking 50,000 people attended.

tour. It was also ironic that a band called Led Zeppelin was flying on a lightweight plane. So by the time they were playing in Chicago and New York the following month, Zeppelin were flying high aboard the *Starship*, a custom Boeing 720 passenger jet.

JULY 6–29 The second leg of tour dates in North America included another sixteen shows, culminating in a three-night stint at New York's Madison Square Garden, for which manager Peter Grant arranged a film crew. These three shows, and further reshoots, would be released as the main portion of Led Zeppelin's 1976 feature film, *The Song Remains the Same.*

On the last day of the tour, it was discovered that more than $200,000 in cash had gone missing from Led Zeppelin's safe deposit box at the Drake Hotel in New York. The group held a press conference, and news of this landed the band's name in headlines, as the amount stolen was higher than that of any other heist in New York history.

AUGUST–OCTOBER During a lengthy break from official activity, some members of Led Zeppelin took to vacationing and exploring new lands. Jimmy Page and Robert Plant both flew to the African continent, Page exploring the pyramids of Egypt and Plant trekking through lesser-traveled roads in Morocco.

NOVEMBER John Paul Jones was said to be especially weary from the road and, further, considering either a leave of absence from the band or quitting it altogether. The extent to which these frequently cited rumors are true has been the subject of debate.

Led Zeppelin had booked some time to record at Headley Grange in Hampshire, England, using Ronnie Lane's mobile recording studio. Because Jones was not going to attend, Led Zeppelin transferred some of their studio time to Bad Company, a newly formed group that was the first to align themselves with Led Zeppelin for their Swan Song record label, which would be formed the following year.

DECEMBER Led Zeppelin renewed their contract with Atlantic Records, laying the groundwork for forming their own record label. Jimmy Page made it known that he didn't want Led Zeppelin to be the only band on the label; he and his bandmates were encouraged to have their label sign and promote other groups, the first of which was Bad Company. According to the terms of the agreement, they would leave record distribution to Atlantic.

The month also witnessed the beginning of additional filming for Led Zeppelin's feature film, including scenes of Jimmy Page climbing a mountain.

Even while John Paul Jones was abstaining from recording sessions at Headley Grange, engineer Ron Nevison was on hand with Ronnie Lane's mobile recording studio to capture Led Zeppelin's late-night improvisations and the genesis of ideas for their next album.

This year saw Led Zeppelin activity take a backseat for the first time in the band's history. Part of this was due to the extended absence of John Paul Jones. Tour manager Richard Cole spent the year working for Eric Clapton. Work continued, for the time being, on Led Zeppelin's feature film, *The Song Remains the Same*. The launch of Swan Song Records was one of the priorities, and with it came side projects in support of the label's first acts: Bad Company, Maggie Bell, and the Pretty Things.

JANUARY Led Zeppelin's recording sessions continued at Headley Grange in Hampshire, England. It was not even determined at this point that the next Led Zeppelin album would include any surplus tracks recorded prior to December 1973.

FEBRUARY 14 Folk singer and guitarist Roy Harper performed at the Rainbow Theatre in London, during which he was joined onstage by three-fourths of Led Zeppelin: all but John Paul Jones. Robert Plant acted as master of ceremonies for the concert. Harper's band for this performance was called the Intergalactic Elephant Band. Jimmy Page added guitar to Harper's songs "The Same Old Rock," "Male Chauvinist Pig Blues," "Too Many Movies," and "Home." John Bonham shared drum duties with Keith Moon of the Who.

MAY 7 The members of Led Zeppelin introduced their record label, Swan Song Records, and held the first of several launch parties, this one at the Four Seasons hotel in New York.

MAY 10 The members of Led Zeppelin threw a second party dedicated to the launch of Swan Song Records. This one was held at the five-star Hotel Bel Air in Los Angeles, which happened to have swans on a lake in front of the property. It was viewed as quite an upscale establishment for a long-haired rock band and the kind of guests they would bring into such a quaint, picturesque location. So while the party lingered on into the wee hours, an anxious hotel manager hovered nearby, doing

Ioannis, New York, New York, *2011*.

what he could to coax people into ending the party so that life could go back to normal.

Eventually, the hotel manager's intrusiveness kicked off some retaliation. People started throwing food at him. Before long, everybody was aiming at each other, setting aloft whatever they could get their hands on: pieces of fruit, entire cakes, even the fine china. Led Zeppelin, now the proud executives behind their own record label, gladly footed the bill for the damages.

MAY 11 Three members of Led Zeppelin—all but John Paul Jones—attended Elvis Presley's evening concert at the L.A. Forum in Inglewood, California. During the show, Presley interrupted a song and informed his bandmates, "Wait a minute. If we can start together, fellas, because we've got Led Zeppelin out there. Let's try to look like we know what we're doing, whether we do or not."

After the concert, the three present members of Led Zeppelin met the King of Rock 'n' Roll. They are said to have gotten along very well. One of the oft-repeated stories of this encounter has to do with Led Zeppelin manager Peter Grant nearly taking a seat that was already occupied by Presley's father, whom Grant didn't see and nearly crushed. Another story of their meeting concerns Robert Plant and his hero exchanging lines in Presley's 1956 hit "Love Me."

JUNE The first album appearing on the Swan Song Records label was released: it was the eponymous debut from Bad Company.

JULY Led Zeppelin manager Peter Grant hired Peter Clifton as the new director of Led Zeppelin's film.

AUGUST Because the footage from Led Zeppelin's concerts at Madison Square Garden shot between July 27 and 29, 1973, was incomplete, the members of Led Zeppelin gathered at Shepperton Studios in Surrey, England, to recreate concert scenes. New director Peter Clifton asked them to wear the same outfits they had worn onstage for the 1973 shows. John Paul Jones refused, resulting in a

discrepancy in outfits that's evident in the film. Also, Jones's hairstyle had changed in the interim, so he was fitted for a wig, which is visible in parts of the finished product.

AUGUST 31 John Paul Jones and Pink Floyd's David Gilmour joined Roy Harper onstage during his set at the free concert at Hyde Park. They performed "The Game," a lengthy track they would record early the following year for Harper's studio album *HQ*.

SEPTEMBER 1 Jimmy Page sat in with Swan Song recording artists Bad Company to perform the blues song "Rock Me Baby" during the encore of their concert in Austin, Texas.

SEPTEMBER 14 Jimmy Page and John Bonham attended the concert by Crosby, Stills, Nash & Young at Wembley Stadium in London, England. Also on the bill were the Band, Joni Mitchell, Jesse Colin Young, and Tom Scott and the L.A. Express. Following the concert, Page and Bonham joined Crosby, Stills, Nash & Young at their afterparty, held at a London restaurant called Quaglino's. There, the two are said to have sat in on the songs "Vampire Blues" and "On the Beach."

SEPTEMBER 24 Jimmy Page joined Bad Company onstage at Central Park in New York, sitting in on the blues song "Rock Me Baby" during the encore. It was the second time that month that the group welcomed Page for a run-through of this song.

OCTOBER 31 A Halloween party held at Chislehurst Caves in England helped Led Zeppelin celebrate the release of Swan Song Records' first UK album, *Silk Torpedo* by the Pretty Things.

NOVEMBER 13 Led Zeppelin announced the details of their upcoming North American tour, set to begin in January 1975, and their album *Physical Graffiti*, which at the time was scheduled to be released ahead of the tour. The press release, issued under the name of Swan Song Records, said the double album *Physical Graffiti* was expected to "ship gold with advance orders of well over a million dollars."

DECEMBER 19 Jimmy Page and John Paul Jones joined Bad Company at the Rainbow Theatre in London during their concert. They guested, along with guitarist Duster Bennett, on the blues song "Rock Me Baby" during the encore.

ABOVE: *Ioannis, Zeppelin III (detail), 2011.*

1975

In the first few weeks of the new year, Led Zeppelin promised fans a new album and a North American tour. One setback, having to do with the album, postponed the record's arrival. Another setback, an injury that Jimmy Page suffered just prior to their tour, could have dealt a blow to the entire schedule. Early on tour, yet another setback surfaced as Robert Plant caught the flu, causing the postponement of one concert date. However, those early setbacks were nothing compared to the major disaster Led Zeppelin experienced by year's end, because of which Plant would go almost five months without walking.

BELOW: *An ad for the New York dates of Led Zeppelin's 1975 tour.*

JANUARY 3 In anticipation of Led Zeppelin concert tickets going on sale in New York on the morning of Monday, January 6, fans began arriving at the Madison Square Garden box office prepared to camp out for the entire weekend in the freezing weather.

JANUARY 4 To accommodate the crowd that had already gathered outside Madison Square Garden, Led Zeppelin concert tickets were put on sale on Saturday evening so that the fans wouldn't have to wait another day and a half outside in freezing conditions. Ticket sales began Saturday night.

The band was to perform three shows at the Garden on February 3, 7, and 12, with further shows scheduled for the nearby Nassau Coliseum on February 13 and 14.

JANUARY 5 Led Zeppelin's Madison Square Garden concert tickets continued to sell through the afternoon, but sales were suspended when rioting in the ticket lines resulted in box office windows being broken. Up to that point, the venue had sold more than 50,000 tickets. On the radio station WNEW-FM, on-air program director Dennis Elsas announced that in light of the developments, tickets would not be sold at the Madison Square Garden box office the following morning. They would be available at Ticketron terminals instead.

JANUARY 6 The remainder of Led Zeppelin's Madison Square Garden concert tickets were put on sale at various Ticketron terminals throughout the New York area. Ticketron also began selling tickets to Led Zeppelin's two shows at Nassau Coliseum. Both sets of New York–area concerts sold out in the morning.

Meanwhile, in Boston, thousands of fans began lining up outside the Boston Garden in anticipation of tickets going on sale at the box office the following morning. It was freezing outside, and so sympathetic officials at the venue opened the arena doors beginning around 11:00 p.m. to allow fans to wait inside. Ticket office manager

LED ZEPPELIN 1975 TOUR
NEW YORK DATES
madison square garden – feb. 3, 7, 12
nassau coliseum – feb. 13, 14

59

Steven Rosenblatt also called on staff to come in early to begin selling tickets overnight.

JANUARY 7 Tickets to Led Zeppelin's show in Boston were originally supposed to go on sale at 10:00 a.m., but ticket sales began much earlier, around 2:30 a.m. By 6:10 a.m., all 9,000 tickets were sold out. At some point, the crowd got out of control, breaking into souvenir stands, raiding dressing rooms, draining fire extinguishers, wrecking a piano, and shattering glass everywhere. The reported total cost of the damages was between $50,000 and $75,000. Steven Rosenblatt, the venue's office manager, was quoted by the local press as saying that he feared the concert would be canceled.

JANUARY 8 The publicists representing Led Zeppelin issued a press release explaining the circumstances of the band's ticket sales in New York City. The message highlighted the fact that 100,000 concert tickets for the metropolitan area had sold out in thirty-six hours. The tickets to Led Zeppelin's three Madison Square Garden concerts took less time to sell out than a four-show stand there by the Who, as well as Bob Dylan's concerts there and the Concert for Bangladesh, publicist Danny Goldberg noted. The press release also praised Madison Square Garden officials Joe Cohen and Tony Avalon, concert promoter Jerry Weintraub, and WNEW's Dennis Elsas.

EARLY JANUARY At some point in early January, before the band left England, Jimmy Page got the ring finger of his left hand caught between the closing doors of a passenger train. He broke his finger. However, rather than cancel the tour, Page developed a new guitar-playing technique that utilized his remaining fingers. While the band decided to add new songs to their concert set lists, Page would not be playing "Dazed and Confused" on tour for the time being, saying it would be too difficult to perform.

JANUARY 11–12 Led Zeppelin performed a pair of European warm-up dates to prepare for their North American tour. At their concerts in Rotterdam, Holland, and Brussels, Belgium, their set lists included, for the first time, a treasure trove of new material destined for the double album *Physical Graffiti*. Five new songs— "Kashmir," "In My Time of Dying," "Sick Again," "The Wanton Song," and "Trampled Under Foot"—all made their debut at this time. One song from Led Zeppelin's fourth album, "When the Levee Breaks," also made its live debut at this time. Backstage in Brussels, Robert Plant filmed an interview with host "Whispering" Bob Harris.

JANUARY 14 With reports that Led Zeppelin's scheduled appearance in Boston was possibly going to be canceled following the damage caused to the venue when the tickets went on sale, the publicity firm representing Led Zeppelin responded with a statement urging city officials

John Bonham at the January 11, 1975, Led Zeppelin concert at the Ahoy arena in Rotterdam, the Netherlands.

to allow the concert to go ahead as planned. It quoted Led Zeppelin attorney Steve Weiss, who said it would be a "great disappointment to the members of the group and to Swan Song" if the show were canceled. Commented Weiss, "In seven years of touring America, Led Zeppelin has never had a concert canceled, nor has there ever been a serious incident at one of their concerts. It is unfortunate that the officials in Boston have so little confidence in the young people of Boston. I do not think there would be any problems if the concert was held."

Ultimately, Mayor Kevin H. White ended up refusing the license necessary for the concert to take place, so the concert was canceled and ticket prices were refunded. Led Zeppelin later announced that a third concert at Nassau Coliseum was being scheduled for February 4, the intended date of the canceled Boston show.

JANUARY 17 BBC 2's *Old Grey Whistle Test* aired host "Whispering" Bob Harris's interview with Robert Plant, on the status of Led Zeppelin's forthcoming studio album, new music, and their record company.

JANUARY 18 Led Zeppelin's North American concert tour opened in Minneapolis, Minnesota. For this tour, the band again rented the Boeing jet they called *Starship*.

JANUARY 20–22 Led Zeppelin performed three shows at the Chicago Stadium in Chicago, Illinois. As Robert Plant took his first opportunity to address the audience in Chicago, he was complaining about the weather and said that he'd gotten "a touch of the flu."

JANUARY 24–25 With Robert Plant's voice continuing to be affected by the flu, Led Zeppelin's concerts nevertheless went ahead in Cleveland, Ohio, and Indianapolis, Indiana. Jimmy Page proved that his three-finger playing technique was working.

JANUARY 27 Led Zeppelin's scheduled concert in Saint Louis, Missouri, was postponed so that Robert Plant could recuperate from the flu. To do so, he remained in Chicago while the rest of the band carried on without him.

JANUARY 29–FEBRUARY 16 As the first leg of Led Zeppelin's concert tour carried on, Robert Plant's voice had yet to recover fully from the flu. As the tour progressed, his sound began to improve, particularly in February. *Led Zeppelin Live* author Luis Rey's analysis of a bootleg audience recording from the concert on January 29 in Greensboro, North Carolina, is that it was Led Zeppelin's worst concert.

In the New York area, *Newsday* music critic Dave Marsh discussed "the title of world's greatest rock and roll group," declaring it had been five years since the Who's last major album (*Who's Next*) and that the Rolling Stones had failed to sell as many copies of their albums as Led Zeppelin had. Marsh listed Led Zeppelin's achievements and settled any question about his opinion by concluding, "The Stones may have the rep, but Led Zep have the numbers."

The final show of the tour's first leg was the makeup date in St. Louis, postponed from January 27, when Robert Plant had the flu. By mid-February, Led Zeppelin's tour had visited fourteen cities for nineteen shows.

FEBRUARY 24 Led Zeppelin's album *Physical Graffiti* became the third album to be released on the Swan Song label. In its second week on the *Billboard* album charts, it reached number one and remained in the top spot for six weeks in all.

Also that day, the owner of the West Palm Beach International Raceway told the press that Led Zeppelin's scheduled appearance there was "definitely canceled." Tickets had been sold for a Florida Rock Festival, scheduled to take place there on March 8, with Led Zeppelin at the top of a bill that also featured Swan Song recording artists Pretty Things as well as Bachman-Turner Overdrive and the J. Geils Band. Led Zeppelin had received a nonrefundable deposit of $200,000 for what would have been their only performance in Florida that year. Speedway owner David Rupp canceled the festival, saying the property would have been unable to offer parking for the anticipated number of attendees.

FEBRUARY 25–28 Mayor Maurice Ferre of Miami sought to bring a Led Zeppelin concert to the Orange Bowl, with proceeds benefiting the Fort Lauderdale Pediatric Child Care Center. By week's end, talks had fallen through, and Swan Song Records issued a press release on February 28 to express their disappointment. In the words of Danny Goldberg, vice president of Swan Song, the group regretted "that they will be unable to play Florida on this tour due to circumstances utterly beyond their control." He continued, "I know that they have a very special feeling for Florida, due in part to the fact that the biggest concert they ever played was in Tampa, Florida, at the Stadium there in 1973."

FEBRUARY 27–MARCH 27 As the second leg of Led Zeppelin's concert tour took place, with sixteen more sold-out shows in thirteen cities, their extraordinary record sales continued. With the double LP *Physical Graffiti* at the number one position in the United States, *Billboard*'s chart of the top two hundred albums also included every one of Led Zeppelin's other records, thereby making Led Zeppelin the first group ever to have six albums placed on the chart at once.

There was good news for other Swan Song artists as well. Bad Company's 1974 debut was still on the charts, as were 1974's *Silk Torpedo* from the Pretty Things and

BELOW: *A ticket from a Led Zeppelin concert that was to be held at the Palm Beach International Raceway in West Palm Beach, Florida, on March 8, 1975; the concert was canceled.*

OPPOSITE PAGE: *Ioannis, Jimmy Page: Physical Graffiti, 2011.*

the newly released *Suicide Sal* by Maggie Bell. All were released on the Swan Song label. A single from the forthcoming Bad Company album was released that month, "Good Lovin' Gone Bad."

In England, where *Physical Graffiti* was also number one, Led Zeppelin announced a series of three concerts to take place on May 23–25 at Earls Court Arena in London. Within hours of the 51,000 available tickets going on sale on March 15, they were completely sold out.

APRIL Led Zeppelin followed up on the success of *Physical Graffiti* by releasing their first U.S. single on the Swan Song label, "Trampled Under Foot," backed with "Black Country Woman." That month also saw Swan Song release Bad Company's second album, *Straight Shooter*, whose first single reached number thirty-six on *Billboard*'s Hot 100 chart. Two other tracks, "Feel Like Makin' Love" and "Shooting Star," would become radio staples for years to come.

BELOW: *An ad for the Vancouver Led Zeppelin show on March 20, 1975, at the Pacific Coliseum.*

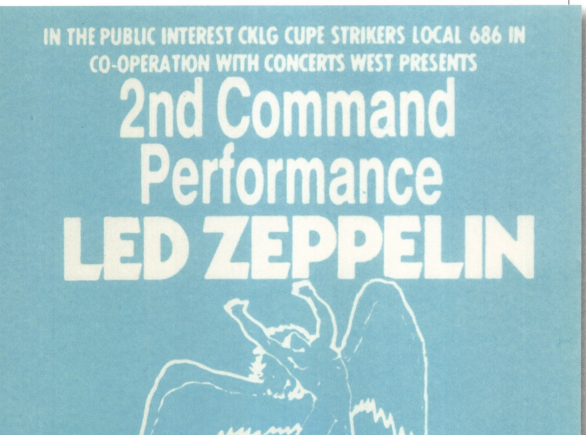

IN THE PUBLIC INTEREST CKLG CUPE STRIKERS LOCAL 686 IN CO-OPERATION WITH CONCERTS WEST PRESENTS

2nd Command Performance
LED ZEPPELIN

THURSDAY, MARCH 20th, 8 P.M.
PACIFIC COLISEUM

TICKETS $7.50 ADVANCE (PLUS 25c SERVICE CHARGE)
NOW ON SALE

ALL CONCERT BOX OFFICES — The Coggery, 130 Water St., Grennan's Records, Rich. Sq., Thunderbird Shop, SUB, U.B.C., Woodward's Oakridge, New Westminster, Park Royal & Guildford. Mail Orders — Box 8600 — Information 687-2801.

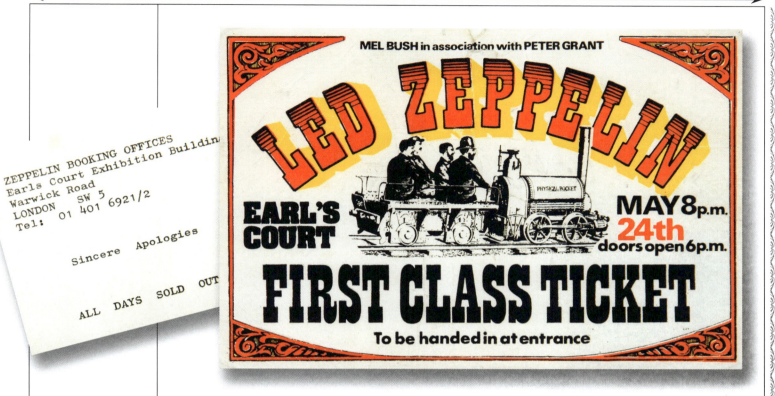

ZEPPELIN BOOKING OFFICES
Earls Court Exhibition Building
Warwick Road
LONDON   SW 5
Tel: 01 401 6921/2

Sincere Apologies

ALL DAYS SOLD OUT

ABOVE: *Led Zeppelin played at Earls Court Arena in West London for five nights, from May 17 through 24, 1975. Here, a notice from the booking office with apologies for all tickets being sold out, and a colorful ticket with an old-fashioned design from the May 24 concert.*

In England, two additional Led Zeppelin concerts at Earls Court Arena were scheduled for May 17 and 18, which also sold out. The total number of tickets sold was 85,000. In preparation for the concerts, Led Zeppelin's sound system was shipped across the ocean in time for rehearsals at Shepperton Studios in Surrey. Giant video screens were also accessed for the event, which was certainly not standard at the time.

MAY 17–25 With their state-of-the-art sound system imported from the United States, Led Zeppelin performed a series of five concerts at Earls Court Arena in London, in front of 17,000 people each night.

JUNE Robert Plant traveled to Agadir, Morocco, with his wife. Jimmy Page joined up in Marrakech, Morocco, for a folk festival.

The second director of Led Zeppelin's feature film, *The Song Remains the Same*, Peter Clifton, announced that his work was nearly finished.

EARLY JULY Jimmy Page and Robert Plant completed their Moroccan vacation after visiting the country's largest city, Casablanca, and Tangier.

JULY 7 Led Zeppelin announced a pair of shows in California that would kick off another set of U.S. live dates "in areas of the country that their winter tour missed." A Swan Song press release stated: "The first dates to be announced are Saturday and Sunday, August 23–24, at Oakland Stadium. 55,000 seats will be sold to each of the two concerts at $10.00, making a $1.1 million gross potential for the two days. The concerts will be in the afternoon, and the Pretty Things (who record for Zeppelin's Swan Song label) and Joe Walsh will also be on the bill."

Concert tickets went on sale for these shows and also for a show scheduled to take place September 6 at the Rose Bowl in Pasadena, California. It would have been the first rock concert to take place at the Rose Bowl.

MID–LATE JULY All four members of Led Zeppelin met up in Switzerland at the Montreux Jazz Festival, after which Jimmy Page and Robert Plant traveled with their families to Greece.

AUGUST 3 Jimmy Page left Greece to fly to Italy, where he was to visit an abbey and farmhouse that had once belonged to Aleister Crowley. In Greece, he left his daughter, Scarlett, under the care of Robert and Maureen Plant, who were also there vacationing with their daughter, Carmen, and son, Karac.

AUGUST 4 While Robert Plant and his family were vacationing in Greece, their car—driven by Plant's wife, Maureen—veered off the road and crashed into a tree. Their daughter, Carmen, had a broken wrist. Their son, Karac, had a fractured leg. Jimmy Page's daughter, Scarlett, was unharmed. The couple in the front seat fared worse: Robert broke an elbow and an ankle, while Maureen fractured her skull, one leg, and her pelvis in four places. Seeing that she was unconscious and bleeding profusely, Plant feared his wife was dead. The driver of a fruit truck discovered the accident and drove the five of them to a local hospital.

Conditions at the hospital were less than desirable. There were more roaches than doctors, and blood matching Maureen's blood type was unavailable.

AUGUST 5 Led Zeppelin tour manager Richard Cole received word of the previous day's auto accident. He quickly arranged for three specialists and a supply of blood to be flown to Rhodes. He also had Robert Plant "kidnapped" from the hospital and airlifted in the middle of the night to London.

AUGUST 8 Swan Song announced, as a result of Robert Plant's auto accident and recuperation, the postponement of Led Zeppelin's tour plans, which included several U.S. dates that month and the next, with other dates abroad to follow. The press release included this statement: "Within the next couple of weeks, doctors expect to have a better idea of when Plant will be recovered and able to perform again."

MID–LATE AUGUST Negotiations continued behind the scenes to reschedule some of the August and September dates for early the following year, and at one point it was announced that the concert at the Rose Bowl in Pasadena, California, had been rescheduled for January 24. Swan Song vice president Danny Goldberg told reporter Mary Hayes, "I'm not going to announce any new concerts until [Plant] can perform. He's not going to sing from a wheelchair. If all goes well and the leg is healing properly, the January 24 date is realistic. If it's not healing at the right rate, we'll have to cancel."

SEPTEMBER Jimmy Page and John Bonham attended *Melody Maker*'s annual awards ceremony in London to pick up seven awards for the band. UK readers had named Led Zeppelin the best group and best live act, with *Physical Graffiti* the best album and Robert Plant the top male vocalist. International readers also picked Plant as best male vocalist, Page as best guitarist, and *Physical Graffiti* best album.

Unable to walk, Robert Plant moved to Malibu Colony in California to continue his recuperation there. He soon grew tired of it, so he asked Jimmy Page to join him and they began writing new Led Zeppelin material. One of the first songs written was "Tea for One," whose lyrics are about suffering from boredom. Also written at this time was "Achilles Last Stand," whose lyrics deal with some of their travels, specifically mentioning the Atlas Mountains in Morocco.

OCTOBER Led Zeppelin rehearsed their new material at Studio Instrument Rentals (SIR Studios) in Hollywood, California.

NOVEMBER Led Zeppelin flew to Munich, West Germany, to record their seven new songs at Musicland Studios. The recording and mixing of their album sessions was completed in eighteen days, with Jimmy Page spending the final two recording his guitar overdubs. Robert Plant sang all his parts from a wheelchair.

An official press release that month included an update on the album recording sessions, Plant's recovery, and the likelihood of tour plans. The singer's elbow had almost completely healed, and his ankle, though healed substantially enough for the cast to be removed, was still not strong enough for him to put any weight on it. There

would be no Led Zeppelin tour until Plant's ankle was fully healed, and nothing would be scheduled until the following summer at the earliest.

DECEMBER Swan Song Records released the new album from the Pretty Things, *Savage Eye*.

DECEMBER 10 Led Zeppelin returned to live in the tax-free haven of Jersey in the English Channel, where they frequented a nightclub in Saint Helier called Behan's. Seeing pianist Norman Hale perform, all four members of the group joined him onstage for an impromptu set of about forty-five minutes' duration. Robert Plant sat on a stool for the performance and tried to resist the temptation to bounce around onstage, which he would have been physically unable to do. They played a list of cover songs, such as "Blue Suede Shoes."

Because of Robert Plant's car accident on August 4, 1975, in Greece, which required a lengthy convalescence, Led Zeppelin's August and September shows that year had to be canceled, including the concerts at the Oakland Coliseum Stadium, in Oakland, California, which had been scheduled for August 23 and 24. An ad (above) for the two shows and an unused ticket (below) from the show on the twenty-third are shown here.

1976

The auto accident in August 1975 had left Robert Plant unable to walk, much less put on a show, thereby shifting Led Zeppelin's priorities from touring to other projects. They entered the new year with an album that hadn't been planned but was very quickly recorded and mixed and readied for release. Time off from touring also gave the band new impetus to work on their feature film, *The Song Remains the Same*.

JANUARY–FEBRUARY One of the biggest impediments to touring—the fact that Robert Plant couldn't walk—got out of the way on the first day of the year: In Paris, he took his first unaided steps since the accident. He later told Lisa Robinson of *Hit Parader*, "I didn't start taking steps until January 1. I was in Paris, drunk, and it was a new year, so I took a step. One small step for man, one giant step for six nights at Madison Square Garden."

On January 23, John Bonham attended Deep Purple's concert at Radio City Music Hall in New York. He'd been friends with bassist and backup singer Glenn Hughes. At one point, Bonham took the microphone to introduce himself and mention that Led Zeppelin had a new album on the way.

Around this time, Plant spoke at length about the events of the past few months in interviews with Lisa Robinson for *New Musical Express* and Chris Charlesworth for *Melody Maker*. He explained why the members of Led Zeppelin were spending a year away from England as nonresidents for tax purposes—to avoid the high taxation rate on unearned income—and the circumstances surrounding the recording of Led Zeppelin's forthcoming album. He also mentioned that manager Peter Grant and tour manager Richard Cole, as crucial parts of Led Zeppelin, were going to be featured in the movie *The Song Remains the Same*.

New Musical Express poll results placed Led Zeppelin as the top band, Robert Plant as the top singer, Jimmy Page as the top guitarist, and *Physical Graffiti* as the top album. At the same time, *Melody Maker* printed letters from readers who were angry that Led Zeppelin had left England for financial reasons.

Late in February, Bad Company's third album, *Run with the Pack*, was released on the Swan Song label. The album also yielded two singles: their cover of the Coasters' 1957 hit "Young Blood" and the full-band original "Honey Child."

MARCH Jimmy Page granted interviews at Swan Song's London office. An interview with Harry Doherty for *New Musical Express* concentrated mostly on Page's thoughts pertaining to Led Zeppelin's music, particularly its changes over the years, how his travels had shaped the music, and what else to expect from Led Zeppelin musically in the future. In his concluding remark, Page said, "We've done a lot of constructive work in the period off the road. It's not as if we've retired."

MARCH 31 Led Zeppelin's *Presence* was released, receiving highly positive reviews from Charles Shaar Murray in *New Musical Express*, Chris Welch in *Melody Maker*, and John Ingham in *Sounds*, a weekly British music newspaper.

APRIL Led Zeppelin's *Presence* worked its way up the UK album charts throughout the month, ultimately peaking at number two in the May 1 issue of *New Musical Express*.

MAY Jethro Tull's Ian Anderson, who chose not to leave England as a tax exile, publicly accused Robert Plant, and also the Rolling Stones' Ron Wood, of misinforming the public when it came to their taxation rate.

The same issue of *Melody Maker* featuring Anderson's interview also included a full-page ad parodying the ad campaign for Led Zeppelin's *Presence*; the ad for the eponymous debut album from Alberto Y Lost Trios Paranoias featured a straightened version of Led Zeppelin's twisted obelisk and said the group "pull[s] the feet from under the world's leading rock bands and leave[s] them flat on their faeces."

MAY 14 Keith Relf, who'd been the lead singer of the Yardbirds, died at his home after being electrocuted. He was thirty-three.

LEFT: *A collectible version of the mysterious object featured on the cover and inside sleeve of* Led Zeppelin's Presence *album, released on March 31, 1976.*

OPPOSITE PAGE: *Ioannis,* Page, Plant, *2011.*

MAY 23 At the L.A. Forum, Jimmy Page and Robert Plant sat in with Bad Company for a four-song set. It was Plant's first time performing onstage since his auto accident, apart from the one-off appearance atop a stool in December. Singers Plant and Paul Rodgers sang from opposite sides of the front of the stage while Page and the rest of Bad Company rocked out to "Train Kept A-Rollin'," "You Shook Me," "Bring It On Home," and "I Just Want to Make Love to You."

Melody Maker reported that John Bonham also attended the concert but could not perform because his arm was in a cast. The same article also carried a retort from Plant in response to Ian Anderson's assertion, "I earn as much as a bricklayer who works really hard, and that's a lot of money. That's about my level of income and that's all I need to live comfortably." Plant's response: "So he only earns as much as a bricklayer, does he? Well, he writes songs like a bricklayer, too, as far as I'm concerned."

MAY 27 A published rumor that Led Zeppelin was to make a surprise appearance at the Marquee Club, alongside the Pretty Things, attracted hordes of fans. In the end, the only member of Led Zeppelin there was John Paul Jones, who was welcomed onstage to play piano for the Pretty Things' encore, "Route 66." *New Musical Express* reported that his appearance was a gesture to Led Zeppelin fans, and that the other band members were apologetic and confused about the source of the rumor.

JUNE

In the United States, Swan Song released Led Zeppelin's *Presence* cut "Candy Store Rock" as a single, backed with "Royal Orleans." In England, *Presence* dropped from the top ten albums on the *New Musical Express* chart. Word also emerged that Led Zeppelin's upcoming movie would be entitled *The Song Remains the Same*, after an earlier album track performed live in the film.

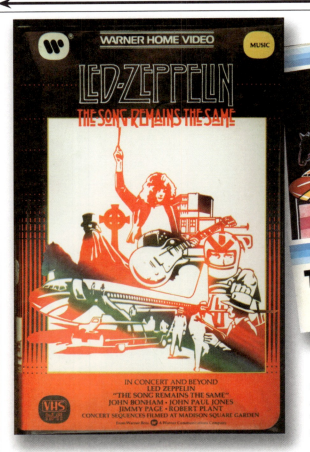

LEFT: The Song Remains the Same— the movie—in VHS and Super 8.

As to when Led Zeppelin would be seen onstage next, published rumors held that Led Zeppelin had been offered available dates at Wembley Stadium in London, so a live date in July or August was likely. However, a Swan Song spokesperson told *New Musical Express*, "Zeppelin would love to get back onstage, and there is an imminent possibility of their doing so, especially now that Robert Plant is almost back to full fitness. But I have no knowledge of any specific date or venue. When they're good and ready, they'll announce something."

JULY During the month of the American bicentennial, *New Musical Express* published a statement from someone who said that U.S. president Jimmy Carter liked Led Zeppelin.

Also, newly signed Swan Song recording artist Dave Edmunds released his first single for the label, "Here Comes the Weekend."

AUGUST *Rolling Stone* magazine published an interview with Jimmy Page in which he attempted to clarify his religious beliefs. He said, "I do not worship the devil. But magic does intrigue me. Magic of all kinds. I bought [Aleister] Crowley's house to go up and write in."

SEPTEMBER As rumors of a forthcoming Led Zeppelin live album circulated, Swan Song Records issued a press release announcing that the double-album sound track to *The Song Remains the Same* had gone platinum in advance orders. Led Zeppelin's first official live album was to be released in October.

Around this time, Jimmy Page had also been expected to provide the sound track for another movie, *Lucifer Rising*, by filmmaker Kenneth Anger. Saying Page was working too slowly, Anger relieved Page of his duties and, according to legend, simultaneously placed a curse on him.

OCTOBER In Montreux, Switzerland, John Bonham recorded an instrumental percussive piece. *Melody Maker* soon reported that a Bonham solo album had been recorded. It was, in fact, the track "Bonzo's Montreux," later included on the Led Zeppelin album *Coda*.

Bigger news that month included the release of Led Zeppelin's *The Song Remains the Same* sound-track album and the film's premieres around the world. Clips of the movie aired on *Old Grey Whistle Test* in England and on *Don Kirshner's Rock Concert* in the United States.

OCTOBER 20 The world premiere of *The Song Remains the Same* was held at Cinema One in New York, with Led Zeppelin in attendance, along with singers Roberta Flack, Mick Jagger, and Carly Simon. Tickets were sold in advance, with proceeds of $25,000 benefiting Save the Children. The original director, Joe Massot, bought a scalped ticket outside the theater, as he had not been invited. A party was held afterward at the Pierre Hotel.

OCTOBER 21 Led Zeppelin attended the L.A. premiere of *The Song Remains the Same*, held at the Fox Wilshire Theatre. As with the premieres in other cities in the United States and Canada, proceeds from the first few days of showings benefited Save the Children.

OCTOBER 22 In Hollywood, a release party was held at the Bistro for Led Zeppelin's sound track to *The Song Remains the Same*. Jimmy Page attended, along with manager Peter Grant and tour manager Richard Cole. Other noted celebrities in attendance included Danny Bonaduce, Linda Ronstadt, and Ron Wood.

OPPOSITE PAGE: *Led Zeppelin arrives at the premiere of* The Song Remains the Same *at the Fox Wilshire Theatre in Los Angeles, October 21, 1976.*

LATE OCTOBER Led Zeppelin returned to England for the London premiere of *The Song Remains the Same*. Robert Plant and manager Peter Grant both gave an interview to *Old Grey Whistle Test* director Mike Appleton, which was shown on television the following week. Their interview can also be seen on the 2003 release *Led Zeppelin DVD*.

NOVEMBER 4 The UK premiere of *The Song Remains the Same* was held at two theaters in London, with Led Zeppelin attending an afterparty at Floral Hall in Covent Garden. Also there were Boz Burrell of Bad Company, Paul McCartney of Wings, and Rick Wakeman of Yes.

NOVEMBER–DECEMBER *The Song Remains the Same* was among the ten highest-grossing movies for four consecutive weeks, according to *Variety* magazine. With the film opening across the UK, Led Zeppelin turned their attention to returning to the stage. In an interview with Nick Kent for *New Musical Express*, Jimmy Page promised, "Something epic is going to happen musically anyway. That's what I feel. This next tour, you'll see." The first song Led Zeppelin rehearsed in London was "Achilles Last Stand."

Led Zeppelin was the cover story of *People* magazine's December 20 issue. It featured an interview with Robert Plant by Jim Jerome, in which he speaks about having children at home as "very stabilizing" compared to his life on the road: "Kids are very stabilizing. Carmen used to think she had two fathers, the one whose singing she heard through the speakers and the one on whose knee she was sitting."

1977

As the year began, Led Zeppelin had just released a feature film whose sound track meant continued success for the band's record label. With Robert Plant fully healed, the band was destined for a tour, for which Jimmy Page expressed high hopes.

JANUARY At Manticore Studios, owned by Emerson Lake & Palmer, Led Zeppelin rehearsed for their upcoming tour of North America.

JANUARY 25 Led Zeppelin's tour dates were announced in a press release from Swan Song Records. The group was to kick off a North American tour on February 27 in Fort Worth, Texas.

FEBRUARY 2 Swan Song Records said that Led Zeppelin concert tickets sold out in record time in eight cities: Baton Rouge (14,500 tickets in five hours), Dallas (10,000 tickets in three and a half hours), Fort Worth (14,500 tickets in three and a half hours), Houston (17,000 tickets in three hours), Los Angeles (54,000 tickets spread across three shows in two hours, plus 18,000 tickets to a fourth show that was added immediately after the others went on sale), Oklahoma City (14,000 in four hours), San Diego (14,000 tickets in one and a half hours), and Tempe (13,500 tickets in a day and a half).

FEBRUARY Only after Led Zeppelin's equipment was shipped to the United States in advance of their tour was the tour postponed because of Robert Plant's tonsillitis. Jimmy Page later told *Circus* magazine, "The last day of [tour] rehearsal was pure magic, and I thought, 'Right. We're going to have a go. We've got the stamina to play ten straight hours.' And then suddenly Robert got tonsillitis."

As for Page being apart from his equipment, he said, "All I had was a dulcimer. After the postponement, I didn't touch a guitar for four weeks. It was a bit unnerving, really. Pacing around like a caged lion—and I'm not even a Leo. Climbing the walls. Sleepless nights, you bet your life."

MARCH Led Zeppelin rearranged the dates of the U.S. tour and announced them in their entirety—the tour would have three legs that would carry the band from April 1 to July 30. All but two of the original dates from the first leg of the tour were pushed back to mid-May or late June; the remaining two were rescheduled as the first appearances of the tour. Hence the tour would open April 1 in Dallas. Also, fifth and sixth nights were added to the concert itinerary at the L.A. Forum, and six dates at Madison Square Garden were announced.

APRIL 1 As Led Zeppelin's tour opened in Dallas, it was evidently an affecting moment for the members of the band. "When we finally did our first date in Dallas, it was a vast emotional release," Jimmy Page told *Circus* magazine.

Robert Plant still harbored concerns about his onstage activity, telling *Melody Maker*, "The first gig in Dallas, Texas, I was petrified. . . . I was really at home with the idea of playing. The only thing I didn't know about was whether I was going to be able to pace myself out, with my foot problems. For the first two or three gigs I was really measuring every move I made, to find if I'd gone too far or whatever."

APRIL 9 The fifth concert of the tour, at the Chicago Stadium, was stopped early due to Jimmy Page's illness. The show consisted of only five complete songs in less than an hour. Page later explained to *Circus* magazine, "They think it was food poisoning. The doctor says no solids. It's the first time we've ever stopped a gig like that. . . . The pain was unbearable. If I hadn't sat down, I would've fallen over."

APRIL 10 On the stage of the Chicago Stadium for Led Zeppelin's fourth and final show there, Robert Plant addressed Page's illness, saying, "I listened to a radio station today . . . insinuating that Mr. Page had been drinking alcoholic substances all day, and it's fair to say that Mr. Page neither smokes, drinks, or takes women or does

OPPOSITE PAGE: *Ioannis, Led Zeppelin Egyptian Pyramids, 2011.*

FOLLOWING PAGES:
Led Zeppelin on stage at New York's Madison Square Garden during one of their June 1977 dates there; they appeared at the Garden on June 7, 8, 10, 11, 13, and 14.

anything like that, so we'd like an apology from the *Loop* tomorrow, and another crate of the same alcohol, please."

APRIL 15 Aboard Led Zeppelin's leased Boeing 707 jet, called *Caesar's Chariot*, journalist Steven Rosen was interviewing Jimmy Page and trying to avoid John Bonham, having been warned about the drummer's temper and aversion to journalists. Rosen later said that he felt a tap on the shoulder, and it was John Paul Jones, who was muttering about his disdain for him after a piece Rosen had written during Led Zeppelin's early days—a piece that called the band a mere imitation of the Jeff Beck Group. Rosen says he and Jones later patched things up after he told the bassist that he had only been trying to make a name for himself as a young writer.

APRIL 19 As many as 20,000 people showed up to the first of Led Zeppelin's two concerts at Riverfront Coliseum in Cincinnati. A few people in the crowd didn't have tickets but were determined to get inside one way or another. Some started throwing bottles at the glass doors. Others were throwing cans, rocks, knives—just about anything. There was little security on hand, but police made sixty-eight arrests. Inside the venue, some fans were pushing their way through the throng so that they could be as close as possible to the stage—even before Led Zeppelin was there. The concert started late, for which Robert Plant apologized.

APRIL 20 For Led Zeppelin's second night at Riverfront Coliseum, Cincinnati's police presence doubled. Officers made twenty-five arrests, including many for public intoxication and disorderly conduct. Paramedics came to the aid of one fan who'd fallen thirty feet off an outside ramp.

Inside the venue, it was standing room only. With chairs on the floor, the facility could hold barely over 16,000 people; take out the chairs, and they could squeeze in an additional two thousand people. But assigned seating meant that people were constantly pushing their way toward the front of the stage. Both nights Led Zeppelin played Cincinnati, Robert Plant warned the audience about roughhousing, and both nights passed without any major incidents.

On the second night in Cincinnati, Plant admonished fans who were setting off firecrackers, saying, "It would be appreciated by a majority of the people here if you could cool it with the firecrackers, okay?" He later commented to *New Musical Express*, "I don't know why the fans toss firecrackers. I think it's horrible. That's the element that makes you wonder whether it's better to be halfway up a tree in Wales. The thing is I look into so many eyes every night, and when I initially look those eyes are sort of sealed 'cause they don't think I'm real, but bit by bit I work on just those pairs of eyes until they glow with warmth, and then it makes it worthwhile, and whooooosh, the firecrackers dim down."

APRIL 27–28 Reporter Jane Scott, of the *Cleveland Plain Dealer* newspaper, reported that scalped tickets to Led Zeppelin's concerts at the Richfield Coliseum in Cleveland, Ohio, were selling for $100 apiece, more than ten times the face value of $9.50. It was during these

FAR LEFT: *Ioannis,* John Paul Jones: No Quarter *(detail),* *2011.*

NEAR LEFT: *Ioannis,* Robert Plant: The Rain Song *(detail), 2011.*

shows that John Paul Jones debuted a new musical instrument, his triple-neck guitar, consisting of a six-string guitar neck, a twelve-string guitar neck, and an eight-string mandolin neck.

APRIL 30 Led Zeppelin played to their largest crowd ever, an audience of 76,229 people at the Silverdome in Pontiac, Michigan. It is not only a record for Led Zeppelin; it is also the biggest draw for any single-act show. *Melody Maker* reported a gross of £467,000.

MAY 1–17 During Led Zeppelin's break between the first and second legs of the tour, Jimmy Page flew to Cairo, Egypt, on a whim. He explained to *Melody Maker* later in the year, "I was going to go to Cairo on the tour break and I was tossing up whether or not to go. And there was this TV program hosted by Omar Sharif about the mysteries of the pyramids. And they showed this old footage of the pyramids with a zeppelin flying in and I thought, 'That's it! I'll definitely go.' It seemed to be such a strange coincidence that that bit of footage should be there on the day I was thinking about it."

Also during the break, Led Zeppelin received a prestigious Ivor Novello Award for Outstanding Contribution to British Music. All the members of Led Zeppelin except John Bonham attended the presentation in London.

MAY 18 The second leg of Led Zeppelin's North American tour kicked off in Birmingham, Alabama.

MAY 25–30 Led Zeppelin performed four shows in five days, all at the Capital Centre in Landover, Maryland, outside Washington, D.C.

JUNE In an interview with *Creem* magazine's Jaan Uhelszki for *New Musical Express*, Robert Plant commented, "Well, one thing that does upset me [is] I see a lot of craziness around us. Somehow we generate it and we revile it. This is an aspect since I've been away from it which made me contemplate whether we are doing more harm than we are good. That's very important to me. . . . What we are trying to put across is positive and wholesome; the essence of a survival band, and almost a symbol of the phoenix if you will; and people react in such an excitable manner that they miss the meaning of it, and that makes me lose my calm and I get angry."

JUNE 3 After only twenty minutes of music, Led Zeppelin's concert at Tampa Stadium in Florida was interrupted on account of rain. The concert was rescheduled for the following day, but city officials forced its cancellation after the wet audience started to riot.

JUNE 7–14 Led Zeppelin played six concerts in eight days at Madison Square Garden in New York.

JUNE 21 Led Zeppelin played the first of six shows at the L.A. Forum in Inglewood, California. Those shows featured not only long instrumental solos from Jimmy Page, John Paul Jones, and John Bonham, but also some lengthy between-song chitchat from Robert Plant. Judging from his comments on several of the nights, Robert Plant was for some reason focused on badges—the backstage pass you needed to get backstage—and badge holders.

JUNE 23 On this particular night, Led Zeppelin's L.A. Forum audience witnessed a rare special appearance from Keith Moon. A friend of John Bonham's, the Who drummer invaded the stage to make some comments of his own and ended up sticking around for Bonham's "Over the Top" drum solo and the show closer, "Whole Lotta Love." Between songs that night, Robert Plant even took a turn on the stool at the drum kit—but then reclaimed his microphone at the front of the stage from a largely incoherent Moon.

JULY Bill Graham's promotion company announced that the final installments of the Days of the Green concert series, featuring Led Zeppelin and two other bands, were sold out. Taking place July 23 and 24, the concerts would include Derringer and another band to be named, which turned out to be Judas Priest. The press release said: "There will be no tickets available at the door on the days of show. If you don't have a ticket, please do not come to the show. Also we caution people to be wary of counterfeit ticket sellers offering counterfeit tickets to these shows."

In England, there was also talk of Led Zeppelin possibly headlining a music festival to be held at Wrotham Park on August 25. The event was canceled because the desired headlining act was unavailable.

JULY 17 Led Zeppelin's concert in front of 57,000 fans at the Kingdome in Seattle, Washington, was professionally recorded. Footage of the entire show is now in widespread circulation as a bootleg.

JULY 23 Led Zeppelin played the first half of a two-show concert series. The concert at the Oakland Coliseum was followed by the backstage beating of Jim Matzorkis, a venue staffer employed by concert promoter Bill Graham.

That night, Zep's tour manager, Richard Cole, was said to have stood guard, with a lead pipe in hand, outside the trailer where manager Peter Grant and security man John Bindon were beating up on Matzorkis. They chose him because of a perceived dispute earlier between him and Grant's son, Warren. Matzorkis was hospitalized as a result of his injuries.

In a 2009 interview, Richard Cole said, "The whole thing was rather a very regrettable thing. Normally, we never stayed after a show. The format was as soon as the show was finished, get the f— out of there and that's it. And it seemed like a good idea at the time that we should just chill out and *not* run out after the show but just stay there."

JULY 24 Before the second scheduled concert at Oakland Coliseum featuring Led Zeppelin and opening acts Derringer and Judas Priest, there was uncertainty about whether the show would actually take place. Led Zeppelin proceeded to go on only after Bill Graham signed a letter

of indemnification stating that neither he nor his company would pursue civil action against individuals in Led Zeppelin's organization over the backstage beating the previous night.

Later, Graham argued that he'd signed the agreement under duress, that it had no bearing whatsoever on any other injured party's ability to sue in civil court, and that it had no bearing whatsoever on criminal charges being filed. The second concert took place, and it wound up being Led Zeppelin's last in the United States.

JULY 25 In the morning, police SWAT teams surrounded Led Zeppelin's hotel in San Francisco, and police arrested drummer John Bonham and manager Peter Grant for one count of assault each. They also arrested tour manager Richard Cole and security man John Bindon for two counts of assault each. Also, the group was named in a civil suit seeking punitive damages.

JULY 26 With nearly a week to go before Led Zeppelin's next scheduled concert date, John Paul Jones separated from the rest of the group for the time being, mostly because his wife, Mo, was with him. The rest of the group pushed onward to New Orleans, where they were to play next at the Superdome on July 30.

However, upon arriving at his hotel, Robert Plant received word that his son, Karac, was suffering from a stomach infection back home in England. He later learned that the infection had claimed the child's life. Plant and John Bonham flew home to England immediately.

AUGUST 14 Jimmy Page performed with Ron Wood and the group Arms and Legs at a charity golf event in Plumpton, England, benefiting underprivileged children.

SEPTEMBER 6 Jimmy Page again took the stage, this time in Brighton, England, at Atlantic Records' annual sales conference. Around this time, the topic du jour in the music press was the future of Led Zeppelin; most of the stories said the group was breaking up.

OCTOBER Jimmy Page invited reporters to Swan Song's office, where he assured them Led Zeppelin was not breaking up.

NOVEMBER–DECEMBER Stories about Led Zeppelin's future continued to be published through the end of the year, some quoting Jimmy Page at length—even on the subject of the supposed Kenneth Anger curse, and about whether the band was just experiencing bad karma. He told Angie Errigo in an interview for *Melody Maker*, "I just don't see how there could be a bad karma or whatever. I think it's just coincidence."

A view of the crowd and the stage as Led Zeppelin performs at the Alameda County Coliseum in Oakland, California, on July 23, 1977. The concert proved to be controversial because of the backstage assault on Jim Matzorkis, a venue staffer employed by concert promoter Bill Graham.

1978

Time stood still for Robert Plant, whose world had been rocked by the death of his son. Touring was definitely verboten, and even just going away from his farmhouse was out of the question. Assault charges against John Bonham, Peter Grant, Richard Cole, and their security man John Bindon continued to plague the band in the new year. John Paul Jones avoided the press, but Jimmy Page was hands-on with selected media, asserting that Led Zeppelin would not break up, that Plant wanted to continue working with Zeppelin, and that further projects were already in the offing.

This year, there were two paths Led Zeppelin could take, but they would first have to assemble to determine the road they were on.

JANUARY In a roundup of the previous year, *Old Grey Whistle Test* pronounced 1977 to be Led Zeppelin's year, over all other artists.

FEBRUARY The criminal charges against John Bonham, Peter Grant, Richard Cole, and John Bindon resulted in all four being handed suspended prison sentences. They were also made to pay fines.

MARCH At this time, Jimmy Page and Robert Plant were not in contact with each other.

APRIL A report in *New Musical Express* suggested a reunion of Band of Joy, the long-defunct group that had at one point included both Robert Plant and John Bonham before they were in Led Zeppelin. While Plant and Bonham's names were mentioned in the article, there was no suggestion that they would be taking part in the reunion concert.

MAY Led Zeppelin's first rehearsal in nearly a year took place at Clearwell Castle, supposedly after Robert Plant's reading of a farming magazine was disturbed when he read a published report that Roy Harper was beginning to do some songwriting with Jimmy Page.

At Clearwell Castle, the members of Led Zeppelin concentrated on writing some new material, including a piece called "Carouselambra." In it, Plant wrote some lyrics that were seemingly critical of Page after his absence from Plant's life at the time of his son's death and burial: "Where was your helping? Where was your bow?"

JUNE News of Led Zeppelin's Clearwell Castle rehearsals hit the press, with *Melody Maker* declaring it an indication that a new Led Zeppelin album and tour were already in the works. At this early stage, they weren't. A spokesperson for Atlantic Records was skeptical, saying, "I don't know what will come of the rehearsals—an album, a tour, or what—but I expect things will be clarified in the next few weeks."

JULY Rumors persisted that Led Zeppelin were going to play England. One rumor held that the band would play an unannounced set in London, opening for Swan Song recording artist Maggie Bell. It didn't happen. Another rumor held that Led Zeppelin would adopt a new name and book themselves in some small pubs. This was not accurate, as it was only Robert Plant who had begun to guest with other bands. Once, he joined up with an act called Melvin Giganticus and the Turd Burglars for a show at Wolverly Hall, near his home.

AUGUST Robert Plant continued to join up with different acts in concert settings, including once on the Spanish island of Ibiza with the band Dr. Feelgood.

SEPTEMBER Joining Led Zeppelin tour manager Richard Cole and his wife, Tracy, as they celebrated their wedding in Fulham, England, on September 15 were Jimmy Page, Robert Plant, John Paul Jones, and Paul Rodgers of Bad Company, among other guests. The following day, Swan Song recording artist Dave Edmunds welcomed Plant onstage for his encore, jokingly referring to him as Robert Palmer, the English singer-songwriter.

A party celebrating two weddings: that of Led Zeppelin's tour manager, Richard Cole (bottom left, in white suit), to Tracy Heron-Webber, and that of Simon Kirke, Bad Company drummer, to Desiree Serino. The group portrait was taken September 16, 1978, at the Golden Lion pub in Fulham, in southwest London. In the back row are, from left to right, two unidentified guests, Jimmy Page, Paul Rodgers, John Paul Jones, and composer Lionel Bart. In the front row are, from left to right, Richard and Tracy Cole, Desiree and Simon Kirke, singer Maggie Bell, and musician Bob Harris.

OCTOBER For the second time in a year, Led Zeppelin rehearsed new material. This time, they did so in London and decided that they would attempt to record it the following month. Also around this time, Led Zeppelin's two-man rhythm section joined Paul McCartney and Wings, along with a host of other famous musicians, to record a pair of tracks under the name Rockestra. In the meantime, *Sounds* published the fourth and final installment of a detailed and comprehensive history of Led Zeppelin prepared by Geoff Barton and Dave Lewis.

NOVEMBER Robert Plant and John Paul Jones emceed a charity raffle organized by the Golden Lion Group, a newly established family business that ran several pubs and gave back to the community by supporting local causes.

Later in the month, Led Zeppelin flew to Stockholm, Sweden, to record at Polar Studios, owned by Swedish pop group ABBA. Plant and Jones, by virtue of the fact that they were usually the first two to arrive at the studio each day for recording sessions, naturally collaborated on some new material, such as the song "All My Love." The lyrics of that song concentrate on Plant's family situation—the loss of his son and his hopes for the future with his daughter, his wife, and their new child on the way.

DECEMBER Led Zeppelin's studio sessions in Stockholm continued into December, giving Jimmy Page some new music to mix at his home studio by year's end.

The tragedies of 1977, which hung over Led Zeppelin like a black cloud at the beginning of 1978, were less at the forefront as 1979 began. With a new album already in the mixing stages and with a new son on the way for Robert Plant and his wife, it appeared that the group was ready to put all those problems behind them and forge ahead.

JANUARY Logan Romero Plant, the son of Robert and Maureen, was born.

FEBRUARY Led Zeppelin returned to Stockholm, Sweden, to continue mixing the songs on what would become their next album. *New Musical Express*, the sole British music paper tracking progress of the album, said it expected the album to be released in a month's time.

MARCH The month passed without the release of a new album from Led Zeppelin, and so would the next few months as well.

APRIL At the end of the month, Jimmy Page presided over a formal ceremony for the grand reopening of the newly rebuilt Phillip's Harbour in Caithness, Scotland. The harbor town had suffered economic hardships following a tragic storm. *New Musical Express* quoted Page as telling the rebuilders, "My craft is my music, and all the way along I've kept hammering away at it to try and achieve excellence. You chaps involved in this project have also striven for excellence and have done a really worthwhile job."

MAY As Swan Song recording artist Dave Edmunds was married, the wedding guests included Robert Plant and John Paul Jones.

Four years after the Earls Court shows in London, Led Zeppelin finally announced the concert that would bring the band back to England. The Knebworth Festival, featuring Led Zeppelin as headliners, would take place on August 4. Freddy Bannister, who had previously promoted both Bath Festivals with Led Zeppelin in 1969 and 1970,

was promoting this concert as well. An article published in the May 26 issue of *New Musical Express* quoted Bannister as saying that his acquisition of Led Zeppelin at this time was "the greatest scoop of my career."

JUNE Ticket sales for the Knebworth concert took place, with promoter Freddy Bannister declaring that tickets were sold out. He changed his tune years later, explaining that tickets had not really sold out, but he had hoped the announcement would spark interest in a second date, planned for August 11.

JULY 7 The second date for Led Zeppelin at the Knebworth Festival, August 11, was confirmed in *New Musical Express*.

JULY 19 Freddy Bannister announced the full lineup of supporting acts that would be appearing on the same bill as Led Zeppelin the following month at the Knebworth Festival. Jimmy Page bemoaned the lineup the day after the announcement in an interview with *Melody Maker*. "The lineup we had hoped for was Fairport [Convention], Dire Straits, Little Feat, and Joni Mitchell."

Well, they got Fairport Convention, the folk quartet that included some friends of the band. The other groups were unavailable. Rejections likewise came pouring in from just about every act that was offered a spot. Concerts at Knebworth House had a long tradition of attracting multiple big names since the festival was first attempted in 1974. That year, when the event was known as the Bucolic Frolic, the acts included the Allman Brothers, the Doobie Brothers, Van Morrison, and Tim Buckley. Bannister had come close to booking Led Zeppelin, but the band backed out when a report surfaced in *Melody Maker* about the booking before an announcement could be made.

Bannister had high hopes when he successfully booked Led Zeppelin in 1979. Even before he arranged any other bands to support Zeppelin, he optimistically allowed his booking to be announced exclusively on the TV show *Old Grey Whistle Test*. He also let the tickets go on sale on June 3, before any other acts were announced.

Ioannis, Knebworth Festival, *2011.*

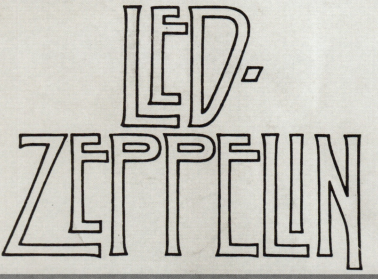

KNEBWORTH 11th AUGUST

Tickets available £7.50 from the kiosk next to the Information tent at the back of the arena, or on your way out — at the ticket kiosk outside the arena.

CHAS AND DAVE

THE NEW COMMANDER CODY BAND

SOUTHSIDE JOHNNY AND THE ASBURY JUKES

TODD RUNDGREN AND UTOPIA

The NEW BARBARIANS

LED- ZEPPELIN

He was reassured by Led Zeppelin manager Peter Grant, who said that the band was about to make history and that Bannister was helping to make it happen. Whose event would be as revered as Led Zeppelin's triumphant return after a four-year absence from the British stage? Bannister's. Even following a noticeable change in the musical climate at that time, Grant was counting on public opinion to side with Led Zeppelin. Bannister just needed the ticket sales to reflect it. Since a second Knebworth performance was in the works for August 11, anything short of a complete sellout for August 4 would mean two things: one, that Bannister wouldn't have earned enough money from ticket sales to break even; and two, that he wouldn't be able to justify green-lighting the second show. Production costs were sky-high, as were the fees the musical acts wanted.

Ticket sales in early June started off with a bang, and Bannister even reported to the press that they had sold out. He now insists this was a tactic to generate interest in the second concert, when in reality, the ticket sales for that first show, while great, did not provide the sellout needed to cover his expenses. Bannister hoped other big names being added to the bill would boost ticket sales and help make Knebworth a sold-out show—two weeks in a row.

Bannister says many of rock's biggest names declined his offers to share Zeppelin's gig. His account is painfully detailed in his autobiography, entitled *There Must Be a Better Way: The Story of the Bath and Knebworth Rock Festivals 1969–1979*. Among the acts he recalls turning him down in 1979 are J. J. Cale, Little Feat, and Roxy Music. In one telling quotation, Bannister says, "No one, it seemed, wanted to play with Led Zeppelin. It was at this point, rather belatedly, that I began to realize just what a reputation the band enjoyed for their egotistical behavior."

Grant, realizing the uphill battle, returned to Bannister with the news that he himself had arranged for another band to play Knebworth. It was the New Barbarians, a side project of the Rolling Stones that included two Stones members, Keith Richards and Ronnie Wood, plus Wood's former Faces bandmate Ian McLagan. "Two out of five of the Stones can't be bad, I thought," writes Bannister. In the end, the New Barbarians backed out of playing the August 4 show because of ongoing studio sessions for the Rolling Stones album *Emotional Rescue*, but the group did sign on for the August 11 show. It was only three weeks before showtime that the group committed to playing, which meant that there was little time to publicize it.

Meanwhile, Led Zeppelin's suggestion of Fairport Convention panned out. Bannister writes that he hadn't been aware the band still existed; he thought they'd broken up years earlier. No, they were actually now down to a foursome. Scheduling was a problem, as the group was organizing its own festival, Cropredy, to take place August 4, and was previously booked elsewhere on August 11. Fairport squeezed in a single Knebworth performance early on August 4.

Another band booked for only one date was Chas & Dave, which played August 11 only. They were offbeat pub rockers who'd just struck a major UK hit with "Gertcha." Bannister, who was already familiar with their

act, writes in his memoir, "They were just fine in the intimacy of a small theater but on the giant stage, trying to project novelty songs to a hundred thousand rock-hungry kids, it was a different matter."

The Marshall Tucker Band was briefly scheduled to appear at both shows. However, the band dropped out by the end of July, to be replaced quickly by Commander Cody and His Lost Planet Airmen. Rounding out the bill for both weeks were Todd Rundgren's Utopia and Southside Johnny and the Asbury Jukes. And that's the complete lineup for Knebworth '79. "Not a vintage support program," recalls Bannister, "but in view of the difficulties I had been experiencing, it could have been worse."

A more damning opinion eventually came from even the least likely of sources, one that few expected would criticize anything Led Zeppelin–related. "In retrospect it was the worst support bill ever assembled for a Knebworth Festival," Led Zeppelin historian Dave Lewis wrote in his *Tight But Loose* Zep fanzine in 1999. In that, his second retrospective on the festival, Lewis admittedly applied a "more objective" view than the one before, which was "published soon after the shows" and "duly reflected my own blind devotion of the time—a view of the proceedings through rose-tinted glasses." Lewis now theorized, "It would seem Peter Grant had little input and perhaps shrewdly let Bannister assemble a lineup that was going to pose little threat to Zeppelin."

Grant told Led Zeppelin biographer Ritchie Yorke years later that he had aerial photos taken both weeks at Knebworth, which, when analyzed by an astronomical laboratory in the United States, revealed approximate attendance of 218,000 the first week and 187,000 the second. Bannister writes that he was never privy to this alleged evidence and that the thirty-six-acre site couldn't accommodate more than 104,000 by a rather conservative estimate, a figure that didn't even account for the massive stage taking up part of the grounds. He also leans back on the ticket sales, which indicated 104,000 paid attendees the first week and the paltry figure of only 40,000 on the second. Bannister's company, Tedoar, Ltd., entered liquidation one month after the Knebworth concerts.

Even if Led Zeppelin drew "only" 144,000 fans to Knebworth, it would have been record numbers for the festival and staggering attendance figures for any band. The actual attendance on the second week may have been much higher than the ticket sales indicated, thanks to the gate-crashing that occurred on August 11. Those who were there can attest to this. Robert Godwin, the noted author of several books on Led Zeppelin, attended both shows and insists he was never in a larger crowd at any time in his life, even at an Olympic event that was reported to have been attended by 150,000 people. That's the way he prefers to remember the final concert in England by Jimmy Page, Robert Plant, John Paul Jones, and John Bonham.

Because it was in that sense a last hurrah, the memory of Led Zeppelin's 1979 Knebworth concerts remains tinged with sadness. Dave Lewis reflected on his own memories twenty years later, writing, "Led Zeppelin at Knebworth could have been, and should have been, a new

beginning. As it was, it turned out to be their last good-bye, but being there to unknowingly wave them off was, for all in attendance, a truly unforgettable experience."

JULY 23–24 Led Zeppelin played a pair of shows in Copenhagen, Denmark, as a warm-up to the Knebworth concerts in England. It had always been Led Zeppelin's tradition, after having been out of practice, to embark on some isolated dates prior to a major tour. In the mind of Peter Grant, those gigs would always provide solace to an unrehearsed band. In addition, Led Zeppelin's rig was now sporting new improvements to the light show, shipped in from the United States, which provided more of a reason for the band to get everything right ahead of time.

These two shows were presented in front of limited-capacity crowds of two thousand, compared to the crowds one hundred times that size that would see Led Zeppelin in the coming weeks. They reasoned that far fewer onlookers would be disappointed if, for example, one facet of the light show were to malfunction unexpectedly.

And that's exactly what happened. Good contingency plan! Knock the kinks out of the way before you attempt

playing in your own country to nearly every fan of yours, young and old. At the Falkoner Theatre on Monday night, technical glitches were inescapable. As Dave Lewis chronicled in *Tight But Loose*, "There were major production problems in assembling the new lighting, the rig proving too big for the arena, which resulted in a blown generator and delayed the gig by nearly two hours."

Eric Kornfeldt's Copenhagen review, published in *New Musical Express*, details just how grotesque these glitches actually were. He wrote: "Come concert day and trouble began early. The stage equipment failed repeatedly during sound check. Then the lighting wasn't receiving the correct power and the crew sent out pleas for a mobile generator. When they finally located one it still proved too weak, though it seemed like it would keep a medium size town in juice. Lasers and lights fused all around, and the band decided they'd only use half their lighting after all."

Onstage, the band was a slicker version of its previous self, with a certain emphasis placed on scaling down the solo numbers. For "No Quarter," Jones held his grand piano solo to within four minutes, which was quite the accomplishment, considering that it was twice that length

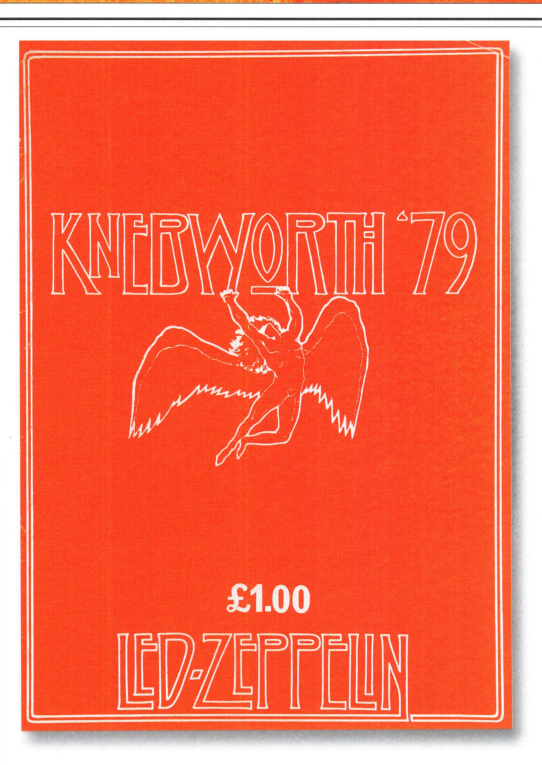

OPPOSITE PAGE AND RIGHT: *The cover of a concert program booklet and two backstage passes from Knebworth.*

not so long ago. Gone from the set list was "Moby Dick," replaced instead by Bonham's minute-and-a-half-long timpani solo, which proved to be an apt segue between Page's four-minute guitar solo and onstage spectacle and the only other new number besides "Hot Dog," which was "In the Evening." This led up to the main set's nine-minute grand finale, "Stairway to Heaven," secure in its position as the pre-encore concert closer since the first days of 1975.

Page did maintain a spot for his solo performance of "White Summer/Black Mountain Side" during the Copenhagen shows and the Knebworth concerts that followed. In fact, it was this instrumental that caused

reviewer Erik von Lustbaden's biggest upset at the warm-up show on July 23. He wrote, in a piece published in *Sounds*, that he opted to find another source of entertainment while the guitarist played unaccompanied onstage: "I went for a piss, bought a bar of chocolate, ate it, had a sit down, made some notes, went back in, and he was still playing it!"

That was the inescapable aura of Led Zeppelin. Even when the band wanted to keep each song to four or five minutes, they hardly ever did. The first six songs of the set were about six minutes or less each, while "Hot Dog"—unrecognizable because the new album hadn't yet been released—clocked in at just over three minutes.

The *New Musical Express* review of the developments in Copenhagen proved reproachful. "A showing like this one in Copenhagen is pointless and ultimately damaging," it said. "They were no more than a quartet of sloppy, uninspired old men, a relic from the past. There was so little feeling inherent in the set that for the most part it was like watching a fully automated factory producing an endless string of chords that neither musicians nor audience cared about."

It's hard to tell how representative these reviewers' comments were of the opinions of the thousands of others who attended.

One audience recording has surfaced from each concert, revealing what Robert Plant said to the faithful gathered there. In his opening remarks on July 23, he acknowledged that "it's been eight years since we were here last time." (Really, it was closer to six years.)

Plant followed this with a resolution that there would be less talking and more playing, although he did use an opportunity after "Hot Dog" to reveal what he might have meant by the lyric "I'll never go to Texas anymore." Plant said, "That was because we were very heavily influenced by the PA and lighting company who charges so much money, we had to write that song, and they got the royalties. That's why only half the lights are working."

Plant elicited fewer comments of note on July 24, except for his sole remark during a hold-up in preparing John Paul Jones's instrumentation for "Ten Years Gone," consisting of the heavy triple-neck guitar and a set of bass pedals. He said, "Very shortly, we shall be doing 'Eleven Years Gone.'"

AUGUST 4 The Knebworth Festival was held, with Led Zeppelin performing for more than two and a half hours.

Before the event, Robert Plant told an interviewer what the concert would be like. "I think the music will speak for itself. It will stand up there as it always has done. There will be new bits, bits from the past, maybe just a little bit different," he said.

At the concerts, Jimmy Page did have some shining long solos, like "White Summer" and "Black Mountain Side," leading into "Kashmir." Then again, between "Achilles Last Stand" and the new "In the Evening," Page played another guitar solo not unlike parts of "Dazed and Confused."

The combined attendance over the two weeks at the Knebworth Festival was supposedly 405,000. Plant was ecstatic in his announcements, which had a "There's no place like home" feel, drawing on the spirit of Albion, which he had referenced years before.

People came from all over the world to see Led Zeppelin that day. Since the festival was held near Stevenage in Hertfordshire, an hour north of London, it was in a central place to which people from all over the United Kingdom could trek. But the audience also came from all over Europe, North America, and Japan. As a result of the wide attendance, the fee picked up by Led Zeppelin for this appearance was reputedly the highest ever in the history of rock entertainment.

Jones said the tunes were "brilliant as ever. It was like the first day that we played together." During the August 4 show, they pulled off a wonderful performance of "Ten Years Gone" from their 1975 album, *Physical Graffiti*. The song required Jones to play his special triple-neck guitar; he also played bass pedals at the same time. While the onstage preparation of this instrument was taking forever, Plant quipped—as he had in Copenhagen—that by the time they got around to playing it, it would be "Eleven Years Gone." The problems encountered in setting up the multifaceted instrument probably account for its omission the following week.

AUGUST 11 The second concert of the Knebworth Festival took place, with a nearly identical set list.

AUGUST 15 Led Zeppelin released their new album, entitled *In Through the Out Door*, just after debuting two of the new songs live—"In the Evening" and "Hot Dog."

SEPTEMBER Led Zeppelin's album *In Through the Out Door* peaked on the UK chart at the number two position. Meanwhile, Freddy Bannister's company, Tedoar, Ltd., entered liquidation, and a report in *New Musical Express* stated that the number of tickets sold at Knebworth was closer to 98,000 for the first show and 48,000 for the second.

OCTOBER All nine Led Zeppelin albums appeared on *Billboard*'s Hot 200 LP and Tape charts, the largest number of albums from one single act to be on the chart at once. *In Through the Out Door* was at number 1, with 1973's *Houses of the Holy* at number 91 and the seven others not far behind.

NOVEMBER All the members of Led Zeppelin except Jimmy Page attended the London presentation ceremony for the annual *Melody Maker* Poll Awards. Of the seven awards, the biggest was the one Led Zeppelin received for band of the year, marking a comeback for the group following their return to live performance. Critics believed it would go instead to the Police, a newcomer on the UK music scene. While accepting the award, John Bonham sang the chorus to the Police's "Message in a Bottle," which had been the country's number one single the previous month. John Paul Jones wore a button on his lapel reading ROCK AGAINST JOURNALISM.

Spokespeople claimed that Page was vacationing in Barbados, but he was actually testifying in court about the recent death of a friend at his house, a story the band desired to keep away from the press.

DECEMBER With Paul McCartney and Wings on tour in the UK, Led Zeppelin members attended some of the shows. Jimmy Page saw them on December 2 in Brighton. John Bonham and Robert Plant saw them on December 12 in Birmingham. Plant, Bonham, and John Paul Jones attended the group's Concert for Kampuchea on December 29 in London and took part in the all-star Rockestra jam at the end of the show.

OPPOSITE PAGE: *A tour button and poster for Led Zeppelin's 1980 Tour Over Europe.*

1980

JANUARY 16 Robert Plant and Eric Clapton were among famous musicians attending a reception for the release of an album benefiting sick and handicapped children. The collection of thirteen rock songs was released to support efforts by the United Nations to work on a number of large-scale issues affecting children. A subsequent UN declaration had officially named 1979 the International Year of the Child.

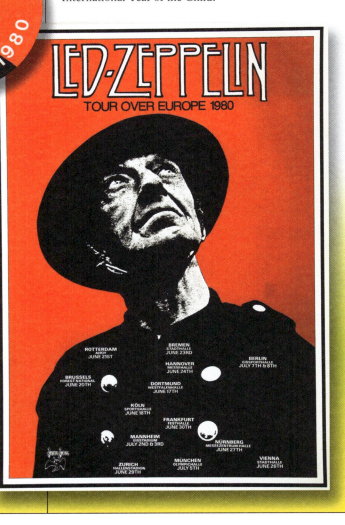

The compilation album, called *The Summit*, was a joint effort between Led Zeppelin's Swan Song Records and budget label K-tel, and hit UK record stores on January 11, 1980. Executives at Swan Song, including members of Led Zeppelin, picked the songs that would appear on the record. Two groups signed to that label appeared on the album. Bad Company contributed "Rock and Roll Fantasy" from their 1979 album on Swan Song, *Desolation Angels*. The last track of the album was Led Zeppelin's own "Candy Store Rock," a song released on *Presence* in 1976.

Among the other huge-name artists appearing on the album were Clapton, Yes, Pink Floyd, Wings, Cliff Richard, and Elton John. Each of the bands or artists on the album kicked in a song that was originally released between 1973 and 1979. *The Summit* was really a great mix of songs, including Thin Lizzy's "The Boys Are Back in Town," Supertramp's "Give a Little Bit," and Dire Straits' "Sultans of Swing."

FEBRUARY Robert Plant joined Swan Song recording artist Dave Edmunds onstage in Birmingham.

MARCH John Bonham gave his last televised interview in a live appearance on the program *Alright Now* with host Billy Connolly. He provided several one-word answers to Connolly but graciously signed autographs for fans in attendance.

APRIL Led Zeppelin began rehearsing in London for their upcoming European tour, word of which had not yet reached the press.

MAY Throughout the month, Led Zeppelin continued rehearsing for their upcoming European tour. The tour itinerary was announced and then revised twice before appearing in final form. The itinerary would see Led Zeppelin kicking off the tour on June 17 in Dortmund, West Germany, and also traveling to other cities in that country as well as to the Netherlands, Belgium, and Austria.

LED ZEPPELIN

"In through the out door"

Lippmann + Rau + Scheller present

CONCERT 80

27. Juni '80

Freitag 20 Uhr
27. Juni '80
Nürnberg
Messezentrum
Halle A

OPPOSITE PAGE: *A poster for the June 27, 1980, Led Zeppelin concert in Nuremberg, West Germany, at the Messenzentrum, which was cut short because John Bonham collapsed, likely from food poisoning.*

BELOW: *A ticket for what was to be Led Zeppelin's last show: July 7, 1980, at the Eissporthalle in West Berlin.*

JUNE 6 Led Zeppelin's tour rehearsals ended early in the month at Shepperton Studios in England.

JUNE 17 Led Zeppelin's first tour in three years began in Dortmund, West Germany. The fourteen-show tour was called Led Zeppelin Tour Over Europe 1980. Each show was about two hours apiece and included at least one song from each of their eight studio albums. The first song of each concert was "Train Kept A-Rollin'."

The dawning of punk music at the end of the '70s had a great effect on Led Zeppelin. Magazines in England were snobbily dismissing Zeppelin as irrelevant and calling them dinosaurs. But punk music reenergized Led Zeppelin, and at the end of the concert, Robert Plant had a message for Zep's audience in Dortmund: "Dinosaurs rule!"

Also that night, for the first time, guitarist Jimmy Page made a regular habit of speaking onstage at each show. He was the first member of the band to address the crowd in Dortmund.

JUNE 26 In Vienna, Austria, Jimmy Page was barely into his guitar instrumental "White Summer" when an audience member threw a firecracker that nearly hit him in the face. Page walked off the stage, and moments later the concert promoter came on to lecture the audience in two languages.

JUNE 27 Three songs into the set in Nuremberg, West Germany, the concert stopped early when it was explained that John Bonham had collapsed from physical exhaustion.

JUNE 30 Led Zeppelin welcomed a special musical guest onstage during their concert in Frankfurt, West Germany. For the encore, they played the song "Money (That's What I Want)" with record executive Phil Carson joining them on bass.

During the band's "Whole Lotta Love" medley, they played the song "Frankfurt Special," made famous by Elvis Presley. The lyrics of that song include two recitations of the words "get the lead out."

JULY 1 At Santana's show in Frankfurt, West Germany, Carlos Santana invited onto the stage a special guest—in his words, "Jimmy Page the great." Appearing onstage together for the first time ever, the two guitarists traded licks on the Elmore James tune "Shake Your Money Maker."

JULY 5 Onstage in Munich, West Germany, Led Zeppelin was joined by special guest Simon Kirke, drummer for Bad Company, for a special five-man rendition of "Whole Lotta Love." Journalist Andrew Baroutas covered the concert for *Juke*, an Australian magazine, saying that Jimmy Page was especially active onstage and the whole band acted quite unlike the dinosaurs they were accused of being.

JULY 7 The final concert of Led Zeppelin's European tour took place in Berlin, West Germany, but it turned out to be the final Led Zeppelin concert of John Bonham's lifetime.

AUGUST Jimmy Page relocated to the Old Mill House in Windsor, England, which he had recently purchased from actor Michael Caine.

SEPTEMBER 11 Swan Song Records issued an announcement from label president and Led Zeppelin manager Peter Grant regarding a forthcoming tour to be called Led Zeppelin, The Eighties, Part One. It included nineteen shows in a North America.

SEPTEMBER 24 Led Zeppelin gathered at Bray Studios near Windsor, England, for the first day of rehearsals. John Paul Jones described it as a day of rejuvenation, as everybody was happy to see each other again for the first time since their tour of Europe. However, John Bonham was drinking throughout the day, having started immediately after he left his own home. Following the day of rehearsals, the band retired to Page's home, where Bonham was carried to an upstairs bed.

SEPTEMBER 25 Overnight, John Bonham died in his sleep, having choked on his own vomit. His death went undiscovered for several hours. In the afternoon, the other members of Led Zeppelin had been waiting for Bonham to emerge. Seeing that he hadn't, Robert Plant's assistant, Benji LeFevre, and John Paul Jones went upstairs to check on him. They found Bonham lying on his back in a pool of vomit. Jones contacted the paramedics, and LeFevre spread the word to the others. Plant departed for Old Hyde Farm to break the news in person to Bonham's family. Page stayed home, and once the news had broken, fans began holding a silent vigil outside the house.

SEPTEMBER 26 Word of Bonham's death continued to spread worldwide, and speculation began as to the status of those North American concerts that had been announced—and, moreover, the future of Led Zeppelin. Meanwhile, police in England determined that Bonham's death was not the result of foul play.

SEPTEMBER 27 Swan Song announced that Led Zeppelin's tour was officially canceled.

OCTOBER A few days before the funeral for John Bonham was held, the coroner ruled the death accidental. Prior to this, *New Musical Express* suggested that Bonham's death was the result of occultist practices by Jimmy Page.

NOVEMBER Led Zeppelin's surviving members met for a discussion of their future as a band. Their decision was unanimous: they could not continue as they were. The decision was then explained to Peter Grant.

DECEMBER 4 Swan Song issued a press release officially announcing the disbanding of Led Zeppelin. The message: "We wish it to be known, that the loss of our dear friend and the deep respect we have for his family, together with the deep sense of harmony felt by ourselves and our manager have led us to decide that we could not continue as we were."

THE INTERVIEWS

Richard Cole

BRITISH-BORN RICHARD COLE WAS AMONG THE FIRST TOUR MANAGERS TO SPECIALIZE IN AMERICAN TOURS OF ENGLISH BANDS. AFTER ACTING AS TOUR MANAGER FOR THE WHO IN 1965, COLE MOVED TO AMERICA IN 1967, WHERE HE WORKED FOR VANILLA FUDGE AS A SOUND ENGINEER. IN 1968, WHEN HE HEARD THAT THE YARDBIRDS WERE COMING TO AMERICA, HE CONTACTED THEIR MANAGER, PETER GRANT, AND SOON BECAME THE BAND'S TOUR MANAGER. WHEN THE YARDBIRDS DISSOLVED SHORTLY THEREAFTER, COLE BECAME LED ZEPPELIN'S TOUR MANAGER, AN EXPERIENCE HE CHRONICLED IN HIS 1992 BOOK (COAUTHORED WITH RICHARD TRUBO), *STAIRWAY TO HEAVEN: LED ZEPPELIN UNCENSORED*.

COLE GAINED VISIBILITY WHEN HE PORTRAYED A GUNTOTING GANGSTER IN *THE SONG REMAINS THE SAME*. TOWARD THE END OF HIS TIME WITH LED ZEPPELIN, AFTER A HOST OF UPS AND DOWNS, COLE'S SELF-DESTRUCTIVE LIFESTYLE AND BAD HABITS BEGAN TO TAKE A TOLL, ACCORDING TO HIS OWN FIRST-PERSON ACCOUNTS. IN RECENT YEARS, HE CLEANED UP HIS ACT AND ATTENDED THE LED ZEPPELIN REUNION CONCERT IN 2007.

THIS EXTENSIVE INTERVIEW WITH THE MOST INSIDE OF INSIDERS, CONDUCTED IN THE SPRING OF 2009, BEGINS WITH COLE DISCUSSING HIS EARLY FORAYS INTO THE MUSIC BUSINESS.

DENNY SOMACH: So when did you first meet Peter Grant?

RICHARD COLE: I first met Peter Grant in 1967 in his office. Mick Wilsher, who was the guitarist with the New Vaudeville Band [managed by Peter Grant, and best known for the pop hit "Winchester Cathedral"]—I bumped into him in the Ship [a pub in central London] just before I turned twenty-one, Christmas '66, when I . . . was looking for a job. And he told me he was with the New Vaudeville Band. And also the agent at the time for the New Vaudeville Band—he put a word in, told me to go see Peter Grant. So I called up his offices in America and I went round to see him in Oxford Street with [producer] Mickie Most.

DS: What were your first impressions of Peter Grant?

RC: Well, my—[laughs]. He was fucking big, that's for sure. He was big, and I always remember him saying to me, he asked me how much I wanted. And I told him and he made a face and I said, "Well, take it or leave it." And I always remember him saying to me, "If you mention anything you hear in this office, I'll cut your fucking ears off." And I just laughed. I thought, "You ain't gonna be able to get over that fucking desk quick enough to catch me."

PAGE 92: *Ioannis*, Led Zeppelin 1973, *2011*.

BELOW: *May 12, 1969: Richard Cole, right, arrives at Honolulu Airport with Led Zeppelin; Robert Plant and Jimmy Page walk with him on the tarmac. Led Zeppelin played at the Civic Auditorium in Honolulu the next day.*

DS: Looking back, how important was Peter Grant to the success of Led Zeppelin?

RC: He was essential. He was essential, you know. I mean, everything was done strategically with Peter. You know, right down to when the sun went down and God knows what else other things he would come up with. And plus, Peter had been a road manager himself, so he knew the road as well. He knew America pretty well. He was very rare because most managers don't know what goes on the road. He did as well, so you couldn't pull the wool over his eyes if you wanted to.

DS: He'd been [American rockabilly musician] Gene Vincent's tour manager.

RC: Yeah, so I mean he was—he could also sympathize with you as well. I remember once saying to him "I can't" or something, and he said, "There's not such a word as 'can't' in my vocabulary. You just fucking get on with it and do it." And that was it. That's just the way he worked.

DS: So here we are in the middle of '68 and the Yardbirds were folded. You'd actually been on the road with the Yardbirds.

RC: Yeah.

DS: So when did you first meet Jimmy Page?

RC: I first met Jimmy Page in 1967, when I was with the New Vaudeville Band. I also did work for the Yardbirds

that come about, and what was the link with Terry?

RC: Beginning of 1968, I went on the road with a band called Creation. . . . When I finished that, I went to New York, and Steve Weiss, who was Zeppelin's lawyer and the Yardbirds' lawyer and God knows who else, got me a job with the Vanilla Fudge. Brian Condliffe, who was the Yardbirds' road manager before me, didn't want to do it [manage them any longer], so I wrote Peter Grant a letter, and he replied to the letter and basically said, "You take on the tour, then." And that was it. So I was back working for Peter. . . .

DS: So when did you first get the call to work with this new group, which essentially were the New Yardbirds, which would soon be Led Zeppelin? When did that happen?

RC: Sometime when I was with Terry Reid, near the end of that. Peter called up and said, "I want you to go with Jimmy and Led Zeppelin. There's this new band." I'd already heard the stuff. I think Peter played it for me when I was with Jeff Beck. I can't remember. I think the new album had been finished by then.

DS: Can you recall your first meeting with Robert, Bonzo, and John Paul Jones?

RC: Apparently, I met Bonzo in the office but I don't particularly remember it. . . . Robert said to me when I was with him a few months ago, I don't particularly remember. All I know is I went out to the airport, picked up the three of them—Jimmy I knew, and these other two guys.

> ## Apparently, I said to Robert, "You can't walk around dressed like that. We'll have to take you and buy you some new clothes." I mean, I don't remember. That's what Robert told me.

near the end of '67; I did a few shows for them. So Jimmy may have come in the van with me, I think, because a friend of mine told me we went down one night and picked him up, so he obviously came in the van with me down to one of the gigs. So that's when I first basically met him. And then when we were with the Yardbirds, Jimmy and I always shared a room together.

DS: What were your first impressions of Jimmy?

RC: Very quiet. I mean . . . I met him at his house. Basically, I think I had to pick up some equipment from there or pick up his instruments, and he was playing me all these different records and stuff. Very hospitable person.

DS: So, just before Yardbirds into Zeppelin, you're working with Terry Reid [the vocalist and guitarist whom Jimmy Page originally wanted for the New Yardbirds]. How did

DS: Robert was this twenty-year-old from the Midlands. You were well versed in traveling the world. Did he eye you suspiciously early on, in the early days of Led Zeppelin?

RC: I suppose so.

DS: Did you sense that?

RC: Yeah, I mean, I suppose he was a bit nervous. I mean, Jimmy was well known. John Paul Jones was also a well-known musician, so for Bonzo and Robert, it was a completely new venture. Both Jimmy and John Paul Jones had been to America before. For those two [Bonzo and Robert], it was brand new. I mean, the same as it was for me when I first went over there. It's a big place. Everything's different, so different. For anyone to go there for the first time, their jaws are just gonna drop.

DS: So can you remember what the first gig [in America] was like? It was in Denver?

RC: It was in Denver and it was in the round. We had a station wagon, I think. I can't remember where we stayed, but the gig was with the Vanilla Fudge, and I knew the Vanilla Fudge obviously because I worked with them, so I introduced them to the band and it kind of made things really easy. They both got on really well. . . .

DS: Once the tour started and things began to lull, was it evident that they were soon gonna be built up? Was there a sense early on that this was gonna happen quickly?

RC: I suppose by the fourth show, when Robert started getting his feet and then I realized what sort of drummer Bonzo was with the drum solo and everything else, but I don't think—every tour, sort of, was the next escalation, so I think it's a bit presumptuous just to stand there and say, "Oh, these guys are going to be enormous." You know, it was step by step.

DS: Did it feel different for you?

RC: Well, they were just easy to work with. They were a lot of fun to be with, so I mean that was really what I went in the music business for.

DS: So at that point, you were still essentially a freelancer going from band to band. Did it become clear that Peter wanted you exclusively for Led Zeppelin?

RC: Basically, the conversation was, we were doing the Carousel Ballroom [which became Fillmore West, in San Francisco] in January '69. And I said to Peter, "Listen, I don't particularly want to be running around with all these other bands. I'd rather just stay with this one." And he just said fine and that was it.

DS: So it was just a done deal and you were committed to that. How would you sum up the individual personalities of Zeppelin? As a summary of working with him, how would you sum up Jimmy? What would you say essentially he brought to the band?

RC: I suppose in a sense he brought some sense of discipline, especially in recordings, because, you know, he was well versed in studios and so was John Paul Jones as well. It's hard to sum up anything with him. You know, I think they all brought something. Without one of them, it's very hard to—

DS: So it couldn't be one without the other.

RC: Yeah. I mean, there were a lot of those sorts of bands that were so intertwined, really, right from the beginning.

DS: Was there a definite feeling of chemistry from right off?

RC: I think once we got through pretty much half the first

tour, then it really started to gel. I mean, don't forget Jimmy and Robert were seasoned musicians and Jimmy had been there before with the Yardbirds, and once the others felt that they were in, then that was it. The whole thing, really, that was it. There was no turning back.

DS: In the early days, in terms of road crew, was it pretty small?

You know, they could almost, like, read each other's minds, especially when they were onstage.

RC: [Laughs] It was never a big road crew.

DS: When you were doing the driving in the early days, what's the snowstorm story?

RC: [Pauses] Oh!

DS: It was the blizzard.

RC: No. Well, no. Yes and no . . . I think it was five shows that we did with the Vanilla Fudge and the last show was [in] a place called Spokane, Washington. And we had tickets to fly from Spokane to Seattle and Seattle to Los Angeles because we had the Whisky [a Go Go] in Los Angeles, which, even though the place wasn't big, it was a big gig because it was Los Angeles, you know, and the press and everything that went with that. And what happened was we couldn't get a plane out and so I decided to drive the car, but all the roads were blocked off and they said we were supposed to get off the road, but I didn't bother. I went around the [cloverleaf off-ramp]. I went up one side because the police were blocking it and drove down the other side. And there was no one else on the road. . . .

DS: [Laughs] You'd worked with the likes of the Who, and you'd been with Keith Moon, and all the antics that came with it. Was it evident that being on the road with Zeppelin was going to be a bit livelier?

RC: Um, yeah, I'd think so.

DS: What would you put that down to? Was it just the sheer—

RC: I don't know, it's just the personalities. . . . I mean they didn't take things too seriously, except for playing, obviously, and getting to the show and that. But they were pretty easy to work with. They weren't—there was no prima donna bollocks in it because, I mean, they wouldn't be allowed between the members anyway because they'd all take the piss out of each other and

then of course you have Peter Grant as well, so I think none of that was sort of allowed, so to speak. . . .

DS: It was evident you were pretty skilled in terms of getting from A to B. What strategies did you come up with on those early tours that helped Zeppelin on the road? Did you have a definite "we should do this"?

RC: Yeah, but it was made up as we went along . . . because most of the things had never been done before.

DS: Because isn't there this thing about you were one of the pioneers of bringing the gear over to America?

RC: Oh, that was the New Vaudeville. Yeah, and also, they didn't bring road managers or tour managers with them from England normally. They'd pick one up in America. . . .

DS: Do you think the on-the-road lifestyle ever affected their onstage performances?

RC: It may have done nearer the end.

DS: But not in the early days?

RC: Not in the early days, no.

DS: Yeah, I think it was the Beatles or Stones. [Note: It was the Rolling Stones, in June 1964; the Beatles performed there in February 1964.]

RC: And so that's why he wanted to do that. And also, it was, like, very establishment, and he wanted to move Zeppelin into that sort of forum. It was a very prestigious show.

DS: Why do you think Zeppelin were so successful in the U.S. from the start, as opposed to the UK, which took a while to tune in?

RC: . . . Maybe because the places you played in America in the beginning were set up—they were used to a different variation of music. . . . We were on with all sorts of different people, whether it be It's a Beautiful Day or there'd be jazz people on the bill with Sly and the Family Stone and Led Zeppelin and things like that. Over here [in the UK], the first run of concerts we did I believe were in the old sort of clubs where the blues and soul bands used to play, which I'd done with Ronnie Jones and the Night Timers, which was like [the London club] Klooks Kleek and the Cooks Ferry Inn and places like that. And that was the one that established them in England. . . . Those places only held two or three hundred people or whatever it was, it might have been five. But every one of those shows, there were people queuing up around the block to go and see them for hours before they even got there.

So I think the public were more aware of Led Zeppelin before the press were, in that sense of it. People go by what it says in the press, so if the press are late to catch on, then it looks as though no one else has caught on. But I don't think that was really the case.

DS: Who were the important promoters that got behind Zeppelin and certainly in America, who were the people that kind of made it happen?

RC: I suppose anyone, really, who gave them a gig. I mean, obviously, you've got Bill Graham on the West Coast. And he was doing New York as well. But then you've got Ronnie [hesitates, searching for a last name] . . . Delsener! We did work with Delsener; we did work with "Philly" Basile. Up in Boston was always Don Law. I mean, I don't think it ever changed from Don Law in Boston. It never changed from Bill Graham on the West Coast, and when I say the West Coast, I mean San Francisco, actually. . . .

DS: Some early Zeppelin performances, just to get some viewpoints from you. You did Carnegie Hall in '69, which hadn't been played as a rock venue for years. Can you remember much about that?

RC: Peter was very good at picking out places of stature. I could be wrong, I'm not sure, but I have a feeling the last band who played there as a band or group was the Beatles.

DS: Royal Albert Hall, January 1970, which is on the DVD. Have you got many memories of that show?

RC: Albert Hall in London is an enormous place to play. I don't mean the size of it but just an enormous sort of venue where everything has to be right. Another one, it's a very prestigious sort of place. I mean that when you play there in London, you've arrived. In those days, that's before Wembley opened up and places like that. . . . The rock business was really small in the '60s, compared to what it is today. And as the years have gone on.

DS: Yeah, it broke out. What's the story then about [Led Zeppelin] appearing as the Nobs in Copenhagen?

RC: When they appeared as the Nobs in Copenhagen it was because I think there was a threat that there was some litigation going to be brought against them by von Zeppelin's granddaughter [Count Ferdinand von Zeppelin was founder of the eponymous German airship company] or something like that and they said, "Oh, fuck it, put it down as the Nobs." I mean, the tickets had all been sold. Everyone was going to the show anyway, so it made absolutely no difference whatsoever.

DS: It still sold out and didn't matter. . . .

RC: Yeah, it was already sold out.

DS: Do you remember going to Iceland?

RC: Oh, I loved Iceland! The reason they actually went to Iceland . . . Led Zeppelin were used as a cultural export of music to Iceland, is basically what it was. It was a hell of a lot of fun there. I mean, we flew in one day, buggered around and went drinking, and then did the show the next day and left the day after; you know, it was one of those sort of things. But I've been back there since. I mean, when we went there in 1970 . . .

DS: It was June. June [22] of 1970.

RC: Okay, so when we went there, there was a bit of road going from the airport and then there was a bit more road when you got into Reykjavik. And I mean it was, like, prehistoric. It was incredible. You've got all those volcanic —moss everywhere, and it was just an amazing place. I went back there in 1990 with the [UK rock band] London Quireboys, and it had completely changed. They had the best duty-free shop I'd ever seen in my life, and all the roads were built. It was just a completely different sort of thing altogether.

DS: Just after that, Zeppelin played the Bath Festival [June 28, 1970]. Memories of that one? Big one?

RC: That was enormous as well. I think we'd done the Bath Festival before [June 1969], but when we did it before, the Bath Festival itself was much smaller. It was Freddy Bannister's venue, and it was basically the same venue as when Freddy Bannister used to promote. I'd done it with the Who and I think maybe some other people. The first one was small, and the one in 1970 was enormous. It was outside in some great big field or something.

DS: Shepton Mallet, yeah. And that's the time when they go on, when the sun's going down.

RC: That's one of Peter's things. When the sun was going down, then you'd have to light the stage.

DS: And that just adds to the atmosphere.

RC: That was, I should think, their biggest show to date at that time. On their own—basically, where they were the headliners. Other festivals are slightly different because a lot of them don't really have a particular headliner.

DS: Around that period, particularly in America, was it difficult dealing with the attitude in some states with Zep being long-haired, sort of hippies? Was that a period where it was quite difficult being on the road? Was that something that was evident in that early '70s era?

RC: Yeah, if you go back to when I left the Yardbirds in

'68 and I think I flew from Montgomery to [Vancouver] and my hair wasn't particularly long. Any of these blocs that have a lot of armed forces in them—I think they were as bad as anyone else. They really, you know—I don't think they liked the fact that—they didn't realize that we were English and we weren't supposed to be in Vietnam. And I think that, you know, just because [Zeppelin] had the long hair and all that, they weren't that pleasant towards us.

> ## And plus, when you got down to the South, they didn't like the long hair, either, so we had to bring in . . . Pinkertons, armed guards, to look after us.

DS: Lots of fun on the road. Obviously, lots reproduced in your book and stuff. Yeah, people talk about the mud shark [see page 170]. How do you look back on that? Is it something that—you know, was it blown out of proportion?

RC: Mmm, yes and no. . . . It happened. We went fishing, and that was the end of it, you know.

DS: Was it more Vanilla Fudge than Led Zeppelin?

RC: Mmm, no, it was about fifty-fifty, really.

DS: Fifty-fifty. Okay, we'll leave it at that [laughs]. Do you remember going to Ireland in 1971? What was Ireland like? And that was during the Troubles.

RC: Oh, God. It was—we played Ulster Hall [in Belfast], didn't we?

DS: Yeah.

RC: And we played the Boxing Stadium [in Dublin]. So we did Ulster Hall first and we left straight after. Because of the Troubles, we left straight after. And I remember Bonzo brought his . . . own chauffeur. So we left Ulster Hall and stayed at the Intercontinental in Dublin, I think it was. And the promoter gave us each a bottle of Bushmills whiskey for the drive [laughs], to get us pissed so we wouldn't see what was going on. And Bonzo and his driver, Matthew, got lost. I mean, it was—he'd seen more than we did because we had the Irish drivers who knew which way to go. So we didn't see much of the sort of damage that had been done and the things that were going on. But the shows themselves were absolutely incredible. I mean, there always has been this—Belfast has always been a tremendous place

to play anytime I've been there with whatever band I've been there [with], and so is Dublin. It's a shame, really, because it's a country that's kind of divided in that sense. But on the other hand, the people's attitude who go to those concerts—I mean, they're there to enjoy the music and that's all there is to it.

DS: . . . Well, the biggest riot was in Milan [July 5, 1971, when crowds, riled up by a group of agitators, clashed with police].

RC: Vigorelli [Stadium].

DS: Not a pleasant experience in Milan, then.

RC: No, no, no. It was [pause]—it was very dangerous. It was [pause]—We, I certainly, I don't think any of us could work out what was going on because all we could see was these—this smoke [Note: It was actually tear gas] going off in different places and we couldn't work out—we thought it was the crowd and weren't really sure—and then what we realized was the police were pushing the crowd toward the stage, and then the crowd, I suppose because people got frustrated, they started throwing bottles and stuff at the band, and then we got the band off the stage and the road crew and just left all

Interior pages from the program booklet of Led Zeppelin's Japan tour, October 2–10, 1972, with a photograph of Jimmy Page and his bow outlined in red and green lines.

the instruments there. And we had a driver called Gus. And I don't know; we just ended up locking ourselves in some room or other. . . . Oh, yeah. I mean, it was very frightening.

DS: I take it Peter was there and he was frightened.

RC: I don't know whether he—I don't think he was there. I don't think he was there. I think I was doing that one.

DS: Good memories of Japan? Always had a good time in Japan.

RC: Well, it was always—Japan was always fun.

DS: Because the set lists were often different in Japan and they seemed to be more relaxed. And you did a lot of sightseeing, and . . .

RC: Well, yeah, I mean, it was easy for everyone, really. I mean, it was easy for me and it was easy for the crew because you had a Japanese crew that really did all the work. They set everything up and did all the communications and you just kind of follow them, basically.

DS: So that was always a good one to do.

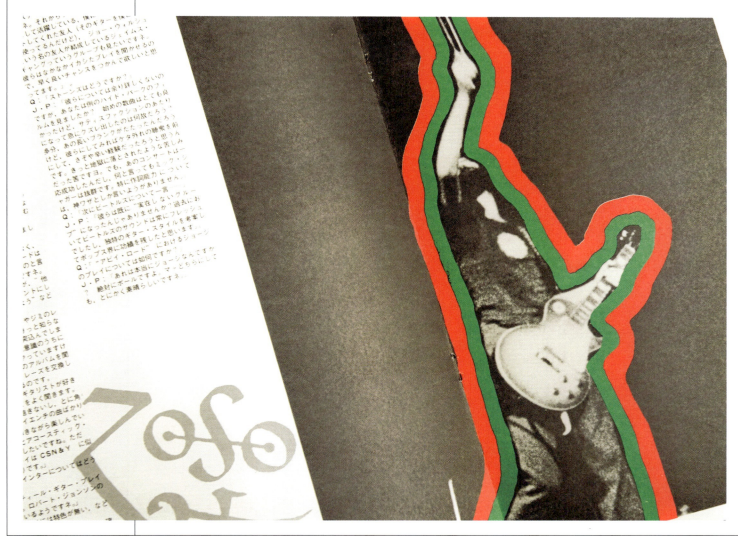

RC: Yeah.

DS: And you went a couple of times. And then you'd move into Bombay.

RC: Bombay and Thailand. We used to go to Thailand first. And then Bombay. And then home again. And that was originally for kind of shopping with Jimmy and Robert, and then they wanted to develop it into doing music. You know, and maybe they got ideas and stuff from there as well. I'm sure they did. . . .

DS: Take us in the Zeppelin world, as it were. How important was Ahmet [Ertegun] to the band's success, do you think?

RC: Well, Ahmet and Jerry [Wexler] were the ones who signed the band in the first place. I mean, Ahmet was a tremendous guy, knowing a good thing when he's seen it, I mean as far as music was concerned. Ahmet was always a wonderful morale booster. Whenever Ahmet came to see us, everyone was very happy to see Ahmet. He was just a tremendous guy, a fabulous guy. And, of course, if Ahmet's behind you, then the whole company's behind you; it's as simple as that. That's the way it was with Atlantic Records.

DS: Someone like [Led Zeppelin PR man and record executive] Danny Goldberg. How important at the time was he? I mean, was he a good influence?

RC: I thought he was. I mean, Danny worked for Lee Solters, and I first met Danny in Paris when Danny and Lee Solters came over. I mean, he got them what they wanted at that particular time, which was major newspaper coverage. And that's what he delivered to them.

DS: Someone like [publicist] B. P. Fallon?

RC: That was a different time. He was for English stuff. They were looking for a publicist. . . . I suggested they get someone like the guy who did T. Rex and people like that because they had a hell of a lot of press coverage and so why not use someone like that, who can do that? So that's what they got when they got ahold of B. P.

DS: Do you think a lot of the books missed the humor that was part of Zeppelin as a general feeling?

RC: Well, they would miss a lot because they were never there. Most of the writers have never met the band [laughs]. It's as simple as that, you know. First of all, you have to realize there were only six to eight people who were allowed in the room. They weren't out there running around with everyone. They were basically very close together all the time. They really didn't go very far from—stray far from—you know, if one band member went out, in a lot of cases, they all went out. You know, together.

DS: So it was quite, again, a camaraderie thing. There wasn't a lot of outsiders let in.

RC: No.

DS: Have you got an example of really where the humor saved the day? Were there times where, you know, it was getting heavy?

RC: Oh, I can't remember. There are so many different times, so many different things, to remember that far back. You know, the funniest one was really in a sense between Bonzo and Robert because they were so close they would start arguing about who paid for the petrol, because Bonzo usually ended up driving his car and then Robert had to pay for the petrol and he didn't give him the money and then it would get into fury and then of course the rest of the band would start laughing and taking the piss and then that would defuse everything. That's about the only one I can remember.

DS: This is all good. On the 1973 tour, you went to Atlanta [May 4] and you got Tampa the next night. I think there's a quote in your book with Peter Grant saying it doesn't get any better than this. Was that a peak?

RC: Well, it was another step up. I mean, it was—that's when we changed from commercial airlines to private jets as well. So it was another step up, where everything had been changed. You know, we went into the stadiums.

> **It was the first time we'd done stadiums. That had to all be sort of reinvented again, how we were going to do it, to get in and out, and what crew we're gonna need and everything like that. So it was completely all new to us again.**

DS: Someone like [publicist] B. P. Fallon?

DS: So that obviously posed a challenge for you. How did you take that onboard, getting them out to 56,000 people as opposed to 15,000?

RC: Well, that's not got that much to do with it in that sense because, you know, you're going in the back way anyway, so you're not gonna—it doesn't matter if you've got 20,000 or 50,000 because they're not gonna see 'em till you're on the stage actually. And then you have to work out how to get out, and the whole idea is to get out while they're not thinking you're gonna get out, and that's the way we used to do it.

DS: Was there an extra pressure with things like death threats and things like that? It was beginning to get a bigger market now. Did you feel that—

RC: There were death threats on a lot of the tours.

DS: And that's something you were used to—

RC: Well, no, no, they'd all have to be investigated. It wasn't that we were taking them onboard. I mean, you know, they had to be—police, FBI, whatever, you know, they were brought in to investigate these things.

DS: So it was beginning to get quite crazy at that point.

RC: Well, it was an extra worry.

DS: And *The Song Remains the Same* movie. Whose idea was it to do the gangster scene with you and Peter? Can you remember much about that?

RC: It was Peter's idea because, you know, it basically featured the four band members and Peter in that part of it. Was it good fun? Not for me, no.

DS: Was it Hammerwood Park [a country manor near Sussex, England, that Led Zeppelin owned from 1973 until 1982]?

RC: It was shot there. Hammerwood Park was actually a house that the band had bought, and it was gonna be studios, offices, and everything else, and I don't know, it all got abandoned somewhere down the road. But so we used it for filming while they owned it. But it's never that easy because you're torn between two things. You're trying to sort out the concert, then you've got the film crew wanting their stuff, you know, and it's not that easy. I mean, you have to make the odd concession, but you can't make too many concessions because you gotta think of the people who've paid to go and see the band.

DS: What are your memories of meeting Elvis Presley? I think it was in '74. That must have been quite a thrill. . . . What was he like as a character? Was he removed from this world?

RC: Well, no, I suppose it's like anything, but when I met him with Zeppelin and when I met him [also in 1974] with Eric [Clapton], he was contained with his own people. I think it's not fair to say he was aloof; I mean, he was Elvis, wasn't he? There was some communication but not a great deal. In comparison, when I went to his house [in 1975], and then that was different. He was on his own territory there. He was relaxed and he was just like anybody else, really, except that he happened to be Elvis Presley [laughs]. You know, and you can't not remember that part of it. I suppose it'd be like going to see the queen when she's in a nightdress or something, you know; he happened to be in his pajamas and dressing gown.

DS: Fantastic. They must be amazing memories. There was the thing with the watch in there . . .

RC: Yeah. He gave me his watch. I was doing these karate things with him and my watch came off and he said, "You've got big wrists," and I was drunk anyway and said, "You can keep the watch." And then he came back and gave me a Bouchard, which was a nice watch.

DS: In your book, you seem to indicate that by 1974, you had questioned your role with Zeppelin. Did you feel you deserved more recognition? Were you a bit pissed off?

RC: I suppose I was going through one of those things. I think I thought maybe they would have made me director of the record company or something like that, you know, so I could go off to maybe something else later. And then I went off—I decided to leave them and went with Eric and then they came back and made me a good offer sometime in '74.

DS: So you actually cut your ties with Zeppelin.

RC: Yeah.

DS: I know you went on tour with Clapton. Did you think that was it with Zeppelin?

RC: I did, but then when I was with Eric down in New Orleans, Ahmet said to me, "Well, are you gonna do the Zeppelin tour in '75?" I said, "Ah, no, I don't think so." And he said, "I think you should do that. You ought to go back and do that." [Laughs]

DS: So it was difficult getting away.

RC: Well, you know, I mean, I'd grown up with them all more or less because, you know, it's . . . it's just one of those things. I think you're tied in with people.

DS: Was it different working with Clapton?

RC: Well, it was a completely different organization. I mean, [manager and impresario] Robert Stigwood was completely different than Peter Grant. I mean, Peter I'd known since I was twenty-one years old. You know, Peter comes from a different school than Robert Stigwood. Peter's more from the streets of Croydon or whatever, and Don Arden [the hard rock manager known as "the Al Capone of Pop" for his aggressive and possibly illegal business tactics] was basically his mentor, so that's the sort of image you're dealing with and I was pretty much the same myself, so I suppose I fit in a lot better than I did with the people in Robert's organization.

DS: Okay, so '75, Zeppelin are back, probably bigger than ever, with a U.S. tour, and five nights at Earls Court: would you view that as the last of the glory days? Because after that, there were troubles and obviously there were all the tragedies that befell them. Did it feel, going back in '75, it was still an invincible sort of operation?

RC: Oh, yeah. We did two warm-ups. Brussels was one, and what was the other, Rotterdam? We did those two and then we went straight in—because we used to work in the winter a lot, when no one else was working, because we didn't have any worry, you know, they used to sell out anyway so we didn't bother, didn't bother about the weather. So when we would start off we would go in the cold weather and we would work our way down to the warm weather. No, I mean, it was just business as normal, really. I mean, they were—'73 [and] '74, it was still 707 jets, suites in hotels, sellouts, you know, this—nothing changed.

DS: Then Robert has his car smash [August 1975]. That must have quite a terrible shock [for you] because you were heavily involved in that. Do you recall?

RC: Yeah, Charlotte [Jimmy Page's girlfriend] called me. I had to get a doctor, we had to get blood—two doctors: one sort of a GP-type doctor . . . and a bone specialist, flown into Greece, and—you know, they weren't in that good of shape. I don't think [Plant's wife] Maureen was that conscious, but Robert was and the children were. And we had to get them out of there, and we only had a small window to get them out because we couldn't— Rhodes had no landing lights at the airport, so you couldn't take off until it was daylight, and then we had to go off at the crack of daylight and we had to get them out of there because they weren't supposed to leave there. You know, they were in the hospital and they didn't want them to leave, so we basically had to kidnap them and get them on the plane and get them back to London.

DS: And then you went to [the British Channel Island of] Jersey. Was the morale of the band, obviously, affected by that? How do you think they coped with that when they went to Jersey and Malibu?

RC: All of them were in Jersey, weren't they? You know, it was, they left what other places they were in and all came over to Jersey, and then Malibu. I didn't go to Malibu. I was looking after the office because obviously I wasn't in tax exile, so I wasn't in Malibu and I don't really know anything about Malibu.

DS: But then you went to Munich?

RC: Munich, we went into [Musicland Studios]—that was to do the record [*Presence*].

DS: Were you involved?

RC: Heavily involved as far as sorting out the hotels and things like that, setting up the thing with the recording studio and that.

DS: And we get to '77, when you said in your book things started to go wrong. I mean, still fantastic audiences, but a lot of incident. Was there a general feeling it was beginning to get out of control?

RC: Well, it wasn't getting out of control. It just seemed to

have got compartmentalized—to me, anyway. People weren't hanging around with each other as much as they used to. They were kind of keeping themselves to themselves a bit more, from whereas before they seemed to do things together a lot more.

DS: Do you think that was the effect of the drugs and just everything—

RC: It more than likely would have had a lot to do with it. I mean, um, you know, it's hard to tell. I'm sure everyone's got their own idea of it. I mean, I don't think Bonzo wanted to be there that much. You know, he didn't like—I think it just got to him a bit more that he didn't want to be away from home so much. I mean, everybody had their own things that they were doing. It was a strange thing because everyone had their own assistants as well, which was pretty crazy because I handled the finances and yet they wouldn't [make] the assistants usually come to me for the money; they would go and get it themselves. And then of course there was so much more work to be done, so I got an assistant to deal with their assistants. And it was just like one thing led to another. It became pretty crazy.

DS: Whose idea was it to bring in [British actor and bodyguard] John Bindon then?

RC: Peter's. I mean, everyone seems to blame me. The truth of the matter is—the band and myself flew to Dallas. We—it's quite memorable, really, because we flew into—you know, people are always giving you funny looks on airplanes, especially when they're in the first class and you're there with long hair and drinking and buggering around. The British Airways pilot managed to park the British Airways 747 next door to our own plane, which had our name on it, and he said over the speaker, "I hope this is all right for you boys from Led Zeppelin. I parked as close to your plane as I could get." And of course everyone looked out the window, and I looked as their fucking faces dropped because there's a plane that's got "Led Zeppelin" on the side of it—another 707. And then we flew into Dallas on that. Peter missed the flight, so he came in the next day, and when he arrived, John [Bindon] was with him. So he must have told the lawyer because the lawyer was involved with the travel agency. By then, I just gave the list of cities, what I wanted and which suite in what city and whatever, so I had absolutely no idea at all because no one had called me and said we need an extra room or anything like that. So it must have all been done between Peter and the lawyer.

DS: Did you know John Bindon?

RC: Oh, John was a mate of mine! I knew him, yeah! I mean, I had absolutely no idea he was coming with Peter. Because he wasn't really security. Peter brought him with him to assist my assistant or look after him. We had security. You know, we had the police department in every

city . . . or great backups, depending on what part of the country we were in. . . .

DS: It was a big operation.

RC: It was pretty unnecessary, and I think maybe, you know, whereas you knew exactly where you are, you really had six people, two bodyguards, a front man, and a lawyer, and that was the end of it, you know. Now it was all stretching out more, and plus, when you've got that many people running around, you don't know what the other one's doing all the time. You know, things get lost with the communications between people.

DS: How do you look back at the Oakland situation [in which a backstage scuffle led to an all-out brawl between Led Zeppelin's and promoter Bill Graham's security teams]?

RC: . . . The whole thing was a very regrettable thing in a strange way because normally, we never stayed after a show. The format was, as soon as the show was finished, get the fuck out of there, and that's it; it doesn't matter where you were. It was one of those shows, I think it was because it was five or six or whatever amount of days off, I can't remember exactly what it was, in between the shows, John Paul Jones's wife was—I believe he was meeting her or she was over there. Jimmy was doing something. We were going to New Orleans after that. There were people there and it seemed like it was a good idea at the time that we should just chill out and not run after the show but just stay there. And Peter had his children with him, you know, and we decided to stay. And unfortunately, Peter's son wanted something off of the door [reportedly a dressing room sign], and the guy gave him the slap, and then it got to Peter's ears and, you know, whether if we'd just left straight afterwards, who knows? Or something could have flared the next day because I believe it was the first concert, wasn't it?

DS: Yeah, you played the next day.

RC: Yeah. So it's hard to really judge it because something could have gone off the next day, except—I forget which day they came around after us. I mean, it may have been the third day they came around after us, after both shows were finished.

DS: Yeah, I think that's when the trouble kicked off and obviously the police were involved, and then soon after, obviously, Robert's tragedy, you know, that must have been very difficult to deal with.

RC: Yeah, because we had all this other business, and then he flew into New Orleans and he'd spoken to his wife on the phone and everything was fine—or either it was fine or he knew that his boy wasn't well, and I don't know how much period of time there was when he found out the boy died. Karac had died. And so, we couldn't use our own plane because the pilots hadn't had enough time

between breaks, so we had to go on commercial airlines to get back.

DS: Did it feel that could be the end, or was there a general feeling after it, or—

RC: I don't [sighs]—I would say it was a very numbing feeling I had, from what I remember I felt. But I don't know whether one would have ever conceived it was the end. It had been very up and down since the accident in '75 after that. Unfortunately, Robert had to put up with a hell of a lot. And so, you know, it was very up and down, but I don't think anyone perhaps wanted to think about—I certainly didn't want to think about, you know, is it the end of it? [Pauses] It wasn't the end of it, though.

DS: So they got back together and then they went to Clearwell [Castle studios in England, in May 1978, to rehearse and write] and then went to Stockholm [Polar Studios, November 1978, to record *In Through the Out Door*]. Did it feel like a rebirth? Did it feel like everyone was back and it was all gonna be good and you've got Knebworth [August 1979]?

RC: Um [pauses]—yeah, I suppose so. You know, it was just the one-off show—well, two shows at Knebworth. I suppose it was, but it was like the beginning of a tour when no one's seen each other much for a while except for, obviously, rehearsals, and then all of a sudden you're all back together again and laughing and joking and carrying on with business.

DS: Do you have good memories of Knebworth?

RC: Well, I must admit my memories of Knebworth aren't that great, unfortunately. [Laughs] I was a little bit not myself, you might say.

DS: So it was getting difficult for you personally?

RC: Well, I was making it difficult for myself. I mean, the job wasn't really any more difficult.

DS: But with all the other stuff going on . . .

RC: Well, the other stuff was really a distraction.

DS: So we get to the 1980 tour and you were not asked to do the tour. That must have been quite a shock.

RC: Well, I wasn't [laughs], well, it wasn't quite like that. I wasn't not asked to do the tour. I was dispatched—Peter paid for me to go and clean up, so I went to Italy to clean up, and I got nicked [arrested] over there, and the tour started while I was still doing other things.

DS: So you're in Rome, where, bizarrely, you got arrested for terrorism. How did that happen?

RC: Well! How'd it happen? I don't really know, except

someone must have thought I looked like a terrorist. I was very dark when I got suntanned, and I was with this punk-rocker girlfriend of mine. Next thing I know, they came around and they nicked me and kept me for six months there.

DS: That's crazy. So, and that was obviously—when you were in jail, you heard about Bonzo.

RC: Yes.

DS: That must have been such a shock. It must have been absolutely devastating.

RC: Well, you know, it's—I was very close with old Bonzo, the old Beast, you know, he was a sweetheart. I mean, again, even to this day, it seems incredible because he was so young. I mean, and so was "Moony" [Keith Moon], he was young. They died within two years of each other, wasn't it?

DS: Yeah. When you were released, did you keep in contact with Peter?

RC: I mean, Peter and I kept in contact—well, Jimmy I'd seen—in 1981, was it?—when the ARMS concert [Note: These were a series of charitable concerts to benefit Action into Research for Multiple Sclerosis, which were in 1983, not 1981] was out there. I didn't have much contact with anyone else. It all sort of dwindled away.

DS: Was it difficult adjusting to life after Led Zeppelin?

RC: Yeah, I would say it was very difficult, especially as I was still drinking and using drugs. I don't think you have a sense of the reality of the thing. It takes a long while to wind down after something like that, you know, to come back to earth again. Also, one of the toughest things is when you're not with a band like that anymore and you had a lot of power and people know that, and they also know you can do things for them, you become pretty "invaluable." [Laughs] You haven't got anything anyone wants anymore.

DS: Is that how you felt?

RC: It's not how I felt; that's what it was fucking like. There were no two ways about it.

DS: That's the rock 'n' roll business, I guess.

RC: Yeah, of course it is, you know.

DS: You provided a lot of background stories, obviously, for Stephen Davis's book [*Hammer of the Gods*]. How do you feel about that, looking back?

RC: Um [pauses]—I would have done better if I had kept them and put them in my book, really. At the time, it's a whole different thing. I was absolutely skinned, I needed

some money, he came up with—offered me some money, and then, you know—I thought, "Well, fine, this is better than nothing."

DS: Yeah, yeah. Did it prompt you to write your own book?

RC: No. No, I never really gave it another thought until, I think it was really more or less 1998 and a mate of mine came to—a friend of mine called Snake, a guy called Roger Klein, who used to be with Sony Records and who works with something to do with Green Day or something, that management company—came and said to me, "I met an old friend of yours called Bernie Rhodes." Well, Bernie Rhodes and I used to share a flat together. We'd known each other since we were kids. . . . He was the manager of the Clash. So Bernie and Roger and I went out to lunch one day, and they came back to where I was living and Bernie said, "What do you want to do?" And I said, "Well, really, I just want to fucking lie about a swimming pool and go sunbathing." "Well, why don't you write a book, then?" And that was what really put the thought in my mind about that, and that's when I sort of started putting the bits together.

DS: And you worked with a guy, Richard . . .

RC: Richard Trubo, yeah.

DS: The reaction to the book from Jimmy, Robert, and John was not entirely favorable. How did you feel about that at the time?

RC: Well, that was just one of those things. I didn't expect it to be, you know. It's very rare they've liked anything written about them. Most people don't.

DS: That's true. And you weren't surprised?

RC: No. No. I didn't write it as a malicious book. That's the thing, and I know that. There's fucking loads of bits missed out in there, believe me. . . . I tried to incorporate as much of it about how great they were as a band, musically, but it wasn't something that, you know, that's what it was like living through those years. And none of us can—the one thing that everybody seems to forget [is] no one sees the same picture. I mean, when I was with Robert at—you asked me a question earlier on where you said, you know, "What was your first impression when you met Robert?" Now, when I went to see Robert in Wembley with Alison Krauss and I was with a friend of mine and I had a suit on and God knows what else, and he said, "I remember the first time I met you, and you said to me, 'You can't walk around dressed like that.' You're all dressed up, you've been shopping . . . " I don't remember saying that, but everybody's got different little bits that they remember about different stuff.

DS: Yeah, it was a lot of years ago. Obviously some people's imaginations have a different take on it. Well, you then became sober and went back out on the road with

t was that same committment that sparked the begin...
years ago, and that same committment that endures today. N...
means one thing: music. Great music.

John Paul Jones

*A ticket, above, to the
Atlantic Records historic
fortieth-anniversary
concert in New York,
held in Madison Square
Garden on May 14,
1988, which featured
more than thirty artists
and culminated in a Led
Zeppelin reunion with
Jason Bonham on drums.
Above right, an interior
page of the concert
program booklet with
a photograph of Robert
Plant, Atlantic Records
founder and president
Ahmet Ertegun, and
Jon Anderson, the lead
singer of Yes.*

the likes of the Quireboys. How did that compare to the
way it was in Zep? Was it very different?

RC: The Quireboys were the most fun I've had with any
band other than Zeppelin.

DS: Well, I know [London Quireboys guitarist] Guy
[Griffin]. Guy comes to Bedford. I know Guy. He's a
great guy. They're still around.

RC: Yeah, I sometimes speak to Guy. They were, like,
very much the old English rock 'n' roll band, you know, I
mean, don't give a fuck and just get on with the job and
have fun and drink and have a laugh, you know, and that
was it. I wouldn't have said they were in it too much for
the money, which is a lot different from most bands. I
mean, nowadays it's really—this is gonna be a career. I
mean, I never thought of the music business as a career.
It was better than fucking scaffolding, but you know
what I mean, it was—it's changed drastically. You know,
nowadays, if you look at the early bands, even
Zeppelin—Bonzo was laying bricks or something, wasn't
he, up until they guaranteed him a certain amount, forty
quid a week or something, to play with Zeppelin in the
beginning or whatever it was. Most bands had jobs!
Nowadays, you won't find very many musicians who
have another job.

DS: Did you have much contact with Jimmy, Robert, and
JPJ in the '90s?

RC: No. I mean, I'd seen Jimmy in 1990 at Donington
[Monsters of Rock concert in Derbyshire] when he was
up there playing with Aerosmith. Aerosmith and
Quireboys were on the same bill.

DS: Were you surprised when Led Zeppelin decided to get
back [together] for the [Ahmet Ertegun tribute in 2007]?
When you first heard, what was the initial reaction?

RC: Well, nothing ever surprises me in this business,
really. I mean, anytime they got back together, they've
only done it for charity, haven't they? The one in '88 was
for Ahmet. It was for Atlantic Records, an Ahmet thing. I
know that they had a very special relationship with
Ahmet, and so, you know, anything's possible for that.

DS: How did you get to go, then?

RC: Jimmy called me and said he's got—I mean, I'd seen
Jimmy around, and he called me up and said to me that
he's got me a couple of tickets. He said, "I told the others
I'll take care of your stuff." And that's what he did. He
got me some tickets.

DS: So . . . it must have been quite an emotional experience. What was it like watching Led Zeppelin without the
pressure of being the tour manager?

RC: Well, it was interesting because I'd never seen them
before, not for that amount of time. Obviously, you get

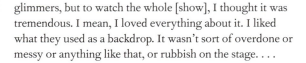

glimmers, but to watch the whole [show], I thought it was tremendous. I mean, I loved everything about it. I liked what they used as a backdrop. It wasn't sort of overdone or messy or anything like that, or rubbish on the stage. . . .

DS: Did you think there was a chance it would lead to more gigs? Did you think they'd find it hard to walk away from that?

RC: I don't think—I don't really ever have a thought on that, whereas you can't read their minds. It's impossible to know what they might do and what they might not do.

DS: You must be proud of the fact that the Led Zeppelin story now has a pretty happy ending. Does it—

RC: Well, it—no, I think . . . It was lovely to see them, and what I think was the nicest thing is there wasn't one bad review. It took them, like, thirty or forty years for the press to figure out what they were.

DS: That was an amazing thing. Looking back over the forty years, what are your personal highlights of working with Zeppelin? What would you say are the things that come into your mind when you say, "That's the bank of the work I did with the band"?

RC: Oh, blimey, I don't know. [Sighs] I suppose for me it was, when I first went in the business, there were two big bands. Well, there were three really, with the Who, in a sense. But there were two big bands, there were the Beatles and there were the Stones, and I thought one day I was gonna be the Beatles' road manager or the Stones' road manager, and I ended up being Led Zeppelin's road manager, and I doubt there's much dispute that they weren't the third biggest band in the world all that long. And so I achieved that, and it was great.

DS: What was it, you think, that made them so special, and why are Led Zeppelin still held in such high esteem? What do you think, in your perspective, makes that now? Why is it? What is the ingredient?

RC: Hmm. [Pauses] Well, you've got the music, first of all. That's the most important thing. I don't think that's aged. I mean, I don't listen to it a great deal. I don't listen to anything a great deal. But when I do listen to it, it hasn't aged since when it was first played to me. . . . When you're involved in it, it's hard to look from the outside because you don't see—I didn't see Led Zeppelin until I went to the O₂ Arena [a large indoor arena at the center of a multipurpose entertainment complex in South London called the O₂] because I was always on the inside. So it's very hard to look at stuff from the outside. . . .

DS: You must be incredibly proud that you worked with such an incredible—

RC: Oh, it was wonderful! Yeah! I mean, you can't—you'd be a bloody fool to say it wasn't the chance of a lifetime. You know, I mean, admittedly, I'd been looking—well, I don't bother anymore, but obviously, I was hoping to get with another big band again, but sometimes you have to say you only get one great shot in your life and that was it.

DS: Can you describe working with Jimmy?

RC: Jimmy's a perfectionist. I mean, both in the studio and out [of] the studio. He's equal in either one.

DS: Working with Robert?

RC: Percy [Plant's nickname], um . . . I mean, Percy's perhaps one of the greatest showmen of all time, really.

You know, I've seen and done things and traveled in ways that I could never have imagined when I left school at fifteen. I was sitting there welding fucking milk cans. I didn't expect to be flying around in a 707 jet.

DS: Would you change anything?

RC: No.

DS: Nothing at all.

RC: No. I mean you can't pick and choose. It would be nice to say I wish I wasn't an alcoholic and a drug addict and if I hadn't this and that, but maybe, you know, the opposite thing is that if I hadn't been drinking and doing things and getting into mischief, I might not have been the right man for the job [laughs]. You know, that's the truth of the matter.

DS: John Paul?

RC: Very steady, and really he was like the rock of Zeppelin in a sense. Very precise, fantastic musician.

DS: Bonzo?

RC: The old Bonze? Well, apart from being the greatest drummer I'd ever worked for, he was just a fantastic person. A lovable man.

Danny Goldberg

DANNY GOLDBERG HAS CHRONICLED HIS LONG AND SUC-
CESSFUL CAREER IN THE ENTERTAINMENT INDUSTRY IN HIS
OWN AUTOBIOGRAPHY, *BUMPING INTO GENIUSES: MY LIFE
INSIDE THE ROCK AND ROLL BUSINESS*, PUBLISHED IN 2008.
THE MANAGEMENT FIRM HE OPERATED FROM 1983 TO 1992
HAD A CLIENT ROSTER BOASTING TOP TALENT IN ALL
GENRES, INCLUDING NIRVANA, THE ALLMAN BROTHERS,
THE BEASTIE BOYS, BONNIE RAITT, AND MORE.

DURING THE DECADE PRIOR TO THAT, HE WORKED AS A
VICE PRESIDENT IN LED ZEPPELIN'S RECORD COMPANY,
SWAN SONG, HAVING ALREADY SPEARHEADED THE BAND'S
PUBLIC RELATIONS EFFORTS. IN THIS INTERVIEW FROM
2008, HE DISCUSSES SOME OF HIS STORIES FROM THE
ZEPPELIN YEARS.

*Danny Goldberg at a
Rock and Roll Fantasy
Camp event in New
York, January 17, 2011.*

DANNY GOLDBERG: Soon after I went to work for a big PR
firm in New York that wanted a rock 'n' roll guy in their
employ, Led Zeppelin became a client.

I got a job working for a company called Solters &
Roskin, and my boss was a legendary PR man who's still
alive. His name is Lee Solters. [Note: Since this interview
was conducted, Lee Solters died at the age of 89.] He was
publicist for Barbra Streisand for decades, for Frank
Sinatra, Ringling Brothers Circus, half of the Broadway
shows. And there came a time that he decided he needed
someone who understood rock and roll because it was
this growing part of the entertainment business, and it
was through a mutual friend, he hired me at a time I was
looking for a job. So I was just assigned things that were
in the office. I was low man on the totem pole.

But when Led Zeppelin's attorney, whose name was
Steve Weiss, approached Solters & Roskin [in spring
1973], Lee Solters said, "You'd better come with me to
meet him. I'm from the Guy Lombardo generation, and
you're the only one here that would understand their
music and would know what to do with them." And we
went there together, we met them together, and that was
the last time Lee ever spoke to them. After that, it was my
client and I dealt with them, and that was why they hired
me, so that they could get and service somebody like Led
Zeppelin.

DENNY SOMACH: By the time you first met with Led Zeppelin,
they were already established as one of the biggest bands
in the world. Why did they want a PR firm at all?

DG: The thing to remember about Led Zeppelin, which is
a little hard for young people to understand today, is for
the first several albums that they put out, for the first several years of their career, they were hated by the rock 'n'
roll press. They had emerged through rock 'n' roll radio,
so the press didn't feel they were part of the birthing of
the band. And the first generation of rock writers—by
1969, when Led Zeppelin's first album came out—was in
their early twenties: twenty-three, twenty-four, twenty-
five; and the audience was fourteen, fifteen, sixteen; and
those critics had the same kind of condescension and
snobbery that older people often have about, "What are
these young people listening to?" And they didn't understand that Zeppelin was really a great band. They were
considered sort of a second-rate version of Cream by the
press, not by their fans.

So when I met them, they had just finished recording
the album *Houses of the Holy*, which is their fifth album.
They'd had this incredible commercial success on the
previous album, which was the untitled album and contained the song "Stairway to Heaven," and they were
selling out arenas all over the world. But they continued
to be condescended to, or "dissed," as we would say
today, by the rock writers, not just in the United States
but all over the world.

Robert Plant and Jimmy Page had gotten fed up with
it. It was like the one mountain they had left to climb,
which was to get that kind of recognition. And they had a
particular competitive sense of the relative stature of Led

Zeppelin compared to the Rolling Stones. And the Rolling Stones, the year before, had done a worldwide tour and gotten massive press. Truman Capote had gone on the road with them, and they were on the cover of *Newsweek*. But statistically, Zeppelin actually had more fans, based on their record sales and even ticket sales at that time. So they wanted a PR firm, and they decided to get one in the United States because they saw the United States as the center of their PR issue, and figuring that good press in the United States would feed back to England. But when I asked around among my friends who'd worked with them earlier in their career and worked with different writers, there were such bad stories about Led Zeppelin . . . people respected their commercial success at first, but once they started getting bad reviews they started getting very hostile to the press, so they wouldn't always give people press tickets. If they met a writer they would sometimes make fun of them or be rude; they had a reputation for being over the top in terms of the way they dealt with women writers. A lot of the rock writers at that time were women. And so I didn't know how I was gonna solve this problem. I was unbelievably excited and also baffled. Plus, they have a character who's their manager who's legendary in his own right.

DS: How would you describe Led Zeppelin's manager?

DG: Their manager was a man named Peter Grant, who was a former professional wrestler in England. . . . He had been this tough guy, driver, security guy, he was three hundred pounds of mostly muscle, thick Cockney accent. They were staying at the George Cinq hotel, one of the most elegant hotels in Paris, but when Peter came to the door of his suite, he was wearing big jeans and turquoise jewelry and not at all trying to dress up for the French. We met with him prior to the meeting the next day with the band. . . . He explained what was on their mind: the Rolling Stones, he wanted to get the recognition that they deserved in his mind. And I said to him, "The band has a reputation of being barbarians to the journalists in the U.S." He chuckled and he said, "Yes, but we're only mild barbarians." And then the next day, when we met with the band, he said, "Tell the boys about the barbarians thing!" He thought it was the funniest thing he'd ever heard.

DS: What else do you recall from that time?

DG: The first meeting was just with Peter, then we saw the show at Palais des Sports. That was the first time I ever saw Led Zeppelin play. I was one of those snobbish guys in my twenties who didn't really get Led Zeppelin! I got that it would be good for my career to work with them, but I had not been a fan until I saw them. I was a little old to be a fan, but I sure became a fan soon after I saw a few of their shows. And then the day after seeing the show, we met with the four guys, "the boys," as Peter called them, and Peter.

DS: What were the boys like?

DG: Robert came over to me afterwards, and he was then twenty-five, but he'd been in the band since he was, like, eighteen. And he says, "Oh, when we were young, we did things, but we're all past that now." And he was so friendly and warm, as he always is. Robert Plant was one of the most pleasant artists I've ever worked with. I can't say that about all the members of the band, especially then, but he was just fantastic. He really was made to be a star. . . . He wanted to talk to the press. He knew how to look you in the eye and [make you] feel special. He knew how to tell a good story and how to be risqué without going over the line. He wanted it! I think it was maybe his family had sort of thought, "Why aren't you getting the recognition?" And he became the main guy that did a lot of the interviews. Jimmy Page would sometimes do them. Jones never wanted to do an interview. And Bonham sometimes wanted to, but we didn't always want him to because he was a bit of a Jekyll and Hyde personality.

God made a rock star when he made Robert Plant.

DS: What were some of your earliest highlights in doing PR for Led Zeppelin?

DG: The first two shows of the 1973 [North American] Led Zeppelin tour were outdoor stadiums. Most of the shows were in arenas, but the first two were in stadiums. The first one was at Atlanta Stadium, and the second one was Tampa Stadium. Tampa had a paid capacity of 56,800, which was slightly more than what Shea Stadium [in New York] had sold when the Beatles played there some years earlier. So I invented the idea that this had broken the Beatles' record for the best show by an artist. Of course, in the intervening years, there'd been these gigantic festivals like Woodstock that had hundreds of thousands of people, but to me those were multiartist shows. And of course if Shea Stadium had held more seats, the Beatles could have sold more tickets; it wasn't that Led Zeppelin was actually more popular in 1973 than the Beatles had been in 1965, but it so happened that Tampa Stadium held about 1,000 more seats.

I knew the critics were not going to say the music was great—not then, not in 1973. And so that became kind of the big selling point, "bigger than the Beatles." And in fact when I saw the Led Zeppelin reunion show in London [in 2007], they showed a little videotape, which I guess is included on the DVD rerelease of *The Song Remains the Same*, from a Tampa TV station where the guy was kind of reading the talking points from my press release, "bigger than the Beatles." You know, so I felt this corny gimmick must have appealed to the band, since they were still using it thirty-some years later.

At the Atlanta Stadium show, Peter was really excited. He loved Led Zeppelin. He was a tough businessman. He was accused—at other times, not when I worked with him—of physical violence. He certainly was intimidating,

A ticket from the May 5, 1973, show at Tampa Stadium, which Goldberg publicized as "Bigger than the Beatles."

he knew gangsters, he was very careful with money, very fierce if he thought anybody was trying to cheat him or the band out of money. But he also was a fan. . . . He got incredibly excited to see a stadium full of people liking Led Zeppelin.

The next day, he called me and said, "I want you to get it in the press that it's the biggest thing to happen to Atlanta since *Gone with the Wind*. So I said, "Uh, well, what do you mean 'get it in the press'?" I said, "Do you want to say that?" He says, "No, no. Just get it in the press." So the mayor of Atlanta, according to the local writer there who covered the show for the *Atlanta Constitution*, had been at the Zeppelin show, so I just made up a quote attributing it to the mayor, Sam Massell. I said he said that it was the biggest thing since *Gone with the Wind*. When it ran in one of the British newsweeklies, my friend Lisa Robinson was nice enough to put that into the *Music Disc* and *Echo* that she wrote for, and it made Peter very happy.

energy spread into any space he was inhabiting, and I knew there was some problem. And I found out later that night that Peter had wanted the band to be paid in cash for the last couple of shows. He said it was to pay bills. I'm not exactly sure what they were going to do with the cash or how all the internal financial arrangements of the band were handled, and there've been different rumors over the years about this, but one thing was sure: that there was $280,000 in cash—this is 1973, so that'd probably be worth, like, three quarters of a million dollars today—[that] was removed from the safety deposit box at the Drake Hotel. The safety deposit box was not broken into, so it was some sort of an inside job. And Richard Cole, the road manager, who certainly had access to it, who was a very close friend of mine and who himself has written a wonderful book about Led Zeppelin called *Stairway to Heaven*, was never accused of it by anybody in the band. He was friends with all of them, so clearly it wasn't he. No one was ever arrested for the crime.

I swear to God, I think that was one of the things that bonded me to the band, getting that corny quote into a British weekly.

DS: The movie *The Song Remains the Same* has a scene about a robbery of the band's cash from a New York hotel. Did you have to handle the press in light of that robbery?

DG: Yes. They ended that 1973 tour in New York. The last three dates of the American tour were in New York City in Madison Square Garden, and the band was staying at the Drake Hotel. I remember being backstage at the last of the concerts, and I saw Peter Grant agitated, talking to Ahmet Ertegun about something, and it didn't look good. When Peter was in a bad mood or upset, I mean, the negative

So it's a bit of a mystery involved and, as I said, there's some inside-job nature of it that someone someday will actually explain what happened. But it was the front page of the newspapers. I remember I spent all these times trying to get Led Zeppelin to be as famous as the Stones, and there it was, on the cover of the New York *Daily News*, "Led Zep Robbed of 300G." And my boss at the time, Lee Solters, an old-school PR guy, said, "See, if we hadn't done such a good job, it would say 'Rock Band Robbed of 300G.'" This was a great PR accomplishment, "Led Zep," because the New York *Daily News* at that time had the biggest circulation of any newspaper in the United States. So Peter called me and said, "Listen, there's all these camera crews here. Will you come and help me deal with them?" So I went up to the suite and said, "Don't you want Atlantic?". . . He says, "Definitely not. I don't want the record company anywhere near here." And that was the first time I knew that he liked me—because Peter was so gruff and, you know, tense all the time. I didn't know if I was hated, or if I was just someone they never wanted to talk to again, and the first time I realized they must have thought I was really doing a good job was when he wanted me and only me to handle this. It was really—although he was upset and the band was depressed and kind of freaked out—it was one of the best times of my life because I knew I had been accepted! And it was easy to do; I just went down. I went to the hotel. I got one of the rooms, the ballroom-type places, meeting rooms, and I said, "Can we have this room for a press conference?" And I told the guy and the people in the lobby we're having a press conference. Peter came out and spoke for a half hour to the different news crews and reporters, and it was incredibly easy to arrange, but it was a very big deal in my career because I was the one he asked to do it.

DS: How did you get to become vice president of Swan Song Records?

DG: Well, a few months later, I got a call from their lawyer, and he said, "The boys want to start their own label." It wasn't called Swan Song yet. Jimmy hadn't thought up the name yet. It was just gonna be the Led Zeppelin label. [The lawyer] said, "Peter wants to meet with you and talk to you about working for it." So I was kind of excited.

They flew me over to England, and a car took me to Peter Grant's house, which was somewhere a couple of hours north of London, and it was some fifteenth-century house surrounded by a moat. And he came down and said, "Jimmy really likes you." That's what he always said; he'd always attribute everything to Jimmy. "Jimmy really likes you, and I need you to be my ambassador in America." And I says, "What does that mean? What's your ambassador?" He says, "You'll deal with the press, deal with Atlantic, just whatever we need done."

So I said, "Well, um, could I call myself vice president?" Because I thought it was just a title that I thought people would respect me more. I didn't want to be known as just a publicist. So he says, "Sure!" So, you know, I made myself a vice president. And that stuff does work, you know. I mean, it did give me a little different image than just being the PR guy, although two-thirds of what I did was PR, but I dealt with the radio promotion department of Atlantic on behalf of the Swan Song artists, and with the booking agents and the concert promoters. So it wasn't only publicity, and it certainly helped brand me as a, you know, then-young executive in the rock business on his way up. I'm eternally grateful to Peter Grant and Led Zeppelin for giving me that shot.

DS: After Led Zeppelin signed Bad Company and they took off, you were sitting there with two of the biggest bands in the world. What was that like?

DG: That was good! Bad Company was really fun. The first record we actually put out was by a wonderful Scottish singer named Maggie Bell, and she never took off completely, but I got to work with the booking agents. There was a very important booking agency called Premier Talent that controlled a disproportionate amount of the rock bands, and they booked both Maggie and Bad Company, and they opened each of them to the big headliners at the time—Black Oak Arkansas, Foghat. Edgar Winter Group, who had been a former PR client of mine, put Bad Company on their whole American tour; it was so important to the band in terms of them breaking. . . . It was totally [Peter's] thing, but it broke in the U.S. "Can't Get Enough" went to number one on the pop chart. The album went to number one. And it was an incredible feeling because it wasn't, then, just Led Zeppelin. It turned out to be the only successful record that was on Swan Song besides Led Zeppelin, but what a start! It differentiated Led Zeppelin's label from the Beatles' label, the Stones' label, which had never broken another big act.

DS: How would you describe the attitudes of Led Zeppelin's members?

> You know, the fans would just chaeer no matter what they did, but these guys were very tough on themselves and very serious about their music, and I think that's why their music and their reputation continue to live on today.

DG: There was a childlike side to them, but they were very shrewd businesspeople, and the main thing I would say about Led Zeppelin is they were very serious about their music. I mean, there were a lot of girls around, there were a lot of drugs around, there was a lot of propensity to—you know, I didn't see them throw TV sets out of windows, but I know they did it. I mean, they told me that when they were younger, they had done stuff like that. But boy, they did a sound check every night. John Bonham would get there an hour early to do a separate drum sound check, and they were fiercely critical of themselves if they made any mistakes during a show.

DS: Do you think John Bonham really is one of the greatest drummers of all time?

DG: I think he's the greatest rock drummer of all time. I mean, there's been amazing drummers in other idioms, you know. By the way, Bonham idolized Buddy Rich, and he was the only drummer I ever heard Bonham say anything good about, Buddy Rich, 'cause he thought he was the best drummer that ever lived, too. He was the biggest John Bonham fan. I think he set the standard—the way

Hendrix did for the guitar—I think John Bonham did for rock 'n' roll drums, I do. I think there's been a lot of great drummers, like I think Neal Peart's an amazing drummer for Rush, Dave Grohl's an incredible drummer, Don Henley, Ringo in his own way, but to me, if you had to pick—if you're on *Jeopardy!* and the clue is, "He was the greatest rock drummer in rock 'n' roll," it's John Bonham.

DS: Do you think the band was justified in deciding after John Bonham's death not to continue?

DG: I wasn't surprised. Robert Plant and John Bonham were very old friends. . . . Robert had been through a lot. One of his sons died of a tragic illness. The death of Bonham, I think, hit Robert particularly hard. . . . For example, Keith Moon of the Who died young, and they had another drummer, no problem. And I think Keith Moon was a terrific drummer, but I think he was not an integral part of the sound of the Who the way that John Bonham was an integral part of the sound of Led Zeppelin. They certainly could have done it and made it work as a business, but knowing them personally and knowing how close Robert was to Bonzo, I'm not surprised that he didn't want to continue.

DS: You were an eyewitness to history when Led Zeppelin reunited with Jason Bonham on drums at the O₂ Arena in London in 2007. What was that like?

A ticket from the Ahmet Ertegun Tribute Concert at the O₂ Arena on December 7, 2010, featuring an illustration of the arena's iconic domed roof and support towers.

DG: Well, it was kind of like the greatest high school reunion of all time. I just went—Peter Mensch, who manages Jimmy Page, got me tickets. I was very appreciative of it. He wanted the people who used to work with the band to be able to go to the show. There were hundreds of people that I recognized from the rock business in the '70s and '80s. . . . It was an older audience, and it was older people on the stage. And you can never,

in your fifties, be the same person you were in your twenties, but the quality of the show was very, very high. And I was particularly inspired by what Jimmy Page did. I mean, he was such an integral part of Led Zeppelin. It was first and foremost a guitar band as much as the other instruments were, and he has been the most erratic over the years in terms of his highs were very high and his lows were very low. And clearly, his high was very high that night, and he was playing as well as I think he ever played. And everybody in the room knew it, and they were very excited. It wasn't just a re-creation of what Led Zeppelin used to be. It was actually a Led Zeppelin show. I mean, it wasn't exactly the same because John Bonham wasn't there, but it was awfully good.

DS: Songwise, what were the highlights?

DG: Well, I always loved "Dazed and Confused." I'm a real headbanger in that respect. . . . I love the whole shtick with the violin bow and the interaction between Jimmy and Robert during that song. I love "[The] Song Remains the Same." The songs, to me, that I remembered from when I worked with them meant a little more to me. And I liked when Robert sings the blues. I think he is a great blues singer, and I think he can really pull it off as much as any white British person ever has. So those were some of the highlights, but my main memory of it was the guitar solos. . . .

DS: What do you think—will the band go out on tour? Where does that stand?

DG: Well, I don't have any inside information. I have an opinion. My opinion is that Robert Plant is having incredible success right now with the work he's doing with Alison Krauss. I think there's going to be more of that. I hear there's another record coming and more touring coming, and I think he's going to run that cycle as long as he can go. [Note: This interview was conducted in 2008; for much of that year, Robert Plant toured with Alison Krauss in support of their Grammy-winning 2007 release, *Raising Sand*.] He spent many, many years trying to get recognized under his own name. He's had successful solo projects but nothing like this. And I think at some point, in a couple of years, that's going to run its course and, you know, one day he'll be looking at the telephone and pick it up and call Jimmy Page, and they'll do a billion-dollar Led Zeppelin tour and we're all gonna want to go. But it's really up to him, as I understand it, and I don't think it's gonna happen right away, but I'd be very surprised if it doesn't happen in the next five years.

DS: Could they do it with a singer other than Robert Plant?

DG: If Robert Plant's not the singer, it's not Led Zeppelin. End of story. No fan would accept that. That, to me, is just absurd.

TICKET ROW 23 SEAT 31
FLOOR - STANDING
ENTRANCE D

BUSCH/CHRISTOPHER

AHMET TRIBUTE CONCERT
MON 10-DEC-07 7PM START
NET PROFITS DONATED TO
A.E.E.F
CHARITY NO. 259420
PRICE 125.00 S/C 12.50 TOTAL 137.50

7-44710 ZTP735 5-DEC-07 16:20

The O₂
www.theo2.co.uk

Larry Magid

As a young booking agent in New York in the '60s, Philadelphia native Larry Magid worked with Miles Davis, Bill Evans, Jimi Hendrix, Cream, Paul Butterfield Blues Band, and Big Brother and the Holding Company. In 1968, Magid returned to Philadelphia to manage and book what was to become a Philly concert venue icon, the Electric Factory. Subsequently, Magid launched the concert promotion firm Electric Factory Concerts. Magid, like pioneering promoters Bill Graham in San Francisco and Don Law in Boston, built the Philly market.

In addition to Electric Factory Concerts, Magid put together hundreds of shows at the venerable Philadelphia Spectrum, a former key venue in American arena rock.

In 1985 and 2005, Magid brought the star-studded Live Aid and Live 8 televised charity concerts to Philadelphia.

This interview, which took place in March 2011, begins with Magid being asked what criteria he used when deciding to book a new band like Led Zeppelin.

LARRY MAGID: There was no real criteria. In those days it was more a gut thing than anything. 'Course, if [rock music talent agent and founder of the Premier Talent booking agency] Frank Barsalona called you, as he would, he had a lot of clout, a lot of sway, and you generally value his opinion and see to his idea. Led Zeppelin was one of them that came out with a lot of hype. He made his mark primarily with British bands even before Led Zeppelin and before Premier Talent. He had a fantastic reputation and he was right an awful lot of times. That was at that point the most important agency; he was the most important agent. And so if he called for Led Zeppelin or any acts like that, we would consider playing them, negotiate for them, and generally played that act either at our club Electric Factory, which operated from '68 to '70. . . .

DENNY SOMACH: As far as Led Zeppelin goes, though, there was a bit of a reputation. Jimmy Page was a known entity.

LM: Well, there were people who were considered players by people who followed bands, especially English bands. My personal view is that a lot of the bands were teen throbs, like the Beatles. Before that or in that era—Herman's Hermits and Dave Clark [Five] and all that—they were Bandstand type of acts. . . . Jimmy Page would be an important figure because he played in prior bands. Same thing as Clapton or Winwood or whoever. . . .

> **So sure, Page meant something and then becoming part of Led Zeppelin would bring more credibility to the band and credibility with the audience.**

DS: So Frank Barsalona calls you up—"I got this band Led Zeppelin." They'd already been out—the first album had already come out—had you heard it, were you aware of it?

LM: We heard everything. Barsalona representing them was important for the band, period. Yes, we knew pretty much everything because we had to know everything. Especially me. I needed to have all that information so I could make a sound decision. So I knew what was real and what wasn't real and I'd have a feel for what was going to succeed and what was hype and wasn't substantive enough. So sure, when Barsalona or [agent] Herb Sparr called, that added to the credibility because that's who the band sought out or they sought out to represent. If you say at the time, well, there was an agent from William Morris—they weren't as up on the other bands. It didn't mean that they didn't have good bands but chances are Barsalona and Sparr were the guys that knew this music—especially the newer music.

DS: The first [Led Zeppelin] show you did was in July of 1969 at the Spectrum.

LM: I thought that we had played them at the Electric Factory. That's what I think. I could be wrong but I think we played them there.

DS: I haven't been able to find that.

LM: Well, maybe I'm wrong.

DS: Could it possibly . . . did you ever play the Yardbirds?

LM: No.

DS: Never?

LM: That was before the Factory opened. The factory opened in '68 so I don't believe we played the Yardbirds, but the Yardbirds, like the Kinks and the Moody Blues, had early credibility. . . . So absolutely, we would have known them. And we worked closely with record companies as well, so we knew what the buzz was and there were people willing to give us that information. Or you took a chance on a new band, say, like, a Ten Years After,

DS: [Tull's Ian Anderson] claims that you were hurrying him up and it took longer, and you screamed at him and he was absolutely pissed off.

LM: Ian?

DS: Yeah—I'll send you the clip. He doesn't name you specifically, but it was a promoter that did a series of shows with us.

LM: I don't recall. And I'll apologize to Ian Anderson when I see him.

DS: Was half the audience there at the time? Was there any problem [such as Led Zeppelin fans arriving late and missing the band]?

LM: The audience was always there. We always had the audience there.

DS: The full audience . . .

LM: We generally had three-act bills, and in those days the audience really wanted to see the opening act because it was like a farm system. We took a specific act and tried to build them into—I remember as an example, we had J. Geils Band on with someone, and because people came early and saw the full set we were able to bring them back six weeks later to the Spectrum and sell out and set a house record. That's just the way it was. Word of mouth, buzz, the whole thing, momentum. And a little good promoter.

DS: When you have new acts coming out did you generally talk to other promoters, like, "How did this band do for you?"

LM: No.

DS: You only concentrate on your market.

LM: People would call me; I'd never call anybody else. . . . But we all pretty much knew each other and we'd talk, and there was no concerted effort to find out, how did Led Zeppelin do in Boston or Detroit. At that point every city had its own personality, just like all the radio stations via the disc jockeys had their own personalities and played what they wanted. Generally because of the live performance being so important, radio generally followed what we did as opposed to later on, where we would wait for somebody to have a hit or some acceptance by radio.

DS: You did a show in '70, '71, '72—now, there's a big discrepancy in Led Zeppelin history and I know you're going to say you don't remember, but there's a hole. They say there was a show on July 19, 1973, in Philadelphia. There's no record of it. However, they played Vancouver on the eighteenth and Boston on the twentieth. Is it possible that there could have been a Philly show, or is it just missing?

Larry Magid, left, with legendary publisher, journalist, and radio and television personality Kal Rudman at Live Aid, July 13, 1985, John F. Kennedy Stadium in Philadelphia.

that the audience became so enamored with that it was easy to build them. The other thing is, Atlantic Records—that was as credible a label as any label that's ever been. If you were on Atlantic, whether you were a rock act or, prior to that, an R&B act, that gave you credibility because they had foresight, wisdom, and taste. . . .

DS: Do you remember anything in particular about the '69 show? Did you book Led Zeppelin by themselves? Did they do two sets or did you have opening acts? Because I can't find a list of any opening acts. Were they one of the first bands to play the whole show that you remember?

LM: No. What happened—one of the shows, they always had support on. One of the shows, I think, I'm going to say Jethro Tull was the opener.

DS: You going to give me the famous Jethro Tull story?

LM: Yes. I was told that Jimmy Page was sick, and unless they were the opening act, they didn't think that he would be well enough to close the show. We convinced Ian Anderson to close the show to follow Led Zeppelin. The real story, we learned a couple years later, was that they just wanted to go to New York earlier so they could party at some club. Famous story to about six people.

DS: It's in every book. And wait till you hear what Jethro Tull said about it.

LM: Well, what did Jethro Tull say about it?

LM: Sure, I'll try to look it up. I know there were two cancellations from Led Zeppelin. One when Robert's son died, and two when he broke his leg.

DS: Robert's son died at the end of August at the end of that tour [in 1977].

LM: I just don't remember dates, I'm sorry.

DS: Anything you can tell me about the last time they played there [at the Spectrum], which was 1975? You did go to the Zeppelin shows, right?

LM: I went to every show for decades, pretty much. I didn't miss much. . . .

DS: Do you remember anything about them as players?

LM: Jimmy Page was one of the top musicians, period. Guitar or anything else. He just had great feel for it and the interaction between him and Robert Plant was great to a lot of people. It was very sensual. But the whole band as a unit was a very strong unit. It was loud, I know that. [Laughs] I remember it being loud so I absolutely went to all the shows. . . . I always said that they didn't need to be that loud, but maybe the younger part of the audience—obviously being a promoter, I'm older than the average person that's going to a show at that time or anytime—maybe they liked it. It certainly didn't hinder their appeal.

LM: Yeah. He's quite an outstanding drummer and he's able to play in a lot of different spheres and influences. He's broad. But you always go with the original, because he's as much prototype for the rock drummer of today than anyone else you can think of. Keith Moon stands out because he could play incredibly well while he was carrying on. Bonham was pretty much straight on. Not many people have the Keith Moon personality on stage, but again, that's the only person that I would equate him to in terms of ability. I know there were other great drummers. I thought they were the two top ones.

DS: Well, this next question is what I'm leading up to—maybe people think there's no way Led Zeppelin could have continued without John Bonham because he was so integral, whereas they feel the Who—it's split. Keith Moon didn't have the kind of presence that Bonham did, so they were able to continue, or maybe they shouldn't have continued when Keith Moon died.

LM: Well, Led Zeppelin did continue, but they didn't call it Led Zeppelin. . . .

DS: But what about the Who, though?

LM: Well, to me the Who epitomize what rock 'n' roll was all about and I just thought personally that they were the top rock band, so, if you say to me as a purist that they should not have continued, I'd say you're right. If you say to me that they should continue as a creative force,

I thought it was louder than it actually had to be, because a lot of bands that are just loud cover up for their lack of ability, but not this band.

DS: Many people say that John Bonham was probably the greatest rock drummer.

LM: John Bonham was a terrific drummer; great musician—one of the top, with the Who's drummer, Keith Moon, who I happened to think was the best one, period. But Bonham was unbelievable and he added to the show as a showman. Remember there's no production values at any time the band got up there, set up, pretty bare stage, maybe a curtain behind them—that was it. They put the drummer on a riser. I thought Bonham was pretty spectacular.

DS: According to [publicist] Danny Goldberg, John Bonham used to do a separate drum sound check for like forty-five minutes to an hour. Do you remember that?

LM: Yeah, he did a long sound check. There were drummers who did that, especially if you had a larger than normal set of drums or percussion instruments. He definitely took a lot of time on stage, as did a few others.

DS: You've since [promoted] Jason Bonham, I take it? How does he compare to his father?

I'm going to agree to that. If you say that they should continue as a business entity, I'm going to agree to that. Unfortunately, we've had a lot of deaths in the music business with musicians with bands, and why should an entity stop in my mind without the ability to replace that person? Bands—jazz bands make personnel changes often. Some great jazz musicians like Miles Davis could have a new band every two or three years, plus he'd go in and record with other people. . . . Yeah, as a purist, those performances, those albums stand as a test, as a milestone, that may never be reached, and who's to judge if they are or they aren't? It's all personal opinion. It's like I said, I thought Led Zeppelin continued because the two key components played together for several tours and recorded several albums; they just didn't call it Led Zeppelin, but we got to enjoy what they recorded and what they performed and I daresay that they those songs would have been part of Led Zeppelin's repertoire had they continued under that name.

DS: You're talking about Page/Plant?

LM: Yeah.

DS: When you first heard that Page/Plant were going out, what did you think?

LM: I thought it was strong. Some shows were stronger than others, depending on albums. And when I say stronger I'm talking about in terms of appeal, ticket-selling appeal, as far as appeal on stage. I never thought that that subsided; Robert Plant and Jimmy Page, regardless of any difference that might have gone on, always were connected with the audience and with each other. Again, sometimes it was just a little too loud. It didn't have to be that loud, but let's blame that on deaf soundmen.

DS: The first time you were called about Robert Plant touring, you played him at the Spectrum. Did you feel that Robert Plant would be able to stand on his own?

LM: You have to speak of the time, so everything evolves, everything changes, everything is different. Plant—probably one of the few people who could pull that off—that's how big he was. And that's how exciting—and I keep using the word "sensual," but that was part of his appeal. And I think that we could attribute a lot of that to his musical integrity. We've seen as the years progressed, whether he was a big draw or a small draw, that he was true to what he felt was important. That message, whether it was blues or the last album with Alison Krauss—he stayed true to music and wasn't making frivolous music. It's the same as Jimmy Page—he's so credible that you'd go see him not necessarily because of the songs but because you knew he was going to give you something credible to listen to and to think about.

DS: That brings me to the first time you were told about the Firm. Did you have any hesitation for them to headline?

LM: No, not really. There were certain people that were credible; that you knew the public would accept because of their credibility. Again, there are hundreds and hundreds of musicians and bands and you narrow it down. They were big. And people wanted to know what they were up to. And yeah, the Firm was strong enough to headline. Now, I don't know if they were strong enough to headline in terms of selling out or doing multiple dates, but that first time around, we felt with our acumen that we could help to maximize their appeal. . . . Now, if they don't do that the second time around, their appeal drops. You don't make a deal just to say okay, I'll make a deal and it's going to sell out. Each deal is predicated on how many people you need to start to make money, to have a return on your investment. We're not fans here—or only fans here. This is a business, not only for the Firm or for Led Zeppelin or Page and Plant or for any group. This is a business. Give us something we can work with and we'll help you sell tickets. In our case, we think we're the difference.

DS: Let's go to Live Aid. I know you were busy that day as the copromoter, but did you get a chance to see Led Zeppelin's set?

LM: Most sets were pretty short, so there were things you could see more towards the middle and end of the show as opposed to the beginning of the show, so yes, we got to see them.

DS: Did you have any concern that Phil Collins might not have made it?

LM: First of all, one of the many great ideas that came out of Live Aid was Phil Collins playing on both sides of the Atlantic. I thought it was a stroke of brilliance, whoever's idea it was, and when the gates opened and Collins came in, or, rather, straggled in—he was obviously very tired—it was a moment of sheer excitement that exploded backstage before it exploded on stage. Had he not gotten there . . . Led Zeppelin would have definitely played. They would have figured something out. It was the cap of a spectacular show; a spectacular event. . . .

It's hard to imagine anybody even beginning to think that they could follow that.

DS: Could you give me an overview of Peter Grant as a manager? He was an integral part and a lot of people say he was the fifth member. I just want you to give me an assessment of Peter Grant.

LM: Peter Grant was one of those bigger-than-life kind of guys.

DS: He's dead now, so don't worry.

LM: I have nothing bad to say about Peter Grant. To me he was a throwback to the English music-hall type of promoter. He was a promoter in every sense of the word. He promoted his bands very well. With Led Zeppelin in the beginning it was almost too much, because of the overtness of the name of Led Zeppelin and all the hype that came out—had they been a lesser band they would have fallen on their face, but [they did not] because of the groundwork that Peter Grant did. He was very protective of his acts and not promoter-friendly. The band always came first. He was a big guy—ex-wrestler, walked with a cane. He did what he thought was necessary and you had to respect him for that, and I did not have a bad relationship with Grant. In the later years, we talked and laughed—he would call me late at night, and I was so surprised, but he was a difficult guy and there was no two ways about it.

I do have a great Peter Grant memory. I don't know if it's a great story. We played Jeff Beck, who was one of the spectacular guitar players of all time—one of the few people who have maintained their integrity over all these years. Peter Grant was his manager at that point. In the band was a young singer named Rod Stewart. Jeff Beck had to be center stage, and Rod Stewart actually sang in front of the drummer, stage right. It was very funny to see the setup. Of course everybody came to see Jeff Beck play, not to hear Rod Stewart sing, because he was this brand-new guy—skinny, scarecrow kind of a guy with a rough voice. We opened the show—I always had three-act shows and we'd take two sets a night. The place held 2,500 people. So the opening act was Ten Years After, and I have to say that they may not have been the best fit for Jeff Beck's group, although Jeff Beck was technically a far superior player than Alvin Lee of Ten Years After. [Ten Years After] came in and they just caught fire; they were a rockin' band that didn't stop from the minute they got on stage. They overshadowed Rod Stewart singing. They overshadowed Jeff Beck; they overshadowed the whole thing. They stole the show. At intermission, Peter Grant came over to me and he said, "We have to change the bill tomorrow. They can't be on the show tomorrow." And I looked at him, thinking he was joking, and I said, "You're kidding, aren't you?" And he said, "No." And I said, "That can't happen; we're committed to these groups and that's not a situation for me; that's a situation that you talk to your agent about, not me. I'm not changing anything."

And . . . the same thing happened the second show, but maybe even more so because it was such a shock to everyone not only in the audience but to the Jeff Beck band themselves. Now it's funny, you can look back on it. Then it wasn't funny to Grant. As I said, he was a very protective manager. He had this incredible guitar player, this brand-new singer, terrific band, and he just followed me up the street while I was walking to my car and he said, "No, they're not going to be in the show, they're *not* going to be in the show!" And I said, "As far as I'm concerned, they're on the show but if you'd like to go on first, before them, or in their slot, we'll work it out for you." And he said, "No, no," and I said, "Then we're going to do this and they're going to play." And he was really pissed off at me and it lasted but it didn't last enough to say I'm not going to play Led Zeppelin for you, or you're not going to be involved. It had nothing to do with that. Not that we were friends, but we talked, we communicated. He knew we were good promoters and the best, at least in this area. And we had a relationship and it got better as we went along. . . .

DS: The 1980 tour: how many dates would they have played for you?

LM: They would have played multiple shows in whatever cities that we were promoting in at the time, or as many dates as we could get that were available. Remember at that time you couldn't say, "Boy, we're doing so well, let's do another ten or twenty dates." When you had to leave, you had to leave. So you'd cram as much in [as possible], and Philadelphia was as important a market as

there was in the late '60s up until the early '80s because of the Spectrum and because we had the ability to do more shows for different reasons than anybody else. . . .

DS: So you don't remember if they would have done two or three nights?

LM: They would have done as many nights as we could have gotten.

DS: Where were you when you got the call when John Bonham had died? Do you remember that, and having to cancel the tour because it had to be probably one of the biggest things you ever had to cancel?

LM: Well, I had a history of Led Zeppelin cancellations. Probably in my office and probably saying, "Shit, here we go again."

DS: What do you think of the possibility of a future tour?

LM: Never.

DS: Why? People say, including Danny Goldberg, that once Robert Plant gets this thing out of his system, it's going to happen.

LM: Perhaps, but it won't be because anybody is offering Robert Plant, in my estimation, a lot of money because he has a lot of money. It would have to be only for the personal aggrandizement, you know, soul-fulfilling, ego-fulfilling, but I think that's what one of their last performances in England was, that to show to themselves and anybody else that they could still do it. Could they still do it? Yeah, but honestly I had no desire to go to London to see the [O$_2$ Arena] show because I saw [Led Zeppelin] at its best; not that this wouldn't be great, but that was at its best because it was at its rawest. This would be more rehearsed, more performed. Would I like to see it? Sure. It would be great for the audience, especially for people who haven't seen them. Would they see it in the same or different light? It remains to be seen. But I, and a lot of others, saw them in their total, and that was enough for me. Anybody like that, you see them and that's it. . . . The original—that stays with you. That's invades your psyche and your soul.

DS: I wanted to get a comment from you about John Paul Jones.

LM: John Paul Jones is a great player. Period. They were four strong performers. Great players. They had a sensuality, they had the songs, they had the appeal, the performance—they were great. It's nice to see them in the various forms, but . . .

DS: There's only one Led Zeppelin.

LM: That's right.

Ioannis, Get the Led Out, 2011.

Mick Wall

AUTHOR, PUBLICIST, AND TELEVISION HOST MICK WALL BEGAN HIS CAREER IN 1977, AT THE AGE OF NINETEEN, COVERING THE UK PUNK SCENE FOR *SOUNDS* MAGAZINE. TWO YEARS LATER, HE JOINED THE PR FIRM HEAVY PUBLICITY, WHERE HE WORKED WITH SUCH CLIENTS AS DIRE STRAITS, BLACK SABBATH, REO SPEEDWAGON, THIN LIZZY, AND JOURNEY. BY 1981, WALL WAS THE PUBLICITY DIRECTOR AT VIRGIN RECORDS, WORKING WITH ACTS INCLUDING THE HUMAN LEAGUE, SIMPLE MINDS, AND CULTURE CLUB. IN THE MID-1980S, HE HOSTED *MONSTERS OF ROCK*, HIS OWN WEEKLY SHOW, FOR EUROPE'S SKY TV.

THE URGE TO WRITE NEVER LEFT WALL, HOWEVER. HIS FIRST BOOK, *DIARY OF A MADMAN*, A BIOGRAPHY OF OZZY OSBOURNE, WAS PUBLISHED IN 1985. SINCE THEN HE HAS AUTHORED SEVERAL MORE ROCK BIOGRAPHIES, INCLUDING THE HIGHLY ACCLAIMED *WHEN GIANTS WALKED THE EARTH: A BIOGRAPHY OF LED ZEPPELIN* IN 2008. AT THE START OF THIS 2010 INTERVIEW, WALL IS ASKED HOW *WHEN GIANTS WALKED THE EARTH* CAME ABOUT.

MICK WALL: The book first came about because I wanted to read a great book about Led Zeppelin and I didn't think such a thing existed. The only book people recognized as being good about Led Zeppelin was [Stephen Davis's] *Hammer of the Gods*. When it came out in 1985 it was a sensation, but it was based on essentially one interview with a tour manager. It came at a time when the '70s and Zeppelin were about as unfashionable as you could get, so it was cool to turn them into whipping boys. There was also what seems a very dated attitude now to the whole sex-and-drugs thing, you know. "Did you know Jimmy Page took drugs?" Whoooa. . . . Who would have thought? "And there were groupies." Whoooa. . . . No way!

I actually tried to convince Jimmy Page to do his own book, particularly after Bob Dylan's *Chronicles* came out. Jimmy didn't want to talk about the sex and the drugs and the magic. I said, "Well, look at Dylan's book. You don't have to discuss anything you don't want to. You could just

A 2012 photograph of Mick Wall, holding a copy of his biography of Metallica, Enter Night.

do an amazing book and it could be very selective." And we came very, very close to getting him to agree to do it. We offered him a significant amount of money. But at the last minute he backed away. And at that point the publisher and I said, "Well, why don't *we* just try and do a really great book about Led Zeppelin? Make it something that grownups will find interesting. You don't have to be a massive Led Zeppelin fan to enjoy it. Let's try and do that great book." So that's what I tried to do.

DENNY SOMACH: What are some things that you uncovered that no one else had expanded upon?

MW: I'd say the musicology of Led Zeppelin, where that music comes from, not throwing up one's hands in horror that they may have ripped off blues or folk artists. In fact, everybody from Lennon to the Stones to Dylan—the greatest rock songwriter of the twentieth century—you know, many of his great songs came from previously existing material or ideas. It's a normal thing, so I wanted to normalize that, but at the same time show to what extent Zeppelin had borrowed so many ideas from the past, but reinvented them and turned them into something new. . . .

is, and what Jimmy himself has told me in the past, is that there was equivocation over whether Plant would make it to the second album. The first album was recorded after they'd done literally just a handful of very, very small shows as the New Yardbirds. Plant had not been an accomplished performer on the stage and he was a little uncomfortable with his role. It wasn't until they got to America in 1969 that Plant eventually became somebody that Page decided would remain as the singer, so there was this sense of chicken-and-egg. We need to get an album out to build momentum. We need to make an album to get a record deal. All these things were done with the people he had available, which at that point were Robert Plant, John Paul Jones, and John Bonham. There was no doubt in his mind that Paul Jones and Bonham would stay; but Plant was never a given until the second album.

DS: And you're saying that Jimmy Page told you this?

MW: Absolutely. The road crew treated Plant very much as the newbie. Richard Cole, the tour manager, treated him no better than a gofer in the early days. It's one of the reasons they had such a raucous relationship later on.

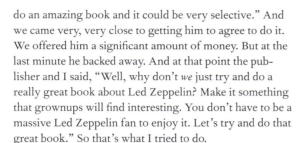

I wanted to show that Jimmy Page was more than a guitarist—that he was one of the great producers of the twentieth century.

DS: You're saying that everybody was borrowing, but I know you're aware that "Whole Lotta Love" wasn't just taken from Muddy Waters's recording of Willie Dixon's "You Need Love," but from the Small Faces, and "Stairway to Heaven" really came from [Spirit's] Randy California. You're aware of that, right?

MW: Well, I think with "Whole Lotta Love," Led Zeppelin clearly stole from both. They stole from Willie Dixon and the Small Faces, who had their own version, which they used to call "You Need Love." But I don't think there's anything wrong with that. I think where we do cry foul in the book is that Zeppelin didn't credit. To this day, Jimmy hates giving credit to anyone. There are examples with people who worked on the reissued *Song Remains the Same* CD a couple of years ago not getting credit. Jimmy is a control freak in that sense. Zeppelin was such a personal vision for him that he didn't even enjoy giving credit even to the people in his own group. I mean, Plant got no credit for any of the lyrics on the first album.

DS: What was the reason? Was it a contractual thing?

MW: It's always been suggested that it was a contractual thing. What the book suggests, and what my own belief

It's one of the reasons why Robert, still, to this present day, has a bad attitude toward Led Zeppelin. Led Zeppelin was Jimmy Page's project. Robert Plant was a guy hired to do a job who wasn't doing it well enough early on for Page to roll out the red carpet in the same way he did to Bonham and Jones.

DS: What about "Dazed and Confused?" Borrowed? Stolen?

MW: I spoke to Jake Holmes, who wrote the original "Dazed and Confused," for the book. Holmes opened for the Yardbirds in New York, and Jimmy bought Jake's album [*The Above Ground Sound*] the very next day, which contained the original version of "Dazed and Confused." If you listen to Jake's version, it's the same tune. It's the same striding bass line. The lyrics are different, but the title was the same. The arrangement is essentially the same. Jimmy appropriated it.

There's a version on a Yardbirds CD that's come out in recent years of a radio performance for the BBC where they do "Dazed and Confused" exactly as Zeppelin would later do it, but with Jake's original words. And Jimmy took all that and stuck his name down as the songwriter and essentially stole the song. He rewrote the lyrics, so it should have been "music Holmes, lyrics and

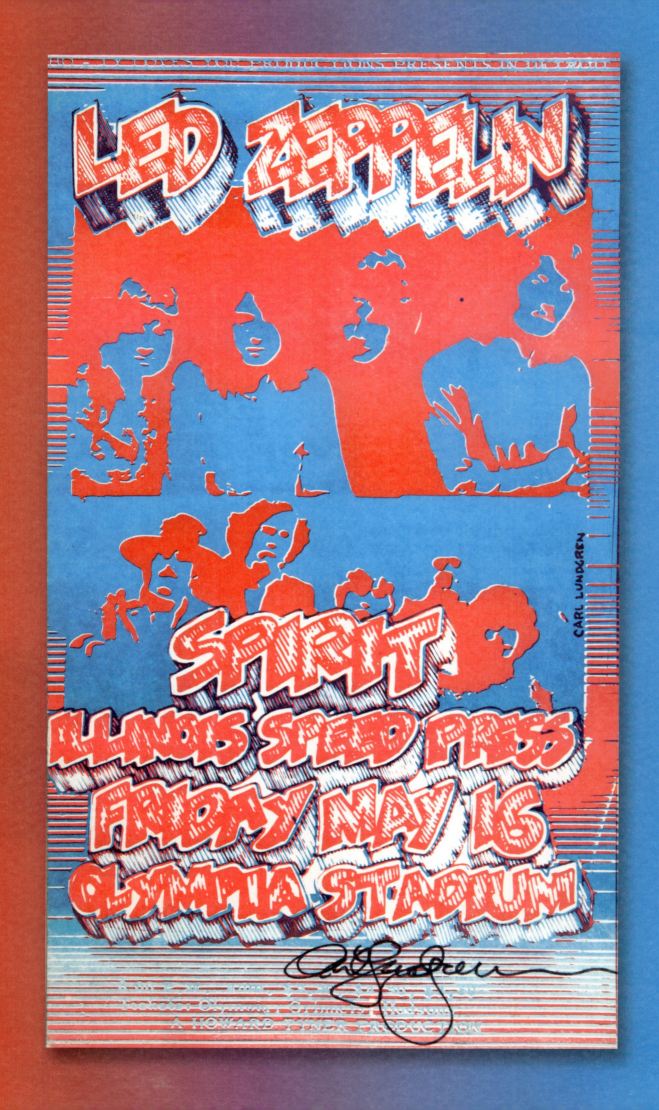

arrangement Page," but he didn't do that. I think it's unforgivable, but what the book tries to explain is where he was coming from, how this happened. In those days going to America if you lived in England, you might as well be talking about a mission to Mars. It was so far away in most people's minds. It was really another planet. The idea that this weird folk song by this completely unknown artist would be something that we would be discussing forty years later wouldn't have even crossed his mind.

According to Jake, and I agree with him, he feels that the kicker is that "Dazed and Confused" is now so synonymous with Jimmy Page, it's the big showcase for Jimmy, and it's finally time to come out and say, "Well, you know what? Actually, Jake Holmes wrote this song." But it's just not gonna happen. And I can understand how embarrassing and sensitive it must be for Jimmy to be put on the spot about it, but the fact is, if you listen to Jake's original and you listen to the Yardbirds' version and then you listen to the Zeppelin version, Jimmy stole the song. [Note: In 2010, Jake Holmes filed a copyright infringement lawsuit against Jimmy Page; the case was dismissed by a judge in January of 2012.]

The question of how much of "Stairway to Heaven" Jimmy took from Spirit's instrumental song "Torres" is I think less of an issue than the whole thing about "Dazed and Confused," "Whole Lotta Love," "Nobody's Fault but Mine," "Bring It On Home," "Gallows Pole," or any of those other really big hot buttons where Zeppelin clearly appropriated existing material.

My own take, having listened to Spirit's tune many times, is that Jimmy loved Spirit. Zeppelin toured with Spirit. In fact, Randy California was using a theremin before Page used it for "Whole Lotta Love," so clearly Page was paying a lot of attention to what Spirit was doing. It's entirely possible that he heard that instrumental piece and appropriated it into "Stairway to Heaven," but here's my take: you know what? It doesn't matter because I think the Spirit piece is very slight. It's charming and it's pretty but it's inconsequential. . . . I don't think Randy California could have written "Stairway to Heaven" in a million years.

a regular show. It was very unusual for any rock artist to attempt to perform there, let alone headline five shows. They could have done more, in fact.

Physical Graffiti was the album that had just come out, which I think in many ways was a kind of zenith of Led Zeppelin. I think *Led Zeppelin IV* is probably their most complete work, but many of the *Physical Graffiti* tracks had been recorded during earlier album sessions along with eight brand-new pieces of material, all put together into what was considered a grand statement. You remember the mid-'70s was the time of double albums. This was Zeppelin making their grand statement.

As a show, it was an incredible thing to see because it was Zeppelin saying, "This is us at our peak." I'm sure they felt they would probably go on and become better, but they never did. In fact, they declined after that. It also came at a moment when they still had their innocence. You look at Robert Plant in those days and he still looks so young and beautiful and in love with the whole idea of Led Zeppelin. But it's almost heartbreaking because what immediately followed the Earls Court shows was this terrible car accident on the island of Rhodes where Plant nearly lost his life. His wife and children were involved. He couldn't walk for several months. There was a question of whether he'd ever walk again. And that coincided with Bonham and Page developing serious heroin habits.

DS: You've written that the Knebworth shows [August 4 and 11, 1979, at Knebworth House, the legendary UK concert venue] were essentially a disaster.

MW: This is actually one of the things the book talks about that's never been talked about before. The popular myth—and I spoke to Jimmy about this just a few years ago and even he was still peddling the popular myth—was that over 200,000 people went to both those shows, 200,000 at the first, 200,000 at the second. In fact, there is no way you could fit in more than 106,000 people at Knebworth and in fact at the second show there were less than 40,000 people there. It was a disaster, ticketwise.

And the band was at their absolute worst. Plant had only recently agreed to come back. He had the terrible

> ## "Stairway to Heaven" is a cathedral. It's a monumental piece of work and if one of the windows in that cathedral happens to be borrowed or an imitation of someone else's window, okay, but that doesn't build you a cathedral.

DS: Let's switch gears from songwriting to performance. Led Zeppelin's 1975 five-night stand at [London's] Earls Court Exhibition Centre has been called one of the most important gigs of their career.

MW: Earls Court was a landmark occasion in the Led Zeppelin story because in many ways it was the culmination of Led Zeppelin on every level, and it was also kind of the beginning of the end. Earls Court is like Madison Square Garden in terms of size and prestige, but it wasn't

car crash in '75. His son had died in '77. And Jimmy was still seriously involved with heroin.

Jimmy had hardly turned up in terms of performance on the final Zeppelin album, *In Through the Out Door*, which was released between the two Knebworth weekends. [Note: According to Swan Song's discography, the album was released several days after the second Knebworth show.] And although the band, being old troopers, were able to come on and put on a show, you've only got to look at the DVD that came out a few years ago, which has some of that Knebworth performance, to see that this wasn't the band that we saw at Earls Court in '75, or on any of those amazing American tours in the early '70s. . . .

DS: I'd like to ask more about the albums—your favorite songs or highlights. We'll start with the first album [*Led Zeppelin*, Atlantic Records, January 1969.]

MW: Well, ironically, I think probably "Dazed and Confused" was one of the big performances on the album. Not even an original arrangement in terms of Led Zeppelin. It was entirely borrowed from the arrangement the Yardbirds had concocted nine months before, but it's still a fantastic moment. It's spooky. It's atmospheric. It's everything that will come later in Led Zeppelin's career. Other than that, I think the other big moments are also derivative in many ways, but again hint of what's gonna come. . . .

DS: *Led Zeppelin II* [Atlantic Records, October 1969] came out the same year as the first. And they recorded mostly while they were touring, right?

MW: Yeah. The first album was done in forty-eight hours, essentially. The second album was done in half a dozen different studios in the United States and the UK. In some cases, Jimmy is playing that guitar while standing in a hallway. In some cases Plant is singing without any headphones on. It was done quick, quick, quick while they were touring, while they were hot, and I think you can hear that crackle in the grooves. I mean, it's a fantastic atmosphere to that record. For me, every single track on that album is a highlight. I think it remains a titanic statement, one of the two or three top Led Zeppelin albums of all time. You could pick any track on that album and it will be amazing. . . .

DS: Now we get to *III* [*Led Zeppelin III*, Atlantic Records, October 1970]. It's really different from the others.

MW: I don't think the significance of *Led Zeppelin III* was understood at the time it was released. There was a general air of dissatisfaction, that wasn't a proper follow-up in the accepted sense to *Led Zeppelin II*. There was disappointment that there wasn't another "Whole Lotta Love" or "Bring It On Home" or "Heartbreaker."

There wasn't this sense of this monumental live band laying it down hot and heavy. In fact, it was the first album where Jimmy Page and Robert Plant had actually written together properly. They retreated to a dilapidated cottage in the mystical Welsh hills—no electricity, no running water, just a roaring fire, a lot of hash and cider, and acoustic guitars. And that feeling's reflected a lot on the album. There are more acoustic numbers.

There's what these days we would call a more low-fi atmosphere to the album, but here's the thing: If they had come out with another album like *Led Zeppelin II*, we'd have been talking Black Sabbath, you know? We'd have been talking Deep Purple, we would have been talking other great groups that essentially perfected a sound and

a format and then ran with it. The reason we still revere Led Zeppelin so much is because they didn't do that. *Led Zeppelin III* is still their least commercially successful album. It's only sold five million where the fourth album has sold forty million, but *III* is one of the most important because it signposted the fact that they were gonna do things differently. They were also hugely influenced by the Band and by Crosby, Stills, and Nash. They all grew beards and it was all about getting it together in the country. So they were influenced by their times, but had the courage to do something different. And that's one of the reasons why Led Zeppelin was always more than just another hard rock band. . . .

DS: Okay, let's go onto to *IV* [*Led Zeppelin IV*, Atlantic Records, October 1971].

MW: *Led Zeppelin IV* isn't just the greatest Led Zeppelin album. It's one of the greatest albums by anybody ever. . . . I once interviewed Jimmy Page specifically about the making of *Led Zeppelin IV* and I said, "If the alien came down tomorrow, would that be the album you'd play him?" and he said, "Absolutely." It contains everything that Led Zeppelin was good at and it also contains "Stairway to Heaven," which is the pinnacle, really, of everything that was interesting about Led Zeppelin— acoustic, electric, a journey, a song that, as Jimmy used to put it, "finds its own time. Finds its own rhythm. Let it go and it finds its own way."

[The album] also had, in typical Zeppelin style, some obvious thefts. You know Memphis Minnie? Her song "When the Levee Breaks" is reinvented. There was no credit at the time. These days Memphis Minnie does get deserved credit, but in fairness to Zeppelin, you know what Page created with "When the Levee Breaks" is way beyond anything you'll hear Memphis Minnie do. Page once described it to me as "hypnotic, hypnotic, hypnotic." It was also possibly their most occult album in terms of many, many references in the lyrics, and in the titles of some of the songs like "Black Dog." And the artwork, and, of course, "Stairway to Heaven," which if you are a serious occultist is absolutely jam-packed with references to that belief system. And at the end of the day, you don't need to know any of that.

It's a bit like *The Simpsons.* You can enjoy *The Simpsons* on a very intellectual level or it can just be a fantastically funny cartoon. *Led Zeppelin IV* is a fantastically good rock album.

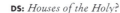

DS: *Houses of the Holy*?

MW: *Houses of the Holy* [Atlantic Records, March 1973], a bit like *Led Zeppelin III*, really got bad press. It kind of disappointed on many levels because it didn't appear to be an adequate follow-up to *Led Zeppelin IV*. In the same way that *III* didn't appear to be an adequate follow-up to *II*. But it's one of my favorite Zeppelin albums. It's joyous. It's completely joyous. There is no "Stairway to Heaven." There's certainly no "When the Levee Breaks." But there are some wonderful moments. "The Song Remains the Same" has this cascading array of guitars. It sounds like a waterfall or a starburst. I mean, just incredibly uplifting.

They were also influenced by the Stones, who'd moved into funk and different styles that they were experimenting with. You've got a funk track. You've even got a reggae track. John Paul Jones comes up with probably his greatest contribution. You've got Jimmy's interest in Indian music coming out in the guitars in "Dancing Days," and you've got wonderful moments like "Over the Hills and Far Away," where this acoustic-electric thing again comes up—Plant telling his fairy tale.

To me it's not a significant album in terms of weight, but in terms of sheer joy, it's a wonderful piece of work.

DS: Let's move on to *Physical Graffiti* [Swan Song, February 1975]. Jimmy Page had wanted to do a double album for a very long time. . . .

Ioannis, Immigrant Song *(detail), 2011.*

MW: We have to remember that in the wake of *Blonde on Blonde*, *Tommy*, even things like *Goodbye Yellow Brick Road* by Elton John or *The Lamb Lies Down on Broadway* by Genesis, there was this belief essentially that serious artists made their most serious statement over the course of a double album. These were the days when most albums only probably lasted thirty-five or forty minutes. So serious artists, you know, would make a double album and show the full panorama of their talents.

So for Page, whose concern always was that Zeppelin didn't get the acclaim they deserved, credibility was always an issue. This was his moment to do something that had a wow factor for the critics. He'd been dissuaded from doing it many times.

DS: There were eight tracks that were recorded for *Physical Graffiti*, and the rest all come from earlier times.

MW: Eventually with *Physical Graffiti*, Page got his own way simply because they did have this wealth of material. These days you'd think about box sets, and extras, and bonus tracks, but back then the best you could do was say, "Well, let's release it as a record."

So essentially *Physical Graffiti* is built around some fantastic moments—"In the Light," "Ten Years Gone"—monumental moments that were all brand new to that time. But also studded with some fantastic tracks. I mean, "Houses of the Holy" clearly had been written for *Houses of the Holy*, but it found its way to *Physical Graffiti*.

"Down by the Seaside" comes from much earlier times. "Black Country Woman" was recorded outdoors, I think at Mick Jagger's country house. Other tracks came from the same sessions that produced *Led Zeppelin IV*, so they clearly had this incredible material—and they didn't know what to do with it. In fact, in those days nothing was gonna be done with it, but they put it together as this double album and I think it was the last truly amazing album they ever made.

DS: Is "Kashmir" the ultimate Led Zeppelin song?

MW: Robert Plant will tell you "Kashmir" is the ultimate Led Zeppelin song, and I think it's one of them. Or, as Jimmy Page put it to me when I asked him, he said "Kashmir" along with "Stairway to Heaven" and "Whole Lotta Love" was one big moment in a journey. "Kashmir" wasn't the biggest and it wasn't the only one, but it was one of them. But for Robert it's absolutely the one. I mean, Robert's told me many times that he wishes people would forget about "Stairway to Heaven" and that the band were more remembered for "Kashmir." Personally, I think it's academic. I think it's amazing that this band were able to do "Stairway to Heaven" and "Kashmir." I mean, the range involved there is incredible.

DS: How do you rate the movie *The Song Remains the Same*?

MW: I personally loved the movie. I've loved it from the first time I ever saw it, up to getting the DVD version recently. But I understand the criticisms. I understand why Robert Plant gets very embarrassed about his scenes as this Celtic troubadour, and you know what? I don't care, 'cause it was a fantastic movie to go and see in the movie houses at the time.

I remember I and several hippie friends went and we sat in the aisle, you know, because you didn't sit on a seat, man. You sat cross-legged in the aisle. You passed the chillum around. And you just dug it. And even to this day, watching the DVD, I love it because it's such a long time ago. It's like a glimpse into a bygone world.

I love the scenes with Grant as the gangster. I love the scenes of Page doing "Dazed and Confused." And going off into his whole magus trip. I mean, Jimmy told me all about the night he did that. He picked a night when there was a full moon. It was recorded at Boleskine House, which was [British occultist Aleister] Crowley's dwelling on the banks of Loch Ness in Scotland.

There was no CGI [computer-generated imagery]. Page really did crawl up that mountain—Crowley's mountain. Crowley was a mountaineer and that whole thing about meeting himself at the top and regressing to childhood, regressing to the old man . . . you know how

> # For me it's one of my all-time favorite rock movies. I don't care who talks about *The Last Waltz* or *Performance*. You know those are great movies, too, but don't take away my Led Zeppelin movie, 'cause it's fantastic!

people go, "Was Jimmy Page really into the occult?" Have you seen "Dazed and Confused" in *The Song Remains the Same*? The bit where you see him with what is supposed to be the violin bow, but turns into the magical wand—the magical weapon, as they say in the occult world—and he's turning it this way and that and you get this spectrum of colors. Here is Jimmy saying, "This is what I'm into and I ain't joking." I love that about him. . . .

DS: Tell me about *In Through the Out Door* [Swan Song, August 1979].

MW: *In Through the Out Door* had some great moments on it, but when I spoke to Robert about it, as far as he's concerned it isn't a proper Led Zeppelin album. People these days tend to ascribe its musical merit to the fact that John Paul Jones took over. Like Robert, I tend to feel that John Paul Jones had as much to do with any success that album had musically as anybody else. I think there are some good moments. "In the Evening" is a good moment. "All of My Love" is interesting. . . .

But it's disappointing because Jimmy Page just doesn't turn up. You know he was at the height of his heroin addiction. He barely contributed to the album. People say, "Well, he played some nice guitar." Yeah, but as I said earlier, that was only a part of what Page brought to Zeppelin. It was the vision, the sonic architecture, the elaborate expertise as a producer. That's what he brought, and there's none of that in evidence on that album. I think it was a sad way to go out, I really do.

DS: You're one of the few authors that actually know the band and talked to them. So I want to ask, because of your credibility, did you talk to the band after the live show at London's O₂ Arena in 2007 to get a sense of their feeling?

MW: I haven't spoken to any of the band specifically about the O₂ show. But a very good record-producer friend of mine had Robert over for Sunday lunch not long after the O₂ show and Robert opened up to him about it. He shared it with me so that I could write about it. At the same time he didn't want to give away a private conversation, but I know from this person,

who's a very credible person, a very well-known record producer, that Robert found the whole thing very cold. Robert called it joyless.

At that point he was working with Alison Krauss, which he felt was the opposite—a very joyful experience. And I got that feeling, too. You know there was a very needy element to that show. Jason [Bonham], Jones, and Jimmy urgently wanted Led Zeppelin to reconvene. Desperately wanted to keep Robert happy and have him agree to do this. And I think it's a bit like when you're urgently in love with a woman who may or may not find you attractive. When you become terribly needy-urgent, it's a repellent. It pushes them further away. I think that's what happened. . . .

DS: Let me clear something up here: Jimmy was supportive of *When Giants Walked the Earth*, and then you had a falling-out, and you were telling me that he saw you somewhere and he said, "I'm doing a Mick Wall." Explain that, please.

MW: Okay. Jimmy and I collaborated for over twenty years on television interviews, magazine interviews, newspaper interviews, radio. Jimmy trusted no one but me for many, many years. Whenever he had something coming out, I'd be called in to do several interviews with him so that he wouldn't have to talk to anybody. Through this we got to know each other, became friends, and hence, my continually over the years saying to him, "One day you must do a book."

[After Page turned down a book offer] I gave up on the idea of Jimmy doing a book and I decided I would do a book. He knew about it. He was comfortable with it. In fact, he rang me here at this house we're in now one Saturday night, very upset. He had a meeting with Robert Plant a few days before and he wanted to make sure that I absolutely got something dead right in my book about Robert, and "make sure you write this and don't forget that." Cut to 2007, and now O₂ is on the table and as far as Jimmy was concerned the O₂ was the first step towards a full-blown re-formation like the Stones, like the Who. Maybe there'll be an album, maybe there won't, but there would be many shows in America and around the world.

Suddenly Jimmy's antsy about the whole thing. Suddenly I'm a bad guy. Suddenly, it's, "Well, when's that bloody book coming out anyway?" Suddenly it's a bad idea. Jimmy always had this thing about people using him—people making money from him. He hates giving credit. He just got really turned off by the whole thing, and it wasn't just me. There were many other people—photographers, record producers that had worked with Jimmy for many years. Suddenly he didn't know them. He thought finally [a re-formed Led Zeppelin] was coming true and at that point I wasn't allowed to go to the O₂ show. All bets were off.

Robert Plant's office was more pleasant about the whole thing, but again didn't extend any particular welcome to the O₂. It was Jason Bonham—whom I've known for a very long time as well—that got me my ticket for the O₂, and who then got his ass fried by Jimmy for doing so. Jimmy was very pissed off that Jason did that.

So Jimmy didn't collaborate. None of them actively collaborated on the book, but the book draws on the many interviews I did with them over the years, and my own inside knowledge and understanding of the situation. Plus new interviews I did with other people. When the book came out, Robert's office called and asked for a copy and I said, "So let me get this right. Robert can't give me a ticket for the O₂, but I have to give him a copy of my book?"

DS: And?

MW: Well, you know, I said yes. I got some copies sent over. And Jimmy also wanted copies so he got copies. Then, just before Christmas 2009, I attended the *Classic Rock* magazine annual awards in London. It's a big star-studded affair. Lots of famous people there and I'm sitting at a table with Slash and Brian May, and at the next table is Jeff Beck, Joe Perry, and Jimmy Page. And at the next table is [ZZ Top's] Billy Gibbons, Pete Townshend, Ronnie Wood—you know, it's one of those.

And I'm saying hello to Ronnie Wood and then he sees Jimmy and they start talking. Now suddenly I was hoping maybe if Jimmy didn't want to say hello just to kind of stay out of his way. At the

same time, I'm hoping he would say hello, and he sees me and he says, "You're a cheeky one."

At the end of the night, I'm asked to do a quick radio station interview—let them know how it all went. And as I'm talking to them, with my back to the main room, Jimmy comes out and he leans over and says into the mike while I'm being interviewed, "By the way, I'm writing a book about Mick Wall," and then he turns and strides off into the night and, of course, at this point I become invisible. The radio interviewer forgets me and goes chasing Jimmy down the street—"Jimmy! Jimmy! Just a quick word!"

So I know they've read it, and I suspect that Robert will be quietly pleased because I do tell the truth and the truth is that Robert still enjoys all the acclaim that Zeppelin brings in. Enjoys it more with the success he's had with Alison Krauss. And enjoys it more that he's not the needy one. Robert was the needy one in the early years of Zeppelin.

Now Jimmy's the needy one. And here's where I remain mystified and why I think the book ends sadly. I am deeply saddened that Jimmy Page still wants to get Led Zeppelin back together. There's nothing wrong with that. Mick Jagger still wants to do the Stones. Townshend wants to do the Who. It must be a tragedy that Page can't do this thing that he wants to do.

Jimmy really is—or certainly was—beyond a rock guitarist. He was an incredibly innovative producer and musician. His influences range from Asian to classical to jazz to rockabilly, blues, hard rock. The panoramic scope of his talents goes so far beyond that of most rock guitarists, and I include Jeff Beck and [Deep Purple's] Ritchie Blackmore. These people do not possess the gifts Jimmy Page has. Why Jimmy Page doesn't make an album about what it's like to be a sixty-six-year-old man in the year 2010, I don't know. I'd love to hear that.

A wristband from the Ahmet Ertegun tribute concert at the O₂ arena in London, held on December 10, 2007; reunited members of Led Zeppelin, featuring Jason Bonham on drums, headlined the megashow.

Phil Carson

As the executive at the helm of Atlantic Records' British arm in the late 1960s and '70s, Phil Carson was a firsthand witness to the emergence of Led Zeppelin, whose avant-garde methods bucked conventional wisdom and achieved musical brilliance. In turn, Phil was so well liked by the members of Led Zeppelin that they insisted he become the liaison between their own newly formed record company and Atlantic, its distributor. After the demise of Led Zeppelin, Phil shifted into artist management for the band's surviving members as well as for Jason Bonham, who remains his client today. This rare interview took place in November 2009.

DENNY SOMACH: How was it that Led Zeppelin came to be signed by Atlantic Records?

PHIL CARSON: Jerry [Wexler, acclaimed Atlantic R&B producer] was very aware of what was happening in England, and he had many sessions with Dusty [Springfield]—and other English artists, for that matter—and he became very cognizant of the great players that there were in England. One of the players he knew about was Jimmy Page. And he heard that Jimmy Page was putting a group together, which was going to be called the New Yardbirds, and he got on the case immediately. He wanted to have the group that Jimmy Page was in.

Jerry had an A&R philosophy, and I've kind of lived my life by his philosophy after he taught it to me. You should never sign a band unless there's a virtuoso musician in it. And he wanted this group called the New Yardbirds because he knew there was a virtuoso musician. His philosophy came from the fact that he felt that a virtuoso musician doesn't play with good musicians; he only plays with great musicians. So if you can find a group that's got a virtuoso in it, rush after it because they're going to be surrounded by other great people.

I believe that he signed the New Yardbirds, which of course later became Led Zeppelin, before he heard a note

of music. I believe he had a meeting with Peter Grant, the manager of the New Yardbirds as it initially was, and Steve Weiss, the attorney, and I think he made that deal without hearing anything the group were going to play because that's how much he believed in Jimmy Page. Of course, Dusty Springfield had told him that Jimmy Page was hot stuff, and Dusty was his yardstick of all that was happening in England at that point.

So Jerry signed the band, [and] later they changed their name to Led Zeppelin, and Jerry never got involved in the production of the group or really had anything to do with them after that. He handed them over to Ahmet Ertegun because he knew that Ahmet was the guy that could move it to the next level. Of course, Ahmet was Jerry's partner and, really, his boss at that time, and it was the right thing to do, to put this fantastic band to the right level at the company. Going back to Jerry's philosophy, if you think about Led Zeppelin, the reason that it became great is because it had four virtuosos in the band. That's why no band before or certainly since, and probably forever, will

Robert Plant on it, and it didn't have John Bonham on it, and it didn't have John Paul Jones on it. [Note: John Paul Jones played guitar on four tracks on *Truth* and Jimmy Page and Jones appear together on the album's "Beck's Bolero" track.] It was the union of those guys that made that album as great as it was. I mean, it was magic! You heard it! It jumped out at you. It was just a piece of pure magic, and live—my God—I mean, that band was incredible! I love the playing of Jeff Beck and Eric Clapton; they're formidable. I mean, I saw Jeff Beck this year, and he takes the guitar and plays it where it's not entitled to go. But as a performer, you've got to give it to Jimmy Page. He's an exciting, visceral guitar player. I mean, there's nobody like him out there. For my money, he's actually the best guitar player—best-rounded guitar player there is. If you count virtuosity and control of your instrument, how you take it into the studio and achieve what you want to achieve and how you perform live onstage, nobody like Jimmy Page before or since—now. He's just incredible!

They knew that I was a bass player and they used to let me come up and play from time to time . . . and that was just a complete thrill for me, but my God! Trying to keep up with John Bonham is almost impossible.

touch the greatness that those guys achieved between them. It was just something quite spectacular.

DS: When did you join Atlantic?

PC: Right in between the release of Led Zeppelin's debut album and *Led Zeppelin II*.

DS: I understand the first album was recorded in thirty-six hours. What do you know about that?

PC: That much I know. I believe it was recorded in less than thirty-six hours. I remember the bill was £1,600, which in those days was about a princely $8,000 or $9,000, and of course it was a blockbuster and deserved to be because it was an incredible record and [set] new precedents in production that Jimmy had learned and precedents that he actually invented.

So he was a formidable force in those days and, obviously, throughout his life has been a most incredible contributor to rock music. Most historians say that Jimmy Page and Peter Grant spotted something, and so did Jeff Beck, that once Cream broke up, there was a void and they were really at the right place at the right time. But of course, they also had talent. But why do you think Led Zeppelin had the career that it did as opposed to Jeff Beck, who had put out his album six months before? The first Jeff Beck album [*Truth*] was an incredible piece of virtuoso guitar playing, but it didn't have

So that was one of the electrifying forces that made it what it is, and you put Robert Plant next to him, and you've got that incredible machine of John Bonham and John Paul Jones behind it, there's nothing that can touch it. It's impossible. I can really say that with firsthand experience, you know. . . . I wasn't that bad a bass player, but my—it was impossible to get to where those guys got. I mean, to this day, I always say when people ask me about my times of actually playing onstage with Zeppelin, I always say, "Listen, John Paul Jones can play a better bass with his feet on the pedals of a Hammond organ than I could ever play on one of his borrowed guitars." But it was a lot of fun and, you know, they would try and—[laughing] John Bonham would try and screw me up any way he could by going across the beat and in and out of it. You know, all the bootlegs will tell you that I sort of managed to hold my own as long as they played stuff I knew, which consisted of three chords in either the key of A or E. I could just about hang in there. But what an experience!

DS: Your real involvement came about for the second album. Tell me the first time you heard "Whole Lotta Love."

PC: It was obviously before it came out, and I had a test pressing, and I remember putting it on, and it scared me. I mean, the middle section of "Whole Lotta Love"—I was listening to it really loud, as one would—and that spiraling guitar and all the things that were coming in and

Clockwise from left: Author Denny Somach, Phil Carson, Robert Plant, and Perry Cooper (Atlantic Records vice president and producer) at the Plaza Hotel in New York, ca. 1983. Plant was being interviewed for the NBC program Friday Night Videos.

going out of Robert Plant's vocal—it was scary music. It just jumped out of the speakers and surrounded you! It grabbed you up and took you places that no other music ever took you. That one track, if you listen to it now, it's phenomenal. It's a life-changing experience. Led Zeppelin was a life-changing experience for everybody—me particularly, for a lot of reasons, but the music—it just changed everything. It was just so incredible.

DS: Speaking of "Whole Lotta Love," there's a story that Peter Grant decided Led Zeppelin was not going to release singles in England. Could you talk about that?

PC: Well, I didn't get the memo [laughs]. Yes. I'd started fairly recently at the company, and I knew that "Whole Lotta Love" could be a huge smash hit. And I decided that that ought to be a single, and I put it out as a single and that was that, and I got summoned to the office of Peter Grant and—it was the first time I met him, actually. You know, there was a huge showdown there, that I released a single without permission, and I said, "Well, look. I'm the record company here, you know. That's what we do. That's how you get a hit." Which of course is how it was those days in the world. And he said, "Well, we don't want a single. You've got to withdraw it." So I left his office. We'd had quite a bit of an argument there, and Peter was a formidable guy, but I wasn't backing down—until I got to [my] office, that is, and got the call from Ahmet, who told me to withdraw the single, which we did. I think I'd shipped—in those days we had various distribution plants. I managed to get them all back except for about 1,200 copies that went out to Manchester, and I think they're changing hands now at like $1,000 apiece! So I wish I'd kept a few. Nobody told me anything about that. What was Peter's philosophy on that? He did allow singles in America but not in England. In that era, the way you would break records was through television, really, because radio sucked in England. I mean, there was no KLOS—no WYSP or WNEW, none of that, none of what we English called underground radio stations because to us, that's what they were. I mean, my God— they play that music on the radio? It's unheard of in England! There were a few because we had the pirate radio ships, but they wouldn't play—they wouldn't even play Led Zeppelin. They were very much pop single– orientated. So the only way to get your records moving was to go on the TV, and the biggest show ever—in the world, in the history of pop music—is, of course, *Top of the Pops*, the BBC television show, and where something like 35 to 45 percent of the entire population of England would watch *Top of the Pops*, so what you needed to do was get a record out there quickly enough, and in sufficient quantity, to get it into the top thirty so that you could appear on *Top of the Pops*. That was why I went about trying to release that Led Zeppelin record in that way. You just didn't have the avenues of promo- tion then. But Peter and Jimmy didn't care. They felt that television was too constricting to get Led Zeppelin across in a *Top of the Pops*–type format where you've got one song and you had three minutes to deliver it in . . .

That was impossible— I mean, as far as Jimmy was concerned—to put "Whole Lotta Love" in a three-minute format on television. So they never did it.

DS: It didn't affect what they did in America?

PC: America was completely different. It had absolutely no bearing on what happened in England. Those were the days that bands would put out two albums a year.

DS: What was the main difference you noticed between the first and second albums?

PC: I suppose it was supreme confidence and authority with which it was played and approached. When their second album was being recorded, they already knew what they had. They'd been to America, they'd seen the success that was available to them, and what it was bringing and what the audience was bringing; they saw what their music was doing to an American audience, and they just took it to the next level. I mean, that album—it was just positively mind-blowing.

DS: Is it true that Jimmy Page and Peter Grant decided to focus on America, as opposed to the UK, when they started?

PC: They'd both had a lot of success in America, and they knew that just because of the pure size of the market it was obviously financially worthwhile doing that. Their actual plan was world domination, and that's what they went after. They certainly did not ignore England. The reverse is largely true: the English journalists were scared of Led Zeppelin and tried to ignore them in the media. It didn't work; they became bigger than any journalists could ever pull themselves up to be.

DS: What was it like working with Peter Grant, who many people say was the fifth member of Led Zeppelin?

PC: He was central to Led Zeppelin's success. Peter knew what he wanted and knew what Jimmy wanted, and he was big enough and smart enough to get it out of every- body else that surrounded him. After the initial showdown between Peter and me on "Whole Lotta Love," we became very good friends, and he realized that with me he had an asset that he didn't have to pay because I got it.

I knew what Led Zeppelin needed and what they had to have, and I knew how to get it for them throughout Europe. And Ahmet quickly realized that I had that capability. I spoke enough German and enough French to get by in those markets. I had a lot of contacts up in the Scandinavian market, so I was able to take the ball and run with it, and Ahmet let me do it, and Peter let me do it. And it worked very well because in those days, there was no such thing as a global record company—as far as Atlantic was concerned, anyway. . . . Of course, there was someone in the record company between Peter and the band who could kind of talk their language and knew what the band needed, so that was a very important factor.

DS: What do you recall about Led Zeppelin's tours in Europe?

PC: Those jaunts into Europe were largely a lot of fun. We were just boys having a good time, and there were a lot of incredible things that happened. There's one amusing story in Sweden, where the head of the record company knew that Jimmy had a real interest in art—had been to art college, and he wanted to do a reception, a sort of high-end reception for them at an art gallery. And I really tried to dissuade him from doing that. I thought the best place to introduce Led Zeppelin would be a place with a few kids around—and there could be journalists, of course; that's what it's for. But let's do it in a club somewhere and have a bit of fun, but the guy said, "Oh, no, no. I'm sure Mr. Page will like it." I said okay.

So we get to the art gallery. And Jimmy does know art. He looks at the art in this place. It was very—it was contemporary impressionist art, but you could've fooled me. It was like paint thrown at canvases. And Jimmy takes a look at this stuff, you know, and he says—he thinks it's really bad art, you know? [Laughs] He notices that it's also not quite complete art because some of the oil is still a little wet on the canvas, and he started to rearrange it on several of the canvases. He must have been right because at a certain moment the proprietor of the gallery certainly saw what was going on and all hell broke loose. "He's defiled this great painting," you know. And because there's a bit of oil running off the canvas

other four, so that gives you a little overview that Jimmy was probably right in the first place.

DS: That brings us up to the third album, which is a little bit more acoustic, and there was backlash from the press. What were your impressions when you first heard *Led Zeppelin III*?

PC: In those days, you had one side and the other side, and there were more acoustic songs on the one side than the other. And the third album did take a bit of getting used to. But having said that, there was some phenomenal stuff on it as well. Everybody who listened to the first half thought, where have they gone with this? But of course, where they went with it was to the next level. People never really got Led Zeppelin. A lot of people didn't really get what they were. They were about broadening horizons and going to different levels and better levels, and sometimes difficult to perceive, and I think that is epitomized with the third album.

DS: That brings us to the fourth, so I want you to talk about "Rock and Roll," "Black Dog," and "Stairway to Heaven." Did you visit any of the sessions while they were doing that?

PC: Yeah, pretty well throughout their career I would go in when invited to a session, which thankfully was quite a lot. "Stairway" was quite fascinating. The first time I heard "Stairway" was when I was invited to lunch one Sunday and I showed up with my then-wife [Jenny], and it was a beautiful house he [Jimmy] had down in Sussex in the town of Plumpton. Beautiful old English house, lovely summer day. And we get there at about 12:30, and Jenny went in to see Charlotte [Martin, Page's girlfriend at the time] to see if she could help with any of the lunch preparations, and Jimmy was out on the lawn playing his guitar. I'll never forget it. He was sitting there with his back to me as I came down the lawn, and he's playing these chords. I stopped behind. These were the introduction chords to "Stairway to Heaven," and it was absolutely riveting. Without any vocal on it. It was fabulous. So that's the first time I heard that piece of music.

> **"Stairway to Heaven" will always be the most played song in the history of rock radio. Once again, it epitomized where Led Zeppelin was—breaking new ground, going to new levels—and that piece of music has stood the test of time. Will time stand up to that piece of music? is all I can say.**

and onto the floor. And a huge argument erupted, and I rather think we had to buy that painting. I think I bought it on behalf of Atlantic, if I remember correctly. I think I charged the group for it later; sorry, Jimmy, but there it is. [Laughing]

Well, we got out of there. The fact was that we paid for one painting, but I think Jimmy rearranged about four of them and the proprietor didn't notice about the

I think the first time I heard it played [by the full band]—because it's a very long time ago and I'm an old fart and sometimes my memory plays tricks—but I rather think the first time I actually heard it played live, before it came out on record, was I think the Bath Festival. I seem to remember that being the first time it was played. I mean, it stunned the audience. Everybody stopped. *What the fuck was that, that just happened?* They just didn't know what it was. And now look at it, the most played song in the history of rock radio.

DS: Some comments about "Rock and Roll"?

PC: "Rock and Roll" shows the roots of Led Zeppelin. I mean, it was a bit of fun. Let's play something that's right out of '50s rockabilly music. Let's have some fun with it. And that's what it is, but once again, it's slightly complex fun. Not many drummers can play the intro to "Rock and Roll"—they struggle through it and come in at the wrong time because, once again, even though it's reflective of something that went before, it's Led Zeppelin, and things are never quite what they seem. So that's why you're gonna see rock 'n' roll cover bands do "Rock and Roll," nine times out of ten they never do it right. They never get the introduction the way it should be. Jason Bonham, of course, nails it every time, but then he was born to it—not many of them can do it right.

DS: Some comments about "Black Dog"?

PC: "Black Dog." That's fascinating. It's the time signatures that make "Black Dog" really what it is. The way that John Bonham stays on the four on the floor going right through a very complex set of time changes that are going around the riff. Because these guys are so excellent at what they do, they could all go off on those tangents and they'd sound altogether united. That, interestingly enough, is something that the early live shows [had]— when they would do different songs in the middle of things like "Dazed and Confused" that would frequently drift off into something else, or in the middle of "Whole Lotta Love," you know, Jimmy would play a little riff and Robert would get it immediately and suddenly they're doing a John Lee Hooker song or an Eddie Cochran song or something by Cliff Richard and the Shadows. It's just amazing where they can go, and they all have this encyclopedic knowledge of music. They know where it's going, but somehow between them, they take it where Led Zeppelin would want to take it, which is a little left or right of center. That's what made it so magic. . . .

DS: How about "The Battle of Evermore"? Keep in mind that Americans have a different perspective, and there's a female vocalist on there named Sandy Denny, who is revered in England but in this country she's known as, "Well, wasn't she in Fairport Convention?" but other than that, they really know nothing. What was it that made Sandy Denny an unbelievable figure in the history of British folk, and how did she get connected with Led Zeppelin? She's the only person outside of Led Zeppelin to get credited for a backing vocal.

PC: I think she's certainly the only person to get a credit on a vocal. She was—Fairport Convention were the band to emerge from the folk scene, which was very big in England. People don't realize how big it was. In its own way, folk was as big in England as country was in America. I guess it was our version of country music,

which is why it became very important. In any town in rural England, and of course a lot of other cities, too, for that matter, there were always folk clubs, and there were jug bands and skiffle bands still playing—and still do to this day. It's a way people get into a pub or some kind of club and just sit around listening to this style of music. And Fairport Convention took it to a different level, added electric guitar and so forth to it. They became a very, very important and iconic band in their day, and Robert knew them well because Robert came from a rural town, too, so he was aware of folk music.

DS: And he was a fan of Sandy Denny's.

PC: Well, of course.

DS: When they brought you the album with no title, no name, no nothing on the cover, I understand there was some concern: how are people gonna know? Would you give us the real story behind that?

PC: [Laughing] "Some concern" is rather an English understatement of how the record company perceived of Led Zeppelin. "You mean there's no title? There's no name of the band on it? Are these people on drugs?" . . . "Occasionally, probably, but that's not the point, is it? This is what they want to do." And because I sort of have to fight those battles with the label and because—by the time the second album was up and running, I was the main conduit between the record company and the band. Not just in Europe, but period. So I was the one who had to face the people in the office and deal with the band. But somehow, Ahmet was always very supportive. I have to say, there's an English expression that it's very difficult to hunt with the hounds and run with the fox. And I was able to do that only because the members of Led Zeppelin and Peter trusted me because I was one of them, and Ahmet never asked me anything that would embarrass or break that trust. It was just a relationship that couldn't happen now. It happened then because that was Led Zeppelin and that was Peter Grant, and there was Ahmet Ertegun, who was the leader of the company and answerable to no one. So you know, that situation just couldn't happen now. Could you imagine, this— [Pauses and tries to think of an example] what's a big band right now? I don't know.

DS: AC/DC.

PC: AC/DC, there you are. They're big enough. [Under his breath] I should know; I signed them. [Loudly, interrupting himself] Oh, sorry. It's not about me, is it? [Laughs] Anyway, um, you can't imagine anyone at Sony being in that position because Sony, as a corporation, is answerable to a lot of people. You know. And if some executive somehow got close to the group, which just won't happen anymore, and he goes into [headquarters] and the president of the company says, "Well, what do the band really think about this?" and the guy says, "Sorry, I can't tell you," he'd be fired. Well, they

couldn't fire me because I was fireproof, but apart from the fact that I was the Led Zeppelin man, I'd signed some of the biggest bands that Atlantic have, so I was able to really hold my own and dictate the way things had to be. And someone had to do that because it was the only way of dealing with Led Zeppelin. They had to have an autocratic force behind them to stand up with the management of the band, which was entirely autocratic. You know, we had Ahmet there. If ever I got into a problem with any of the midlevel executives, the guys I'd count as my peers, I'd just say, "Well, look. You just speak to Ahmet. This is the way it's going to be. If you don't like it, talk to Ahmet and then just call me again. We'll finish it off." That happened a number of times. Didn't make me very popular, I have to say, but. . . .

A Houses of the Holy *button featuring the iconic Giant's Causeway imagery.*

DS: You always had your bass playing to fall on.

PC: See, I could always do that.

DS: Let's move on to *Houses of the Holy*. After the fourth album was so huge, was there any concern for you as the record label? Were you like, "What are they gonna follow it up with? What's gonna happen?" Or did you not have concerns with a band like this, that you knew that every album they did might be different but it didn't matter, it was gonna be great?

PC: By the time that *Houses of the Holy* came out, Led Zeppelin were expected to change the rules with every release. *Houses of the Holy* was no disappointment to anybody. It just moved Led Zeppelin onto the next level, where they wanted to be. It certainly didn't diminish their popularity in any way. And it became, like everything else, an important record. Obviously, . . . no Led Zeppelin album will ever catch up to the fourth album, in the same way that no AC/DC album is ever going to catch up to *Back in Black*. Every band has its pinnacle of commercial success, which is not necessarily its pinnacle of artistic success, and *Houses of the Holy* could really be that pinnacle of artistic success. That's why it sold incredibly well. . . . *Houses of the Holy* was, was—it was very well received, actually. I have to say I don't recall any critical dismissal of *Houses of the Holy*, so I think by that time in the way the group was going, people had kind of begun to have an understanding of what the group was.

DS: In England, all these bands recorded studio and live sessions specifically for BBC broadcasts. Could you explain why this was, as well as the concept of "needle time?"

PC: BBC was the only place you could get a record played. The musicians' union in England had come to some bizarre arrangement with the BBC that there is only a certain amount of hours in the day when they could play records, so there's a limit. Programming had to reflect those guidelines. So if you got a band that went into the studio and recorded a song for the BBC in a BBC studio, that didn't count as needle time. That was a BBC session where the musicians in the band got paid union rates through the union, so the union's all happy and so forth, and everybody got along quite nicely. It's just a way of getting a song played without it being played off the record.

DS: Did you attend any of the Led Zeppelin BBC sessions?

PC: Absolutely, sure, yeah. There weren't that many. I only recall two or three BBC sessions, and generally they would take place in a small studio with an audience, and you would run it just like it was a regular show. Obviously, it was kind of staid because the studio is set up like a studio and would have a small audience. But that's how they used to do that. And we did that. There weren't many in the days of Led Zeppelin, actually, but two or three, I think.

DS: Led Zeppelin's BBC recordings could be heard again with the 1997 release titled *BBC Sessions*. How do you think those recordings hold up?

PC: Well, the playing is, of course, pretty damn good. I mean, there were very few nights when Led Zeppelin were less than great. The recording, of course, was not as good as it would have been if Jimmy Page was supervising it himself and actually being in the engineering booth when it was being done, but of course he couldn't be in both places at the same time. And unlike making a record, where he could record something, go back and listen to it, and then go and do it again, you didn't have that opportunity. Having said that, the BBC engineers do know what they're doing. They got the sounds down pretty well, and I think by the time they released some of those sessions, Jimmy did have a chance to work a bit of magic on them, so they're probably a lot better than they were on the day. But I'm glad they were done because the record would not have existed otherwise.

[*Houses of the Holy*] is a brilliant album! It's different [from] the others, but once again with Led Zeppelin, they changed the rules as they go along, and they would disappoint the audience, in a way, if they did not do that.

DS: How important to the success of Led Zeppelin was the fact that Jimmy Page was also producer, which was not something that was done in those days?

PC: It was fundamental to the success of Led Zeppelin that Jimmy Page was the producer because Jimmy wrote all the songs with Robert and the other two on occasion, [and] he knew exactly what he wanted to get, and he was able to get the best out of everybody. He was a taskmaster, Jimmy Page. I mean he'd really go to the wall to get what he wanted, and he got it. In every record they made, there was a great deal of input from Jimmy that really made it all happen.

DS: As the record label, had you hoped Led Zeppelin would do a live album and film it?

PC: The era of live albums was on us in the mid-'70s, and it was something that the band were resisting and then thinking about. They'd tried—had several false starts on it, by the way. They'd recorded a couple of shows. They had a BBC-TV producer called Stanley Dorfman direct a couple of sequences. But it never really took off until the '73 tour, when they decided to really try for it. That was a bit of a nightmare for many, many reasons, and getting it done and the cost of it all and so forth. They never thought they'd get their money back on it, by the way, and neither did Atlantic. It cost so much, at the time, to do. But of course now, I think it's the biggest-selling music DVD of all time.

DS: What do you remember about the premieres of *The Song Remains the Same*?

PC: The premieres were fascinating events and fortunately I was able to coordinate both of them and they were quite interesting things to put together. We had a couple of parties in England to celebrate the release, one which we had in a set of caves, and the other we had in an abandoned building in Covent Garden. I just thought that the best place I could take this to where they wouldn't get destroyed was caves or an abandoned building. And they worked out to be very interesting

parties, and we did something quite interesting with the premiere in England. Again, it's a long time ago and it's in my dotage, but I would say that—I think we had it in about four theaters simultaneously and I worked out a way where we perfectly timed the start so that just as the credits were about to roll, the band would walk in. Everybody was seated, they would walk in, you know, go up to their seats at the back of the theater. At that point, the house lights would start dimming and they would never take their seats; they would just walk out the back so that nobody would know they weren't [staying] there, and then they would go to the next theater and that would be how we went about things.

DS: You were a key person in setting up Led Zeppelin's Swan Song record label. What changed once Swan Song existed?

PC: They wanted to have their own label to create—not so much just for Led Zeppelin but they felt that they would like to have signed some other bands and tried to do for other bands that they believed in what could be done for Led Zeppelin. I suppose it was similar to the way that, like, Frank Sinatra and friends getting the Warner–Seven Arts thing started. They wanted, like, musicians to have a label for musicians, and so we had this whole plan where we would buy this old country mansion. It was called Hammerwood Park, fondly enough. And I would run the label, and I would start getting artists together, and I did all the proposals for it and so forth.

This was one of those times when they trusted me to get all the groundwork done because they didn't want Ahmet to know they were thinking about this until they were ready to present it to him properly. And I never told him. So we got it all together, we had it all in place. And Peter took it to Ahmet, who called me—of course he obviously knew that I had been involved in setting it up, but he said, "Look. I'm your friend here. If you want to go with them, I completely understand it. But just understand what will happen if you do that. You'll be locked into this one artist for the rest of your career. And eventually something will happen that will go wrong, and you've got nowhere to go if you work for one artist."

WORLD PREMIERE

Nº   24

TUESDAY, OCTOBER 19, 1976 AT 8:30 PM

AT

CINEMA 1

60th ST. AND 3rd AVE. N.Y.C.

Proceeds for the Benefit of **SAVE THE CHILDREN FEDERATION**

ADMIT ONE   **DONATION $3.50**

A ticket for the October 19, 1976, New York premiere of The Song Remains the Same.

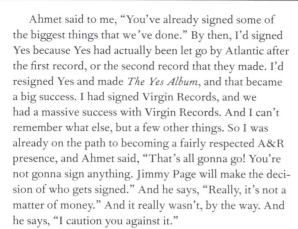

Ahmet said to me, "You've already signed some of the biggest things that we've done." By then, I'd signed Yes because Yes had actually been let go by Atlantic after the first record, or the second record that they made. I'd resigned Yes and made *The Yes Album*, and that became a big success. I had signed Virgin Records, and we had a massive success with Virgin Records. And I can't remember what else, but a few other things. So I was already on the path to becoming a fairly respected A&R presence, and Ahmet said, "That's all gonna go! You're not gonna sign anything. Jimmy Page will make the decision of who gets signed." And he says, "Really, it's not a matter of money." And it really wasn't, by the way. And he says, "I caution you against it."

And I thought about it very deeply. It was a turmoil for me because these guys were my friends, and Peter was my friend. But he—it has to be said—he was becoming difficult even for me to deal with because he had his personal demons that he was struggling with and it made communication very, very, very tough, so

PC: Yeah, because Jimmy was a very discerning A&R man. They had more than that. Bad Company was of course the biggest success. But they had Dave Edmunds, who had some major hit records. They had Maggie Bell, who never had a big record in America but who was an incredible blues singer and did pretty well in Europe. They had the Pretty Things, which almost became big again—didn't quite make it. So all the artists signings were really very good signings.

DS: What were your thoughts when you heard Led Zeppelin's first album on Swan Song, *Physical Graffiti*, was going to be a double album?

PC: For me, I really felt there was nothing Led Zeppelin could do which would not become a success. They just were so totally on the pulse of what was happening that I knew there would be things on it that would work. On any of the albums they made, that was always the case—after *Physical Graffiti* as well.

Physical Graffiti was a challenge for a number of reasons. It took them a very, very long time to record, for a start, but once again, by the time it was ready to come out, the public wanted a Led Zeppelin record, so it sold very, very well.

I decided not to do it. And then all hell broke loose. This must have been 1974. I remember it now because I was getting married in 1974, and they were all invited to the wedding. And they decided as a band, "Well, we're not gonna go." But John Paul Jones came. I mean, I must always—business has nothing to do with personal friendship—and he came along. But there was a period of business between Peter and me and the rest of—maybe all of the band, and maybe they felt that I'd let them down. In retrospect, I absolutely do not regret that decision.

DS: What were your impressions of Bad Company when Led Zeppelin first signed them to Swan Song Records?

PC: Well, Bad Company was just terrific. And to have them—I mean, my God—Mick Ralphs from Mott the Hoople and Simon Kirke from Free and Paul Rodgers from Free and Boz Burrell from King Crimson? It was once again the Jerry Wexler description of virtuosity and why it should work. That band was raw, energetic, and incredible. And off we went with Bad Company!

DS: Other than the Rolling Stones and the Beatles, there were very few artists [with their own labels] who had success of any kind. But Swan Song was the first artist label that had other bands and had any success.

DS: Forget "Stairway to Heaven" for a moment. A lot of people say "Kashmir" is the definitive example of Led Zeppelin. Do you agree?

PC: "Kashmir" has been regarded as a definitive Led Zeppelin song for all of the right reasons. It brings into play the virtuosity of every musician in it. The imagination of Jimmy and Robert and the influences they got by traveling in Morocco. It brought a lot of things together and made it into a most phenomenal piece of music, and that is probably why a lot of people regard it as probably the high point of Led Zeppelin's creativity. I still am a "Stairway to Heaven" boy personally, but you have to give it to John Paul Jones, particularly for the use of the Arabic scale of music, of the way he approached those things, and the way the guitars come through. But then we would refer to Jimmy as the "Jimmy Page army of guitars" because the overdubs were just mind-blowing in their perfection and immensity. And that's a high point.

DS: What do you recall about *Presence*?

PC: *Presence* took a long time to get together because Robert had had a very serious accident, and fortunately there's really little trace of it left now. But my God, that was bad. . . . If you ask Jimmy Page about all the things he's done, I think "Achilles Last Stand" would be one of his personal high points of recording and playing. So there were some amazing things on *Presence*. *Presence*, once again, became a very big record, as they all did, and as time goes by, everybody revisits Led Zeppelin records and everybody seems to have their favorites. *Presence* seems to be emerging slowly as an important record. I think in sales terms it's obviously way behind a lot of the others, but as people reinvestigate Led Zeppelin, that is starting to pick up as an album that deserves the interest.

DS: What is that object on the cover?

PC: If I told you, I'd have to kill you. [Laughs]

DS: The final Led Zeppelin album was *In Through the Out Door*. Obviously, nobody knew it was going to be the final album.

PC: No. On that album, John Paul Jones had really come through as a writing force and Jimmy was possibly a little less involved at that point for various reasons. But Jonesy stepped up into the breach there and created a lot of fascinating music for the band to play, and I think it's quite an important record for a lot of reasons. Of course, one of the most notable things was the packaging, where nobody could think of how to package it, and Peter Grant came out and said, "Ooh. Let's put it in a brown paper bag." So we did. [Laughs]

DS: And there were six versions of it!

PC: Oh, my God, there were six versions of it, some of which, if you smeared water on them, they would change color! Did you know that?

DS: No, I didn't.

PC: I bet they don't do that anymore, but we had it in some special ink. So now everybody out there is going to try to smear a little fingertip over the print. These people should call in and tell me if that happens! Because the ink we used was—had some chemical in it that would respond to the addition of, would you believe, saliva, and if you wet your finger and rubbed it over certain areas of the cover, color would appear. I'll bet they don't do that anymore because the cheap bastards that make it now probably won't pay for that extra-special ink. We never told anybody about that, by the way. It was just one of those Zeppelin little things that we'll do.

DS: Where were you when you heard of John Bonham's passing?

PC: I remember that day. Really, too well. I was in my office in Berners Street in London, and I got a call from one of Peter Grant's assistants down at his house. He said, "Peter wants you to come to the house. Drop everything and come immediately. He's sending a helicopter." Peter lived about 105 miles southeast of London, with roads that weren't that great, but my house was almost

halfway to his house. And I thought, well, you know, by the time I get down to Battersea—which was the closest place you could get a helicopter. . . . I drove hell for leather down there and I got there and went straight up to see Peter and he told me the news. I didn't know till I walked through the doors what had happened. It was a terrible day. Terrible day.

DS: What were your thoughts on them continuing or not continuing, and why was there that lapse in time before they made the official announcement?

PC: Well, the release that we made, I drafted that release with Peter that day. I don't remember—I thought we put that out pretty quickly, didn't we? That we could no longer continue as we are . . .

DS: It was about thirty to forty-five days after.

PC: Was it as long as that? God, I don't remember that. I mean, because that decision was made very quickly. Very quickly. So they just all thought that that was what it was.

DS: What was your involvement in the *Coda* album? Was it just a contractual obligation, something they wanted to get out?

PC: *Coda* is—no, certainly not a contractual obligation. *Coda* is a sort of a musical term that suggests finality, and it was something that they just wanted to round off everything at that time that was available to be put on a record, just to say, "That's it. That's the end of the recording time for Led Zeppelin." I had very little to do with its composition because it was totally a Jimmy Page thing. I mean, he put it all together, and out it came. It was never positioned in the minds of the band that it was gonna be a great album.

> It was to say, "Hey, that's all we've got. It's over. Please take it. Buy it if you want it. It's out there." That was the attitude of *Coda*.

DS: Was there any discussion of going on with any other drummer the way the Who did?

PC: No. There was none. None whatsoever. That was a joint decision. They talked with Peter, and they felt that would be the end of it at that point.

DS: What did you think when you saw them reunite at the Atlantic Records fortieth anniversary?

PC: I thought it was quite remarkable that Jason had stepped in the way he did. It didn't surprise me because I remember doing Knebworth [in 1979] and we were doing the sound checks there and Jimmy was messing [with] his guitar and John wanted to hear how it sounded, and everybody was on the stage milling around, and John said to Jason, who I think may have been fourteen at the time, or maybe less, actually, "Play a bit. I'm gonna go out and have a listen." So John wanders out to the front and soon there was Jason, who started playing something. I think he may have played the riff of "Trampled Under Foot," actually, and Jimmy's like, head down, starts playing the riff, you know. Robert saw all of this go on. He started singing, and Jonesy obviously saw Jason. They'd lock in and start to play. And they're blazing away. Jimmy has no clue that it's Jason Bonham on the stage behind him, by the way. You know, because Jimmy had his hair down, sweating, he's playing away and suddenly he looks up and he sees John Bonham in the field about four hundred feet away from him and he looks around and saw Jason playing. That was the first time I saw Jason play with the four guys. It was quite a moment.

DS: Since you mentioned Knebworth, could you explain what is the Knebworth Festival?

PC: Knebworth was an old English country home with a big ground on it that the owner of the place used to let out to do rock concerts. Led Zeppelin did two concerts, and I think we drew 200,000 people, something like that. It was a huge, massive event. And the audience loved it! They just loved the return of Led Zeppelin to British shores. It was remarkable.

DS: What do you remember about the Frankfurt concert toward the end of Led Zeppelin's 1980 tour?

PC: I suppose the most notable thing is that I personally remember that I played there. I played the encore. We did "Money," if I recall correctly, the old Beatles song. Packed audience, great vibe, it was [close to] the last date of the German tour before we had set up to go to America. None of us knew, of course, that it would be the last time the band played, you know, with John Bonham. Ahmet Ertegun was there; I do remember that. He came along. . . .

DS: What did you think of their appearance at Live Aid?

PC: Live Aid was an interesting experience. By then, I was managing both Jimmy and Robert. I was managing the Firm, with Jimmy and Paul Rodgers, and I was out with Robert on tour. The Live Aid thing came up, and word came—well, I think Robert was going to do it on his own at first and then I seem to remember he said, "Well, why don't you call Jimmy?" That's right, because Jimmy had played in the Honeydrippers, which Robert, Ahmet, and I produced. Jimmy played guitar on one of the tracks. I think Robert suggested that I give Jimmy a call. He said he wanted to do Live Aid as part of the Honeydrippers.

Robert had already had the call to do Live Aid. So Jimmy said, "Well, if I have to come, why don't we do it as Led Zeppelin?" So after a while, that kind of sunk in, and yeah, that's exactly what we did.

But the day of the Led Zeppelin appearance, it was not that great. I had a lot of trouble with the guy who was directing and the people who were producing Live Aid. Because in those days, Phil Collins was the hot tamale, you know, and the network—which I believe was ABC—had selected a sports director to direct it, and he had no clue. He had no clue of what was up there. I said to him, "This is Led Zeppelin! Don't you understand Led Zeppelin are gonna do Live Aid?" He said, "They're gonna do Live Aid, but they're not gonna be in the broadcast." "Are you crazy? This is the greatest rock group of all time, and you don't want them in the broadcast section?" Remember there was a whole day and only two hours got broadcast initially. So I had to fight with these people for days, and eventually Bill Graham was helping [and] we agreed that Led Zeppelin would be in the broadcast part, but of course Phil Collins was gonna play drums because by then it had become the Phil Collins show. Nothing to do with Phil Collins, by the way, who was one of the most self-effacing individuals you will ever meet. It was because ABC network people thought "Phil Collins: ratings," you know.

Phil was a great player, so they were happy to have him play drums, but already it was a mess because Phil played in London, got on the Concorde, and came here to Philadelphia, so he's already in three time zones and having to get onstage and play to 120,000 people and a big television audience. And then, of course, the actual director. And it starts being taped and the damn camera's on Phil Collins through most of the thing. So I threw a total wobbler in the truck. I got thrown out of that to find that Jimmy's guitar tech had forgotten to tune Jimmy's guitar. I mean, it was not a high point of Led Zeppelin's appearances.

DS: You were one of the promoters for Led Zeppelin's O₂ concert. Can you give us some background?

PC: The whole point behind the O₂ thing was it was a tribute to Ahmet Ertegun, who was my boss, my friend, and I wanted to put together a show for Ahmet. And I asked Robert and his manager, Bill Curbishley, who was a very dear friend of mine, and Harvey Goldsmith, the English promoter, "Could we do something? Maybe take the Albert Hall and do a tribute to Ahmet. Robert wants to do it. Let's see if we can get Eric [Clapton], all the people that loved Ahmet, to come and do something for Ahmet." And it started out beautifully. That's how it was going to be. It was going to be one band and Eric would play and Robert would sing and we'd have a few guest people. It was going to be a real heartfelt tribute really put together by two of the musicians who revered Ahmet so much and were very good friends of Ahmet Ertegun.

But from that, it grew, and Eric said, "Look, I don't mind doing this as Cream," which is something that is not easy for Eric to do. He said, "Look, I'll do one night

IT IS A GREAT LIFE THIS LIFE OF MUSIC
LED ZEPPELIN
RONNIE WOOD
BILL WYMAN'S
RHYTHM KINGS
PAUL RODGERS
PAOLO NUTINI
FOREIGNER
10TH DECEMBER 2007
O2 ARENA LONDON

AHMET ERTEGUN
TRIBUTE
1923 - 2006

as Cream." Then the other idea came up that we'd do one night of Led Zeppelin and one night of Cream. That was fantastic. We'd do that at the Albert Hall. All very heartfelt stuff, and we'd get various artists to play the first half of each of those two shows and that would be the tribute.

By then, Jimmy had another manager, Peter Mensch, great manager. He and I had a great relationship. I credit Peter with breaking AC/DC. And he did a really tremendous job for them, and I think he could have done a very good job for Jimmy, but somehow it got a little bit too big. And it was decided we were going to do it at this other arena, the O₂. At that point, Eric said, "No, I don't want to do that. I don't really want to do an arena show. I don't like arena shows with Cream. I'm not gonna do it."

Led Zeppelin by then were committed to do it. So they say, "Well, we'll do it." And we decided we were gonna have a first half of various artists who would play and the second half would be Led Zeppelin. But then the Led Zeppelin thing kind of took it over. It became a Led Zeppelin show, which it could have had the right to become because Led Zeppelin coming back after twenty-three years is just an amazing situation. But the grandeur of it all somehow tended to overtake it a little, and of course when we put the tickets on sale, we had as few as 10,000 tickets actually for sale by the end of the day because a couple of thousand went to the charity.

Because the whole thing was really a tribute to Ahmet to perpetuate something in his name, which was the Ahmet Ertegun Education Fund, which provided scholarships at major universities, and our goal was to keep something forever in Ahmet's name. . . .

Of course the thing went crazy. I mean, we had 20 million people hit the website looking for ways to buy tickets, [and it] froze the website. The website was the same website the Olympics use to sell all the tickets the

The cover of the commemorative book for the Ahmet Ertegun tribute concert, December 10, 2007.

a rock throughout the whole thing. If you look at some of the video that's out there, you see them crowded round that drum riser because Jason knew every subtlety of every Led Zeppelin song that they played, and boy did that kid rock! [Laughs] "Kid." I call him a kid because I've known him since he was two years old, but did he rise to the occasion that day! He was phenomenal.

DS: Will that performance ever be issued on DVD?

PC: Well, they've got it. It's all on multicamera, high-tech, high-def, state-of-the-art stuff. They spent a fortune getting it done, and the board of the Ahmet Ertegun Education Fund agreed it should come out, and as far as they're concerned they can do what they want with it. It's just a question of what the three guys decide.

DS: For all us regular people, what was the backstage like at the O₂ Arena?

PC: [Laughs] The backstage was extremely well policed. You know, you couldn't get in there unless you had the appropriate passes and there were certainly enough security guys to stop you, to the point of Harvey Goldsmith getting thrown out himself because he didn't have the right pass to get into the Jimmy Page area. Harvey, uh, didn't like that too much, I have to say [laughing]. There was a huge furor about that, but everybody who played there was in very good heart. Our friends from Yes, Chris Squire and Alan White, opened the show with Keith Emerson of Emerson, Lake & Palmer, and did "Fanfare for the Common Man," which was pretty neat. And of course Foreigner closed the first half and did an incredible performance of "I Want to Know What Love Is" with an eighteen-piece choir from a girls' school in Portsmouth, and that really set the tone for Led Zeppelin.

> **But my God, during that half-hour break with the sense of expectancy and anticipation from the audience, you could just feel it. I mean, it was an amazing, amazing event.**

Olympics have. At the end of the day, we actually had two million credit card registrations to buy the 10,000 tickets that we had. So it became somewhat unwieldy to put together. There were other things that could have been done better, but doing it at all was incredible and is a marvelous accolade to Jimmy, Robert, and John Paul Jones with the help of Jason to go and give their time to that incredible thing, and my God, did they rise to the occasion! It was just electrifying.

DS: What was the high point of the show for you?

PC: [Without hesitation] The moment they started. And it was just incredible. The high point, I guess, continued, and watching them relate to Jason Bonham, who was like

DS: Last question: do you think they'll tour?

PC: No. I don't think they'll tour. I do not write off the fact that they may perform again. There may be something that is close to everybody's heart that is a reason for performing again to do something very special, but I don't think they'll do what we will call a tour.

DS: Is there anything final you'd like to say?

PC: Led Zeppelin, for me, was an absolute life-changing experience. It was a hell of a roller coaster, had its enormous ups and some pretty devastating downs, but I wouldn't trade it.

Dave Lewis

A Led Zeppelin archivist, historian, and megafan, British-born Dave Lewis is editor and publisher of *Tight But Loose*, the long-running Led Zeppelin fanzine he founded in 1978. For over three decades, Lewis has chronicled Led Zeppelin in books, magazines, and on the Web. His books include *Led Zeppelin: The Final Acclaim* (1983); the exhaustive, groundbreaking *Led Zeppelin: A Celebration* (1991); the definitive log of every known Led Zeppelin gig and tour, *Led Zeppelin: The Concert File* (cowritten with Simon Pallett, 2005); a chronicle of Led Zeppelin's historic, final 1979 UK concerts at Knebworth (2009); and, most recently, *Led Zeppelin: Feather in the Wind—Over 1980* (2011), about the band's 1980 European tour.

In addition to consulting and appearing on numerous television and radio programs about the band, Lewis has contributed Led Zeppelin features to a variety of magazines, including *Classic Rock*, *Mojo*, *Q*, and *Record Collector*. Lewis conducted the final major interview given by Led Zeppelin's larger-than-life manager, Peter Grant, before his death in 1995. In this interview from March 2010, Lewis is asked about Led Zeppelin's legendary 1979 Knebworth shows.

DAVE LEWIS: They played Knebworth twice, on August 4 and 11. They'd turned it down in 1974. There was a plan for them to play then . . . but it didn't come off. But five years later [they] played to about 300,000 people in those two weekends, and it was very memorable. If you ask a lot of Led Zeppelin fans out in the UK where they saw Led Zeppelin, it tends to be at Knebworth. . . .

DENNY SOMACH: And that turned out to be the last time they ever played [in the UK].

DL: Yeah, we didn't know it at the time as we turned up to wave them off. It should've been a new beginning, but unfortunately it was the end. . . .

DS: Take me through who else played, what that was like, the vibe of the audience. Walk me through it.

DL: Sure. Well, when they announced the dates, which was end of May, I was in the middle of doing the second *Tight But Loose* magazine. This was the fanzine that I created in 1978. It went to press, and a day later they announced the Knebworth shows. It had been very much kept under wraps. And there was one TV announcement and two adverts in the weekly music press. So [it] wasn't a big thing, there was no Internet, no YouTube, no nothing. But off the back of those two adverts and that one TV announcement, they sold 100,000 tickets in about three weeks. So it was a massive event. It was a chance for people in the UK to see Led Zeppelin for the first time in four years. You know, they hadn't played [in the

A recent photograph of Dave Lewis.

UK] since the [1977] Earls Court show, so the excitement was fantastic. And for me personally, to be going to see Led Zeppelin again and to report it in the *Tight But Loose* magazine, which I was obviously going to do, was incredibly exciting. So it was a big plan really to get near the stage, we definitely wanted to do that. My friends from Bedford came with me. There was four of us that went up. . . . We left Bedford and reached the Knebworth site at seven o'clock on Thursday; this was obviously something like seventy-two hours before Led Zeppelin were going to come on stage at Knebworth on Saturday. When we got there, surprisingly, we weren't the only ones with the idea. There were lots of people camped out already to get the best vantage point. . . . About seven o'clock, we were on the Knebworth site and we were able to go down to the stage and see the setup, and John Paul Jones's piano was there, and he had Bonzo's [drum] kit. It was incredibly exciting to think that we were gonna see Led Zeppelin again in this fantastic setting—open air, 100,000 people. Incredibly exciting, so that was fantastic. The sound check was later that day and in fact, I could say I may have been responsible for making sure the sound check got off on time. Because around five o'clock we were at the top of the Knebworth house, just where the arena is, and this Cherokee Jeep came in and swung round. And I looked over and Robert Plant was in the driver's seat with a couple of the load-in guys, and he came over, wound down the screen, and said, "Mate, where's the stage?" And I thought, "Oh, I think I'll tell him where the stage is." And so we showed him where it was, and they actually recognized me from when I went to see them fly out in 1977, [when] I went to Heathrow airport. So, fantastic that we'd already met Robert. He looked great, he looked fantastic. The sound check went ahead. Unfortunately, they cleared everyone out of the arena, so we only heard it outside. We couldn't see it, but we could hear it, and we knew what we were in for. The next day was an incredible day.

bit of convention, it was pretty quaint—a folk outfit, folk-rock. Commander Cody, who may have gone down in the U.S. but didn't quite come over the same way in a quaint English field. Todd Rundgren was okay, but everyone was here for Zeppelin. . . . At about eight o'clock, the stage was cleared, but there was another hour wait. And again, the tension was incredible. You just knew. I could see Peter Grant walking on the stage; you know, I think he wanted to make sure everything was absolutely perfect. It was incredibly exciting. What we didn't know as well was quite what the presentation was gonna be—we didn't know what they were gonna look like, you know; obviously punk rock had kicked in and were they gonna look contemporary? Was Jimmy gonna have his dragon suit? Had things moved on? Where did Led Zeppelin fit into all this now? It was a lot of questions being asked, they had a lot to lose that day, and we didn't really know what it was gonna be like other than the stage was huge. We soon found out because about 9:40, the music faded, the lights came onto the stage, it went dark, and all you could see was silhouettes. And then the first chord of "The Song Remains the Same" blared out from Jimmy, and the moment he played that chord, the screen at the back unfolded and a green light cut across to show a vivid image of Led Zeppelin behind us, on stage in total sync video, which had never been done, certainly not to that extent in the whole of the UK at any point. It was incredibly exciting. So for the next two and a half, maybe three hours, we were in Zeppelin heaven. The set list was great. They were a bit rusty, they were nervous, you know they were gonna be, but I think most of the occasion was something unforgettable for everyone that was there and I don't think there ever was such an emotional Led Zeppelin gig because they did have a lot to lose. And I think the fact that it had gone so well, I think it was a big relief amongst all of them, particularly Robert, and it was incredible. And there were some very moving moments during the show—

> **You had thousands of people coming on this site. . . . It was like being on bloody Planet Zeppelin. It was a unique atmosphere.**

So all that went on; obviously we wanted to be near the fun, so we queued by the gates, this was on the Friday night. Now, another thing happened: about three o'clock in the morning, somehow the gates were pushed down and we all had to run through, and it was quite a funny crush, actually, looking back, and it's a surprise nobody got injured. We all had to run through to the arena and try and get the best place we could. We did—we were right in the front, you couldn't have been nearer, and then there was the twelve-hour wait. . . . It was a long day. I have to say the support acts weren't very good. I think it was personally done to make sure no one outsung Zeppelin, not that they were going to. But we had a fair

none more so than at the end, when they went on for the encore, the crowd spontaneously began singing what is one of the well-known soccer anthems here, "You Never Walk Alone." Robert came back on and began singing it and then Bonzo came in. It was a very emotional moment. I think they knew the crowd was still with them and there was still a whole lot of good days ahead for Led Zeppelin. And when we came away, no one could have thought this was the last time. I mean, they did come back the second week [but] the emotion wasn't quite the same. They played very well, but again it was very exciting to see Led Zeppelin again on stage. And you just felt that they had new places to go, and it did feel like a new beginning. They had a new album coming out: *In Through the Out Door*. And in fact one of the outstanding performances in the day, "In the Evening," was an unheard track, it was from the new album. So it did feel like they were new days for Zeppelin and just spurred everybody on and it should've been a new beginning, but unfortunately we were witnessing the end, but it was a very exciting and emotional end. . . .

DS: The second weekend, was it the same set of support acts?

DL: The second week we had New Barbarians, which was Ronnie Wood and Keith Richards, which was an added attraction, I think, to help sell the second week. . . . That was the only change from the previous week. And then Zeppelin came on but it was pretty much delayed. In fact they got fined for that show; Freddy Bannister got fined because he overran into, like, one o'clock in the morning. But another great show, and again it was just this sense of there's more to come. There was a definite sense that this was a new beginning. The press reaction was mixed, as it always is, but again Led Zeppelin didn't play for critics, they played for the fans, and certainly over those two weeks they played for the fans in such a way that I think that everyone that went away from that gig felt that there was more to come for Zeppelin. And they more than lived up to their reputation, so great days, you know, 1979, the whole summer, it was one of the last really great British rock festivals of that era, and very innocent times. . . . And I think Peter Grant was very keen, always, to present Led Zeppelin in the best light. One of the things he said to me once was, "Led Zeppelin don't play concerts, Led Zeppelin plays events." And I think Knebworth was one of the best events they ever played.

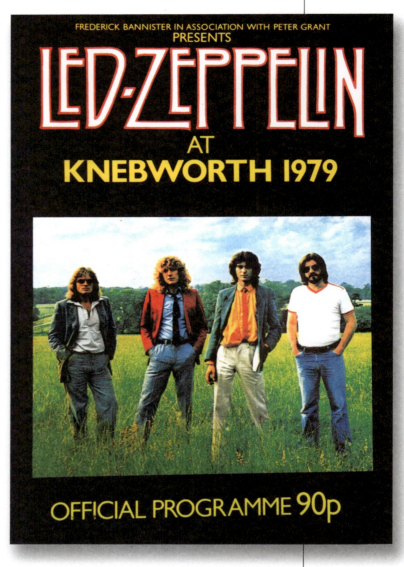

FREDERICK BANNISTER IN ASSOCIATION WITH PETER GRANT PRESENTS

LED-ZEPPELIN

AT KNEBWORTH 1979

OFFICIAL PROGRAMME 90p

> **I canvassed lots of fans to give me their memories, and their memories were real rites of passage—you know, their mum and dad letting them go to a gig for the first time. . . . It was very innocent. You felt you belonged to something. And I think Led Zeppelin was always like that. There was a massive relationship between their fans and the band.**

DS: Peter Grant: was he the fifth member of Led Zeppelin?

DL: Peter Grant was undoubtedly the fifth member. Jimmy Page is Led Zeppelin's pioneer because he brought the band together. It is his band, it was his band, it was his concept, out of the Yardbirds, to have this light-and-shade band in a four-piece way with lots of chemistry between the musicians, which, luckily, they got. But the business side of it, the strategic side of it, was definitely Peter Grant. It could not have happened in the way it happened. I think had there not had been a Peter Grant, this band of musicians who was called Led Zeppelin would have been big but they would never have been

on the scale it was. He set the timing of what they should do, his connections, particularly in America, with the U.S. college circuit . . . and the stadiums. He was a pioneer of that. And an evening with Led Zeppelin, which is a slogan that he wanted to present the band in and did so from the second and third tours, this thing where there wouldn't be a support act, it was all the one act, that was unheard of at the time. There was always a bill of two or three acts. It was just the way it was done. His relationships with [promoter] Frank Barsalona, with people like that, Bill Graham, forged Led Zeppelin into the concerts of the stratosphere. It became a word-of-mouth thing that you had to see Led Zeppelin. . . . Every time they went back to America there was bigger demand, because

something had happened. You know, the way the album releases were planned, not that it was like a military operation. The good thing about Peter Grant—again and again it is something he told me when I interviewed him—was that as far as he was concerned the music was them; he never ever got involved in that side of it. He was often in the studio to see how it was going, but that was for Jimmy, Robert, John Paul Jones, and Bonzo to sort. His was the strategic planning of what would happen and where. . . It was a lot of creating the myth that they didn't play TV, that they didn't talk to the press. . . . He knew that that guided the mystique, no doubt about it. He wanted to elevate Led Zeppelin to a place far beyond any other band. I mean, again, I think it's something that Robert Plant said once: "It's not just a case of the fact that we think we're the number one band. It's how far behind whoever is number two is behind us." They had that arrogance and self-belief, and I think a lot of that came from knowing that Peter Grant would take care of things. And I would mention [road manager] Richard Cole as well—very crucial in that operation. As Rich Cole said to me a couple of months ago, "It was six of everything: it was six limousines, it was six bands of groupies, whatever." It was a very insular operation. . . . They were like a band of Gypsies, and often it was just them against the world. And they often felt like that, particularly with the critical reaction they got. But at the end of the day, when they played to the fans, that was the reaction that made them as big as they were.

DS: Why was it that the new album wasn't rushed out to coincide with Knebworth? Wouldn't that have made sense? Or was that just typical record company politics?

DL: It certainly would've made sense. But I have to say, in a rare mistiming, the sleeve design. . . . In this day and age, that would be seen as commercial suicide. In Led Zeppelin's era, it didn't really matter—you know, it didn't really matter that we didn't get it at Knebworth because the next week when it came out, it came out on the twentieth, we all went out to buy it. It really didn't matter. And in the States it was the same. So I think that, for once, I think that some of the sort of logistics got the better of them, but it didn't really matter in the end.

DS: Okay. I want to talk to you about the evolution, first of all—this is not your first book, correct?

DL: Indeed not, there's been several books. . . . So I've been busy, you know, I've always wanted to chronicle Led Zeppelin in the best way I can. And then the Knebworth book was published by myself last year, and I got a plans ahead to do a book on their final tour of Europe. . . . [Note: That book was published in 2011.]

DS: How's that coming?

DL: Yeah, yeah, that's moving a lot. . . . I was very lucky to have attended five shows of that [European tour]; I had massive stage access. And it's a tour, really, that is a bit of a lost tour for Led Zeppelin, because it was a very back-to-basics tour. It was a tour that was done to get them back to the people after Knebworth, you know, it was the old question: what to do next? And I think Peter Grant found out they needed to regain contact with their audience and it got very big. And they wanted to go back to America—Robert was pretty tentative on that after some of the tragedies that happened before. And I think Europe was a testing ground to see if they could still do it in a smaller way—you know, cut the light show, cut the set list. It very much felt like a rejuvenation on a lot of those gigs, and I think they would have gone to America with renewed vigor, I think they really would have taken that. So—and because there was hardly any press coverage of that tour—I call it the lost Led Zeppelin tour, and I think people would be very interested to know exactly what happened. There were fourteen shows across Europe during that summer, and I'm very keen to chronicle those and get viewpoints from people who were there and since I was lucky to be there—so it's another string to the bow, the Led Zeppelin story. . . .

I wrote *The Complete Guide to the Music of Led Zeppelin* a few years ago, and it was done solely to really encompass all of the musical aspects of the band in a track-by-track format, which really gave people insight to the songs, every song that they recorded. And I was very pleased to do this because I think it really appealed to not only older Led Zeppelin fans, but newer fans who didn't really know much about the band that were just coming to them new, because that's something that certainly has been apparent in the last couple of decades. So it encompasses every fact that you're gonna need to know about those tracks, and everything that went into making those tracks what they are today, and those albums what they are today. So it's like a summary of everything that Led Zeppelin were able to achieve musically from '68 to 1980.

DS: If you don't mind, I'd like to mention just some random songs, and you say, "This is what blah blah blah . . . ." Let's start with "Black Mountain Side."

DL: "Black Mountain Side" is based on Bert Jansch's "Black Water Side," which came out in the '60s. Jimmy was a great advocate of playing folk sort of guitar, and sort of folk tunings with the guitar. And I know he saw Bert Jansch and the folk bands during the '60s and another guitarist, John Renbourn, so those songs had gone through the passage of time, I think. And when it came to doing *Led Zep I,* I think he was keen to incorporate instrumental work very much in the light-and-shade sort of strategy that he wanted for the band. And I think "Black Mountain Side" was just the right track to put in the middle of side two, before "Communication Breakdown"—again, typical Jimmy timing. There's been criticism, of course; it wasn't actually his track and his composition, but he will say it was street music, it came through the times. And plenty of other folk artists have certainly covered it, but as an example of his guitar picking, his guitar tuning, in a folk medium, you know, it's a masterpiece.

The cover of the program booklet for the two Led Zeppelin concerts held at Knebworth House in Hertfordshire, England, on August 4 and 11, 1979.

DS: It really was an extension of "White Summer." . . .

DL: Yeah, "Black Mountain Side" in a live setting was incorporated with "White Summer" and "White Summer" was a guitar piece that [Page] recorded with the Yardbirds on the last Yardbirds album, *Little Games*. But when he took it out with Zeppelin he was able to bring elements of the "White Summer" track into "Black Mountain Side" and vice versa, so it became a long, rambling, onstage sort of epic, which was very much a centerpiece of the early Led Zeppelin shows—and a demonstration obviously for Jimmy to really show his prowess. . . . On the album version, all you're hearing is "Black Mountain Side." There's no elements of "White Summer" in that. It only became part of that when they played it live. And the best version of that is probably on the BBC's album, which was recorded in 1969, which was a really fantastic version.

DS: Talk to me about "Ramble On."

DL: "Ramble On" is a centerpiece of *Led Zep II*. There are many facets of that track which make it so outstanding—there are two exemplary guitar solos, not just one. You see Jimmy Page going out on a tangent in between the verse and chorus, and both of them are just magnificent. The drumming from Bonzo is very clever; it's just a tom-tom drum that prevails all the way through the track. You then got the Tolkien-influenced lyrics of Robert Plant, and you've got some amazing bass playing from John Paul Jones.

If there's ever a track that shows the chemistry of what Led Zeppelin is about, then "Ramble On" is it.

DS: The third album, which is probably the most misunderstood—I'll take you through a couple of these. Start with "Friends."

DL: . . . John Paul Jones in the '60s was very much a session arranger, and worked with a lot of string orchestras. And I think he wanted to bring that swirling sound to that track. Acoustically, it's obviously very much based on some of the tunings that we talked about in the folk idiom. And then, the very positive vocals and vocal feel that Robert Plant's got on it. There's an Eastern influence as well coming in there—I think it was the first of the Eastern influences coming in. In fact, it's quite well known that a year later, when they're in Bombay, or a couple of years later, in 1972, they recorded a version with a Bombay orchestra. So I think you're getting there the esoteric

Zeppelin—the "we're not just about Marshall amplifiers, we can do very different things." Yes, it's a bit misunderstood, or was at the time, but what people have to quickly learn about is that Led Zeppelin wasn't going to be one dimension. This was gonna be many colors of the musical spectrum, and Led Zeppelin within a hard rock format could go into blues to rock to Eastern to acoustic to loud to soft in a way that no other band could.

DS: "Celebration Day."

DL: "Celebration Day" is a story of being in New York and on the road and the fast pace of New York and just what they were seeing when they were going through this incredible touring period where they toured the States relentlessly in those first two years, and a lot of those images I think came out into the lyrics and it's matched with a very forceful and dominant drum sound and rhythm section from Jones and Bonzo. It's got that amazing intro, which is part of the fact that the track went wrong in the studio. When they came to do the intro and play it back, part of the tape was lost, so they had to loop it in from "Friends" and you get that revolving sound that comes in, which again I think shows what a master craftsman Page was in the studio. And he often sort of stumbled on techniques like this and part of the track going wrong, and [engineer] Eddie Kramer—who actually didn't work on the album—said something to me recently: "Sometimes it was best to leave the mistakes in," and I think Jimmy was always good at that and some of those off-cut things you hear before the track all added to the atmosphere of being in there in the studio with Led Zeppelin. I think "Celebration Day" is a very punchy, forceful rocker that showed that as much as the acoustic side was gonna come through, they could still rock with the best of them when they wanted to.

DS: "Out on the Tiles."

DL: "Out on the Tiles" was a phrase that Bonzo used often. One of the things that's often missed with Zeppelin is the camaraderie and humor they had, it often gets missed in the sex, drugs, and rock and roll. They had a great time together, and there was a lot of English banter, and "Out on the Tiles" was an English expression for "Let's go out to have a drink and have a good time." And it was used as the title on a track that is very much Bonzo-led—he's got the credit on it. And his drumming on that is absolutely amazing. It was one of those great-to-be-alive sounds. They didn't play it live that often, surprisingly; they did it a few times during 1970. And it's got that long fade-out solo from Jimmy. . . . Playing it now, it just makes you feel good.

DS: The next song I want you to give me a little bit about is "Hats off to Harper."

DL: "Hats off to Harper"—to Roy Harper. Roy Harper was an English folksinger who had carved a real strong reputation with a series of his albums in the late '60s,

early '70s. I think Jimmy first saw him at the Bath Festival in '69, I believe. And he was a big admirer. And they began to seek each other out and create a bit of a rapport. Robert was also a big advocator of his work. And they just liked the fact . . . that Roy Harper just got out there and played his songs and wasn't bowing to any commercial possibilities. . . . The track itself is just a bottleneck blues, it's not actually in the vein of what Roy Harper did, it was another "in" joke. . . . I can almost imagine how they were doing this bottleneck blues and it was just a nice way to end the album. And then someone would have shouted out "Hats off, what about Harper?" . . . The people they liked became very much a part of their world, and there were people like [Scottish blues-rock singer] Maggie Bell and a few others. But Roy Harper was always essential to their influence. They, I think, really wanted to pay some homage to him, and they did in that track.

DS: Talk to me about "The Battle of Evermore." I want you to explain to the American audience why Sandy Denny is so revered. We only know her as the woman who fronted Fairport Convention, but she was really revered in the UK and there are tributes to her.

DL: Well, "The Battle of Evermore," when Robert Plant wrote it, he was trying to hop back I think to the medieval wars and the town criers that used to be around and tell people the news. And it's like he's telling a message from the battlements and what's gone on and he felt he needed a foil to tell that tale. So as much as he was going to be the vocalist, there had to be someone almost answering part of the lyrics, so I think there was only one person in England, a female singer, that was gonna take that gig and that was Sandy Denny. The reason Sandy Denny was so revered, and still is, is she had the sweetest voice and could sing over a melody with such ease and contentment, and also such power. And Fairport Convention . . . were part of the Zeppelin world. Their paths crossed quite a lot, particularly when they were touring. And I think there was a sense of camaraderie with those players, so Sandy was asked to do it and I remember one of the quotes she said about the session was that by the end of it, she was totally breathless trying to keep up with Robert. It's an incredibly powerful performance, but I think Sandy Denny plays such a key role in that and there was no one else that could've done that at that time in the studio the way it was done. You hear it now and it's got a whole texture to itself; I mean, it sort of jumps out on that album as being something extremely special. It's almost hallowed ground. It has been played live since, it's a track that Robert has got a lot of affection for. In '77 they did it live and John Paul Jones took the vocals, and he always told me that if there was a job to be done musically and no one else would take the gig, he would always get the gig. So who was gonna sing? Oh, Jonesy will do it. But since then, Robert sang it with Alison Krauss and he did it also at the Fairport's Cropredy Convention festival, which Fairport Convention would hold every year, a couple of years ago.

So I think he's got great affection for the track, great affection for Sandy Denny, she was a very special vocalist. And I think again it was the sweetness of tone that she was able to bring that made it so special.

DS: "No Quarter."

DL: "No Quarter" was, I think, the beginning of the ethereal Zeppelin moving into very different territory. Based on a very simple piano riff that became a synthesized piano riff. It was a track that kicked around for a while. It started in '71 for the fourth album, which was at a faster arrangement. It was then slowed down, and it was kinda Olympic in . . . the spring of '72. What you've got there is a very ethereal, searching journey song, as Robert Plant used to introduce it—it was about an endless journey. And the texture to that track is quite unique. . . . I can remember when it was aired on the *Old Grey Whistle Test*, a TV program we had in England in the '70s. Led Zeppelin didn't appear on television, but they allowed this track to go out cut to a piece of very mysterious film, and the impact of it was quite striking. . . .

DS: I want to ask you about "In My Time of Dying."

DL: "In My Time of Dying"—I think Robert would've heard that track, he was a great advocator again of Bob Dylan's early work, particularly the folk albums. The first three albums. . . . [Robert] was able to combine [the lyrics] with what he would call a chanting song, a sort of a blues song of these guys that would be out in the field . . . and it was very much a workout song. And what you got in the middle of it all is Jimmy playing this incredible bottleneck solo. And the drum sound, I would say, is probably the best-recorded drum sound of any Led Zeppelin track. When Bonzo first comes in, in that first couple of minutes it's like bringing the house down. And I think all those blues elements Led Zeppelin were very good at doing came out in that track. And it's an eleven-minute marathon. When I first heard it on that album it left me completely breathless, and I think it probably does still to any listener. It's Led Zeppelin pushing their creative talents to the absolute limit. It reaches a zenith at the end, where you've got this piece where Robert's chanting, Jimmy's going crazy on the bottleneck, Jonesy's in there, Bonzo's in there; again, it was Led Zeppelin in their world and their world of blues. It was a blues manifestation that I think, again, only they could have produced.

DS: "Achilles Last Stand."

DL: "Achilles Last Stand," possibly their finest creation for many reasons. When Led Zeppelin recorded the *Presence* album, their backs were against a wall. Robert Plant had a car accident in Greece, all the time plans were curtailed; everything about their world was suddenly stopped. What they did was to go into Musicland Studios in Munich and create an album very quickly, the fastest album they'd done since the first album. And all the adversity was channeled into making this incredible album very quickly. I think it's a very underrated Led Zeppelin album. It's only a basic guitars-, drums-, bass-formatted album—there's none of the experimentation that one would've expected. But because of that, it's so forceful. And there's no finer example than "Achilles Last Stand," which is the opening track. It's spiritually and lyrically . . . out there, getting Robert searching for the answers "Where the mighty arms of Atlas hold the heavens from the earth." Within that, you've got Jimmy Page crazing up what can only be described as a landscape of guitar orchestration. It's one of John Bonham's finest performances; John Paul Jones is in there with the chugging bass line. For me, again, it's Led Zeppelin pushing themselves far beyond what anyone could've expected. It's a ten-minute marathon and by the end of it, again, they've taken you on a journey.

there was a lot of questioning of what Led Zeppelin was all about from Robert, I think, particularly towards the end. . . . And I think, in the latter era, it's a bit underrated, I think it's a track that people need to go back to because I think it was missed a bit at the time. You know . . . it's a bit long [10:52]. It's much more than that. . . . "Carouselambra" has got a lot to offer and was an indication of two things. One, John Paul Jones's pivotal role within the band, and also the fact that they had new ground to take and new ground to go through in the studio.

DS: And finally, this track—no one knows where it fits—I hope you'll explain it to us. "Hey Hey What Can I Do."

DL: "Hey Hey What Can I Do" is a very interesting track because it was only released on the B side of "Immigrant Song" in the U.S. and then it came out on a sample album, *New Age of Atlantic*, here and I think in the States.

And Led Zeppelin were great at taking their listeners onto journeys and, again, I think ["Achilles Last Stand"] is one of the finest journeys that they've ever taken their audience on. Even today it stands as one of their finest creations.

DS: "Carouselambra."

DL: I think "Carouselambra" was an attempt in 1978, when it was first put together, to capture the grandeurs of Led Zeppelin, as I would call it. Another epic, long, rambling track. What's great about it is that it's led by—as much as the *In Through the Out Door* album—it's led by John Paul Jones. He was completely relentless in coming up [with] ideas for that album. He had just acquired a new keyboard setup called a GX-1. Stevie Wonder had one, I think, and he was one of the early people that got this synthesized sort of keyboard setup. And within that, that riff in "Carouselambra" became very prominent, and when they first worked on it in 1978 at rehearsal at the [legendary rehearsal studio] Clearwell Castle, it was already beginning to sort of develop into a lengthy track. When they got to Polar Studios [in Stockholm, Sweden,] the following year, or later that year, they were able to extend it in such a way that, again, I think was a throwback to the "Achilles" tempo and the "Achilles" sort of arrangements. Jimmy's in there as well, and it's significant that Jimmy plays a double-neck on that track, one of the very few tracks that he plays it. You can hear it in the slowed-down piece. And at the end he was going into different territories and I think it was indicating that there was new work for Zeppelin, there was new places to go. It was a track that, again, lyrically, Robert has got this searching theme. He said it's about different events that were going on at the time, and there were lots of tragedies going on around them, and

What I like about it is it's a semiacoustic groove, it's almost both sides of Led Zeppelin, and is very much born of the Led Zeppelin–Free era. It was cut at the same time. It's one of the first examples of, I think, Jimmy playing mandolin on that. And it's just a warm, semiacoustic groove, probably unlike anything else they did at the time, very commercial, would've made a great A side, in fact, I think, and could've been a top-forty hit. I think there's a lot of warmth in that track still, particularly amongst Page and Plant. It was a number that they played live in 1995, when they got back together for the Unledded tour, and it was a crowd pleaser. It's one of those good-time sing-along numbers that, again, just made you feel good. And there was—as much as they were many things, Led Zeppelin could be the ultimate feel-good band, and I think "Hey Hey What Can I Do" is a great example of that.

DS: What did you make of *The Song Remains the Same* as far as the movie, and how do you think it relates?

DL: Well, it's much maligned, as some folks would say. Again, you gotta go back to an era where I was a very naive Led Zeppelin fan. . . . When I read about that there was going to be this fantasy sequence and Robert was gonna be King Arthur and Jimmy was gonna climb the mountain . . . and John Paul Jones was gonna be Phantom of the Opera and Bonzo was gonna get out on the drag circuit and do what he does best, I thought it

was fantastic. I thought, oh, God, this is going to really mirror offstage what they do. And also, I think, everybody wanted to see Led Zeppelin live, everybody wanted to see what this was all about because there'd been so little footage. You know, there'd been the Danish TV, and a couple of other things, [but] at the time none of that had been seen. And I can vividly remember again the clip that was shown on the *Old Grey Whistle Test* of "Black Dog." And it was just amazing to be watching them in action. Transfer that to the big screen. I went to the premiere, I went to the first three nights, and saw the film over thirty times in the cinema. I couldn't stop going 'cause it was the only chance to see Led Zeppelin live at the time because they weren't touring. It was the next best thing. In hindsight, yes, it's cheesy, yes, obviously, [it's] something like [what] *Spinal Tap* has sent up admirably, but what you got there is some fantastic live footage still. Not the best footage, I think there's better—I think the 2003 DVD really demonstrated that with Earls Court footage and certainly the Knebworth footage. But it's a time where—I think Jimmy once summed it up: "It was where we ended our sets with 'Whole Lotta Love.'" And that it's a quaint period, where the '73 tour was getting big-time for Zeppelin, and you've got the [hotel vault] robbery involved in there. And yes, some of the fantasy sequences are a bit "quaint," is the word I'd use. I think one of the things—and you can laugh at it now, and I'm sure they do as well—and when it came out, again, on DVD a couple of years ago, it was still fantastic to watch. It's that amazing scene where you see John Paul Jones at his house and his wife hands him a telegram from Peter Grant and he goes, "Tour dates? This is tomorrow!" Now, Peter Grant was the most strategic person ever to organize a rock band, so to send a telegram saying to his band member "You got some gigs tomorrow" is laughable and I love the cheesiness of it. But the fact is, it stands up, you know, it's still seen a lot on late-night movie shows and it's still a great way of seeing a lot of good Led Zeppelin. It's not the best footage, but at the time it's what we had. And you have to remember, if there wasn't anything else, we took whatever it was and bowed down in front of it. I mean, it got slaughtered in the press. . . . In hindsight, overlong, coulda done with some good editing, but still some fantastic pieces in it. I will stand by it.

DS: Now, give me the background on *Tight But Loose*.

DL: Okay. Led Zeppelin came into my world in 1969. I was a young kid. I loved the Beatles and the Stones; the Who; I liked the Hollies, I liked the Dave Clark Five. I listened to the weekly pop show we used to have on the radio in England called *Pick of the Pops*. Alan Freeman was the DJ. And one afternoon he played a track called "Whole Lotta Love" by Led Zeppelin. My world was never the same after that. I wanted to know everything about this group: I wanted to know where they were, what they were doing, what they looked like. I wanted to know what their albums sounded like. I very quickly did,

and it quickly became a way of life for me. I was lucky enough to see them in 1979 at the Empire Pool at Wembley, and again at the Ally Pally [Alexandra Palace in London] in 1972. As I got older, it got to a point that if Led Zeppelin were going to be playing in England, I was gonna be there. When they played Earls Court I went to all five shows. Incredibly, I got backstage on the last night and I got to meet all of them. And it was the beginning of a period where I really wanted to extend my enthusiasm for them and channel it in some way. Now, Led Zeppelin didn't do fan clubs—that was for the Osmonds or David Cassidy—but I felt they needed a platform of communication between their fans. And a couple of years later, I did a piece for *Sounds* magazine, and out of that I decided to do a fanzine, ironically, that was born out of some of the ideas that some of the punk rock bands had got, where they'd just done do-it-yourself fanzines, you didn't even have to print it properly, you could handwrite it, which is exactly what I did. I called it *Tight But Loose*, after a phrase used to describe the band by both Jimmy and Robert in 1977. I began it in 1978; handwrote the first one, kicked it off, had a really good relationship with the record company. Peter Grant also saw it had good intentions. I guess I was just in the right place at the right time. I mean, I was a fan, and suddenly I was at the side of the stage, watching them in Europe, in Munich, and Cologne. Very exciting, incredible days. The untimely death of John Bonham obviously brought that era to a close, [but] didn't stop me writing about the band for the next ten years, and then I revived the magazine in 1991.

DS: I hear that when the band became aware of the magazine they were excited.

DL: With the *Tight But Loose* magazine, as it grew and they got to see it, there was a good rapport . . . it got to a point where I would take the issues into Swan Song and they would be passed around and I would get feedback. And I remember one issue Jimmy said, "Why are there more pictures of Robert in it than me?" It was a fantastic way of becoming, like, almost part of their world almost by accident. But I think the good thing about it was they saw the intentions were good; they had a very rocky relationship with the press, and I think they found it was quite a quaint way of connecting with their audience. And they allowed me good access to do that . . . lots of information came directly from the source. I particularly remember John Bonham saying to me on the last show of [the Europe] tour when I was in Munich with them, saying to me, "Give me a call in the summer, I'll tell you what we're up to, we're looking to go to the States." You know, it was that sort of relationship, which I was very lucky to forge. And indeed I did call him in that summer, and he told me excitedly that they were going to go to America in October, and that's the sort of thing that I was able to use in the magazine exclusively.

I can remember a very memorable experience and it's one that I hold very dear. On September 18, a week before John Bonham's death, I went into the Swan Song

MEL BUSH in association with PETER GRANT

presents

LED ZEPPELIN

EARL'S COURT 75

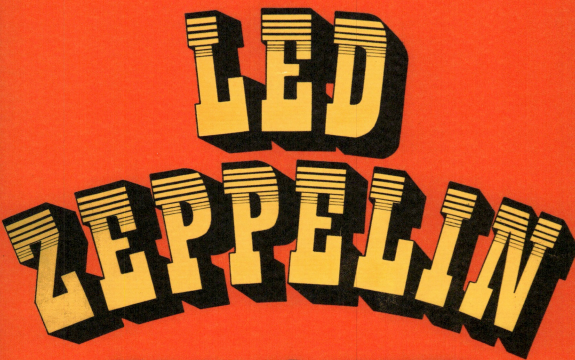

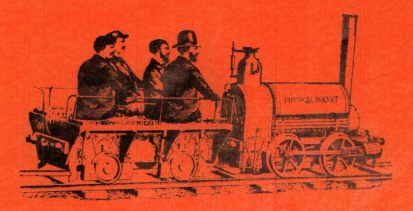

OFFICIAL PROGRAMME

office and Jimmy Page was in there and he was conducting some business about the tour. And I was allowed to go and see him in an upstairs office that was sort of off-limits for most people; I was allowed to go in and he was looking at a cut-down model of the PA and the stage they were gonna use in the upcoming U.S. tour, and he showed me where the light show was gonna be. And it was an incredibly intimate conversation we had, and he told me how he felt that Led Zeppelin still had so much more to do, and I was able to use all this. . . . It was very ironic that the issue that I put together the following week had all this information in it, exclusive information, just as the news came through that unfortunately John Bonham had passed away and the Led Zeppelin era was drawing to an end and indeed came to an end the moment John Bonham passed away. So that sort of relationship, I think, made *Tight But Loose* a very special magazine, and the issue that came out afterwards, again, was a tribute to that. And all these years later, I think I'm still able to mirror that enthusiasm for their music and to share with like-minded people that enthusiasm. People love reading and finding out about this world of Led Zeppelin and I've been extremely privileged to be in the center of that for many, many years. . . .

The cover of the program booklet for the Led Zeppelin concerts at Earls Court Arena in West London, May 17–24, 1975.

anniversary concert in] '88. I don't think anybody could've foreseen how it exceeded the expectations of anybody and everybody. Certainly myself. Several reasons for that. They looked right: I've always said, when they looked right and they felt right, it worked. And I think if you looked back to Live Aid and the Atlantic '88, it didn't look right. It did look right that day [at the O₂ Arena]—they didn't look like old guys trying to relive former glories. They played on a massive stage. I've always said Led Zeppelin worked better on a massive stage. . . . The backdrop production was unbelievably clever; if you look back to the way they used the backdrop at Knebworth, it was an evolution of that. . . . The set list was just perfect—nothing was overplayed, nothing was overdone. The fact that they could do a track like "For Your Life," never ever played live by Led Zeppelin, and just send it into the stratosphere, was just so unbelievably admirable. The fact that they could play "Stairway to Heaven" halfway through the set, and it did not become this millstone around their neck, but become just perfect and just a perfect sort of delivery, and as Robert said afterwards, "Amen, we did it." Well, they did do it. What they did at the O₂, they could come away with a happy ending. And Led Zeppelin, up until that day, didn't have a happy

It's a very special bond, I think, between the fans, the band, and myself, and it's something that I'm extremely proud of and . . . when I was lucky to have access to them, I'll never forget their sort of generosity. . . .

DS: Go back to the [2007 Ahmet Ertegun tribute concert at the] O₂ Arena.

DL: The O₂ was an incredibly exciting occasion. I mean, here we were seeing Led Zeppelin again. You know, the buildup to it was incredible, I was at the press conference when it was announced in September, when Harvey Goldsmith said Led Zeppelin were gonna be back doing a full set at the O₂. . . . But then you get to the day and you think: exactly what are we gonna get? I thought it would be good; I thought it would be better than Live Aid; I thought it would be better than Atlantic [Records' fortieth

ending. Whatever happens next, and, you know, we could say it's a shame that they didn't go on further and do a few more shows—maybe there will be some shows one day. There'll never be a show like the O₂, not least of which because it brought people from all over the world, from thirty different countries, who had this massive, massive interest in Zeppelin and this massive bond. It was like being on Planet Zeppelin . . . and I met some amazing people that weekend. And all of us went away knowing that Led Zeppelin, in 2007, still meant as much as it did in 1969. And it was an incredible last performance. And if it is the last performance, it's a happy ending.

Ron Nevison

OVER THE COURSE OF HIS ALMOST FOUR-DECADE CAREER, MULTIPLATINUM RECORD PRODUCER AND ENGINEER RON NEVISON HAS WORKED WITH LED ZEPPELIN, THE WHO, THE ROLLING STONES, MEAT LOAF, BAD COMPANY, OZZY OSBOURNE, JEFFERSON STARSHIP, KISS, GRAND FUNK RAILROAD, HEART, THIN LIZZY, CHICAGO, AND MANY MORE OF ROCK'S BEST-KNOWN ACTS. IN THE 1980S, NEVISON WAS ONE OF THE TOP PRODUCERS WORKING WITH VETERAN ROCK ACTS. AS THIS INTERVIEW—CONDUCTED IN LOS ANGELES IN SPRING 2009—KICKS OFF, NEVISON IS ASKED HOW HE GOT INTO THE BUSINESS.

RON NEVISON: I started working for the Festival Group [a company that specialized in sound reinforcement for rock concerts and festivals], learning the trade. . . . I started out just setting up the sound systems, worked into a monitor mixer, and then after a couple of years I was doing major acts, working [the] front-of-house sound mixer, [for bands] including Derek and the Dominos and Jefferson Airplane. In fact, I was at Woodstock with the Jefferson Airplane.

Somewhere along the line, I was doing a tour with Traffic, and I was with Chris Blackwell, who owns Island Records [Note: Island Records is now owned by Universal Music Group], and I said, "Chris, I'm burned out." Nowadays, the front-of-[house] mixer arrives with the band [in] a briefcase a half hour before the gig. In those days, we loaded the truck up, we drove to the next gig, we unloaded it, we set it up, [got] two hours' sleep, and drove to the next location. It was a little bit different in the '60s. And I got burned out. I told Chris I wanted to go into the studio and apply what I had learned as a mixer for live performances. And he said, "Well, hey, I have a studio called Island Studios in London, and you can work there whenever you want." So I took him up on it. I moved to London, started working in the studio, and that's basically how I started my work as an engineer.

DENNY SOMACH: What was the first act that you worked with?

RN: I worked on a lot of different projects, but the first big album I did as an engineer was the Who's *Quadrophenia*, if you can believe that. And I just lucked out. . . . I got hired by a company called Trackplan that Pete Townshend owned. Trackplan was designed to [build] studios for musicians, and so I was assigned the job of building a mobile studio for Ronnie Lane, who was the bass player of the Faces. So I built that studio, and then I built a studio for Ronnie Wood, who was still with the

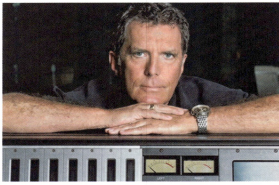

Faces [and] who was about to go to the Rolling Stones . . . When they were ready to do *Quadrophenia*, the Who had built a studio on Battersea, which I had nothing to do with, and the control room was not ready, and so they said, "Let's get Ronnie Lane's mobile and cut the tracks with that." And of course I was the guy that built it, so who was better, they thought, to engineer the sessions? . . .

DS: Talk to me a little bit about some of the other bands. Were you sought after, or did you just work with bands that came to Blackwell's studio?

RN: No, no, this was years after Blackwell's studio. I was only at Blackwell's studio for six months or so. Most of the years, I was building studios and doing various sessions. . . .

After the *Quadrophenia* thing, Led Zeppelin were at [legendary rehearsal and recording studio] Headley Grange, where they had recorded a couple of different sessions, *Houses of the Holy* being one, and they had used the Rolling Stones' mobile truck, which was the only other one in town, and maybe it wasn't available. And maybe they had decided I did a good job on *Quadrophenia*. They might have called up Pete Townshend to ask my qualifications. I don't know. I never really found out about that.

But I got the job, and I went down to Headley Grange with Ronnie Lane's mobile, which was in an Airstream—caravan, they call them in England—trailer, here. And [we] worked on the *Physical Graffiti* album; also at that time I did the first Bad Company album with the same mobile studio and at the same location, Headley Grange. . . .

DS: If my research is correct, you were the engineer for Led Zeppelin's November–December '73 and the January '74 sessions for *Physical Graffiti*. Is that correct?

They weren't real critical of what the sounds were like. They were more into the whole vibe of it, which was very interesting.

RN: That's correct, yes.

DS: This happens to be what most people consider the most interesting period in Zeppelin history, from a song-writing perspective. So I really want to, first of all, start out by asking you: what was a typical day like, working with Zeppelin? You're at Headley Grange, living there as well, right?

RN: Right. Well, it's a story. It's a story. I started [off] living there, and what happened is they would get crazy in the middle of the night and wake me up. "C'mon, let's record, let's record, let's record." So I talked to the manager, and I said, "You know what, we're not getting anything done in these night sessions." And he said, "Maybe you should go back home, lock the studio up, and then come back at noon and work till midnight or something and then go home." And I said, "I think you're right. I think that's what we should do." So that's what we did, and we got a lot more work done than just doing all-night sessions and not getting anything done.

But a typical day was, I guess we'd start at noon, and they were very, very well rehearsed. The interesting thing that I got from working with them, especially on the basic tracks, is that John Bonham really was the first drummer that I ever heard that just played just from the guitar. I mean, he played every guitar lick. And most drummers play with the bass player and play the rhythm and keep time. But this guy was—and that, I think, is the signature of Led Zeppelin in my mind, and I've talked to other guys who've worked with them, like [recording engineers] Eddie Kramer and Andy Johns, and they agree that was a kind of unique aspect of working with them. . . . The way Page and Bonham worked together, I think, is what made them so successful.

. . . And we would cut the basic tracks. Sometimes John Paul Jones would play Clavinet [a type of electronic keyboard] instead of bass for some of the songs, and then he'd throw the bass on afterwards because the Clavinet kind of gave the vibe for the track. And sometimes we'd have Robert sing a live vocal, and sometimes he wouldn't. But there was no click track [a system of audio cues used to synchronize sounds], there was not anything like that, and you know, they didn't seem overly concerned with the sounds. . . . Some bands that I've worked with, you know, were just on me every minute to kind of change this or to make that closer or take that away. . . .

DS: Did Zeppelin do any writing in the studio, or was everything already flushed out ahead of time?

RN: It was pretty much flushed out. They were pretty prepared. They knew exactly what they were doing. And you have to also understand that I didn't know—because I didn't do the recording for the whole album—I didn't know until it came out that it was a double album. I did all the tracks from these sessions that you described in November, December, and January—"Kashmir," et cetera, et cetera. They decided at some point to use tracks from the previous sessions, from *Houses of the Holy* [and earlier], and make it a double album. I didn't really know that. So I only ended up doing half the album and not all of the overdubs. . . .

What typically happened with them was when they worked in a mobile studio like this at a house, it was basically to get the drum sound that they wanted. And once they did some of the basic overdubs and the drums, they would then move into a studio and use the engineer at the studio. So if you look in the credits of Led Zeppelin's albums, there are multiple engineers. . . . I think that Eddie Kramer and Andy Johns—and Glyn Johns, I think—probably did the most work with Led Zeppelin. That's my recollection.

DS: Were you aware of any additional material that you recorded with them that's not been released?

RN: No, everything that I . . . I could probably remember most of the things. "In My Time of Dying," "Kashmir," "Custard Pie," "Sick Again." . . . Do you know why it was called "Sick Again"? Because that's the sound the hi-hat made [whispering]: "sssickagain, sssickagain, sssickagain."

DS: That is a great story.

RN: I just remembered it!

DS: I don't know how you could have forgotten that.

RN: Well, you know, you have to understand I'm sixty-three years old and this happened in 1973. People ask me, "What microphone did you use for that?" Like I remember. "What guitar did he use on that?" I've done three zillion records since then, and, you know, there are some things you remember—selective memory—just as there are some things you don't. . . . "Kashmir" was originally called "Driving to Kashmir." I have some old cassettes from rough mixes, and it was called "Driving to Kashmir." I think Robert Plant had taken the summer before and driven through northern India and Kashmir and came up with that. [Note: The details of this trip do not appear to be correct; Plant has stated he wrote the song about an experience driving through Morocco and that he has not traveled to Kashmir but might save that for his final trek.]

DS: I asked Keith Emerson, who was part of the opening act for Led Zeppelin at the O₂ Arena reunion concert in London in 2007, What is the definitive song of Led Zeppelin's? And he said, "It's obviously 'Kashmir.'" I've heard that from more people than I have "Stairway to Heaven." When you were recording "Kashmir," did it seem to you that it was going to be the classic that it was, and do you agree that it is the definitive Led Zeppelin–sounding song?

RN: It might be the definitive Led Zeppelin song, but it's certainly unique in its sound with the orchestrations. And when I recorded it, we recorded drums and guitar. There was no vocal on it. And they weren't sure how long the verses on it were going to be, so it was a lot longer originally than it came down to. And of course, I was not around for any of the rehearsal, so I hadn't heard it before. So I didn't know what to make of it. If you listen to it with just drums and guitar, you wouldn't get such a vibe from it. It wasn't until they put the bass on and put the vocal on and started—and I wasn't around, since they took it to a studio, Olympic Studios, I think, to do all the orchestrations, which, by then I was working with the Who again, by that time doing the *Tommy* film, so by that time I wasn't a party to that, either. It wasn't until I heard it finished that I went, "Oh, my God." So that was very interesting.

DS: Now I'm going to ask the question that I'm sure you knew was going to come. Give us the Ron Nevison story about you completely erasing the guitar track on "The Rover." [Note: There is a notation on the sleeve of *Physical Graffiti* stating that for this song, "Guitar lost by Nevison."] What's the deal here?

RN: Well, the deal is that I didn't work on "The Rover." "The Rover" was not part of the songs that I did—and no tapes were ever sent to me from that. And I never worked with Led Zeppelin in the studio, so I really don't know—I've talked to Robert Plant about this ten years ago, and he doesn't know how this [came about]—but I suspect that somebody else erased it and blamed me. That's the only thing I could say. Because "The Rover" was not part of the sessions that I did.

DS: When you first saw the notes on the *Physical Graffiti* album come out with a reference to the incident, what did you think?

RN: I thought, "What a ridiculous thing to put on an album liner!" That's what I thought. And, you know, I

have no answer for that. I didn't work on that track, and I didn't have those tapes. It wasn't till later that they decided, in the studio, not with Ronnie Lane's Mobile Sound, to kind of take those tapes out of storage and start finishing those things off like "The Rover," et cetera, and they did that at Olympic and I was never with them at Olympic, so there was no way that I could ever erase that. So let's put that to bed. But you know what they say about publicity? I get asked that a lot, so let's perpetuate it. . . .

DS: At the time they were doing this, arguably they were the biggest band in the world.

RN: Yeah, arguably, yeah. I would think so.

DS: You had, in Jimmy Page and John Paul Jones, two very seasoned session guys who probably knew quite a bit about the studio and everything else, and Jimmy Page is obviously the producer listed on all the records. What did you think of Page's studio knowledge and technique in working with him? Was he more than you were normally used to because of all the years of session work?

RN: Well, he was the producer. He was the writer, the producer, and everything. And I was a little shocked when I first started recording; he would run in the control room and pull the guitar down. And I thought maybe he didn't want anybody to hear mistakes or anything like that. No, he just wanted to hear what the drums sounded like exactly, because that's what they were keeping. You know, the guitar was something he was going to do over. . . .

> **[Jimmy] wanted to hear what the drums were doing before he signed off on the track, so it confused me a little bit at first, but it was the right thing for him to do. He was brilliant all the way around.**

DS: What about someone like a John Paul Jones, who also had a lot of studio experience and had worked with numerous engineers and producers over the years?

RN: John Paul Jones was not only a great musician and bass player but he was also a great arranger. He did a lot of the arrangements, the orchestrations. And so it was a perfect band, no question. A voice like Robert Plant?

Interestingly enough, when I first went down to Headley Grange to do those sessions, something—I never really found out what, but for personal reasons, John didn't come for a week. So we didn't leave and pack up. We just started doing old Elvis songs. They didn't rehearse any of this stuff. We just did—we stayed there for a week recording old songs and messing around and tweaking until he turned up.

DS: Did you run tape on that?

RN: Oh, yeah! Yeah, they have tape on that. Yeah. So that was fun. That was fun doing that, and so that actually helped me get into the whole swing of things.

DS: Had you seen them live either prior to or afterward?

RN: No, never saw them live before that. Yes, afterward I believe I have. I think it was Madison Square Garden, I believe.

DS: During the recording of *The Song Remains the Same*?

RN: I don't remember, to tell you the truth. But I do remember us going up to London one night to see Monty Python live at the Drury Lane theater [the Theatre Royal, Drury Lane] on the West End of London. You know, Monty Python in the early '70s was a huge hit in England, and to see them live after watching them hilariously for a couple of years was really amazing. So all of us went up: the roadies, everybody went up, and we watched that. Took a night off and did that.

DS: Were there any other musicians who came in during any of the sessions that you did for *Physical Graffiti*?

RN: Not at Headley Grange. It was just the four.

DS: Did Page pretty much keep a lid on visitors?

RN: Oh, yeah. There were no visitors. They probably had three roadies, myself and my assistant, Ron Fawcus, and Peter Grant, the manager, and the road manager, Richard Cole. That was it the whole time.

DS: Now let me ask you the magic question that I ask everybody and I get all sorts of answers. What was Peter Grant like? They say he was a larger-than-life character.

RN: . . . Yeah, he was. Larger than life, indeed. I didn't like the guy. He was a creep. What can I say? He treated everybody lousy, and he was a strong-arm. He was a hoodlum. That's all I can say about him.

DS: Do you think, though, that that mentality he had ended up being very helpful and a big part of the success of Led Zeppelin?

RN: Well, I think you can argue that those kind of tactics work. [Laughs] And he was very protective of the band, and obviously at that point they had their own label with Swan Song through Atlantic, and he was very close to Ahmet Ertegun and they had control over the whole thing.

DS: What did you think of Ahmet Ertegun?

RN: You know, I met him a couple of times and he seemed like a genuinely nice guy. And, of course, I really appreciated what Ahmet did for blues in this country [the United States] because he really was instrumental—he and his brother—in forming Atlantic Records, to bring blues out of the black society and make it more mainstream. If you remember in those days, especially in the late '6os, a fabulous guy like Jimi Hendrix had to go all the way to England to get noticed, where Jimmy Page and Clapton and guitar players like that were already playing the blues. And the blues here was just confined to black radio. And so I think that Ahmet created a—much like Chris Blackwell, by bringing Bob Marley and Jimmy Cliff and all those artists from Jamaica did with Island Records—I think Ahmet did with Atlantic.

DS: So you didn't have that much interaction with Peter Grant. Was he someone who would come to Headley Grange?

RN: Yeah, he would come once a week, something like that. . . .

DS: Have you had any interactions with any of the members since then?

RN: No. I mean, I've seen them over the years. I ran into Plant in L.A. about seven or eight years ago, and I haven't seen Jimmy Page, and of course I will never see John Bonham again. So, that's the answer to that, I guess.

DS: What do you make of the O$_2$ Arena reunion show? You didn't attend, right?

RN: No, I did not. Just to have them out again is phenomenal.

DS: Do you think that they will do a full-blown tour?

RN: I don't know. That's hard to say. I don't know why they don't. It seems to be Robert Plant that's the one that's not kind of signing onto it.

DS: Danny Goldberg says that Robert spent too much time trying to get his own identity and now that he's got it, he doesn't want to lose it. But he says once that gets out of his system, he thinks that in 2010, they will tour as Zeppelin. [Note: They did not tour in 2010.]

RN: I think he's right. It seems that he is the only one who seems to be not into it. But certainly I think it is inevitable. And probably with Jason Bonham.

DS: Did you, by any chance, either live or on HBO, see the Atlantic fortieth anniversary concert [in 1988]?

RN: I did.

DS: What did you make of their performance there?

RN: I thought it was brilliant. Brilliant in some ways and a little rusty in other ways. I was just so excited to see them, I guess my judgment's a little colored, I don't know. . . .

DS: Having done the *Physical Graffiti* album—obviously, it was a high-profile project to work on—what immediately happened after you worked on that? Were there other people who said, "Wow, you've worked with Zeppelin? We want to work with you." In terms of your career and other artists, were there other artists who particularly wanted that sound?

RN: Let me finish with the *Physical Graffiti* sessions by saying I had signed on to start the *Tommy* film in February or January of '74, I guess, and because John Paul Jones was late starting these sessions, I had to leave these sessions a week ahead of time, and they weren't really happy about it. But I had a year's worth of work to do with the *Tommy* film, to record; with the *Tommy* film, everything was recorded ahead of time, and then they shot. There was no spoken word in the film; it was all recorded. So I really felt like, you know, I didn't want Pete Townshend to go get another engineer. It put me in a real spot. Here I am leaving Led Zeppelin for the Who, and I was in a quandary, to tell you the truth, but it was something I had to do, so I didn't do the last week with them at Headley Grange.

DS: You talked about a session that you did for NARAS [the National Academy of Recording Arts and Sciences] with Eddie Kramer and Andy Johns. How did your approach to Zeppelin differ from theirs?

RN: I was as curious to hear what they were going to say. It was interesting because there were one hundred or more producers and engineers from the producers and engineer's wing of the recording academy. We each picked a track of Zeppelin, and we talked about it. They'd play the track. Of course, I picked "Kashmir" and I brought up the fact that the day we cut "Kashmir" I had just gotten my first Eventide phaser, which was like a phasing device. Up till then, the only phasing you could do would be taped phasing, which was a technical thing you had to do. So I just threw it on one of the drum tracks so that the cymbals went like [imitates a cymbal sound being processed through a phasing effect], and when they came in for the playback they loved it, and of course I didn't know until the album was finished that they actually used it. So that effect was kind of an accident that affects what you hear. But it was part of that kind of Middle Eastern or Asian provocative vibe that they had on that track.

So we would talk about that, and they would talk about tracks that they produced, and I don't remember exactly anything special that they said that stands out in my mind, but it was a fun night. . . .

DS: [When you worked with Bad Company] were you consciously or unconsciously trying to achieve a sound similar to Led Zeppelin?

RN: Not at all. Not at all. That's why I didn't use the same drum room. No one could accomplish what John Bonham did in that room. First of all, the drums on Bad Company were a totally different kind of sound. And that establishes the band sound. They weren't a metal kind of—I don't know if you can call Zeppelin metal, but Zeppelin really started a whole kind of sound, and I don't think I saw Bad Company as following in their footsteps at all. There was pretty much a straight rock 'n' roll, four-four time, there weren't intricate time signatures and all of that kind of stuff. And it was really soul-based, you know, a soulful singer like Paul Rodgers . . .

DS: I understand you engineered a Bert Jansch album [*L.A. Turnaround*, in 1974], and Jimmy Page was heavily influenced by him, particularly on "Black Mountain Side" off of the first Zeppelin album. Were you aware of Jansch's influence on Page when you did that, or was it just another project?

RN: It was just another project. You know who produced that album? One of the Monkees, Michael Nesmith.

DS: You're kidding.

RN: No. And I did it, again with the Ronnie Lane mobile studio, at this mansion that the record company Charisma had at that time . . .

DS: You worked with Heart. Were you aware of what big Zeppelin fans they are?

RN: Yeah, I think that's why they hired me. They do Zeppelin songs in their live sets. When I saw them perform, they did "Rock and Roll" at the end of the show. Ten years ago, I did an album called *The British Rock Symphony*, and I had her [Ann Wilson] come. I went up to Seattle, and I had her come and sing "Kashmir" and sing "Stairway to Heaven," and she did a duet on "Kashmir" with Roger Daltrey. Then I had Paul Rodgers come down; he was living up in British Columbia at the time. He came down and did a Beatles medley of "Norwegian Wood," "Come Together," and "Penny Lane." So I had them both working [on this project]. . . . I tried to get a bunch of people, including the singer from Yes, Jon Anderson, and they just weren't into it, so I had to start looking for others. We had to get away from the concept [that] they would all be British singers, so that's when I thought, who does Robert Plant better than Ann Wilson? So she was up for it, and it was fun.

Eddie Kramer

SOUTH AFRICA–BORN EDDIE KRAMER IS A PRODUCER AND AUDIO ENGINEER WHO WORKED EXTENSIVELY WITH LED ZEPPELIN. OTHER ARTISTS HE WORKED WITH INCLUDE THE ROLLING STONES, KISS, JIMI HENDRIX, DAVID BOWIE, PETER FRAMPTON, SANTANA, VANILLA FUDGE, AND JOE COCKER.

IN 1968, KRAMER MOVED TO NEW YORK CITY, WHERE HE WORKED AT THE RECORD PLANT STUDIO TO ENGINEER HENDRIX'S DOUBLE ALBUM *ELECTRIC LADYLAND*. IN 1969, EDDIE WAS HIRED TO RECORD THE WOODSTOCK FESTIVAL, AND OVERSAW BOTH THE ALBUM AND THE MOVIE.

BEGINNING IN 1969, AS AN INDEPENDENT PRODUCER, KRAMER ENGINEERED *LED ZEPPELIN II*. THIS WOULD BE THE FIRST OF FIVE ALBUMS HE ENGINEERED FOR THE BAND. HERE, IN AN INTERVIEW FROM THE SUMMER OF 1983, KRAMER DISCUSSES HOW HE ADDED HIS OWN TOUCH TO "WHOLE LOTTA LOVE."

Eddie Kramer at Electric Ladyland studios in New York, June 29, 1993.

EDDIE KRAMER: At one point [while recording *Led Zeppelin II*] there was bleed-through of a previously recorded vocal in the recording of "Whole Lotta Love." It was the middle part, where Robert screams "Wo-man. You need it." Since we couldn't rerecord at that point, I just threw some echo on it to see how it would sound, and Jimmy said, "Great! Just leave it."

DENNY SOMACH: What's your opinion of Jimmy Page as a guitarist?

EK: [Page] is the sort of guitar player who, when he's on, when he's hot, when he's burning, and he's really inspired, he can pull off the most amazing things. He himself admits that he's not the world's greatest guitar player, but he feels that on a good day, he's equal to anybody. And, I think in those days he was really . . . he was particularly sharp. Let's put it that way.

DS: How did engineering for Led Zeppelin compare to working with, say, Jimi Hendrix?

EK: Working with Zeppelin was a different kind of a challenge, because here was a band that was a four-piece . . . an amazing singer, an incredible drummer, a really powerful guitar player, and of course the bass player, John Paul Jones, had this symphonic background because he was a classically trained musician. So the soundscape was bigger, certainly heavier [than Hendrix]. That's for sure. Zeppelin is known for their heaviness and also their delicateness. There's an interesting parallel between their dynamics and what Jimi Hendrix would do.

DS: What's the deal with the studio chatter at the top of "Black Country Woman" [from 1975's *Physical Graffiti*]?

EK: The beginning of "Black Country Woman," it goes, "Oh, what about that airplane, then? Gotta get this airplane out." That's moi! And Robert says, "Nah, leave it in," and you can actually hear the airplane, actually before the click, you actually hear [makes fluttering airplane sound] and then you hear the click, and then he says, "Nah, leave it in," and then they start the song. Why is that? Because Robert—actually, Jimmy and John Paul Jones were outside on the lawn [at Headley Grange] on two bar stools with their acoustic guitars and they cut the basic track outside and obviously during the performance this plane went over.

So when Robert was outside singing his vocal he heard it and said, "What the hell's that?" So those are some of the accidents we used to leave in.

George Hardie

GRAPHIC DESIGNER AND ILLUSTRATOR GEORGE HARDIE DID THE ARTWORK FOR SOME OF THE MOST ICONIC ALBUM COVERS OF THE LATE '60S AND '70S. WORKING WITH THE FAMED BRITISH DESIGN GROUP HIPGNOSIS, HE CREATED THE ICONIC BLACK-AND-WHITE DIRIGIBLE ON *LED ZEPPELIN* AND THE PRISM ARTWORK ON PINK FLOYD'S *DARK SIDE OF THE MOON*. IN THIS INTERVIEW FROM THE EARLY 1990S, HARDIE IS ASKED ABOUT HIS CONTRIBUTION TO THE LED ZEPPELIN CATALOG, STARTING WITH THE BAND'S DEBUT EFFORT IN 1969.

GEORGE HARDIE: I worked on this cover half my life ago and at least half of the brain cells I then possessed are now long gone: let this explain inaccuracies.

The first work I ever did for the music business was to add typography to a friend's photograph on a Jeff Beck cover. The photographer was Stephen Goldblatt [a prominent cinematographer]. He suggested to Beck's management that I might have some ideas for a new group called Led Zeppelin.

I was summoned to an office on Oxford Street. I walked up through Soho and passed the Marquee Club, where a very small queue was forming to see a group called Led Zeppelin. I climbed five floors and reached an attic office: RAK Records.

I sat waiting, biting my nails. Opposite me sat four musicians biting theirs: Led Zeppelin. Every so often, one of them, a blonde, would set off down the stairs to the marquee and arrive back, puffing, to report on the growth of the queue: Robert Plant.

I was ushered into an inner office to meet Peter Grant, the giant of a man, dressed accurately as a cowboy: Led Zeppelin's manager. He talked. I showed him some ideas. These were rejected by a thin, dark-haired man who produced a book open at the famous photograph of the zeppelin [the *Hindenburg*] on fire: Jimmy Page.

The rough I showed was a multiple sequential image of a zeppelin, clouds, and waves, based on an old club sign in San Francisco, recently visited, and owing a lot to [iconic graphic designer] Milton Glaser. The image as a logo appears on the back of the album and was used as part of *Led Zeppelin II*, as far as I can remember.

So I set to, and with my finest Rapidograph dot stippled a facsimile of the famous photograph some seven inches square on a sheet of tracing paper. I was paid £60 [about $140 at the 1968 exchange rate], which I had paid into an American bank account and spent during a trip to New York thirteen years later.

I think the drawing made a good and memorable cover, but this was more to do with the photograph and Jimmy Page's choice of it than with my skill as a dotter. I missed *Led Zeppelin II* and *III* but later became involved again through Storm and Po [cofounders Storm Thorgerson and Aubrey "Po" Powell] at Hipgnosis. We did some very enjoyable work for them.

As to working on the original artwork for this printing, the longest task was writing this piece. I delved deep in a plan chest and found the original tracing paper, unsullied, in a clean folder on which one of my partners had written years ago, "G's pension fund."

This U.S. Navy photograph of the Hindenburg, *the famous 804-foot German zeppelin, shows the ship just before it crashed to the ground at Lakehurst Naval Air Station in Lakehurst, New Jersey, on May 6, 1937.*

Cameron Crowe

CAMERON CROWE IS A SCREENWRITER AND DIRECTOR WHOSE BEST-KNOWN FILMS INCLUDE *JERRY MAGUIRE*, *SAY ANYTHING*, *FAST TIMES AT RIDGEMONT HIGH*, AND THE SEMI-AUTOBIOGRAPHICAL *ALMOST FAMOUS*, ABOUT A TEEN-AGE MUSIC JOURNALIST ON TOUR WITH AN UP-AND-COMING ROCK BAND. BEFORE GETTING INVOLVED IN THE FILM INDUSTRY, CROWE WAS A CONTRIBUTING EDITOR AT *ROLLING STONE* MAGAZINE, FOR WHICH HE STILL OCCA-SIONALLY WRITES.

CROWE WAS A FAN OF 1970S PROGRESSIVE AND HARD ROCK BANDS. ACCORDING TO HIS EDITOR AT *ROLLING STONE*, BEN FONG-TORRES, "HE WAS THE GUY WE SENT OUT [AND] COVERED THE BANDS THAT HATED *ROLLING STONE*." LED ZEPPELIN WAS ONE OF THOSE BANDS, AND HERE IN THIS INTERVIEW FROM THE SUMMER OF 1982, HE REMINISCES ABOUT HIS 1975 LED ZEPPELIN FEATURE IN *ROLLING STONE*, BASED ON HIS EXPERIENCES TOURING WITH THE BAND.

CAMERON CROWE: I had written about Led Zeppelin for the *L.A. Times* and I had spoken to Plant and Page and John Paul Jones—to all of them. I was sixteen. But it worked to my advantage because they really kind of . . . take you under their wing a little bit. They used to say, "Hey, are you sure you aren't missing out on school?" and stuff like that. "No, no, no, no, no." You know? "Let's rap—come on, Jimmy!"

They were great to me, so [an article I wrote] came out in the *L.A. Times* on their '73 tour that they really liked, you know? And they were on the cover of the calendar section.

So later when they came back in '75, they remembered the story and let me on the road to write about them again, for *Oui* magazine at the time. But *Rolling Stone* I had begun to work for, so they were saying, "If you can get us a story, go for it!"

So in the process of being on the road for three weeks, Plant decided to do the interview for *Rolling Stone*; John Paul Jones, Bonzo, all decided. Page was holding out, so

it came down to the point where it was gonna be a cover story and Robert would be on the cover. Page wouldn't speak, but the others would, and Jimmy started to con-sider it. And I remember one night on their plane he said [in a high voice, trying to impersonate Jimmy], "Cameron, why should I do this interview? Why should I do it?"

I was saying, "Well, you know, there are a lot of fans out there who really are on your side, and if you really felt like [you've] been wronged in these record reviews, here's a forum for you to defend yourself." [Again, in higher voice] "I don't have to defend myself."

"Well, why don't you say all the things you've always wanted to say to *Rolling Stone* magazine and it will be printed in *Rolling Stone* magazine?" And he kinda liked that, plus he liked the idea that I had just interviewed Joe Walsh . . . and he loved Joe Walsh. So Page did the inter-view and it was fantastic. It was like, we spent hours and hours, and he told me all these stories. It was fantastic. And agreed to be on the cover. They did a photo session one day at the Plaza in New York. All the band except for Page was in this room waiting, and the photographer—who was my roommate—Neil Preston, was there. It was like, "Is Jimmy gonna show up? Is he gonna show up?" And it was like [makes sound like a door chime—bing bong]. Page walks in with this bouquet of dead roses and he says, "This is how I want to be on the cover of *Rolling Stone*." You know, so it's like, Led Zeppelin with Page up front with this smirk on his face and this arrangement of dead roses in his hand. It was a great picture. The camera malfunctioned and it clicked off a shutter-beat behind and none of the pictures turned out, so it had to be a composite of some live shots, which was a big disappoint-ment, but the story ran and it was great. Jann Wenner, who was the publisher of *Rolling Stone*, called me up to San Francisco and, like, kind of congratulated me—wondered why it was such a positive article, but ran it anyway. That kind of put me even more down the road, you know, they made me a contributing editor not too long after that.

Cameron Crowe, right, with actor Billy Crudup on the set of Almost Famous, *October 31, 2000. The semi-autobiographical film was based on Crowe's experiences as a teenager traveling with Led Zeppelin in the 1970s, when he was a writer for* Rolling Stone.

Jason Bonham

Jason Bonham at the drums during his show Led Zeppelin Experience *at the Warfield theater in San Francisco, November 24, 2010.*

JASON BONHAM IS THE SON OF LED ZEPPELIN DRUMMER JOHN BONHAM AND HIS WIFE, PAT PHILLIPS. HE FIRST BEGAN PLAYING DRUMS AT THE AGE OF FIVE; HE APPEARS IN THE FILM *THE SONG REMAINS THE SAME* AT AGE SIX, DRUMMING ON A SCALED-DOWN KIT. IN 1983, AT THE AGE OF SEVENTEEN, HE JOINED HIS FIRST BAND, AIRRACE.

IN 1988, JASON JOINED JIMMY PAGE ON HIS SOLO ALBUM, *OUTRIDER*. FOR THE ATLANTIC RECORDS FORTIETH-ANNIVERSARY CONCERT, HELD IN NEW YORK LATER THAT SAME YEAR, BONHAM APPEARED WITH THE THREE SURVIVING MEMBERS OF LED ZEPPELIN FOR A PERFORMANCE AT MADISON SQUARE GARDEN.

IN 1989, JASON FORMED HIS OWN BAND, BONHAM, AND THEIR FIRST RELEASE, *THE DISREGARD OF TIMEKEEPING*, HAD A HIT SINGLE, "WAIT FOR YOU." THE BAND BROKE UP AFTER THE RELEASE OF THEIR SECOND ALBUM, AND HE CONCENTRATED ON SESSION WORK AND GUEST APPEARANCES.

JASON, ALONG WITH HIS SISTER, ZOE, REPRESENTED HIS FATHER WHEN LED ZEPPELIN WAS INDUCTED INTO THE ROCK AND ROLL HALL OF FAME IN 1995. FROM 2004–7, HE PLAYED LIVE WITH FOREIGNER AND ALSO PLAYED DRUMS FOR THE 2007 LED ZEPPELIN REUNION CONCERT AT THE O2 ARENA IN LONDON.

IN 2009, JASON JOINED THE GROUP BLACK COUNTRY COMMUNION, WITH GLENN HUGHES, JOE BONAMASSA, AND DEREK SHERINIAN. MOST RECENTLY HE HAS TOURED WITH HIS OWN BAND, PLAYING A FULL SET OF LED ZEPPELIN MATERIAL IN CONCERT AS JASON BONHAM'S LED ZEPPELIN EXPERIENCE. HALFWAY THROUGH THE TOUR, IN THE AUTUMN OF 2010, JASON ANSWERED A SERIES OF QUESTIONS ABOUT HIS FAVORITE LED ZEPPELIN SONGS, HIS MEMORIES OF GROWING UP WITH LED ZEPPELIN, AND HIS EXPERIENCES PERFORMING ALONGSIDE HIS FATHER'S BANDMATES AT LED ZEPPELIN'S REUNION CONCERT IN 2007. EARLY IN THE INTERVIEW, BONHAM IS ASKED HOW THE CURRENT JASON BONHAM'S LED ZEPPELIN EXPERIENCE TOUR IS GOING.

JASON BONHAM: It's going absolutely fantastic, beyond my wildest dreams. I never imagined in a million years that the reaction would be the way it is. I can't describe it. It is unbelievable. . . . The final bits of the puzzle were only being put together twenty minutes before we went on. I was in the dressing room, narrating into the computer, trying to do the voice-overs for the screen, the images we have, changing that around. I then ran out and said, "Give this to your guy. This is now going to be the intro to the show." I found a piece of music that I wanted to use. And he said, "What about the middle section? What are you gonna do in the middle of the video?" I said, "Don't worry, I'll wing it. I'll just talk to the audience." And from that moment, it began to write itself. . . . The show went fantastically, and all the production people that had been wanting every little detail covered said, "That's the best way. Keep it that way. It's real when you talk to the audience and you're talking through the video footage. It really works." So that was very, very cool. And then . . . every night it just got better and better and better to a point where it became unbelievable. It really became very overwhelming—so emotional, it was hard to contain. By four songs in, you—I was, you know, sucking air and, you know, trying not to break down.

DENNY SOMACH: For fans, there was some element of surprise, as you didn't name any of the band members ahead of time. But it sounds like it was also a surprise for you how well it was going to go.

JB: Yeah. Well, the reason I didn't want to name anybody was the Internet can sometimes not be the greatest place. I know that. I've seen enough comments before the start of this tour that were—there was a couple of comments that really shouldn't have . . . I almost threw the towel in and didn't want to do it. That soon went away. The doubt went as soon as we started the first show. As soon as we went to the production rehearsals and I saw the size and the scale of this thing and I went, it was an arena, and I was like, "Wow, this is phenomenal. This is just gonna be very, very special." So the reason I kept them quiet was I didn't want anyone to simply type the name in, do the Google search, and then it would be, "Oh, that guy. Fine." So I really wanted to be judged on what we do when we play [more] than what we've done in the past. Come to the show. And so far, my wishes always were: come to the show with an open mind, and hopefully you'll walk away going, "I did not expect that." And so far, we've done that. It really has worked, and the reviews have been phenomenal. I mean, I couldn't have asked for a greater way to really do this. This was beyond my—I never imagined it.

DS: How did you come across [singer] James [Dylan]?

JB: I found him on the Internet doing the Virtual Zeppelin. I flew him to Florida. I wanted to see if he could do it in real life, so he came down. He was a Virginia boy with his work jeans on and his worker boots and his T-shirt that was twenty times too big

for him. So I said, "Listen, if you can lose fifty pounds and start honing in the image, you can do this. You can sing, definitely." And he hadn't been out on the road or even sang pro forever, I don't think, which made the [production] company very nervous. They were like, "Uh, we're investing a lot of money in this. And this guy's a complete newcomer." But yeah, as soon as he started, everyone was like, you know, you know they don't expect it coming out of him because he looks more like [punk rocker] Chris Daughtry than he does Robert Plant. And that was a key moment as well. When I saw the way he looked, I was actually more—I was grateful for the fact that he didn't look like Robert. . . . So he worked out great. . . .

Obviously, I've known Tony [Catania], the guitarist, for a long time. [Bassist] Michael Devin became involved through—there was another guy playing bass originally, but he just didn't seem to work out. He wasn't prepared to do some of the hard work, learn the songs . . . but he's a good guy. I just said it's not gonna work out. My sister lives in L.A., Zoe Bonham. She said, "I know a couple of bass players." So she chose to tell me about Michael. He came in. Loved his vibe. Great guy. Irish-Italian Boston boy. He's one of those guys, hit first, ask questions later. I said to Michael while we were rehearsing, "You wouldn't happen to know somebody who plays lap steel and keyboards and bass guitar." And he goes, "I actually do," and Stephen LeBlanc came in, and the final bit of the puzzle was done. And then we started doing rehearsals.

> **The last thing I wanted to do was surround myself with a bunch of look-alikes. That just would be too cheesy for me and just not right. I didn't want to tarnish the Led Zeppelin experience I did have, which was playing with them at the O2 and all my moments with them throughout my life.**

DS: Before you hooked up with the production company, who were also responsible for the Beatles tribute *Rain*, had you been thinking about doing a tribute to your father over the years, or is this just something that came up toward the thirtieth anniversary?

JB: Never, never imagined doing it again . . . I never thought of it this way. I never thought [of] it in this size. So it was seeing *Rain* and the possibility of having this budget that you can create the show that really gives it everything you need to give it, to create. What I wanted to do, if I was going to do it, I said it's got to be done in the most tasteful and professional way. And they were like, "Yeah, we totally agree." . . . Just going out and playing the music was not—never crossed my mind. It had to be a personal journey, my personal moments. So once we started, I started to think about that and everything, and the images. And finally, Mom didn't give me the images [of John Bonham] till a week before the tour. [She] doesn't like that footage going anywhere because she always feels that someone—it's gonna get out and it's gonna be all over the Internet. She's always been very personal about that.

DS: Has she seen the show yet?

JB: No, not yet. She's gonna see it out in L.A. She was supposed to come to Toronto, and she watched a couple of things from Montreal that were online, and she broke into tears.

DS: Didn't you phone her from the first gig?

JB: Yep, yep. One of the first gigs, I held the phone up and said, "Hi, Patricia." That was hilarious, first gig. But she watched two things from Montreal: "Stairway" and "Kashmir." And she broke into tears and said, "I'm gonna need a little bit more time to prepare myself for the show."

DS: How did you decide what songs you were going to do, to narrow it down?

JB: We've all got favorites. For me, there had to be a story behind most of them. "Your Time Is Gonna Come," for instance, was my first-ever memory of Zeppelin, and that's a very vivid memory so that had to be in there. A strong image of Zeppelin to me was always the black-and-white "Babe I'm Gonna Leave You" from Danish TV, so that song had to be in there. Plus, I was trying to do them in order, a timeline. Once we get to a certain point, we start out of context and then go into context. But we change it every now and again because once the websites get up the set list . . . just to make it interesting.

DS: Do you mind fans filming and posting it on the Web?

JB: No, not at all. Actually, I prefer that than the producers put out the official [video]. What they thought was good, I disliked completely. I didn't like it at all. It didn't have any vibe. . . . It was multicamera, shot with [sound] direct from the board, no cheers, no vibe—it didn't—that's not the show. This show, you have to be here, and you'll experience that tonight. Unless you've seen one before, everyone says, "You can't describe the show until you're there." Every show is different. It's an emotional thing. It's a feeling, and everyone gets it. So for me, I loved it when we first started seeing the little clips [online]—you know, somebody posted a little bit of "Since I've Been Loving You" and somebody posted "When the Levee Breaks." It's great. That builds the buzz. People say, "Oh, yeah, I can't wait to see the show." For me, when we did the official one, that was opening itself up for criticism, especially when it's not the right sound . . . and I told them that, and I felt very sad that they would just do something without even asking the artist. [In the voice of Peter Grant] It wouldn't have happened back in the day. [Laughs, then continues in Peter Grant's voice] Just to exploit another nickel . . .

DS: Since this is a tribute to your dad, give us a few comments about your favorite memories.

JB: Wow, favorite memories, um . . . [Pauses] I don't know. I don't really have any real, real favorites. There's just—to me, they're all good.

DS: Wasn't he always having you play [drums] when people would come to the house?

JB: I don't know if that was my favorite memory. I was like, "Oh, my God, here we go again." They were fond memories, but some of my favorite memories were [when] I was racing [dirt bikes] in the tip of west Wales. It was a four-hour drive. When he was home, we were doing those races on my dirt bikes, he was the one that was up at 5:30. He was the one that was making the sandwiches, loading the car, getting the hamper ready, would wait for the last minute to wake me and then would go, "Come on, let's go in the car." And we'd listen to [Fleetwood Mac's] *Rumours* over and over again on the eight-track. They were good, fond memories. And I remember over and over again telling him to stop smoking because I couldn't stand the smell of smoke in the car. And he'd . . . have the window down with his cigarette, driving in his Range Rover. Just real funny memories. When we went to Knebworth together and he got stopped for speeding on the way, it was quite funny. It was a new Porsche.

DS: You were playing in the sound check [at Knebworth] and Jimmy Page heard it. What is that story?

JB: Yeah. The story was, I rehearsed at home. Dad said, "I want you to get up and play 'Trampled Under Foot' at sound check." So I rehearsed it to the album version and he said, "Jimmy changed the guitar solo. He'll go on a bit longer. Just look to him to put his hand up and turn to you and that's it." So we get to the point and Dad gets me on the drums. I'm thirteen. They start the song, and Jimmy hadn't noticed me walk on. He didn't see me walk on. And Dad went out front. He actually said to Chris Welch, the journalist, that this was the first time he'd ever seen Led Zeppelin play. So, yeah, it was very cool.

DS: How many shows did you have a chance to see?

JB: In '77 I was at Tampa with the riot. [Laughs] I was there. It was a bit of a scary moment. I saw the Madison Square Garden show, one of the Madison Square Garden shows on that tour, '77. Of course I saw Knebworth. Other than that, Earls Court. I saw an Earls Court show. That was about it.

DS: What was the first band you were in?

JB: My first band was a band called Airrace. We did a lot of touring. There was a twenty-five-year anniversary and I went and played with them, just a couple of shows with them, which was quite funny. The original lineup.

It's funny, I went from the O₂ to the "Oh, my God, what am I doing?" We went and played some show in somewhere in England. There were about nine people there and a dog. And this was like about a year after the O₂ event, so obviously it was quite amusing. . . ."

DS: Speaking of the O₂, what were your best memories of that?

JB: Memories of the O₂ . . . well, the whole six weeks prior, really, for me. Getting to know the boys. To be around them for that time. One of my favorite moments was the first day, June 10, 2007, when we got together. We went out for dinner, and we were in a busy Indian restaurant and we were sharing a table with other people. And no one had a clue what we were discussing, really. And we were in a busy place in London where there was—I felt like a journalist because I was, just, question, question, question all the time. And I said, "Oh, yeah, by the way, you know the story in Japan when apparently Dad samurai-sworded his room into pieces? Is that true?" [Pauses] And Jimmy and Robert look at John Paul Jones. [Pauses] And John Paul Jones says, "Actually, it was me." And I'm like, "What?" He goes, "Yeah, your dad fell asleep, drunk, passed out, whatever." He said, "And I took the sword out of his hand, chopped his room up, and put the sword back in his hand, so when he woke up he thought he'd done it." So I loved those kind of moments, the six weeks, loads of great stories they shared with me. The real ones. You know, the real stuff. [Winks] "We can tell him now; he's old enough." So it was—I cherished every moment. It was a great thing.

DS: Alan White [drummer for Yes] told me you were trying to do séances, everything you could to get the reunion tour going. Were you disappointed that they didn't continue? Did you think they might? And is there still a shot?

JB: Well, we did continue for a year. Jimmy and John Paul and myself, we carried on for a year of writing and did some great new material and we were gonna have a new band, you know. It was gonna be a new project. When that stopped, I was devastated—I knew Robert wasn't gonna do the other one [carry on the Led Zeppelin name with his participation] because we'd sat

and talked long about it, you know. But that's something that was up to them.

DS: What was the problem with getting a vocalist?

JB: I don't know. You'd have to ask them [Led Zeppelin]. I was just enjoying every moment playing. . . .

DS: You grew up in the video age, whereas Led Zeppelin did not do TV or anything. You have a completely different outlook, correct? You did do videos with [the band] Bonham.

JB: Yeah . . . I'm a lot more into that side of things.

DS: Were you aware that [Robert Plant's son] Logan Plant has a band and was playing in New York?

JB: Yeah, I've seen him a few times. We all went to see him when we were rehearsing for the O₂. I haven't seen him for a while, Logan. He's actually—he's definitely got his—he's a good-looking front man, that boy, I can tell you that. He's a good-looking kid.

DS: Could you give us a view from the top at the O₂? You're sitting there in the center. Fans flew in from all over the world. What's going through your mind as you're sitting at the drums?

JB: What was going through my mind while I'm onstage? "I hope my mom's okay." That was my main thing that's in my head. "Hope she's not upset." That was going through my mind most of the time. . . .

DS: And what did she think?

JB: She was great. She dealt with it great. My grandmother, my dad's mom, was there as well. My dad's sister, she didn't deal with it very well. She was in tears at the very start. As I say, for me, when we went on, really the things that [were] going through my mind were, "Is Mom okay?" and just, I was just trying to impress the three guys onstage. I wasn't really dealing with the audience. On this tour, I've met nine people so far from the front row. I've got pictures. And every time I've met them, they give me a picture. "That's me, that's me." . . .

A ticket from the canceled October 30, 1980, Led Zeppelin concert at the Joe Louis Arena in Detroit.

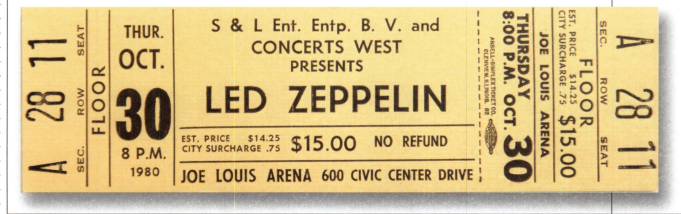

These two guys, a bit older than me, they were camping out in Montreal every day [in 1980]. Five days they camped out. They were sixteen years old. And the door opens and the guy says, "I'm sorry. John Bonham died this morning. Led Zeppelin will not be coming." And these two guys waited thirty years, and one brought his own son to my show. And he broke down into tears and says, "I feel, you know, this is my way of finishing where I started those years ago." . . .

DS: You mentioned what songs are in the show, but what are a couple of your favorite Zeppelin songs?

JB: "Kashmir" is always great. . . . For me at the O₂, "Kashmir" was the moment I knew when we come to that song, I was like, "I'm gonna nail this one now. I'm ready." So I remember I had this little metronome rhythm watch so I could monitor the tempos and start them in right where I wanted them to be. I remember

There's a lot about this tour. A lot of people reminiscing . . . and people have their ticket stubs from the [Zeppelin] show that didn't happen in Chicago—it's just unreal.

DS: Are you a collector? Do you collect?

JB: Not really. Then again, yes and no. I have very good friends. Sam [Rapallo], who runs the Zeppelin website—I have a two-terabyte hard drive of everything that there is, that is out there now, from every bootleg to every radio [appearance]. . . . He just recently gave me an interview of Dad in a newspaper in 1970 where he talks about, "My son plays drums. He's four years old. His technique's not great, but he's got good time." And he says, "My dream is for him to play with me side by side at the Royal Albert Hall." Yeah, it's a weird thing, I had no idea, when we started putting the "Moby Dick" parts together, that the part I do is from the Royal Albert Hall. So I do get to play with him at the Royal Albert Hall after all these years. But it's strange, 'cause now I'm the old guy. He's the kid.

Ioannis, John Bonham: Moby Dick *(detail),* 2011.

looking and I just turned it down two beats. I said I really wanted to hold it back. But "Kashmir" has always been one of my favorites. It works great live. It's the simplicity that's just so killer about it. We've started to do "How Many More Times," which is still so much fun to play for a drummer. It's a lot of scat, free flow, just go for it, in Dad's approach. "Good Times Bad Times," singing on that one. We also do "What Is and What Should Never Be." "The Lemon Song" has been working out fantastic. I love playing "The Lemon Song." I've never done that before. We do a lot of early stuff, which Zeppelin had stopped doing. They stopped doing some of those things. When we started, the first few dates, we were doing "I Can't Quit You Baby" as well. We changed that around. Some of my favorite songs to play—"Celebration Day," "Rock and Roll" into "Celebration Day" into "Black Dog," so it's fun.

DS: Do you have a favorite Zeppelin album?

JB: *Physical Graffiti* without a shadow of a doubt. I like all the elements on it. "In the Light." I'd love to do, one night, I'd love to say on a tour, "Could we do one night where we just do *Physical Graffiti* from start to finish?" I just love the album. "In My Time of Dying," "Ten Years Gone," fantastic!

Chris **Dreja**

CHRIS DREJA SPRUNG FROM LONDON'S FOLK SCENE, ALONG WITH FUTURE YARDBIRDS GUITARIST TOP TOPHAM. INFLUENCED BY LOCAL FOLK AND BLUES GUITARISTS, THE TWO FRIENDS SWITCHED FROM ACOUSTIC TO ELECTRIC GUITARS. COINCIDENTALLY, IN THEIR FIRST PUBLIC PERFORMANCE PLAYING ELECTRIC GUITARS, THEY SHARED THE BILL WITH A YOUNG JIMMY PAGE.

DREJA AND TOPHAM WOULD BECOME THE CORE OF THE METROPOLITAN BLUES QUARTET, WHOSE OTHER ROTATING MEMBERS INCLUDED KEITH RELF, JIM MCCARTY, AND PAUL SAMWELL-SMITH. THE BLUES QUARTET EVOLVED INTO THE YARDBIRDS, WITH DREJA PLAYING RHYTHM GUITAR, FIRST BEHIND ERIC CLAPTON AND LATER JEFF BECK. EVENTUALLY, DREJA SWITCHED TO THE BASS, WHERE HE REMAINED UNTIL THE BAND BROKE UP IN 1968. DREJA IS ALSO CREDITED AS A SONGWRITER ON NUMEROUS YARDBIRDS TRACKS.

AFTER THE YARDBIRDS BROKE UP, PAGE IS REPORTED TO HAVE OFFERED DREJA THE POSITION OF BASSIST IN A NEW BAND HE WAS FORMING (LATER TO BECOME LED ZEPPELIN). DREJA DECLINED IN ORDER TO PURSUE A CAREER IN PHOTOGRAPHY. HE PLAYED IN THE YARDBIRDS REUNION BAND BOX OF FROGS ("BACK WHERE I STARTED" WENT INTO THE TOP TWENTY IN THE U.S.) IN THE 1980S, AND HAS BEEN PART OF THE YARDBIRDS' RE-FORMATION SINCE 1992.

IN THIS 2011 INTERVIEW, CONDUCTED WHEN DREJA WAS IN NEW YORK WITH THE YARDBIRDS, HE TALKED ABOUT WORKING WITH JIMMY PAGE, FIRST AS A BANDMATE AND LATER AS A PHOTOGRAPHER. (HE SHOT THE GROUP ON A NUMBER OF OCCASIONS, INCLUDING, FAMOUSLY, FOR THE BACK COVER OF THE FIRST LED ZEPPELIN ALBUM.) AT THE TOP OF THE INTERVIEW, DREJA WAS ASKED IF, WHEN KEITH RELF AND JIM MCCARTY LEFT THE YARDBIRDS, HE WAS PLANNING TO BE IN THE NEW LINEUP THAT WAS FORMING.

CHRIS DREJA: No. Basically, I would have carried on with Jimmy as the Yardbirds because, you know, I loved that band. But Jim and Keith both pulled out of our last

Chris Dreja performs with the Yardbirds at New York's B.B. King Blues Club, September 7, 2011.

five years seemed like twenty years, a long time. And I couldn't wait really to get away and get out and not be so reliant on these crazy guys. [Laughs] You know, because they were all a bit wacky by then. And I wanted to wake up in the morning and do my own thing, and my own thing was my other passion, photography.

DENNY SOMACH: Okay.

CD: So he never asked me. He knew I didn't want to do it. And in fact, I worked very loosely with Peter [Grant] for a couple of weeks and then went straight into photography, came over to New York, and didn't see them for a while.

Everybody always asks me about that, you know. On the guitar, I have a regret. But not joining Zep on the bass? Not particularly. I wouldn't have been good enough. John Paul Jones was the *perfect* fit.

DS: Even though you weren't going to be in the band, you were going around with Jimmy Page, seeing others basically audition for various parts. What do you remember about that?

CD: I'd already gone to the audition with Peter and Jimmy. We'd gone up to Birmingham or just outside Birmingham to check out John Bonham and [laughs] the other one. And funnily enough, we all loved John Bonham. He was a hell of a drummer. Amazing drummer, you know. And [as for Plant] it took a little while, because of the voice that he had at the time was a little bit, sort of—he totally made it his own afterwards. . . . So I'd already met them, and Jimmy had auditioned them and kind of said, "Okay, that's good," and then of course John Paul Jones—his wife rang [Jimmy] or something and he said, "Hey, mate, I've been playing sessions with you for all these years. Can I join your band?"

And of course it was a perfect fit because John Paul Jones is a real gent and a wonderful musician. It was a perfect bass player fit for him.

American tour, saying they didn't want to tour anymore. You can't take a horse to water and make it drink. So I knew that was the last tour. And also, we'd been traveling and maybe playing five hundred shows a year, because in those days that's kinda how you made your money. So we were a bit brain-damaged. It was, like,

DS: Any other candidates you remember watching?

CD: Well, there was another young singer—well, he was young at that time. Reid?

DS: Terry Reid?

SOUVENIR PROGRAMME

ROY ORBISON

THE WALKER BROTHERS

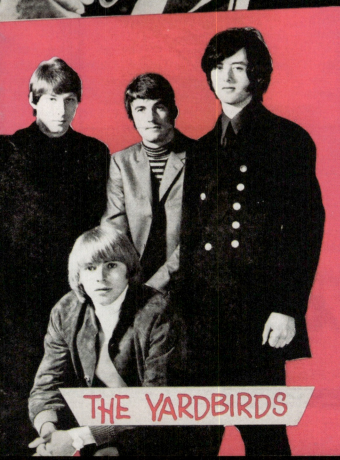

THE YARDBIRDS

THE **BIG** SHOW

JANUARY 1967 EDITION

CD: Terry Reid was a small guy with a huge voice. Soul type of guy.

DS: Did you have any influence on Page?

CD: I think Jimmy was checking out all sorts of people, not always that I was privy to. I think the biggest influence we would have had on Jimmy, frankly, would have been a lot of our arrangements prior to the inception of Led Zeppelin. Because when I listen to things like the [live album recorded at New York's] Anderson Theater, and all sorts of later takes, the arrangements that were going on for some of that stuff was amazing. I can't even believe it myself: wow, did we do that? You know?

DS: So Jimmy's formed his new lineup of the Yardbirds, and you're going into photography. And you get to shoot the back cover of their first album as Led Zeppelin.

CD: The first [photo session] was before I went to work in America as a photographer, and I had a small studio in a place called Putney, which is just on the outskirts of London. I'd worked with Jimmy before on photographs, and we had collaborated and done some quite interesting things. And of course I was friendly with both Peter and Jimmy, and they knew I'd gone into photography, and so they asked me to take the back liner shot for the cover—for twenty-one guineas, I may add, which is [a] pretty cheap price, guys. [Laughs] Only kidding.

But anyway, I got to do this photograph and they turned up in my studio, and I remember Robert had a little jersey on and John Bonham had another little jersey on. These guys were poor. They had no money at that time. And they looked kind of scared and a bit naive and kind of, "Well, what's in front of us? What's the future gonna bring?" You know. And I think that was very much captured in that first photograph, especially when you strip out all the type from the back album cover.

DS: In a recent interview, you mentioned that at a later photo session with Led Zeppelin, years after the first album, the band members "had changed and grown in stature." Could you explain what specific changes you noticed in them?

CD: [It was] maybe two and a half, three years later. John Bonham was well out of it, and Robert Plant was much more, you know, just a man from the caves. And they'd all grown into their roles by that point. But it's just an amazing side-by-side of looking at these two semiportraits of this band, you know, of what was coming and then what happened later.

DS: Do you remember any specific changes with John Paul Jones?

CD: Not really. John Paul Jones was always Steady Eddie, I always thought, kind of a little aloof. I don't think he got quite into all the mayhem that came—maybe he did, I don't know. But he seemed to be very bright, very

intelligent, a thinking guy, and of course, you know, he did all the arrangements with Jimmy and even a little of the production as well, you know.

The two that really changed—because I remember once, I was working in New York in a studio, well out of music at that point, in photography, and Peter rang me up and he said [imitating Peter Grant's voice], "Oh, do you want to come down? The boys are playing at Madison Square Garden and they'd like to see you. Would you come down?" So I went down. Well, the last time we played, it was like five, ten thousand people. Nothing. And we got to Madison Square Garden, and of course it's a concrete joint, isn't it? And I met them downstairs in the dressing rooms, and they were really nice, really polite, you know, and then Jimmy said, "We have to go upstairs and play now, so join us in a minute." And I remember walking up the concrete gantry behind the stage, and everything was moving. It was like, "Jesus, what's going on here?"

And of course in those days, they started out with "Whole Lotta Love," and by that point, they had this mega, mega PA system, you know. Because in my day, nearly everything came off the stage. And they had this huge voltage, and the whole building was—and it was a four-piece. I couldn't believe it. Wow, you know! [Imitating Peter Grant's voice] "So what do you think now? They're pretty good, aren't they?" [Laughs]

DS: Here's one thing that for a while I've wanted to clear up with a person like yourself. Ten years ago, I'm talking to John Paul Jones and I'm asking him about playing bass on some of the Yardbirds' singles—

CD: He did, yeah.

DS: —and he denied it up and down. [Imitating Jones] "No, I didn't. I didn't do that."

CD: Well, he—[pauses] well, I think he, he did on a couple. Because I think they were [producer] Mickie Most sessions. And Mickie Most was all about singles. In fact, he had a cupboard with a drawer in it and he'd open the drawer and all these cassette cartridges would be coming out. And he'd say, [imitating Most] "Well, this will be a nice one for you boys to, you know."

[Most] never'd touch the albums. *We* did all the albums. But of course, Mickie was a real producer, and in those days he wanted real vocals by twelve [o'clock], backing track by one, come back and mix by four, dinner and home by five. He wasn't into, sort of, the looseness that we were working at. So, yeah, he did get—he got session guys in. And of course Jimmy was a big session guy. But I don't think he'd be—he didn't play on *all* of them, I know that. Uh, maybe a *couple*, John Paul Jones.

DS: Top Topham.

CD: Top Topham, yes, my great friend at art school, whose father introduced me to the blues. Thank you so much! He did. He was in the navy, and he brought back

The Yardbirds, along with Roy Orbison and the Walker Brothers, performed in the Big Show—an Australian concert series—in January 1967. This concert program served as a souvenir of the event.

all this wonderful blues music, and that's how Top and I formed the original Yardbirds, and we were at art school, that great art school experiment, along with Eric Clapton, the Who, and so many people that didn't do art but did do music [laughs]. And Top Topham was a budding guitar player, and he was originally in the band when Giorgio Gomelsky was managing the Stones. He gave us the gig at the Crawdaddy Club, and by then we were working every night of the week. Eight nights a week. My father was quite happy about that. But Top's parents, they saw a future for him in art, and they kind of grounded him from going professional [as a musician]. And that, of course, is when we asked Eric to come in and play with us.

DS: What do you make of Top's recent claim that Jimmy Page approached him three times in 1968 with an offer to join his New Yardbirds lineup?

CD: I don't know what to make of that! I, I'm not—you know, rock and roll is a funny, odd business. I really don't know. I'm intrigued! I have heard that, but I just, I mean, I don't know. I couldn't verify it.

DS: Do you remember somebody auditioning for Jimmy's group on vocals and mellotron?

CD: No. No. That wouldn't work.

DS: It's been written you filed a cease-and-desist order against Jimmy Page and Peter Grant prohibiting them from continuing to use the Yardbirds name in England. Could you explain what your intent was?

CD: We had dates left over from our tour, I believe in Scandinavia. And of course, Jimmy was hot to trot. Everybody else—well, particularly Keith and Jim— kind of refused to do it, and that was the end. So I guess Peter and Jimmy were thinking more, "Let's fulfill those contractual dates, and then let's think again," you know. Well, I did nudge him a bit to think again. [Laughs] And I guess that's why they'd become Led Zeppelin.

There was no hard feelings, but it wouldn't have been right, I think, from them to—the New Yardbirds? It was a bit odd, that, you know? It's a bit kitsch.

DS: I think they recognized that, too.

CD: I think so.

DS: Do you think it came down to—clubs don't want to promote them unless they used the familiar name of the Yardbirds or New Yardbirds?

CD: Well, it's possible. I mean, the business was as scummy then as it is campy now at times. Maybe they thought, "Well, who are these guys? We don't know them. But we know the name the Yardbirds." So it's possible that's why, but I think mainly because it was to fulfill contracts

that we had elsewhere. And I think I would have done the same as well under the circumstances.

DS: Do you know the significance of today's date, September 7, specifically forty-three years ago today? It's the anniversary of the first of those Scandinavian dates that Page, Plant, Jones, and Bonham played together.

CD: I heard that those original gigs were so effing loud. You know, they were playing in, like, pub back rooms and things, and they just didn't take any prisoners! Well, a bit like the Yardbirds, really. We didn't take any prisoners.

I always remember a very great story. I came back from New York. [Peter Grant] invited [my wife and me] over to his house, and by this time he was, like, living in a semimansion. [Laughs] Amazing! And he had a cook and a chef and a butler, and it was extraordinary. Last time we went round there, we were kind of—pretty much ordinary guys, you know? And after dinner was served, Peter said to me [imitating Grant], "Come into the music room. We've just come from the studio, and I wanna play you this." And he rolled up the most amazing joint. Mind-blowing, you know? We went into the music room; there was all this fabulous gear in there, and he said, "The boys have just done this, and I think it's gonna be really successful." And it was "Stairway to Heaven." [Laughs] Unbelievable! I was getting the first listen, pretty much, from the studio. And I remember, there was one mistake in it that . . . Jimmy fluffed one note, which I'm sure they went back and redid. But I always remember hearing that and thinking, "Wow, this is pretty good. That drumroll, how does he do that?" [Laughs] Fantastic moment!

DS: What do you remember about "Dazed and Confused"?

CD: It was Jim [McCarty] who found that, as I understand that. The guy [Jake Holmes] was sort of a psychedelic country player. I think he picked it up in the Village here in New York and came to one of our shows and said, "I think we should try this. This is kind of really Yardbirdy kind of music." And we arranged it. Jimmy had a good . . . we all had a good part in the arrangement, how it developed. It became very electric. Because it was a lot acoustic originally. And it went on to become very much a part of our repertoire—short-lived because we weren't around for that much longer at the end. I guess Jimmy then took it on to Led Zeppelin. But you can't screw with dates, guys! [Laughs]

DS: Meaning . . .

CD: Meaning that I don't know what was going on there, really. But it seemed to me that Jake Holmes wrote the song and [the Yardbirds arrangement] was pretty faithful to that . . . and it kind of went on to be a very much sort of Zeppelin song written by them, and I don't quite know how that all happened.

Mark Stein

MARK STEIN IS THE NEW JERSEY—BORN VOCALIST, KEY-BOARDIST, COMPOSER, AND ARRANGER BEST KNOWN AS A FOUNDING MEMBER OF VANILLA FUDGE. THE BAND'S ORIGINAL LINEUP—VOCALIST AND ORGANIST STEIN, BASSIST AND VOCALIST TIM BOGERT, LEAD GUITARIST AND VOCALIST VINCE MARTELL, AND DRUMMER AND VOCALIST CARMINE APPICE—RECORDED FIVE ALBUMS BETWEEN 1966 AND 1969 BEFORE DISBANDING IN 1970. LED ZEPPELIN OPENED FOR THE BAND FROM 1968 TO 1969. CITED AS ONE OF THE FEW AMERICAN LINKS BETWEEN PSYCHEDELIA AND HEAVY METAL, THE BAND REUNITED SEVERAL TIMES OVER THE YEARS, MOST RECENTLY WITH ALL FOUR ORIGINAL MEMBERS. RETURNING TO THE STUDIO IN 2007, VANILLA FUDGE RECORDED *OUT THROUGH THE IN DOOR*, A LED ZEPPELIN COVER ALBUM. IN THIS INTERVIEW FROM THE FALL OF 2009, STEIN IS ASKED ABOUT THE FIRST TIME HE HEARD LED ZEPPELIN.

A recent photograph of Mark Stein on the keyboard.

MARK STEIN: I remember one night hanging out with a couple guys at [Vanilla Fudge manager] Phil Basile's house in Long Island. Ron Terry was our agent back then. So we're getting ready to do this tour out in the Northwest, I guess it was late '68 or early '69. [Ron Terry said,] "I gotta play a track from this new band, it's a band called Led Zeppelin, and they're going to be opening a show and just got signed to Atlantic." So he plays this track and it's called "You Shook Me," right? It goes [singing] "You shook me, you shook me all night long." That's the first time I ever heard that, you know, and Plant's vocal does that, you know, ascending thing and Page's slide guitar goes down with it and I said, man, what was that? And Ron goes, holy shit, and I go, wow, this is a pretty amazing new thing going on. . . . Next thing you know, we were playing a gig, I think it was Albuquerque, or—

DENNY SOMACH: Denver?

MS: That's right, the Denver show [December 26, 1968, at the Denver Auditorium Arena], and this is the show where Vanilla Fudge was headlining. And this new band Led Zeppelin was the first band on the bill. And I think Iron Butterfly might have been on that show, and—

DS: Spirit?

MS: Spirit. But I didn't get to meet any of the guys at that time. We started doing some shows; I remember it was brutal weather—the worst snowstorm in recent history [the bands played December 27–30, 1968, at the Seattle Center, the Pacific Coliseum in Vancouver, the Portland Civic Auditorium, and the Kennedy Pavilion at Gonzaga University in Spokane]. . . . So we were doing one of the coliseums and Led Zeppelin was opening the show for us. I was in the dressing room and knock, knock on the door and this kid, John Bonham, says, I just want to meet you

guys. This innocent-looking kid just walks in. We said come on in, man, pleased to meet ya. So a couple of the guys with Jimmy Page were walking in and we're hanging out, and before you know it, "We love you guys, we're listening to your record, and it's just great to be playing on a show with you guys." . . . [Bonham] said, "Can I meet Carmine?" I say, "Carmine, come here, here's John Bonham, from Led Zeppelin." So they started talking, and developed a really great relationship over the years. I think Carmine got him his first [drum] endorsement at the time. So then it was just a bunch of young kids—wide-eyed, bushy-tailed, innocent, beautiful guys. And we got on great together, and I thought, wow, they were just an amazing band. And people started taking to them right away. So we just started playing a bunch of shows together and it was a really great marriage.

DS: Did you get a chance to see their set?

MS: Yeah, we used to stand by the side of the stage and watch them. I remember going up to Robert the next morning, and saying, "Robert, you know, you guys are great. But you know what? I think you should just move around on stage a little more." I say to Jimmy—he was playing a Telecaster at the time—I know it sounds ridiculous, but I think I said, "I think you should get a little bigger amps. You guys have everything it takes to be this really great band." People talked to me over the years and think I'm giving them a lot of shit but this is the truth—it's how this all started evolving. It just came on so quick, with so much momentum; it just started this Led Zeppelin wave. And before you know it, they were just killing the audience.

DS: . . . So you did those five dates with them. And you really had a chance to see the whole set there in the early stages. Now, what did you think after you saw them in the five days?

MS: Well, they just started evolving, like I said, so quickly. They were getting tighter, more and more confident. They were just in total sync with each other. Plant and Page were amazing. They were just in love with each other on stage. It was so sexual and exciting and powerful and dynamic, and the rhythm section with Jonesy—John Paul Jones—and Bonham was obvious. And they were just getting stronger and stronger; the legion of fans just started growing and growing. If I could fast-forward to a gig, I guess it was in [July] '69, we were doing the Terrace Ballroom, I guess it was in Salt Lake City. . . . They opened for us for the first tour; the second time in the United States we were sharing the bill. Some nights they'd be headlining. There was one night again in Salt Lake, where we were opening; no, they were opening for us—forgive me. So they go on stage, and I'm standing in the audience, and they just played the most incredibly powerful show. And I was just blown away. I was scared to go on after that. . . . That's how intense it was. I tell you what—they inspired us to play one of the most intense shows that we've ever played. So it was kind of like two heavyweight fighters on the same bill that night.

DS: Okay, now tell me, let me fast-forward a little bit; I think there's a story where you ran into John Paul Jones when you were driving around L.A.? Would you tell me that story?

MS: I don't know. Unless you're talking about the one in Malibu.

DS: Malibu.

MS: Oh, yeah! I guess that had to be in the '70s. I was with Patty [Mark's wife, Patty Stein] and at the time I was living in Thousand Oaks. . . . We were driving in Malibu one day, taking a drive, and I said, "Patty, that's John Paul Jones walking down the street!" So I pull over and say, "Hey, Jonesy!" He says, "Holy shit, Mark!" We got outta the car, shook hands, and gave each other a hug, and he introduced me to one of the roadies. And he says, "This is Mark from Vanilla Fudge, they broke us in." It had to be, I don't know, maybe '74? . . . He invites me into the house, you know? And I walk in the house and there's Peter Grant, and there's Robert Plant, and I say

> I'm standing next to (Zeppelin road manager) Richard Cole, and I mean, they were just blowing me away and blowing the audience away. They wouldn't let them off the stage, and I said to Cole, "Jesus Christ. How do you follow that?" He said, "Look, just go up and play."

DS: What kind of difference did you see from the December–January dates to that second tour four or five months later?

MS: Well, in the initial days it was a group with incredible talent and a future that was more, really, experimenting with themselves and the audience, becoming stronger and stronger, to suddenly, in such a short time, becoming this incredibly powerful band that was just blowing everybody away. It was just like a heavyweight fighter that was kicking the shit out of everybody. Nobody wanted to fight them. We were the only band that would tour with them. It was amazing. But it was a short time after that that they were, you know, kind of blowing us off the stage. And that was kind of like getting to our demise, and ultimately they took off and became the rock gods that they became.

DS: A lot of people say that there was a fifth member, [band manager] Peter Grant, that had a lot to do with it. Did you ever meet Peter Grant?

MS: We were great friends. We met in England and our first tour in '67 in England. I remember meeting him when he was managing the Yardbirds. This big heavy dude, who was very powerful and didn't take shit from anybody. He was the perfect manager for them. I mean, he opened up more avenues, controlled more things than people can imagine. I have to say that he was one of the most influential figures since the beginning of big-business rock and roll. He made a lot of things happen. . . .

oh, my God, how ya doing? And actually, I think it was about the time he hurt his leg, he was in a cast.

DS: Yeah, he crashed, it was August '75.

MS: Yeah, that's when it was. He was in a cast, and we were just talking about the old days. So I don't know, they were getting ready to go play, and were rehearsing at SIR [rehearsal studio] that night and they invited me over to rehearsal. So I went down to rehearsal that night and they said, "Keep it quiet." Nobody knew that Zeppelin was rehearsing that night. I was just hanging out with the guys and Peter and it was awesome, it was just wonderful being with them guys again. Actually, there was a keyboard there and I started playing, we actually started jamming on something, I don't remember what it was but I did get to jam with Zeppelin that night. The next day, I remember, it had gotten all over the streets. Carmine called me up, I remember, and says, "Hey, is this the new keyboard player of Led Zeppelin?" I said, "Yeah!" You know, it was, like, an awesome night, so you can't keep a lid on that stuff, right?

DS: Any other festivals where you played that Zeppelin played?

MS: Yeah, I remember the Seattle Pop Festival [July 25–27, 1969]. That was really cool. And everybody was on that show—Vanilla Fudge, Zeppelin, the Doors, Ike and Tina Turner, so many of them. I tell you, everybody

An ad for the Seattle Pop Festival, July 25–27, 1969. Led Zeppelin and Vanilla Fudge shared the bill with numerous other acts.

SEATTLE POP FESTIVAL

25, 26, 27 JULY
GOLD CREEK PARK
WOODINVILLE,

CHUCK BERRY	GUESS WHO
BLACK SNAKE	IT'S A BEAUTIFUL DAY
TIM BUCKLEY	LED ZEPPELIN
THE BYRDS	CHARLES LLOYD
CHICAGO TRANSIT AUTHORITY	LONNIE MACK
ALBERT COLLINS	LEE MICHAELS
ALICE COOPER	ROCKIN FU
CROME SYRCUS	MURRAY ROMAN
BO DIDDLEY	SANTANA
THE DOORS	SPIRIT
FLOATING BRIDGE	TEN YEARS AFTER
THE FLOCK	IKE & TINA TURNER
FLYING BURRITO BROTHERS	VANILLA FUDGE
	THE YOUNGBLOODS

LIGHTS BY THE RETINA CIRCUS

TICKETS AVAILABLE AT THE FOLLOWING LOCATIONS:

DISCOUNT RECORDS; CAMPUS MUSIC - UNIVERSITY DISTRICT   BANDSTAND MUSIC; BELL, BOOK AND CANDLE - BELLEVUE
WAREHOUSE OF MUSIC; THE BON MARCHE - DOWNTOWN   KERN'S MUSIC ; FARMER'S MUSIC - BURIEN
SHORELINE MUSIC - NORTH SEATTLE   ALL HOUSE of VALUES STORES

RECORD ALBUMS FEATURED AT ALL HOUSE of VALUES STORES

MAIL ORDER : BOYD GRAFMYRE PRODUCTIONS, po box 3146, seattle 98114

$6 one day , $15 three days

was so stoned that day—drinking, and doing this and that. Wonderful days.

DS: Did you get a chance to see their set?

MS: Robert Plant jumped up on stage just before I went on, and I was drinking a lot, I remember. I went to grab him. I was hugging him and he says, "It's great to see you, too," and I said, "Man, I really love you," and I was like, "Wait a minute, man," and I wouldn't let go of him, you know? We developed such camaraderie from the early days, and then all the madness that evolved. . . .

maybe he didn't recognize me because my hair was long or whatever, but I says, "Hey, Rob, Rob, turn around." And he says, "Mark! Mark! I was thinking it was somebody from the press, I was just sloughing you off, you know?" And he says, "You haven't, uh, you haven't, uh, heard any mud sharks, have you? [Note: This is a reference to a notorious rumor involving a groupie, members of Led Zeppelin's entourage, Stein, and a fish.] That was all a bunch of rubbish, wasn't it?" And he goes, "I never heard anything like that, either, I don't know where that came from." Then we started laughing. But we were all hanging out backstage, all the guys and Zeppelin, and all

Just as the sun broke and the night started, Zeppelin went on and it was just a sight to behold. They were just at the beginning of the total command of rock and roll in those days.

DS: Okay, so aside from Seattle, any other dates that you remember? I want to talk about—you played the Atlantic Records fortieth anniversary, where they got together. Did you see them at that show?

MS: Yes, I saw them at that show.

DS: Okay, so could you give us, like, a sort of view-from-the-top type of analysis from that night and Vanilla Fudge playing and also seeing Zeppelin?

MS: I remember the Atlantic fortieth anniversary . . . and everybody that was anybody on Atlantic was there. . . . It was just like a kid in a rock candy store. And I did see Led Zeppelin take the stage, and I believe it was Jason Bonham that was playing drums with them on that show, and yeah, you know, it was so many years later and Robert was trying to do a lot of the vocals he did when he was so many years younger. So they were good, but it wasn't, obviously, you know, the spontaneity and the greatness that they had in earlier years. And that kind of bothered me, to be honest, because there were a lot of people that saw Zeppelin for the first time, and I saw them when they were in their heyday, when they were amazing. And I used to hear a couple of people saying, "You know, I saw Zeppelin and they were kind of like this and that," and I said, "You know, look, you got to remember, Zeppelin were phenomenal in the early days and all through the '70s and into the '80s, so don't judge Led Zeppelin by what you saw that night." The guys had been through hell and back, and it was decades later, so I don't think it's fair to judge them that way. Judge them by their earlier performances, judge by what you've seen on DVDs. But boy, I remember going up to Robert Plant and I hit him on the back, and he turns around and

these bands and beautiful atmosphere. . . . It was one of the great rock festivals, in my view, of all time.

DS: Well, since you did mention that incident, I got to ask you about it.

MS: Patty, my wife, and all my grandkids—please put your earmuffs on. I really don't have the right answer for this, but go ahead, ask the question.

DS: What is the story, and it's been documented in books— have you ever read *Stairway to Heaven* or *Hammer of the Gods*?

MS: Yes, I read *Hammer of the Gods*. I'm in it.

DS: Well I know you're in it. So what is this magical story that is mythical, whatever, mud sharks, Seattle, the Waterside Inn, is that it?

MS: Edgewater.

DS: Edgewater Inn.

MS: It was the Edgewater Inn in Seattle. Well, this was actually during those few days at the Seattle Pop Festival. It was just partying, it was us, Fudge and Zeppelin, partying, and at the time I had a Super 8 camera and I was taking pictures of, you know, on the road and everything, and shows and this and that. I don't know, I walked into the room and it was Bonham and Page. I guess they were throwing fishing lines out the window right into the water and just . . . fishing! They were Englishmen and loved to fish. Everybody was hanging out, drinking, and I guess they . . . I don't really remember what they caught. You know, this story has been over-under-

Commemorative pins from the Atlantic Records fortieth-anniversary concert at Madison Square Garden, May 14, 1988.

sideways-down like a million times. I can't get specific on it because I really don't remember.

DS: Is there a story there and you're just not telling it or . . .

MS: Yeah, there's a story there, there's a story there. There was some groupie chick running around . . .

DS: Because you know, if I ever run into the other three guys I'm going to ask them.

MS: Honestly, I don't really think they were in the room. I was just taking pictures of everything that was happening while they were catching, whatever, mud shark or

snapper or whatever the hell they caught. And they were just partying, and there was a chick there, and we were doing the usual rock-and-roll craziness and, you know . . . I'll leave the rest to the imagination.

DS: Okay, all right. And you said earlier about that footage?

MS: Well, I gave the Super 8 to [Vanilla Fudge road manager] Bruce Wayne. You know, it was—I never at the time thought it was going to turn into this majestic rock-and-roll road story. I said, here, take this thing. I was just a kid myself. What was I—twenty, twenty-one? I said I don't know where I'm going to get this developed, take care of it. And I never heard anything after that. That's the truth.

Joe Perry

ANTHONY JOSEPH "JOE" PERRY IS THE LEAD GUITARIST, PRINCIPAL COSONGWRITER, AND COPRODUCER OF AEROSMITH. IN THE LATE 1960S, PERRY AND FUTURE AEROSMITH MEMBER TOM HAMILTON FORMED THE JAM BAND. AFTER STEVEN TYLER, BRAD WHITFORD, AND JOEY KRAMER JOINED PERRY AND HAMILTON IN 1970, THE JAM BAND BECAME AEROSMITH. THEY ARE THE BEST-SELLING AMERICAN ROCK BAND OF ALL TIME, HAVING SOLD MORE THAN 150 MILLION ALBUMS WORLDWIDE. THEIR HIT RECORDS INCLUDE THE AUSPICIOUS DEBUT ALBUM *AEROSMITH*, AS WELL AS *TOYS IN THE ATTIC*, *ROCKS*, *PUMP*, AND *GET A GRIP*. THEY HAVE WON FOUR GRAMMY AWARDS AND WERE INDUCTED INTO THE ROCK AND ROLL HALL OF FAME IN 2001.

DURING AN INTERVIEW FOR THE GIBSON GUITAR WEBSITE, PERRY STATED, "PEOPLE CALL AEROSMITH THE AMERICAN STONES, BUT WE WERE ALWAYS THE AMERICAN ZEPPELIN."

PERRY IS A CLOSE FRIEND OF JIMMY PAGE, AND WHEN LED ZEPPELIN WAS NOMINATED FOR THE ROCK AND ROLL HALL OF FAME, PAGE ASKED JOE TO INDUCT THEM.

IN THIS INTERVIEW, GIVEN IN THE FALL OF 2011 EXCLUSIVELY FOR THIS BOOK, PERRY, AN ACKNOWLEDGED LED ZEPPELIN AND YARDBIRDS FAN, IS ASKED IF IT'S TRUE THAT THE JAM BAND PLAYED "TRAIN KEPT A-ROLLIN'," A STAPLE OF THE YARDBIRDS REPERTOIRE, AND WHETHER STEVEN TYLER'S EARLIER BAND, CHAIN REACTION, PLAYED THE SAME SONG.

JOE PERRY: Yeah, I can't say I remember hearing Steven's band play it but I know it was a song they had in their repertoire. . . . When we did finally did get up and jam it was a song we both knew, so yeah.

DENNY SOMACH: It must be a favorite because I believe, if I'm not mistaken, that it appears on three of your live albums.

JP: Well, it's always been a kind of touchstone of our set of songs. It was one of . . . the first songs we learned together in our set when we were playing clubs and things. . . . We just really played for the fun of it and to get the people dancing. We weren't really concerned with trying to get a hit record or anything like that. That was never any kind of goal. We just happened to get up and play. The fact that they knew the songs, this hard rock song, this protometal song, gave us a common language, so to speak. . . .

DS: Did you ever see the Yardbirds live?

JP: No, unfortunately. I heard they played at a couple ballrooms in the area. It was after the fact. I didn't get a chance to see them. I know Steven saw them play once or twice. He had a friend who somehow managed to hook up with those guys at a club somewhere and got Steven's band an opening slot on a couple of shows. Because a lot of bands that came over with their guitars and all the local bands—the best local band would open the show wherever these bands would play. That's how Steven got to meet them. He was about four or five years ahead of us in the music business, having a record deal and having a single in the jukebox and being in New York City.

DS: The song "Livin' on the Edge"—did you nick a line or two from [the Yardbirds'] "Mister, You're a Better Man Than I"—is that correct?

JP: I didn't—I didn't write the lyrics.

DS: Okay, but you know what I'm referring to?

JP: [Laughs] Yeah, yeah.

DS: [Laughs] When the lyrics were presented to you and you were playing it, did you recognize it at the time?

JP: Of course. I was here when we wrote the lyrics. We debated whether to use it and we figured, why not? It's a great line. It fit the song. It was a kind of a tip of the hat, you know?

Joe Perry performs with Aerosmith at the BankAtlantic Center in Sunrise, Florida, August 10, 2010.

DS: Okay. Now, I also understand that somehow there's some Yardbirds influence in "Walk This Way." Is that correct? There's a riff in there . . .

JP: No, I can't say directly or anything like that. The only thing that would be any kind of lineage would be the fact that I heard that Jeff [Beck, the Yardbirds' guitarist in 1965–66] was a fan of the Meters, that funk band from New Orleans. I didn't know that and I happened to live next door to one of the DJs for the local FM station and . . . he was one of the writers for the music paper and he was really good friends with the DJ Maxanne Sartori [a Boston radio personality]. So we used to hang out and he would play me different stuff and I learned about the Meters from him. That kind of tied in with our being hip to James Brown; Joey [Kramer, the Aerosmith drummer] played in this soul cover band when we met him so we got turned on to James Brown. Not only did I have a little bit of education in the blues but also, for a white kid from the suburbs, I probably knew a little more about funk than the next kid. I was really into the Meters. I figured it would be really cool to write a song. I was discovering how to write songs and I figured, why don't I write one and aim down that road? Try to steer this car into that set of woods. And that's where the influence for "Walk This Way" came from. It's kind of a distant lineage there to the Yardbirds with Jeff Beck being in the Yardbirds and a fan of the Meters and me being a fan of the Meters as well. . . .

DS: Right. Let me move on to Zeppelin. Did you ever see Zeppelin in the early days?

JP: No, I missed them. They are one of the few bands that I did miss.

DS: You saw them later on, though, right?

JP: Yeah. The first time I saw them was when they were doing five nights at Madison Square Garden, which was pretty huge and still is even more so. That was the first time I saw them.

DS: Did you get to meet them at that point? Because I know over the years you and Jimmy Page have become friends.

JP: Yeah.

DS: When was the first time you actually met them?

JP: Well, I met them—we were both staying at the same hotel when they were doing that run at the Garden [in 1977]. We were on tour or we were recording; I'm not sure which. I remember walking into Jimmy. He was wandering around the halls at four in the morning. We bumped into each other and hung out for a while; quite a while.

DS: Did he know who you were? Was he aware of the band?

JP: Yeah. And he invited me to the show. We went to the show the next day and I saw him there. At that point they were really at their peak. They were starting to reach that point where they were putting out amazing records and their shows would sometimes last two to three hours and take long solos and things like that. So it was over the years—every couple years I'd bump into him. After [Aerosmith] got back together we really started to become friends. It's funny because we didn't really talk too much about guitar or things like that. Mostly we talked about family. He had just gotten married again and was having kids. . . .

> When (Jimmy) was over here, we'd have him come over and when I was over in England, we'd go over there and hang out. Just over the years we've had a relationship. 'Course he knew Steven from the Yardbirds days, so we became friends.

DS: You did play with them a couple times, like at Donington and at the Marquee [in August 1990]?

JP: Yeah, we had quite a weekend. We were playing at the Donington festival and I'm not sure how it hooked up but we were going to play the Marquee Club. It was something we always wanted to play. It was like playing the Whisky a Go Go for an English band, or CBGB.

DS: You were doing a night at the Marquee . . . was it planned that Jimmy Page was going to get up and play?

JP: Well, we talked about it and he said, yeah, I'll do that and we'll jam and have some fun. As it turned out the sound check was the high point because we got to play about eight Yardbirds songs with him. . . . Working out the songs and which ones we were going to do was an amazing thing for us. Talk about a dream come true. To play "Shapes of Things" with Jimmy Page—it was great. And then he took the bus with us out to Donington the next day or the day after, whenever it was, so we spent three or four days hanging out with him.

DS: Did you play any Zeppelin songs on that show?

JP: Yeah. I think we did. I think we played "Immigrant Song" and "Whole Lotta Love," maybe. I don't know. It's probably on the Internet. . . .

DS: I know recently, or about a year ago, you did talk about the rumored sessions that Steven was doing, some rehearsals, with Jimmy Page and company. What was the story on that?

JP: Well, I wasn't there, so all I can do is tell you that everything I know is what I had read in the paper mostly from the British press and from the few people that were there that I know. . . . Whenever Jimmy gets together and plays, or Steven or I'm going to be someplace, you know, everybody's kind of listening and watching what's going on.

DS: Did you hear anything from Jimmy Page directly?

JP: Well, I talked to him a few months afterwards and asked him if what I read in the paper was true and he confirmed that it was, indeed, true. So all the stuff that was in the paper was pretty accurate. . . .

DS: Do you have any idea what you think Jimmy Page's next musical situation will be? He just recently launched a website after all these years, and there's all these stories that he's about to do something. Are you aware of anything, musically?

JP: Well, I'm always hearing about him and wanting to get together. I know he'd really like to do Zeppelin. And that's always around the corner. You never know when Robert's going to change his mind . . . we don't talk that much about it. We've even talked about doing things together. In fact, when Steven was off doing the *American Idol* thing, one of the things that crossed my mind was I know Jimmy was thinking about doing some stuff and we've talked over the years about how it'd be great to play together in a kind of someday kind of way. Someday got a little closer for a few minutes but I really don't know. I can't really say what he's up to. I know he travels a lot and I know he wants to play. I don't know; we'll see.

DS: Do you remember when you got the word that Jimmy wanted you to induct him into the Rock and Roll Hall of Fame—where you were and what your reaction was?

JP: We were in Argentina. He and Robert were on their way back—they had either just done some gigs in Japan or they were promoting something.

DS: That was probably the Page/Plant tour [1995, in support of Unledded].

JP: Yeah, maybe. All I know is they knew we were in Argentina, so they took a side trip and we hung out with Jimmy. He said, do you want to have lunch, so Billie [Perry's wife, Billie Paulette Montgomery Perry] and I . . . went down to have lunch and Jimmy asked if I would induct him into the Hall of Fame. I was really flattered— I mean, I was kind of speechless for a few minutes. Robert asked Steven if he would do it. It took us a few minutes to get over that. Of course, I'm not much of a public speaker, but I think everybody got the vibe of how we felt about doing it and being the ones.

DS: Do you remember what songs you played with them at the induction?

JP: I'm pretty sure we played "Train Kept A-Rollin'" and "Immigrant Song."

DS: Was it "Bring It On Home" that you played? [Note: This is the song that they played together.]

JP: I can't remember. I was pretty stunned that night, I have to say.

DS: [Laughs] How important was Jimmy Page's production to the success of Led Zeppelin? Do you agree that his production technique was a big part of the Led Zeppelin sound?

JP: Well, I think he was definitely a pioneer in that part of things. First of all, I don't think he gets anywhere the credit that he deserves for being the producer he is. If he was nothing else and just a producer, he'd be right up there with the top ten producers from that generation. It's incredible the way he used the studio to get different sounds out of guitars and experiment. Like I said before, I never really got a chance to ask him a lot of questions about the studio, about playing, about the bands—guitar player's questions and those kind of things. *Guitar Player* [magazine] did a series where they had younger guitar players interviewing their idols or their friends—older guitar players or whatever—so they asked me if I'd interview Jimmy, which I did, and this was after being friends with him for twenty years. I finally got to ask him about his guitar strings on the first album. Stuff you'd think I would have asked him first off. So it was great; I got a chance to ask him some of those questions. He was pretty close to the vest, being a typical English musician. They have their secrets and they keep them pretty close. They don't want it out there. He told me stuff that he knew I wouldn't be talking about to anybody else, but since it was an interview he was a little tight-lipped about it.

DS: Were there particular songs that you asked him about?

JP: Not so much that, but just where he was at during the first record. Some bands, it's like the first time they've ever been recorded, the first time they've ever heard what they sounded like coming back through speakers. Or they were a band that had multiple chances to be in the studio and played with a lot of different bands and written a lot of different songs and kind of knew what they were doing when they did their big record, so to speak, and Jimmy was definitely one of those, having the track record that he had before Led Zeppelin. Everything from little Jimmy Page at fourteen and being on talent shows, to being the leader of the New Yardbirds, and coming to America and watching what was going on at the rock shows, and following his buddy Jeff Beck around and watching his shows, and the Who, and just kind of studying what's going on. All that stuff, and spending thousands and thousands of hours in the studio as one of the top studio musicians— when he went in to do that first record, and assemble the musicians he assembled, I mean, he knew what he wanted. . . .

His backlog of blues knowledge and what he knew as a musicologist, and [his ability] to tie all that together, was just brilliant. He knew what he wanted to do.

He knew what kind of guitars he wanted to use acoustically and what kind of compressors and what kind of microphones, and what kind of tape machines. He knew all the stuff he wanted to use on the first record and he certainly wasn't a snob. Because of what it was going to take to launch Zeppelin, they were going to have to work hard and stay on the road. He knew how to get sounds. He wasn't married to any particular studio. He knew what sound he wanted, and he knew what it took to get that, so he could substitute an LA-2A [leveling amplifier] for a different kind of compressor to get a certain sound. Or substitute this amp for that amp to get the sound he wanted. It's like George Martin said, it's all in your ears, or all you need is ears. . . .

Jimmy was incredible at getting those sounds and knowing what he wanted to hear. That's why they were able to travel and do those records in various studios all over the place wherever they were touring; whenever they had time off, they went in and recorded.

DS: He was notorious for changing engineers on just about every record.

JP: Well, he knew what he wanted. Technology changed really fast during those periods, so I'm sure he wanted people that were right up at the forefront. When you're on the road, you don't get a chance to spend a lot of time in some of the big studios over a long period of time as they're getting new tape machines, new equipment. Especially if you're in some backwater studio in Minneapolis or you're in the commercial room—the place where they cut commercials in Ohio. Or in a radio station and cutting leads, you might not have the cutting-edge equipment. That's why you want to bring in people who know the latest stuff. I think that's probably the reason why you keep changing people out. I mean, the last time he recorded at Olympic Studios might have been a four-track machine with a two-bus board, and the next time he went in there, they might have had a sixteen-track machine, so you want the guy who was used to that. And the compressors were getting better; there were a lot of things. And some of the things didn't sound as good as the old stuff. And so he'd stick with it. He was always looking for new ways to make the guitar sound different. Using the violin bow—some of the tricks you might see someone use, he'd take it, bend it, and turn it into something new.

DS: Give me an example of some of your favorite Zeppelin tunes and why. They don't have to be the obvious ones.

JP: Well, I don't know. I think that some of the later ones—he was really smart in that he knew that once they broke, the first couple of records—the songs would be the backbone of their career. They were going to be the ones that everyone would want to hear. After establishing themselves as being a heavy metal band—if you could call that music heavy metal—or a hard rock band, then he felt they were free to experiment. He knew that all they had to do was put one or two hard rock songs on there—or three or four, and they could really experiment. He knew all of the British folk songs and the medieval folk songs, and they would incorporate world music into their sound, and he wasn't afraid to do that. He knew that live, they would always be able to excite the audience by playing their first batch of records.

DS: Like "Dazed and Confused" and "How Many More Times?"

JP: Yeah, he was very canny about that. He was able to go off and experiment and try different things. It didn't really matter to him to play any kind of format or have the song be under three and a half minutes. If it felt like it needed to be seven minutes long, then that's how long it was going to be. One riff would change to another; one flavor would change to another flavor. Also, that was a reflection of how music was. He was clearly listening to how other bands were doing things. I know that him and Townshend had a kind of friendly bet going about that: Jimmy could do in one song what it took Pete to do in a whole rock opera. You know, changing the energy and the vibe and telling a whole story. So Jimmy set out to do that, and I think he did, in "The Song Remains the Same." . . .

DS: Is the definitive Zeppelin song for you "Whole Lotta Love," "Kashmir," or "Stairway to Heaven?"

JP: I don't know. I'd have to say "Song Remains the Same." And then a couple of other songs on [*Houses of the Holy*] are amazing. There are some songs that go from one end to the other. It shows off Jimmy's playing. . . .

DS: With a song like "Kashmir"—did that take you by surprise?

JP: No. I think it was just one of the best ones that they ever wrote. Obviously, the Moroccan, African section of the blues influenced them. The blues kind of went off in three different branches. The way they came over from that music that formed the grandfather to the blues as we know it—the Delta blues and Chicago blues and so on. The blues—the music that was the forerunner, they were influenced more by the Moroccan, that northeastern form of African music. They incorporated that as well as the Far Eastern Indian modal scales and things like that. They were able to experiment with that and they did. He was amazing at being able to pick the talent that was able to help him translate what was going on in his head, what he saw down the road.

DS: Give me just a word or two about John Bonham as a drummer. People say that he was the ultimate rock drummer. What's your feeling about that?

JP: Well, I think he definitely—as Jimmy was probably the ultimate rock producer for that kind of music, you can't define what kind of a band Led Zeppelin is; they're not a heavy metal band, they're not a hard rock band, they're not a blues band, they're not a blues-rock band, they're all of those bands. They're a folk band. They're a world music band. They're all of those. I think that John Bonham's genius was that he could—as was John Paul Jones—he was able to help form that vision. Obviously, Jimmy was the leader and driving force but they all worked together to form this thing—this Led Zeppelin. . . .

One of my favorite tours that I ever saw Jimmy play was when he toured with Robert and they brought that Egyptian band with them. They had the hurdy-gurdy player and they brought all these world instruments with them and some of the top players and that really showed what Zeppelin was all about because they created that music live. There was no tape. There was no sampling; it was the real thing.

DS: Did you ever read *Hammer of the Gods*? The reason I ask that is, Stephen Davis, who wrote that, also wrote your biography, correct?

JP: Right.

DS: What did you think of *Hammer of the Gods*?

JP: I thought it was good. I thought that it was a little sensational, but you have to make a living, you know. I think a lot of the things they did—music wasn't the only thing they pioneered, let's put it that way. . . . I think that Bonzo was definitely going neck and neck with Keith Moon. I don't know what it is about drummers, but the two of them, they must have read what each one was doing and kept trying to top each other. Unfortunately, they topped each other to the point where they both went over the cliff. That was just an incredibly sad, sad thing, that we lost both of them, because they were both groundbreaking drummers. Incredible. The stuff they did on the side, they also lived out to the ultimate.

> ## It was almost like going to church, seeing them perform live. I mean, it was really magical; it was a magical thing because they incorporated so much music and the music they used.

Ioannis, Jimmy Page: Achilles Last Stand *(detail), 2011.*

Simon **Kirke**

SIMON KIRKE IS AN ENGLISH ROCK DRUMMER AND SONG-WRITER BEST KNOWN AS A MEMBER OF BAD COMPANY (THE FIRST BAND TO RELEASE AN ALBUM ON LED ZEPPELIN'S SWAN SONG LABEL) AND, BEFORE THAT, THE BAND FREE.

IN 1968, KIRKE, ALONG WITH GUITARIST PAUL KOSSOFF, SINGER-SONGWRITER PAUL RODGERS, AND BASS GUITARIST ANDY FRASER, FORMED FREE. OVER THE NEXT FOUR YEARS, FREE WAS INFLUENTIAL IN THE UK AS WELL AS THE U.S. THEIR BIGGEST HIT WAS THE NUMBER ONE "ALL RIGHT NOW." AFTER FREE DISBANDED IN 1973, SIMON AND RODGERS—JOINED BY GUITARIST MICK RALPHS (MOTT THE HOOPLE) AND BASSIST BOZ BURRELL (KING CRIMSON)—FORMED BAD COMPANY.

MORE RECENTLY, KIRKE HAS TOURED WITH RINGO STARR'S ALL-STARR BAND ON THREE OCCASIONS. HE TOURED WITH A REUNITED BAD COMPANY IN 2009 AND HAS BEEN PLAYING WITH NEW YORK ROCK BAND ZETA VANG AS A SIDE PROJECT. THIS INTERVIEW TOOK PLACE IN SEPTEMBER 2011.

DENNY SOMACH: Bad Company was one of those bands that just came out with that single that just exploded. I'm sure it was a combination of things—we'll talk about the Peter Grant part of it in a minute—but were you surprised at the immediacy?

SIMON KIRKE: Uh, I was pleasantly . . . not that surprised. And I don't want to sound arrogant. You know, we'd been around the block. All four of us had been in very well-known bands. But we'd all been tugging this great big boulder behind us—you know, we'd had this drug addiction . . . and Mick had had this growl with Ian Hunter [lead singer of Mott the Hoople]; he was fed up with it. And finally we're in a band where all the four guys are healthy. . . Not only that, but we've teamed up with possibly the best manager on the planet, who is aligned with the best band on the planet, which is Led Zeppelin, and Peter Grant. And it was like all the elements coming together. "Can't Get Enough" was a wonderful song to play, it was the first song we recorded as Bad Company, and you can hear me tuggin' out "One, two, three, yeah!" And we just exploded. And as I said, with that management of Peter Grant, we couldn't fail.

DS: Did you know Peter Grant? . . . Because you were [Swan Song's] first signing. How did that go?

SK: No. Well, we sat round the table in Paul's cottage in the country, and we were so stoked about the way that this band was sounding, and Paul's great, you know, he takes the bull by the horns and says, "Who's the biggest band in the world right now?" And he says, "Led

Simon Kirke in a recent photograph.

Zeppelin." And we says, "Right," and he says, "Who manages Led Zeppelin?" And we didn't know. We didn't know. So we made some phone calls, in the days before the Internet, you know, we really had to find out. Peter Grant. How do we get his number? Finally got his number, we called him—I mean, Paul called him. Because he's got some moxie, Paul, and we were there, and he says, "Hello, Mr. Grant. I have a band," and we heard Peter say, "I know." So it was already out and amongst the little fraternity that Free and Mott and King Crimson were put in a band together. And he came to see us, he drove across England, and he was very, very clever. This is what happened: he said, "I'll be at your rehearsal at two o'clock." So we play our set, we play ten songs that we know . . . we play and play. Two o'clock comes. Three o'clock comes, three-thirty, four o'clock. No Peter Grant. Son of a gun—he finally walks in and he's huge and, like, 320 pounds, ex-wrestler, sunglasses, and we says, "Oh, forget about everything that we [just] said about him." "Peter, good to see ya. Sit down, we'll play you the set." He says, "Don't worry, I've heard it." We says, "What do you mean?" He says, "I've been out in the car park for the last hour in my car listening to you through the window." He knew that we'd be a little bit nervous, so he just listened to us muck around through the set because no one was there. He says, "I think you sound great, I'd like you to be on LZ's new label." And then he offered to carry some of my drums out to the van. I said, "Man, you've got a friend for life." And that was Peter Grant.

DS: So aside from him being your manager—because everyone who has ever known him has said, "I gotta great Peter Grant story!" And such and such—he met [Bob] Dylan . . .

SK: You know, Zeppelin were a hard bunch, particularly Bonzo. I mean, they were a hard bunch to keep down. In fact, only Bonzo, and without getting into specifics, Bonzo used to get into a lot of trouble. I believe it was in Hollywood and there was a party the night that Zeppelin had done the three nights at the Forum or whatever. And Dylan was introduced to Peter Grant. He said, "Oh, I'm the manager of Led Zeppelin," and Dylan said, "Oh, don't tell me your troubles," 'cause, you know, Bonzo was being Bonzo. Peter Grant stories—I've, I've got some, yeah. I've got some Peter Grant stories.

DS: Did you read—there's a biography that Chris Welch wrote.

SK: *The Man Who Led Zeppelin?*

DS: Yeah.

SK: Oh, really? I like the story about in the pirate radio days when, you know, ships used to come out and he used to go out to these pirate ships and Frisbee these 45s of Zeppelin's singles, trying to get them on the deck of Radio Caroline. I mean, there's a wonderful story in

those days, and he used to go out with Mickie Most, who was a famous producer back then, the pair of them used to skipper this little craft out. And then one day, Mickie threw the anchor over and forgot to tie it to the rope. . . .

DS: All right, that brings us to some Zeppelin questions. Let me start by saying, you had the pleasure—or the task—of opening for Zeppelin at the O₂ Arena. Tell me what that was like.

SK: Oh. Well, you know, initially, the lineup had been finalized, and someone suggested to Harvey Goldsmith, the promoter, that there's a track called "Fanfare for the Common Man" by Aaron Copland, and it would be a good idea if a band of well-known musicians, a supergroup or whatever, would open it up. And the first choice was Keith Emerson, because he was quite classically trained, and he quickly called Chris Squire [of Yes], who called me and [Yes drummer] Alan White to do percussion—and it snowballed from there. So we rehearsed, and everyone was kind of, "Oh, I wonder how Zeppelin are gonna sound." Because obviously, Bonzo wasn't around. But Jason was—and I knew Jason was a great drummer. And rumors were coming in—they sound great, they sound terrible, they sound great, la la la. So when they hit the stage on the night, I believe they started out with "Good Times Bad Times," and it was like 1969 or whatever, I guess—they sounded great. And parts of that show were absolutely outstanding, not least of all because Jason played drums so wonderfully, and "Kashmir" was the best thing I ever heard on stage by a rock band ever. . . .

DS: Okay, now, I think I've spoken to everybody—to the other three guys—what was going on backstage?

SK: They were very much themselves. They kept themselves to themselves. I had a guitar that I'd offered to have autographed by them for the Wounded Warrior project over here. So I'd taken it over and I'd given it to Bill Curbishley, who managed Jimmy and Robert. I said "Is there any chance of me going to see them?" Because they knew who I was, and he says, "No way, man, I'm really sorry." He said, "They're all sealed off, no one's going in, except road crew and me." I said "Okay." Anyway, I gave him the guitar and they did sign it. But no, so everyone was a bit keyed up, and I think they were as keyed up as anyone because of what was expected of them—that this was Zeppelin, man, and they had played for years and years and years and, you know . . .

DS: What was your relationship with John Bonham?

SK: Oh, I loved him. We were pretty much from the same age, you know, I think he was born a few months before me—I was born in July '49, and he was born, I believe, a couple of months before that. [Note: Bonham was born in May 1948.] So we were pretty much on the same level in terms of time. My very, very first memory of Bonzo was when Free came to New York, opening for Blind Faith. We were in this Irish bar on Eighth and Forty-Eighth;

we'd just arrived—we were terrified because we'd been turned over by the customs in JFK, I mean turned inside out, because of our hair. It was '69. It was a rough time to be a hippie. So we were absolutely terrified. First time I'd seen a gun on the hip of a police. Anyway, so we're sitting there nursing our little Budweiser or whatever, and the barman comes over and he's got four pints of Guinness and he puts them down on the table between us and he says, "That's from that guy over there." And it's Bonzo. And he says, "Welcome to America, guys," and he didn't know us. Maybe he'd heard of us and he got up and walked up. And that's the first time I'd ever met him. And I loved his drumming, you know, I thought he was the most stupendous drummer—not because of his power, but because he had a lovely touch. And a lot of drummers would agree with me that he had a very delicate touch—he was a bit like John Daly, you know, the golf star who could hit it a mile but he still had that very silky touch around the greens. Well, Bonzo was like that. He had a very, you know, he just had a great feel.

DS: Did Bad Company—I know that Zeppelin didn't usually have other acts—but did you ever open for them? Ever play a festival with them?

SK: No.

DS: Did you ever see them? Other than the O₂ Arena?

SK: Oh, yeah, yeah! I got a great story! We were in Houston and we had a night off. At the time, Bad Company and Zeppelin were touring independently of each other across America. And Peter Grant said later it was one of the proudest moments of his life to see the two planes on the Houston tarmac. Anyway, we had a night off. Zeppelin were playing in Houston, I believe it was the Summit—and we went along to see them and they were just amazing. They were a great jamming band. I mean, a lot of people think of them as that hard three-minute-playing band. But they could jam forever. Anyway, here comes this John Paul Jones solo on these keyboards, oh, God, what's it called? Somebody can fill me in on this . . .

DS: "Trampled Under Foot"?

SK: No, not "Trampled Under Foot." Ah, bugger, it'll come to me. [Note: We believe he's referring to "No Quarter," the live versions of which included expanded keyboard solos from John Paul Jones.] Anyway, so he's playing and there's lasers going and he's doing this incredible [fingering] thing on the keyboard, dry eyes, the crowd are going nuts, and I'm behind him looking up at him with my mouth open—and he turns around to me and he goes, "It's easy." That's all I can say.

DS: Do you remember what year that was?

SK: '77.

DS: '77. So that brings us up to 1980. They do a very short tour of Europe [including a show in Munich on July 5, during which Kirke sat in on drums], didn't get a lot of coverage at the time because everyone thought, well, they're coming to America, it's no big deal. The punk thing was happening, so it ends up that you played with them on what turns out to be the last date. So pick that up for me.

SK: Oh . . . what happened . . . I was at a loose end, Bad Company were kind of gone on hiatus, so Peter called me up and said, "Listen, we're in Germany, why don't you come and hang out with us for a few days? Come over from England." It's not a long trip. It's like an hour flight. So I went over to Frankfurt, they were playing there, and after the show Bonzo came up to me out of the blue and says, "Hey, Kirkey, would you like to play drums on 'Whole Lotta Love?'" I said I'd love to. Because no one had ever played with them on stage other than . . . Ronnie [Wood]. Okay. And it was an honor. And I said, "Oh, God, I'd love to, yes! Where do we rehearse?" He says, "In my bedroom in the hotel." What? I thought we'd have two drum kits in the studio. So I go up in his room and he's got two twin beds, and he sat on one bed and I sat on the other, and we're facing each other, you know. And with our hands on our knees and thighs he ran me through all the different time changes. He says, "I start off duh duh duh duh," and I says, "I know the beginning, John, I have heard it a few times." And he says, "No, listen, listen, pay attention." He was like a college professor. "Pay attention! Because after three minutes, I stop, Jimmy goes [vocal drum beats]." Anyway, we ran through all this, and the next night, I went on and they put another kit next to John's, and . . . I'm getting quite, quite emotional. 'Cause really, that was their last gig, and it was the last time I ever saw John, because he died a couple of months later. And it was great. I believe you . . . have a copy of it somewhere.

DS: You did "Whole Lotta Love" and "Rock and Roll"?

SK: I can't remember. It was [more drum beats] yeah, it was great! And at the end I'm sweating bullets because I sweat when I play. Bonzo is as cool as ice; he says—can I swear on this program? —"That was fucking great." And that was the last I ever heard from him.

DS: Didn't know you were making history?

SK: No, I didn't.

Ian "Mac" McLagan

IAN MCLAGAN IS A GENUINE, DYED-IN-THE-WOOL ROCK 'N'
ROLLER, HAVING TOURED AND RECORDED WITH THE
ROLLING STONES, BOB DYLAN, ROD STEWART, BONNIE
RAITT, BRUCE SPRINGSTEEN, AND TAJ MAHAL, TO NAME
BUT A FEW. IN 1966, MCLAGAN JOINED THE SMALL FACES,
THE BRITISH ROCK PHENOMENON THAT DOMINATED RADIO,
SALES CHARTS, AND CONCERT VENUES WORLDWIDE. AFTER
THE BAND DISBANDED IN 1969, MAC COFOUNDED ITS
FOLLOW-UP, FACES. SINCE HE CUT HIS DEBUT SOLO ALBUM,
TROUBLEMAKER, IN 1979, MCLAGAN HAS BEEN MAKING
MUSIC THAT CARRIES ON THE BRITISH ROCK TRADITION
THAT HE HELPED ESTABLISH WITH THE SMALL FACES AND
FACES. IN THIS INTERVIEW FROM THE SUMMER OF 2010, HE
RECALLED A PRE—LED ZEPPELIN ROBERT PLANT.

*Ian McLagan on
the keyboard at
the Wychwood
Music Festival, in
Gloucestershire, UK,
June 2006.*

DENNY SOMACH: Is it true that Robert Plant used to come
to a lot of [Small Faces] gigs? You said he was a fan.

IAN MCLAGAN: He would come to the gigs in Birmingham,
and he would run us errands, you know, go out and get
us tea or cigarettes and stuff. He was a little bit younger
than us, you know. He obviously loved Steve's [Steve
Marriott, Small Faces founding singer-guitarist] voice
and he's a man of great taste.

DS: Okay, so Small Faces did "You Need Lovin'."
The band was playing it already when you joined them.
Led Zeppelin takes it, even down to the original
arrangement . . .

IM: Well, here's the whole story. "You Need Lovin'"
from the Small Faces was actually a riff taken from
"You Need Love," which Willie Dixon wrote for
Muddy Waters. Now, Steve used to use these vocal
licks—he used to do stuff from James Brown, Ray
Charles, you know. He'd do little screams and shouts
that were theirs, and he threw them all in a jam. "You
Need Lovin'" is basically a jam. And when Robert Plant
heard it, he remembered those licks, and when they cut
"Whole Lotta Love," that's basically taken from our
song. But ours is taken from Willie Dixon's. They [Led
Zeppelin] got sued, and finally they paid Shirley Dixon,
Willie's daughter, some royalties.

DS: I understand you have a great Peter Grant–Bob
Dylan story.

IM: During the Faces, I think it was '72 or '73, we were in
L.A. and we played the Palladium one night, and then we
had a party at the Green Parrot Café. It was like an after-
show party—and Bob Dylan came. Peter Grant was there.
And Peter Grant went up to Bob Dylan and said, "Hello,
Bob, I'm Peter Grant. I manage Led Zeppelin." And
Dylan said, "I don't come to you with all my problems."

DS: Is there any truth—this was in a couple of books—
that Jimmy Page was looking into taking on Steve
Marriott as his vocalist? Could you talk about that?

IM: Yeah, well I've heard this several times. Steve was
actually the first choice for the Stones, after Mick Taylor.
He was Keith's choice. But I don't think Mick [Jagger]
would have allowed Steve, with a voice like that, to be in
the Stones. But also, Jimmy Page wanted Steve for the
Yardbirds, for Zeppelin, yeah.

DS: What do you think about Zeppelin going on without
Robert Plant?

IM: Well, without Robert Plant, I dunno, it'd be different.
I mean, he's still alive, right? I think Robert Plant's got
another career now.

Chris Squire

English musician Christopher Russell Edward "Chris" Squire is best known as the bass guitarist and backing vocalist for the progressive rock group Yes, founded in London in 1968. In 1981 he joined the short-lived rock supergroup XYZ (which stands for "ex–Yes and Zeppelin") with Jimmy Page on lead guitar and former Yes member Alan White on drums (Squire and White left Yes in 1981 but rejoined it in 1983). Robert Plant decided not to join the band, which did a few demos but never got off the ground. In this interview, which took place in 2008, Squire is asked about opening the Ahmet Ertegun tribute concert at London's O₂ Arena in 2007.

Chris Squire on stage with Yes at the HMV Hammersmith Apollo, London, November 17, 2011.

CHRIS SQUIRE: Well, that was a great show. Yes, of course, it was really for the Ahmet Ertegun charity following his departure from this world the year before. . . . He was one of the great rock 'n' roll business characters and was responsible for signing Yes, Bad Company, AC/DC, Genesis, and of course Led Zeppelin as well. So I was asked by Phil Carson, who . . . said that Led Zeppelin was going to reform with Jason Bonham, John's son, playing drums. They would play the second half and the first half would be a variety of Atlantic acts. He asked if I would open the show with Keith Emerson doing [Emerson, Lake & Palmer's] "Fanfare for the Common Man," with Simon Kirke from Bad Company playing drums and Alan White playing timpani parts. We had about eight or nine orchestral horn players as well, because it's an Aaron Copland piece. Basically, it's an orchestral piece that Keith adapted for ELP. We had a day's rehearsal. It was a little nerve-racking. But it came off great. I'm sure at some point there will be a film of it surfacing.

DENNY SOMACH: Did they film it?

CS: Oh! It was definitely filmed!

DS: Have you seen the YouTube clip?

CS: No, I haven't. Is that from someone's cell phone? [Laughs]

DS: Yes. It looks great.

CS: Does it?

DS: Yeah, I'll show it to you later. But you stayed for the whole concert, right?

CS: Yeah. Well, Bill Wyman had a band, his band on there, then they had various guests. . . . Second half, Zeppelin played; the last time I had seen them was the Atlantic fortieth [anniversary concert] in 1988 at Madison Square Garden, where their performance left a little to be desired. But in all fairness, Jason was nineteen years old or something then, it must have been difficult for him doing that show in his father's footsteps. But twenty years later, you know, Jason's become a great drummer. The whole power of Zeppelin really comes from the drums, actually. And he played magnificently—and the whole band did.

DS: How do you rate John Bonham as a drummer?

CS: Well, he was extraordinarily good. As I said, the Zeppelin thing stemmed from the power of the drums and then they hung the hooks of the guitars and the keyboards around the power of the drums and of course Robert's great singing as well. But John Bonham was very important in that band.

Jason, now, is accomplished enough to follow in his father's footsteps.

DS: Now, you have a unique perspective on rock 'n' roll history. I'm going to point this out. Your first high-profile gig was opener for Cream's farewell concert. And now you get to open for Zeppelin.

CS: Yeah. [Laughs]

DS: I can't think of anybody else who has that kind of perspective.

CS: I know. Plus we've also headlined a lot of shows! [Laughs]

DS: Yeah, I know, but that's gotta be pretty amazing. Cream on the one hand, and now exactly forty years later, you're doing the Zeppelin thing.

CS: Yeah, I actually went to see the Cream show at the Albert Hall in London [in May 2005]. I know they played in New York as well. The one in London, strangely enough, I have to say wasn't quite as exciting as the original one [the Cream farewell concert at Albert Hall in 1968] had been. But the party they threw after that show—it was like the last great rock 'n' roll expense party. It was fantastic. I had great conversations with Tom Hanks and all these other interesting people who had been invited to that, so that made it a lot of fun.

DS: You did have a period in the early '80s when you and Alan and Jimmy Page were going to form a band.

CS: Yeah, that was after John Bonham had passed away, and Jimmy was very upset about that but at the same time he didn't want to not do anything. He moved into my area of Surrey, England, where I was living at the time. Our houses were quite close. He came over to my studio that I had there and listened to some things I was working on. He said, "Oh, I like that, I like that." He also had a studio that he bought from Gus Dudgeon, who was Elton John's producer, in the same area. And so we went over to that place and he was quite happy to just play along with the songs I'd written because he just wanted to keep his chops up, I guess.

DS: Back to the O₂ show: did you stay for the Zeppelin set?

CS: Yeah! I have to say they were extremely good. I was kind of thinking, I wonder what this is gonna be like. I think they rehearsed for four or five months for this show and it was very, very good. [Laughs]

DS: What was it like—the crowd, the enthusiasm?

CS: Oh, obviously it was great. Everyone that I knew that knew I was playing on the show [asked], "Can you get me a ticket?" and of course there was a limited supply. But my brother wanted to come and bring his kid. Everyone wanted to see that show. But for the people that were there, it was worth it.

DS: What was the backstage like afterward?

CS: Crazy. There was every rapper or film personality you'd ever seen on TV all crammed back there, wandering around in different parts. It was kind of confusing, really. It was one of those nights. Very special.

DS: I don't know if you saw the papers, but they announced today that they're going to go out without Robert Plant.

CS: Again?

DS: They announced it today. Officially. They're not going to call it Led Zeppelin. They're calling it something else. It didn't say what they're going to call it and they didn't mention the singer, but it's that guy they've been rehearsing with [possibly Myles Kennedy, lead vocalist and rhythm guitarist for Alter Bridge, based on rumors at the time; the project never materialized].

CS: Yeah, was he not in a band opening for AC/DC at the Garden last week? Someone just told me that I should catch the opening act, that's the guy who's

gonna sing with Zeppelin, but my schedule didn't allow me to see them. . . .

DS: What do you think of this new trend of people getting new singers? I mean, Journey did it, and . . .

CS: Yeah, well, I'll tell you a funny story. This agent I know, Keith Nesmith, who works for a company called the Agency . . . called me when he was in London 'cause he was doing the Journey show, and he said you should come along and see the show just so you can see the possibilities of getting a stand-in, replacement, whatever you want to call it. And I said okay, so I went along and sat up in the balcony. And it was great because the Filipino guy [Arnel Pineda] sang like Steve Perry, he moved like him. All the fans cared about was hearing the songs. They knew them. It was a great show. I have to say, I had a great time. And then afterward I went backstage to meet Neal Schon and the other guys, and there was Jimmy Page [laughs], and I said, oh, funny seeing you here!

DS: Now, speaking of Jimmy Page, that's the natural lead-in—

CS: You know what's going to happen? Whatever name they call it, by the time it gets to the local level, "Zep's in town!" [Laughs] . . .

DS: So you actually had a band—you and Alan [White] and Jimmy [Page] did some stuff at your house?

CS: Yeah, we did some of it there, and then Jimmy also had a studio in that same part of Surrey, which he actually bought from Gus Dudgeon. . . . We did most of the serious recording there. I made the demos at my studio. . . . The idea was that Robert was going to come and join in but I think I heard Alan say that the music was too complicated. I don't think it was that. I think it was just too soon for Robert. He didn't want to just jump back into another project. He was still upset, I guess, about John's death.

DS: Some of those songs later surfaced on Yes albums and a track on the *Scream for Help* [a 1984 horror film] sound track and something on a Firm album. Would you set the record straight?

CS: Yeah, well, "Can You Imagine," on *Magnification*, was one of the songs I recorded with Jimmy. It was rerecorded with Yes and the orchestra that we used on the *Magnification* album. There was another song that I'd written that did pop up on a Firm album without any credit to me.

DS: Was that "Fortune Hunter?"

CS: It was something like that. I think it was the first track. . . . And so I kind of thought, that's interesting, you know [laughs], and I thought, well, if that album goes into the top twenty, I might [laughs] . . . I don't think it went that well, so . . .

DS: We do have a lawyer here [at the radio station].

CS: Yeah. [Laughs] So I left that alone. And then there was another bit of music that we'd written. A segment of that did turn up in another Yes piece that we recorded in San Luis Obispo, and I can't remember . . .

DS: "Believe It?" One of the songs is on the *Drama* album, right? The reissue? "Satellite?"

CS: Oh, "Satellite." Apart from the demo I did with Jimmy, and the demo I made myself at home, that has never actually been rerecorded. So that is still out there.

DS: We have it now; we're about to play it!

CS: You do? [Laughs]

DS: Yes!

CS: Which version do you have, the one with Jimmy?

DS: Yes.

CS: Wow.

DS: You need a copy because you lost yours, right?

CS: I wouldn't mind having one.

DS: I'll make you a copy. I have the four songs that never surfaced, correct?

CS: Well, not really, although they're out there on the Net.

DS: Will you do a setup for us? You're doing lead on them, right?

CS: Yeah, I'm doing all the singing. All the music was mainly my music, and Jimmy was like, "Oh, I don't care that you wrote it. I just want to play right now." That was his stance at the time.

DS: I want to ask you a question that I know the answer to, and you've told me over the years, but I want to ask it on the record. And now that [Led Zeppelin manager Peter Grant is] dead, you don't have to worry about it. Could you tell me what happened to the XYZ tapes? Didn't somebody come to your house and ask you for them?

CS: Ah, no, that's not true. No, nobody asked me for them.

DS: I heard a story that Peter Grant came and asked you for them.

CS: No. [Laughs]

DS: Tell the Peter Grant story.

CS: I once went down to Peter Grant's house to discuss a new project with him and we were discussing it for about ninety-six hours straight. . . . We weren't getting anywhere.

DS: He put a cigarette out in your hand, didn't he?

CS: No, no, no. We had a good relationship. It was quite funny because my dad, while he was alive, knew I was involved in that project and he said, "Well, the obvious name for that band would be XYZ. Ex-Yes-Zeppelin." So there I was at Peter Grant's house, and said that's the natural name for this project. Yes is on hiatus, we're not sure what's going on with that. And Zeppelin presumably is not going to be anymore, and Peter Grant kept saying, "Yeah, but I don't like the idea of Yes being before Led Zeppelin." And I said, "But Peter, it's the alphabet. It's X Y Z." "X Z Y? I don't know." And we had that same conversation for about ninety-six hours. [Laughs]

DS: There's a book out in England of his life story written by Chris Welch and they're supposedly turning it into a movie. What was Peter Grant like? Was he like a bigger-than-life figure?

CS: Well, yeah, he happened to be at a certain place at a certain time. Like most of those [people with bad] reputations, [situations] probably happened once, then passed down the line and got overblown . . . no, he was actually a quite a gentle guy, you know, in many ways. He liked to get high. I'm sure he wouldn't mind me saying that. He was a good guy.

DS: Do you have a favorite Zeppelin song?

CS: Yeah, "Kashmir."

DS: You played in Germany and Jimmy Page came to see you and ended up playing with you on an encore. Tell us about that.

CS: Yeah, that's true. I think it was Stuttgart. Pretty sure. Or Dortmund.

DS: It was Dortmund.

CS: Was it Dortmund? Well, my memory is intact, that's good. That was after Jimmy and I had done that [XYZ] project. As I said, it was too early for Robert to be involved so we just put it on the back burner and it stayed there. But when Yes were out promoting *90125* in '84, Jimmy was doing something out there in Germany and he just came and jammed on a couple of tunes.

DS: The Beatles tune "I'm Down."

CS: Yeah, is that what it was? It probably was. Yeah, he came and jammed on a Yes song that we did at that time that was a cover of the Beatles "I'm Down."

Alice Cooper

Alice Cooper performs during his No More Mr. Nice Guy tour at the Scottish Exhibition and Conference Center on October 31, 2011, in Glasgow, Scotland.

SHOCK-ROCK PIONEER AND 2011 ROCK AND ROLL HALL OF FAME INDUCTEE ALICE COOPER HAS RELEASED SEVEN PLATINUM ALBUMS THROUGHOUT HIS LONG RECORDING CAREER. HE IS BEST KNOWN FOR THE HITS "SCHOOL'S OUT" AND "I'M EIGHTEEN," BOTH OF WHICH ARE COUNTED AMONG *ROLLING STONE* MAGAZINE'S 500 GREATEST SONGS OF ALL TIME. BUT MANY PEOPLE ARE SURPRISED THAT ALICE HOLDS THE DISTINCTION OF BEING THE VERY FIRST ACT TO SHARE CONCERT BILLING WITH LED ZEPPELIN IN CALIFORNIA.

THEY PLAYED A SERIES OF SHOWS TOGETHER IN JANUARY 1969 AT THE WHISKY A GO GO IN LOS ANGELES, FINISHING JUST ONE WEEK BEFORE THE RELEASE OF LED ZEPPELIN'S FIRST ALBUM. AT THE START OF THIS INTERVIEW, CONDUCTED IN THE FALL OF 2008, ALICE IS ASKED WHAT HE REMEMBERS ABOUT THOSE SHOWS.

ALICE COOPER: You have a better memory than me, knowing the actual dates on that. I know I have a slide that somebody took that said "Alice Cooper and Led Zeppelin This Weekend Only."

At the time, we were just local bands, as far as we were concerned. We didn't even know who Led Zeppelin was, you know, who they were. It just was another band. We figured they were from the Valley or something until we got there, and of course we saw Jimmy Page. And us, being Yardbirds fans, realized that he was in the Yardbirds, and that was a big deal to us.

So we were immediately humbled by that because here was a Yardbird. Before that, nobody had really heard of Jimmy Page. He might have played some lead for the Kinks and things like that, or on sessions, but honestly, nobody had heard of him. So we got there, and they had British accents, which was kind of like a surprise to us.

DENNY SOMACH: What were some of the songs Led Zeppelin played?

AC: We were more interested, at the time, in the musicianship than what the songs were. When you hear a guitar

player like that, and a drummer like that, and a singer like that, you go, "Okay, these guys are something!" Mostly blues, blues-rock. Most bands back then played blues-rock: Savoy Brown, Fleetwood Mac, Paul Butterfield—everybody was a blues band back then, except us. We were the only one that wasn't a blues band.

I mean, [Led Zeppelin] played a lot of standard stuff. They did "Train Kept A-Rollin'." They did "Babe I'm Gonna Leave You." All the blues things. And then I'm sure they did some of the songs off their first album, but we didn't really recognize them because we had never heard their album.

DS: Who played first, you or Led Zeppelin?

AC: We just sort of like said, "Well, who goes on first? Doesn't matter to us."

We flipped a coin. I think we went on first the first night, they went on first the second night. But we really got along. They were just a great band, as far as we were concerned. They were a cut above a local band, that's for sure.

The first night, we were the opening act because they had the flu. They were really sick. Everybody threw up at the Whisky at one point or another. The dressing rooms were these tiny little dressing rooms up on top. British bands were white. These guys were sort of a see-through blue-white, because on top of being really white they were really sick, so we said, "Guys, we'll go on first. You guys try to get it together." And so we did the first set, and then they came up. Somehow, they got through it. But it sounded great to us!

DS: Did they make it through every night?

AC: I don't know how many shows we did with them. I think it was a three-night thing, and I think they played the first two nights, and then [Jimi Hendrix's Band of Gypsys drummer] Buddy Miles took over. You know, Buddy Miles was an old buddy of ours. He played with another great band, Mike Bloomfield's

Electric Flag, and so we knew Buddy from that. Another blues band!

As far as Led Zeppelin went, they were just sick, and that was all we knew. All we knew at that point was we needed to do two sets a night, and everybody had to do two sets, and at the time we were doing theatrics on that little, tiny stage. I think we were more worried about getting through the theatrics and everything, and doing our songs, rather than who we were playing with.

DS: Had you ever seen Jimmy Page perform with the Yardbirds before?

AC: Well, the funny thing was that we had played with the Yardbirds. We opened for the Yardbirds when we were, like, seventeen years old, in Phoenix at the VIP Club. It was Keith Relf, Jeff Beck, Chris Dreja. . . . I think at that time it was Chris Dreja on bass and Jimmy Page and Jeff Beck on guitar, but I'm not quite sure. It might have been Jimmy Page on bass at the time.

We had learned all the Yardbirds songs. That was our biggest influence. So to be opening for them—and the fact that we did their entire set before them—and they were standing there giving us the thumbs-up and laughing. I guess it was a big compliment to them that here was this little band doing all their songs. And then of course they got up onstage and blew us away—because they were the Yardbirds.

How would you like to be Jimmy Page getting into the Yardbirds and them handing him a bass and saying, "Well, we have a lead guitar player, some guy named Jeff Beck." And him going, "Well, okay, I'll wait until the other guitar player leaves so I can play guitar." How about that for a tandem? Beck and Page in one band. And then before that, it was Clapton!

DS: What do you recall about the individual members of Led Zeppelin?

AC: Jimmy Page was always one of the finest guitar players in rock 'n' roll, even back then. He wasn't as refined as he is now, of course, but I didn't know anybody who played like that! He was way above anybody we knew. And I don't think he had really done the bow technique yet. I don't think that came about until a couple of Zeppelin albums later, when he started doing stuff like that. At this point, he was just a rock 'n' roll guitar player. [Note: Jimmy Page had been using the violin bow onstage and in the studio for some time already.]

Bonham hit the drums hard. I don't think that Bonham hit the drums harder, though, than Buddy Miles, or another drummer named Frosty from Lee Michaels. There were a couple drummers that just annihilated the drums. John was one of them. And he was a really good drummer.

There's always going to be the controversy: who's better, Bonham or Keith Moon? You know, it depends on whose corner you're in. I've always said Keith Moon was the more versatile drummer, but John Bonham really hit the drums hard.

DS: Your band, at one point, was called the Nazz. Did that name come from the Yardbirds song "The Nazz Are Blue"?

AC: Yeah, we used to do "The Nazz Are Blue." That was a song we really loved. We looked at that word "Nazz" and went, "That's a great name for us, since we do Yardbirds songs." It's a bit of a tribute to them [Note: No relation to Todd Rundgren's Philadelphia-based band, the Nazz].

DS: Have you seen Led Zeppelin since then?

AC: After that, no, I didn't really see them. I saw Plant and Page on their tour . . . in the '90s. But that wasn't Led Zeppelin. It was a different drummer and bass player at the time.

In fact, what they're probably gonna do, if they do go out without Robert Plant—can I make a prediction? I'm gonna make a prediction that they go with David Coverdale—only because he's got the hair, he's got the look, he's got the pedigree, and he can sing. On Whitesnake's first album, he sounded like Robert Plant! I think he could do just about any song that Plant did. It's just weird to me that Robert Plant is not doing this.

DS: What was your reaction the first time you heard "Whole Lotta Love"?

AC: "Whole Lotta Love" could easily be a Yardbirds song. It had that Yardbirds feel to it. You could really tell where this band came from. And so every time I hear, to this day, "Whole Lotta Love," to me it just shows what their roots really are.

DS: What do you think is their best song?

AC: Well, I think people will always say "Stairway to Heaven" is the song they're known for more than anything else, but when I think of the uniqueness of them, I think more "Kashmir." . . . So I would say "Kashmir" was them in their produced state rather than their live rock 'n' roll state, like "Whole Lotta Love," so I would go with "Kashmir."

> **I think "Kashmir" was more of a production. It was more purely Led Zeppelin than any other song.**

Asia's John Wetton on guitar and Carl Palmer on drums at the Variety Playhouse, August 18, 2010, in Atlanta, Georgia.

John **Wetton**

ENGLISH PROGRESSIVE ROCK MUSICIAN JOHN WETTON PLAYS BASS, GUITAR, AND KEYBOARDS; HE IS ALSO A SINGER AND SONGWRITER. WETTON DID STINTS AS A PROFESSIONAL MUSICIAN WITH BANDS SUCH AS KING CRIMSON, ROXY MUSIC, AND URIAH HEEP. HE IS ONE OF THE ORIGINAL FOUNDING MEMBERS OF THE SUPERGROUP ASIA, WHOSE EPONYMOUS DEBUT ALBUM IS ONE OF THE BEST-SELLING DEBUT ALBUMS OF ALL TIME. HERE, IN THIS INTERVIEW FROM SEPTEMBER 2009, HE SHARES A BRUISER OF A MEMORY ABOUT AN ENCOUNTER HE HAD WITH JOHN BONHAM AT THE FAMOUS SUNSET "RIOT HOUSE" IN MAY 1973.

JOHN WETTON: One night when King Crimson were playing in Los Angeles, we were staying at the legendary Riot House [a nickname for what was then the Continental Hyatt House on Sunset Boulevard and is now the Andaz West Hollywood Hyatt], I was in the bar, as one is, with John Bonham and John Paul Jones, and the party then moved up to Bonham's suite. I remember John Paul Jones sitting there and he stood up and said, "I'm leaving now because a fight is just about to happen." And I said, "What fight is that?'" And he said, "The fight between John Bonham and the bass player." I said, "You're the bass player." And he said, "No. Tonight, John, *you* are the bass player." [Laughs]

And off he went to bed. And the next morning I was comparing bruises and I said, "You were right." And he said, "He always picks on the bass player. He gets into an argument and then inevitably it will be a fight."

That's my one and only Led Zeppelin story, I'm afraid.

Jake Holmes

JAKE HOLMES IS AN AMERICAN FOLK-POP SINGER-SONGWRITER AND ADVERTISING-JINGLE WRITER. HE IS THE ORIGINAL (THOUGH UNCREDITED) WRITER OF "DAZED AND CONFUSED," ADAPTED AND POPULARIZED BY JIMMY PAGE FOR THE YARDBIRDS AND LED ZEPPELIN. ALTHOUGH LED ZEPPELIN DOES NOT CREDIT HOLMES WITH AUTHORSHIP OF THE SONG, WHICH APPEARS ON THE FIRST LED ZEPPELIN ALBUM, A MARCH 1968 YARDBIRDS LIVE RECORDING FROM THE FRENCH TV SERIES *BOUTON ROUGE* OFFERS THE CREDIT "BY JAKE HOLMES, ARR. YARDBIRDS." ANOTHER LIVE PERFORMANCE, RECORDED THE SAME MONTH IN NEW YORK CITY, IS INCLUDED ON THE ALBUM *LIVE YARDBIRDS: FEATURING JIMMY PAGE*, UNDER THE ALTERNATE TITLE "I'M CONFUSED." NOTABLY, IT IS THE ALBUM'S SOLE TRACK WITHOUT A SONGWRITER CREDIT.

TO THIS DAY, IT IS NOT WIDELY RECOGNIZED THAT HOLMES WROTE THE CLASSIC ZEPPELIN SONG. PAGE, WHILE ON TOUR WITH THE YARDBIRDS IN 1967, SAW HOLMES PERFORM "DAZED AND CONFUSED" IN NEW YORK CITY. WITHIN MONTHS, HE HAD ADAPTED IT FOR THE YARDBIRDS, AND, LATER, FOR LED ZEPPELIN. FOR REASONS THAT REMAIN UNCLEAR, PAGE CLAIMED SOLE SONGWRITING CREDIT FOR "DAZED AND CONFUSED" ON LED ZEPPELIN'S DEBUT ALBUM. HOLMES LATER SENT PAGE A LETTER REGARDING SONGWRITING CREDITS BUT RECEIVED NO REPLY. IN JUNE 2010, HOLMES FILED A LAWSUIT AGAINST JIMMY PAGE FOR COPYRIGHT INFRINGEMENT IN UNITED STATES DISTRICT COURT, CLAIMING PAGE KNOWINGLY COPIED HIS WORK; AS OF THIS WRITING, THE SUIT HAS BEEN DISMISSED (ALSO SEE PAGE 121).

EARLIER IN HOLMES'S CAREER, HE WROTE SONGS THAT WERE RECORDED BY FRANK SINATRA, NINA SIMONE, THE FOUR SEASONS, AND OTHER GREATS. ON HIS OWN, HE RECORDED TWO WELL-REGARDED ALBUMS FOR TOWER RECORDS IN THE 1960S: IN JUNE 1967, *THE ABOVE GROUND SOUND OF JAKE HOLMES*, WHICH FEATURED THE ORIGINAL "DAZED AND CONFUSED"; AND IN 1968, *A LETTER TO KATHERINE DECEMBER*. HE LATER RELEASED RECORDS FOR POLYDOR AND COLUMBIA RECORDS. HIS MOST SUCCESSFUL SONG WAS "SO CLOSE, SO VERY FAR TO GO," WHICH REACHED NUMBER 49 ON THE *BILLBOARD* CHARTS.

IN THE 1970S, HOLMES MOVED INTO WRITING ADVERTISING JINGLES. HE WROTE THE U.S. ARMY RECRUITMENT JINGLE "BE ALL THAT YOU CAN BE" AND COWROTE THE FAMOUS "BE A PEPPER" JINGLE FOR DR PEPPER, AND HIS VOICE CAN BE HEARD ON NUMEROUS COMMERCIALS.

EVEN AS HIS JINGLE CAREER FLOURISHED, HOLMES NEVER GAVE UP SONGWRITING. HE COWROTE HARRY BELAFONTE'S 1988 ALBUM, *PARADISE IN GAZANKULU*, AND RELEASED A NEW SOLO ALBUM IN 2001 CALLED *DANGEROUS TIMES*.

IN THIS 2007 INTERVIEW, HOLMES DISCUSSES HIS UNIQUE STATUS IN ROCK 'N' ROLL HISTORY.

JAKE HOLMES: I'm sort of the Sasquatch of pop music.

DENNY SOMACH: You started out with music in [Greenwich] Village. Could you give us a little background?

JH: Yeah, I started out at the Bitter End, actually, with a duo [with his wife, Katherine Grier] called Allen & Grier. We did parodies of folk songs.

DS: Which one were you, Allen or Grier?

JH: I don't know because neither of us had our right names. It was Fred Weintraub, who owned the Bitter End, who named us, and he took my middle name [Allen] and my wife's middle name [Grier], but I'm not sure if she was Grier or I was Allen. . . .

DS: What year was this?

JH: Uh, let's see. When was the *Titanic* sunk? It goes back a ways. I guess it was in the early '70s—no! Late '60s!

DS: Did that particular duo record?

JH: Yeah, we did an album called *It's Better to Be Rich Than Ethnic.*

DS: What did that come out on?

JH: That came out on a record company called Tower Records, which was a subsidiary of Capitol, which went into the woodwork along with Veejay [Records] and a few other nefarious labels.

DS: After that, then what happened?

It was a very interesting way for acts to perform, to be able to have this opportunity to have a week at a place and to develop your material, which doesn't happen too much now with rock acts. They don't get that chance.

JH: After that, I actually went off as a single.

DS: Weren't you also in a comedy troupe?

JH: Yeah, with Joan Rivers. That came later. Fred Weintraub was sort of one of these master manipulators. He was sort of like a folk Boyz II Men manager [laughs]. He was putting together all these groups like the Serendipity Singers and the Bitter End Singers, and so he put together what

Jake Holmes ca. 1970.

he thought would be a really neat idea, which was a comedy trio with music, and I was sort of the music guy. And then this guy Jim Connell and Joan Rivers. And we did these "sketchy" kind of comedy things infused with music, and that was a pretty rocky thing. . . . We didn't get along too well after about six months, but we stayed together for about a year and toured and did all that stuff.

DS: But you didn't record with that particular group?

JH: No.

DS: And then did you go solo at that point?

JH: Yeah. You probably know better about it [laughs]. I'm a little vague in the past.

DS: All right, not a problem. So tell us about the making of *The Above Ground Sound of* . . . That was on Tower Records also, right?

JH: That was on Tower. Yeah, right. We actually did this tour. We did a college tour, which was a very good idea for young acts. They would set up coffeehouses in different colleges in the lunchroom or whatever, and we would play for a week. . . . I had a bass player, Rick Randle, and my guitar player, Teddy Irwin, and we pretty much would spend the days writing and doing crazy things sometimes, writing songs. That was where the album kind of got built up. And we never had a drummer. We just used—I was sort of the drummer. I was the rhythm guitar drummer, and Teddy was the lead guitar, and Rick was this incredible bass player who played a lot of things. On that album, there's a song called "Lonely," which is in four-four and he's playing three. There's this little slow three against it, so it's like [hums a fast rhythm] and he's like [hums a slower rhythm that doesn't match up]. So it was really interesting music, and that's—I think you're kind of leading up to "Dazed and Confused," but that's where "Dazed and Confused" came out of. And that was sort of, kind of this six-eight thing that had this distending line, and we just kind of worked it out. . . .

DS: Has that album ever been reissued on CD?

JH: It is out on CD. You can get it on the Internet. . . .

DS: You mentioned what we were gonna talk about in a few minutes anyway, "Dazed and Confused." What is that song about, before we go into the history of it?

JH: Well—my version? [Laughs] My version is about being left by somebody and not understanding why. That was pretty much it. It was not a drug song. Believe it or not, the three of us didn't do drugs. My guitar player did do alcohol, and my bass player was schizophrenic, so he didn't have to do drugs, and I was too out to lunch to do drugs, so we didn't do—we were kind of like not drug-free. We were just sort of drug-naive. And we did a lot of psychedelic stuff [music], but it was basically because it

was four in the morning and we were kidding around. So that was our drug, just working. So it kind of grew out of this sort of late-night craziness. . . .

> **And it was sort of weird and all that, but it was basically a song about—was more my love song as opposed to being some sort of psychedelic rambling trip.**

DS: Do you remember the actual day that you wrote it, or was it written over a period of time?

JH: I don't. I really don't. Some things I do remember, but that one I don't remember.

DS: Do you remember the first time you played it?

JH: No.

DS: Or played it for even the other two guys? You wrote it solo, right?

JH: Yeah. I wrote the song, and then I sat down with them and we worked out an arrangement. I mean, that song is a half down—and maybe more in terms of Teddy's solos in there, 'cause Teddy is just amazing. He's an amazing guitar player, and his solo work was amazing in that song. So, I don't remember. I really don't. That whole thing is sort of a blur.

DS: Obviously, it was featured in your live shows, correct?

JH: Oh, yeah. That was pretty much our closer, 'cause it would just rock out. . . .

DS: Do you remember the Yardbirds coming to see you?

JH: Yeah. Well, they didn't come to see me. I played with them at the Village Theatre [in New York], which ended up being the Fillmore East maybe about a year later. . . . I think it was Janis Ian and the Yardbirds and me, and we were on the same bill.

DS: Wasn't it the Youngbloods?

JH: That could be! I thought it was Janis Ian. I played twice there, and I'm not sure. I don't remember. I know the Youngbloods were on one of those bills that we were on.

DS: Let me see if I have it here. [Pulling out a replica of a flyer] Is that it?

JH: [Laughing] Oh, my gosh.

DS: We do our research here, Jake. . . .

JH: I remember the date, and I do remember performing it, and I remember the theater, and I remember working with the Yardbirds. And they went out, rushed out and got my album, I guess, from what I gather.

DS: That's what the books say. Did you have any interaction with them at all? Did you meet them?

JH: Yeah, I mean, you know, but you meet them, hello, and that's it. [In a deep British accent] "Nice to see ya, boys, okay." That was about it.

DS: So that was late '67, correct?

JH: Yep.

DS: So then they come back [to New York] in '68 and play the Anderson Theater and there's a live album recorded there. You're aware of that?

JH: Their album.

DS: It was out for, like, two weeks and then disappeared. When's the first time that you found out they had covered the song?

JH: Years later.

DS: How many years later?

JH: Oh, much longer. I never knew up until maybe five years ago. I never realized the Yardbirds had actually recorded the song with my name on it. I didn't know that. I had no idea that it was—they had taken it and just kind of used it. And then later on, Jimmy Page just took it and took my name off it. But at that point, I just—I thought, "Well, okay." I thought, actually, in those days, what they st—[hesitates] took was the six-eight descending line and the title, and pretty much everything else is up for grabs. And you think of it as blues, almost, and you think, "Well, okay." And I remember that the rules back then were different than they are now. There's intent now. There wasn't intent then. It was, first, it was songs—because there were more songs. It was like the first, I think it was the exact first two bars of a song, that was kind of the rule that you had. And if they match, then . . . you could sue somebody for it. But it was a little more amorphous than that. And I didn't care that much. It was weird. I really didn't care.

DS: Did you know that Led Zeppelin had recorded it?

JH: Yeah, I did know that.

DS: And when did you find that out?

JH: Oh, when the album came out.

DS: The first one.

JH: Yeah.

DS: And what was your reaction?

JH: I thought, "Oh, hey. That's cool." I was a little bit weird about that stuff. I wasn't interested in Led Zeppelin. That wasn't my world. I was in another whole world. So they were sort of off to the side to me, so I thought, "Oh, well." And then, it wasn't until about twenty years later that I really thought this wasn't fair. But by then it was too late to do anything.

DS: I'm trying to get to the point of how you found out about it. You got the album, or somebody told you?

JH: I saw it at a record store, and I guess friends of mine said, "Wait, you know, isn't that your tune?"

DS: Were you aware it was the centerpiece of their show?

JH: No, I had no idea.

DS: And that there's a twenty-minute version of it on their live album?

JH: I had no idea. I still didn't. You're telling me something I don't, to this day . . .

DS: Then you'd better brace yourself. You know the Yardbirds are back together?

JH: Yeah!

DS: And they perform the song.

JH: Yeah?

DS: And they just released a new album with it. Just came out this week.

JH: Really? I hope my name is on it.

DS: Nope. Not this one. . . . Could you tell us—I know you're in the Songwriters Hall of Fame, right?

JH: Yeah.

DS: Could you tell us some of the jingles that you were responsible for writing?

JH: "I'm a Pepper, you're a Pepper." The Sears "softer side of Sears." "Be all you can be," the army.

DS: And did you sing on all those commercials, too?

JH: Yeah. Yeah. That's my voice going [sings] "Be—all that you can be." I was younger then, and I could get up to those notes. Um, yeah. I've done pretty much most of the stuff I've sung on. Recently, the silly Charmin thing, the goofy—

DS: Post–Mr. Whipple, right?

JH: Yeah, post–Mr. Whipple. A lot of stuff. The list goes on and on.

A recent photograph of Nancy Wilson (left) and Ann Wilson of Heart.

Ann and Nancy
Wilson

THE AMERICAN ROCK BAND HEART FEATURES SISTERS ANN AND NANCY WILSON. THE MULTIPLATINUM GROUP FIRST CAME TO PROMINENCE IN THE 1970S, AND EXPERIENCED A MAJOR RESURGENCE IN 1985 AND IN THE 1990S.

ALSO IN THE '90S THE WILSON SISTERS PUT TOGETHER AN INFORMAL ACOUSTIC GROUP CALLED THE LOVEMONGERS, WITH SUE ENNIS AND FRANK COX; IN 1992 THE GROUP RELEASED A FOUR-SONG EP THAT INCLUDED A LIVE VERSION OF LED ZEPPELIN'S "THE BATTLE OF EVERMORE." THE WILSONS HAVE ALSO BEEN KNOWN TO COVER ZEPPELIN CLASSICS LIKE "ROCK AND ROLL," "STAIRWAY TO HEAVEN," "IMMIGRANT SONG," "BLACK DOG," "THE RAIN SONG," AND OTHERS.

IN 1995, THEY RELEASED *THE ROAD HOME*, WHICH WAS PRODUCED BY JOHN PAUL JONES. THIS INTERVIEW WITH THE WILSONS TOOK PLACE IN AUGUST 2010.

DENNY SOMACH: Did you ever play "Immigrant Song" or other Zeppelin tunes live?

ANN WILSON: We did play "Immigrant Song" live. After my solo album, we did it because it was on my solo album. It was really fun to do. I mean, there was no other reason to do a cover than to pay it homage. And because it's just a great experience as a musician and people love it. That's the reason. But we did it on the solo album because [producer] Ben Mink had some ideas for it. He visualized that song sort of literally as a horde of Huns or Vikings or something that start out on the horizon as a little black line and get closer and closer and closer until you're completely overrun. So that's how this song is arranged. It starts out very gentle and then by the time it's over, you're just completely flattened. [Laughs] So we had fun arranging that.

DS: You covered "Stairway to Heaven" and it was a bonus track on one of your reissues, correct?

AW: This version of "Stairway to Heaven," we didn't really intend to release it ourselves. We were at this point a club band playing in a club. "Stairway to Heaven" was on the charts at that point, and we were just covering it in a club. And later on, years later, our record company decided they needed more padding for an album they wanted to rerelease [as] a compilation—or a bonus track or something—for *Little Queen* so they fished around and found this old club stuff from way back when. I'd always forget the words because there's a million words to this.

NANCY WILSON: [Laughs] There's a lot of words.

AW: And if you don't pay attention, you can get lost real easy.

DS: What about the live version of "Rock and Roll?'

AW: Same thing—the live version of "Rock and Roll" we started doing in clubs because *Zeppelin IV* was out—it was on the charts. Everybody wanted to hear it. We wanted to play it. And "Rock and Roll" is just a great way to get people to drink beer and dance and get excited.

DS: And "Black Dog" and "Misty Mountain Hop"?

AW: Yeah, we did "Black Dog." That song took forever to learn because it's got the rock 'n' roll slide rule, where there's a beat set up on the bottom and on the top they

slide the slide rule over to the right a click and everything's a little bit off. And for musicians, that is like heaven to try and learn that kind of stuff because it's so tricky. So that's why we did that one and also because the words are incredibly sexy, and over the top [laughs].

"Misty Mountain" we did just because it's such a mother. It's got this [sings the chords] thing going that's just relentless and the words are just incredibly cool.

DS: And you also did "Battle of Evermore"?

AW: Yes, we did.

NW: We always have Zeppelin somewhere, don't we?

AW: "Battle of Evermore" is long. It's probably, I don't know, it's seven minutes or something.

NW: Seven or so . . .

AW: Another song with a whole book's worth of lyrics and very Tolkien-esque . . .

DS: Would one of your fantasies be to sing "Battle of Evermore" with Robert Plant?

AW: Well, speaking for myself, no, it wouldn't, because that version is quintessential. With Plant singing, it's quintessential. Although I did hear Plant sing it with Alison Krauss and that was pretty awesome.

NW: Amazing.

AW: The point is I don't think I'd want to do it because I'm more drawn to the Plant part than I am to the female part.

DS: Have you ever met—I know you worked with John Paul Jones on one of your albums, correct?

AW: Yes, we did.

DS: Did you ever get feedback from any of the members of the band about your covers—are they aware that you covered so many of their songs?

AW: We did work with John Paul Jones on our *The Road Home* album and—no, we've never gotten feedback from any of the members of Zeppelin about us doing their covers. It's been eerily quiet. But I understand that. I mean, why should they comment, really?

DS: Well, I'm sure you've crossed paths with them over the years.

AW: Yes, we have crossed paths over the years but the topic of conversation never comes around to the songs that we have covered by Zeppelin.

DS: The reason I'm asking you now is we're approaching the thirtieth anniversary of John Bonham's passing and as

a tribute we're gathering comments on how LZ was an influence.

NW: Our dream was just to get into see Led Zeppelin [laughs]—just to go to their shows.

AW: Oh, of course. Yes, Led Zeppelin was a major influence on Heart from the beginning, as were a lot of other people, but I think that when John Bonham passed, it was in effect really the end of Zeppelin because they knew in their very core soul of their band that it would never be Led Zeppelin again without him. He was the velvet hammer. He was the heartbeat of that band. Except for the one time at the O$_2$ Arena, a few years back, they never replaced him but with his son.

NW: Well, his son—

AW: Yeah, but with his son. I find that really, really admirable that they would remain true and authentic to their original band like that.

DS: As opposed to the Who, who put Kenny Jones in after Keith Moon died.

AW: I don't want to compare the two band's ethics in that. I'm just saying that Led Zeppelin never wanted to become a tribute band to themselves. That's why they didn't go out and find a singer to replace Robert Plant when he didn't want to go on tour recently. I mean, they just said, okay, that's good. Let's let it lay. And I think that's really beautiful.

DS: Were either of you at the O$_2$ Arena show?

AW: I was.

DS: Could you give me a little thumbnail sketch?

AW: I was blown away. I was also very jet-lagged because we flew from Seattle just for that show but—and so it seems a little dreamlike but it was amazing. It was amazing on a whole lot of levels, not the least of which was, where we were sitting, just about everybody famous in the world was also sitting. . . . People from all over the world from all walks of entertainment and sports and news and everything. But the band itself, I thought, really did a great job for just having one shot at it. And I was nervous for them because I know [what] it's like to be on the other side of the footlight, so to speak. Just imagine all that world attention—all the thousands of people, like, coming from every corner of the planet to hear them do one set. One chance. To be Led Zeppelin for the world.

NW: No pressure!

AW: No pressure or anything [laughs] and they did great, I mean, they really did sound great, they looked great, they were great. And it was really cool because afterward there was this big party and of course, everybody went there expecting—hoping to see Zeppelin, but they were too cool to appear. [Both laugh] Which I thought was the ultimate rock statement. It was completely cool.

DS: Do each of you have a favorite Led Zeppelin song?

AW: Oh, it's so hard to choose just one.

NW: Well, okay, I'll start. *Today* my favorite Led Zeppelin song is "The Ocean."

AW: On this day, my favorite Led Zeppelin song is "The Rain Song."

DS: Anything more to add about Led Zeppelin's overall influence on Heart?

NW: Of course Led Zeppelin was a really big influence—because I think Ann learned a lot of her singing technique from Robert Plant—and Aretha Franklin, too—but she didn't always used to be the lead singer; she was the chick singer in a band that would occasionally do a ballad. Then they started doing Led Zeppelin and none of the guys could sing that high, so they asked her to try it and she really got into it so that's one of the things that makes us unique is that it's a very heavy rock group and there's this girl who can do anything—her voice. And I sing, too, but I'm more of a player. And I'm starting to think of myself as a singer, too. I love it. . . .

> **We used to play full sets of Zeppelin in clubs because Ann has this uncanny Robert Plant thing that she can do—it's really amazing.**

We still play "Rock and Roll" occasionally, because we stopped doing it last year and we just heard from the fans in the States [who] were so disappointed that we weren't playing it anymore, and so we had to acquiesce to the pressure of playing it and we love playing it.

I remember we were at Milton Keynes [in England] in '82 with Queen, or maybe it was Leeds, and Robert Plant came to the show to see us because he loved "Barracuda" and some of the things we'd done that sounded like Zeppelin. We all knew that he was coming but we couldn't tell Ann because we knew she would just freeze and stand there. So we're standing on stage and we break into that song and I look over and Plant is standing right on the stage with us and we're all smiling at him and we're going, "Don't tell Ann." It's a good thing her eyesight's not that good.

DS: No ambition for her to do a duet with him one day?

NW: Well [laughs], we said something like, "Why don't you come out and sing harmony with us?" and he said, "I can't sing harmony." In clubs we used to do "The Crunge," "The Rover," and a whole bunch of stuff . . . and we also did a lot of Deep Purple. When I joined the band we started doing more original things in clubs.

DS: Your producer, Ron Nevison, did a number of Led Zeppelin albums, didn't he?

NW: He engineered *Physical Graffiti*. That's why we really went for him—we were looking for a straight-ahead rock sound in that old-fashioned sense.

DS: I think of Heart as more of a Led Zeppelin band.

NW: There's no way Heart will ever be a New Wave band!

Ioannis, Zeppelin III *(details), 2011.*

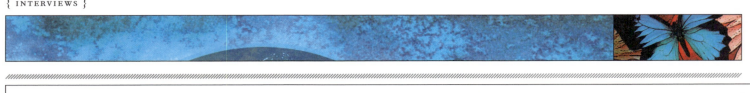

Bob Geldof

Sir Robert "Bob" Geldof is an Irish singer, song-writer, actor, author, and political activist. In the late 1970s he fronted the Boomtown Rats, which had several hits. Geldof cofounded the charity super-group Band Aid in 1984 to raise money for famine relief in Ethiopia and organized the global charity concert Live Aid the following year; efforts for which Queen Elizabeth II granted him an honorary knighthood. In this October 2011 interview, he discusses what it took to get Led Zeppelin to partici-pate in 1985's Live Aid, and why they are the only act not to appear on the event's official DVD.

BOB GELDOF: Jimmy [Page] is difficult with this stuff; Robert's one of the guys, you know, hang at a pub, get up on the pub stage—do karaoke—really a regular guy. One of the great stars and voices of rock 'n' roll. Just a cool guy. . . . Jim is—it's not that he's been starry, it's he's been particular. He's hugely proud of Zeppelin and their achievements, quite rightly. And so he really didn't want to do it because Bonzo wasn't there. Robert wanted to do it because Robert will just get up and play. But he [Jimmy] just wasn't sure about putting Zeppelin back together . . .

[Phil] makes it to the stage in time for Zeppelin. [Note: Live Aid was a dual event with venues at Wembley Stadium in London and the JFK Stadium in Philadelphia. Phil Collins performed first at Wembley and was then flown by Concorde jet to play drums for Led Zeppelin at JFK the same day.] So Jimmy got caught up in that—the enormity of the event—the fun of it. But he hated that gig. He didn't like his performance specifically. He blamed Phil, which is unfair. Phil played with three bands that day, I think. When it came to putting out the DVD twenty years later, when we found the tapes, I think Zeppelin are the only band that aren't on there. I pointed out to Jimmy that it didn't really matter; that this would end up on the Internet. Not through us, but someone has this on a VHS even though they were very rudimentary. . . . He said, well, he didn't care. He wasn't gonna put his official name on it. And he didn't want to rerecord it because no one else was. But very cool. I mean, they're the only band who aren't on the thing even though some of them weren't that great. . . . But they [donated] money to Band Aid, which is amazing.

I can't stand it when people go on about rock 'n' roll. You know, oh, so-and-so—how do you get all those egos together? They're the least egotistical people. Like, cer-tainly around each other, you know, it drives me nuts. In general, they're a better class of person—a better person and a more intellectual sort of person than 99 percent of the twats who ask me about them.

George Michael (in yellow shirt), Bono and Paul McCartney (at the mike), Freddie Mercury (in red shirt), and Bob Geldof (right foreground) at the Live Aid concert, Wembley Stadium, London, July 13, 1985.

Jimmy Page

Interview by Long John Baldry

IN THE 1970S, JIMMY PAGE'S MISTRUST OF THE MUSIC PRESS KEPT HIM FROM GRANTING MANY IN-DEPTH INTERVIEWS. HOWEVER, THE LED ZEPPELIN GUITARIST MADE AN EXCEPTION IN 1977, WHEN HE WAS APPROACHED BY MUSICIAN AND ACTOR LONG JOHN BALDRY (1941–2005).

LONG JOHN BALDRY WAS AN ENGLISH BLUES SINGER WHO PERFORMED WITH NUMEROUS BRITISH MUSICIANS AND ACTUALLY HELPED SEVERAL OF THEM BECOME ESTABLISHED. ROD STEWART, ELTON JOHN, MICK JAGGER, JACK BRUCE, AND CHARLIE WATTS WERE ALL MEMBERS OF HIS BAND AT ONE TIME OR ANOTHER. IN 1963, BALDRY JOINED THE CYRIL DAVIES R&B ALL STARS WITH A YOUNG JIMMY PAGE ON GUITAR. HE HAD A NUMBER ONE RECORD IN THE UK IN 1967 WITH *LET THE HEARTACHES BEGIN*. IN THE LATE '70S, BALDRY MOVED TO CANADA AND WORKED AS A VOICE-OVER ACTOR.

THE CONVERSATION BETWEEN BALDRY AND PAGE TOOK PLACE IN 1977, DURING LED ZEPPELIN'S HEYDAY, BEGINNING WITH A LOOK BACK ON THEIR COMMON HISTORY AND CONTINUING WITH PAGE'S PERCEPTIONS OF THE DEVELOPING MUSIC SCENES IN LONDON AND ELSEWHERE, RIGHT ON THROUGH THE PUNK MOVEMENT. PAGE ALSO RECALLS THE FORMATION OF LED ZEPPELIN, DISCUSSES THE GROUP'S FIRST TOUR AS A NEW LINEUP OF THE YARDBIRDS, AND OVERVIEWS THEIR EARLY SUCCESSES AND STRUGGLES. HE CONCLUDES WITH SOME FORWARD-THINKING AMBITIONS FOR HIS GROUP, SOME OF WHICH, UNFORTUNATELY, WOULD NOT SEE THE LIGHT OF DAY.

AT THE TOP, BALDRY ASKS PAGE ABOUT HOW CYRIL DAVIES IMPACTED BOTH HIS PERSONAL AND ARTISTIC LIFE.

JIMMY PAGE: Well, [Davies] was the first person that I heard play the harp. Initially, he'd been playing with [legendary British blues musician and radio personality] Alexis Korner and had been drawn into, sort of, [American blues musicians] Sonny Terry [and] Brownie McGhee's style because of Alexis's style of playing. . . . And I don't know whether they'd been instrumental in bringing over Muddy Waters. . . .

LONG JOHN BALDRY: Well, they were part of the scene at that time. . . . As a matter of fact, I think it was the Marquee people who first brought Muddy over.

JP: Well, of course, he was really—as was everybody— totally bowled over by Muddy, and he felt that, you know, with that style of electric guitar playing, bottleneck,

Elmore James, and the harp being used in the way of Little Walter, this was the way things should be going. And of course there was this conflict between him and Alexis to the point that there was only one decision for him to make, and that was to get out. Now, there was nobody that was really into—nobody who really had this sort of fantastic textbook of the blues, you know, behind them, as did those two people, Alexis and Cyril. And so to form a band, he had to turn to rock 'n' roll musicians and break them into it, gently, by turning them on to the sounds. . . . I'd been involved with playing, like, Chuck Berry numbers. But this is really getting right into the nitty-gritty of the thing, you know. And the band that he had with Nicky Hopkins, who could play note-for-note perfect Lafayette Leake and Otis Spann stuff, and [drummer] Carlo Little, and, um . . .

LJB: Ricky Brown on the bass . . .

JP: Yeah, Brown, but the other one, the chap that followed, the chap who died . . .

LJB: Cliff Barton ?

JP: Yeah, Cliff Barton was—I never heard a bass player play like that, ever. He played slap bass almost, and boy, oh, boy, could that chap play! And between the two, the rhythm section, they had all these eights worked out— [sings a fast-paced descending bass line] which, of course, [Yardbirds bassist Paul] Samwell-Smith took over and was quite a trademark later for the Yardbirds. And the Muddy Waters things that they were doing, you know, and which the Stones started using—I mean, everybody was influenced, without any doubt, by Cyril Davies and his band, his approach on the electrified harp. Everybody! And yet over the years, you know . . . it always surprises me that Cyril's name never comes up. There's very little on record. . . .

LJB: I think it was certainly one of the most explosive bands I've ever been in. That combination . . .

JP: That was the thing that made the pendulum swing right over, you know. And when the Beatles came out with "Love Me Do" and all this sort of stuff, and "Please Mr. Postman," it seemed sort of pathetic compared to anything that was going on then.

Jimmy Page performs with Donovan and the London Contemporary Orchestra at Royal Albert Hall, London, June 3, 2011.

LJB: I always thought that Merseybeat or whatever was going on—

JP: Was rubbish!

LJB: —was sort of syrupy compared to what we were doing in London.

JP: Yeah, I mean, there was so much balls going on.

LJB: Why do you think it started off in London? Obviously, London being a big metropolis, the capital of England, but it was totally a London thing. I know the Animals had something going up in Newcastle, but it was without exception, really, a whole London thing in many ways, really.

JP: First of all, record collectors had a hell of a lot to do with it. Now I know that, personally speaking, it helped me a hell of a lot knowing this guy was collecting blues and R&B because, you know, I'd just take the things and get to know the numbers and work them out from there, and of course it was at a lot of expense because this stuff was never, ever on the radio. And Eric [Clapton] knew a chap called Charlie Radcliffe, who again was another collector and he got a lot of stuff from him, you know . . . things like that, you know. And some of these rare things, you know, Blues Boys Kingdom label, B. B. King's first and only record label that he had, put out one— "Motherless Child," I think was the title. All these sort of things that collectors had. And there just seemed to be a hell of a lot of record collectors around London, and with Cyril's sort of, as you said, explosion that came on the scene, it turned so many people on that that was it! Now, what did they have anywhere else? They didn't have a Cyril. They didn't have anybody else, I think, and then of course the Stones, and Mick's personality, and Brian Jones's musicianship, you know. I mean, they used to do Muddy Waters numbers to the tee. I mean, it was just spot-on, you know. Really, really good, and still are. The Yardbirds were, with Eric, were blues, blues-based, but they were still into this sort of "Good Morning Little Schoolgirl" stuff, you know. When Jeff [Beck] joined, it gave [manager] Giorgio [Gomelsky] the thing that he'd been wanting for a long time, which was for the expansion of the group to take other areas of music and really basically land him on the pop market. But I would say it was Cyril and the Stones.

[Note: At this point in the discussion, the tape cuts off and picks up with Page addressing a new topic.]

Yes, Eel Pie [a hotel on Eel Pie Island in the Thames that was a blues and jazz venue in the 1960s]. I always remember some little old lady who used to collect tuppence from you for your entry to and fro across the little bridge across the Thames [laughing]. Fantastic! But the hotel itself was a beautiful place, really lovely. It—I don't know when it would have been built, what, about 1900, 1910? It was a real character piece. . . . It was truly alive, a jumping place, fantastic. And there was never any bad music, there was always good. But the Marquee was the

one. That was the nucleus. And the reason why it took off and was always so full and packed was purely because of, you know, this brand-new—to the public—this brand-new era, just as punk rock is now. People are clamoring now, you know. You get the secretaries going down there, you know, curiosity seekers going down there. Not just people with safety pins [laughs].

LJB: Well, Cyril Davies never saw the new Marquee [Club] in Wardour Street. He died before that place opened. It was the original Marquee Oxford Street that he played in. What do you think he would have made of the new one in Wardour Street had he still been alive?

JP: Well, he would have obviously given an injection into the atmosphere, which it needed. I remember when I joined [the Yardbirds] after this whole deal with Samwell-Smith going down, the first gig that I played was at that new Marquee, and in fact we did two dates there. For some unknown reason, we always played with problems, you know, gear breaking down and fuses busting, but we did two gigs there.

Then we [Led Zeppelin] started to move on to the Albert Hall and the larger places, and we made a decision to go back to the clubs and do a tour of the clubs. And obviously it was going to be the Marquee in London [spring 1971] and we went there and it sounded really odd! The actual sound, the acoustics! And they'd built a bar, and the bar took up half the size of the Marquee, so it was like it had just become a—I don't know, how do you put it—the business side of the record industry or something, sort of the hangout place for that. The musical aspect became second place as far as I could see.

LJB: I remember that particular tour you did with Led Zeppelin, the club tour, because I came down to see you on that particular evening, squashed against the wall at the back of the crowd. Enjoyable evening! A bit on the loud side, but then of course you had been used to playing the larger venues before coming back into the clubs.

JP: Yeah, it was amazing, really, because the lady that I was with was pregnant at the time, and the whole sort of rumbling induced the pregnancy because she had the baby within hours after that! [Laughs] That gig, actually, it was quite funny.

LJB: Well, it induced a nosebleed for me for that particular reason. [Laughs]

JP: [Laughing] Oh, I'm sorry about that. It wasn't a fight, was it?

LJB: No, my nose actually started to bleed with the intensity of the physical vibration coming from the stage because the equipment you brought in I think was probably louder than anything I'd ever heard before.

JP: Ah, yeah, but it wasn't—I mean, we had a lot of light speakers to the PA but they weren't all turned on, obviously. Yeah, it took some adapting, obviously, because

Ioannis, Page, Plant *(detail), 2011.*

even with our first tour of the States we went straight into those auditoriums as a support band, you know, those sort of 15,000 [seating capacity] jobs.

LJB: You did actually work as a support band in Led Zeppelin? I thought it went out immediately as a headlining.

JP: Oh, God, no. No, our first tour was, you know—well, our first year was working just all the time, it was a twenty-four-hour job all the time because you just had to. There was no [halfway]. You just had to do it. I mean, over here [in England], we had a hell of a lot of trouble getting the Yardbird label off our backs, you know? In the States, there had been a sort of clamoring [for] two guitar heroes, and I was fortunate enough to have made a bit of a dent in that. Consequently, we were assured a certain amount of an audience because of that, you know? But over here, there was sort of reticence on behalf of the promoters and colleagues and things to just put "Led Zeppelin." It had to be "Led Zeppelin featuring Jimmy Page" or "The New Yardbirds" even though we had done a couple of dates—well, our first tour together with the band was in Scandinavia. In fact, it acted as a warm-up tour to the British thing, British clubs, and from that we came back and recorded our first album, having run through most of the material. But curiously enough, that was an old commitment that the Yardbirds had to fulfill, and so we called ourselves the New Yardbirds for that, purely to save a lot of trouble and suing and everything. After that, it was Led Zeppelin, but as I said, we had a lot of trouble.

But in the States, our first few dates were with Vanilla Fudge, who at that time were at sort of a peak, you know, still doing really well. And matter of fact, we didn't get any billing at all then, but we did the Whisky a Go Go, and we were billed immediately as Led Zeppelin.

And then we went to the Fillmore West. And there was Taj Mahal opening. We were on second. And top of the bill was Country Joe. Now, at this point of time, well—let's precede it by a few years. We all know about San Francisco and the vibe that went on in San Francisco, and it always given me the image of sort of a big family setup, you know, all the bands jamming with each other and playing in the park, and it was just, like, a really good vibe. But by the time that we arrived on the scene, it was getting a bit jaded. People were getting just a bit fed up with it all. They were waiting for something new; once it became merchandising on Haight-Ashbury and all that sort of thing, the thing got a bit sour. And the Cream, I think, had just broken up at this point. Hendrix had received some bad publicity, which was the usual sort of thing, where he'd played a concert—and for some astronomical fee [$50,000 for one gig], [which] to the press meant more than the concert or the appearance and everything else, so really the timing as far as it went was just right for something new to come on the scene. Well, we went on after Taj Mahal and the place just exploded, you know, it was incredible! And poor old Country Joe didn't know what had hit him. And I remember the last night of three nights, he just had anybody and everybody coming up and jamming with him, from out of the

Ioannis, Jimmy Page 1972 *(detail)*, 2011.

audience. But I do remember sitting in a dressing room suddenly hearing a really sweet guitar being played. "Who's that?" And it was Steve Miller. I always liked his playing.

LJB: Those guys always used to hang out and play together, Steve Miller and Elvin Bishop and all those blues . . .

JP: But I was never really too knocked out with any of that San Francisco rock. I liked Steve Miller. And another band that I really liked and really impressed me, for the variety of their music and technical capabilities, that I thought were San Francisco but in fact they were from L.A., was [psychedelic folk band] American Kaleidoscope. They were just stunning to watch because they just pulled so much out of the bag and you never knew what was coming next. That was fantastic. And, well, there weren't many bands that I really—Spirit was another band I liked. I thought they were very good. But around that point, they were just really waiting for something new. I mean, we were just going out there and really, really doing our balls and really enjoying it.

It was just—we were all so happy to be playing with each other.

LJB: And the length of your performances as well. I suppose the Led Zeppelin must really hold the record for the length of sets you played.

JP: [Laughing] I guess so, yeah.

LJB: Two-and-a-half-, three-hour sets.

JP: That all started in Boston Tea Party. That was another club. Gosh, they just wouldn't let us stop. We were even playing sort of Beatles numbers. "I Saw Her Standing There" and things like that, that we didn't even know completely, but anything, you know! We'd gone through all the Chuck Berry repertoires, and it was an incredible night! That night, we played for about three hours, but actually how we got into these long sets was the fact that—and it's always been our greatest problem for tours, and that's the program, knowing what to drop when you've got new material and everything. And we were doing acoustic sets as well. It seemed—well, it didn't even feel like three hours, anyway, when we got into these three-hour sets. Originally, it was getting sort of between two and three-quarters, three hours, but then, like, it was sometimes, we'd do three and three-quarters purely because we'd stretch the numbers. And I think it was, again, that's something that people got to know us for. I mean, they'd know that if they came along to see us, they'd never see the show exactly the same way because there were numbers that had areas for improvisation and, obviously, the improvisation would change every night, you know. And I think that's what kept us on our toes, really. If we'd have been the sort of band that played note-for-note perfect, we probably would have broken up a long time ago.

LJB: How long has Led Zeppelin been together? It must be ten years already.

JP: Nine.

LJB: That's not a bad record.

JP: It really took about four years to get to know each other, if you know what I mean. There was a musical respect right from the start, right from the initial rehearsal, which we held in a little tiny, weenie place . . . and I think we did "Train Kept A-Rollin'." Yes, and this was the first rehearsal, and there was just a great beaming smile from everybody. We knew it . . . was definitely right. And then from then on, it was just a point of— well, Robert had already been to my place and we had discussed the sort of ideas that I had. One good example of this is "Babe I'm Gonna Leave You," which I had on a Joan Baez LP, and I played him that version of it and he looked at me and said I was mad.

It's very curious, this sort of—the roots, so to speak, roots coinciding. Jeff [Beck] and myself. I remember being in Miami. It was just at the time that everything was being tied up with Atlantic and Jerry Wexler and everything. And [manager] Peter [Grant], just at the end of it, said—'cause we'd already recorded, you see—he said, "Oh, I've got some of Jeff's new material." It was for the first album, *Truth*, and he said, "He's done 'You Shook Me,'" and I thought, oh no! Because, you see, we'd done it as well. And both totally unknown by each other that either had done it, you see, and I thought, oh, God, it's going to sound exactly the same! Because we were both in love with that [Muddy Waters] EP, the one that had "Little Brown Bird" on it and "You Need Love." Fortunately, his was totally different. But it always annoyed me, actually, that people related our LP to Jeff's—Jeff's came out first—and said it was, you know, a similar sort of theme and concept because it wasn't. . . .

LJB: Yeah, and of course, right in the beginning of Led Zeppelin, coming from the Yardbirds days, a good deal of the material you recorded and performed onstage was blues—

JP: Very blues-based.

LJB: —in feel, or whatever. Has it strayed very far from that now, Led Zeppelin today, or do you think that that blues feeling that was there in the beginning still hangs on today?

JP: Well, it's inescapable. It's inescapable, I mean, there's even been talk along the line, say, two years ago, of just doing a club tour and just doing blues, you know, just doing a whole blues set. But we'd never get away with it because we'd just be heckled the whole time for the other numbers that people wanted us to do. But anyway . . . as far as [for me], personally speaking, it's more [about] composition and orchestration.

You see, I've written this twenty-minute piece, which involves acoustic guitar, basically. [Note: Page is referring to "Carouselambra."] The whole thing is built around a flamenco-style, mock classical, and fingerpicking sort of style, and it's quite a complex thing. And yet the electric portions come in, too, so the band is employed as well. The whole piece goes through four different moods, and the idea originally was to write a piece—I mean, it could be just instrumental, but it's a challenge, really, to take it into a vocal. It has four vocal spots. And I wanted to literally do work on something on the seasons, but when we did "Rain Song," Robert used three of the seasons in that. So you could do it around the elements or anything, which can relate to fours. Who knows, by the time he actually tackles the lyrics of it? But I've always—one of the things I've always wanted to do was to orchestrate, like, a sort of measured piece using guitars and especially now you can do anything, make a guitar sound like anything, really. And use the guitar—give it a certain treatment to take on the positions of woodwinds or strings or the brass, whatever, you know, within an orchestra. And those pieces that I just mentioned, for those other songs, you know, it's just little tastes of what can be done. And that's really my next step, and [laughs] I'm just waiting for my studio to be finished so I can do it. But I think it will be very—well, you know, the timing's right for something like that, you know. I've had quite a lot of it written. I've worked on it a little more now, but I didn't think the timing was right. It was too much of a step; people wouldn't have been ready for it.

Ioannis, Jimmy Page: Achilles Last Stand, *2011.*

You know, I've always felt that the initial overall atmosphere and vibe and identity that shines forth in our first LP has been sort of with us ever since and we just sort of explored and embellished upon those things.

Robert Plant

SINCE LED ZEPPELIN DISBANDED, LEAD SINGER ROBERT PLANT HAS ENJOYED A SUCCESSFUL SOLO CAREER. IN 2007, HE RELEASED THE ALBUM *RAISING SAND* WITH BLUEGRASS ARTIST ALISON KRAUSS, WHICH WON THE 2009 GRAMMY AWARD FOR ALBUM OF THE YEAR.

CONSIDERED ONE OF THE MOST IMPORTANT SINGERS IN THE HISTORY OF ROCK MUSIC, PLANT HAS INFLUENCED A WHOLE GENERATION OF SUCCESSORS. *ROLLING STONE* MAGAZINE READERS SELECTED PLANT AS NUMBER ONE IN THE MAGAZINE'S BEST LEAD SINGERS OF ALL TIME POLL IN 2011. PLANT, ALONG WITH THE OTHER MEMBERS OF LED ZEPPELIN, WAS INDUCTED INTO THE ROCK AND ROLL HALL OF FAME IN 1995.

THE FOLLOWING WAS TAKEN FROM AN INTERVIEW CONDUCTED IN 1982, WHEN PLANT WAS ON A MEDIA TOUR IN SUPPORT OF HIS POST-ZEPPELIN DEBUT SOLO RELEASE, *PICTURES AT ELEVEN*. IT WAS ONE OF HIS FIRST MAJOR INTERVIEWS SINCE ZEPPELIN ANNOUNCED THEY COULD NOT CONTINUE AS THEY WERE IN 1980. NEAR THE TOP OF THE INTERVIEW, HE IS ASKED WHY LED ZEPPELIN HAD TO END.

ROBERT PLANT: Well, really, if you're in a four-piece band for a long time, and you didn't absorb any other players and you don't take in any other sidemen at all, even on a temporary basis, then what you've got is perfect. You work within it. It's great. You're quite happy. When it's tough it's tough, and when you're really hitting it, it's great. Really, the four-piece format was the ultimate situation and then [upon the death of drummer John Bonham] it was no longer a four-piece format. It was pointless turning round and round and going, "Well, what shall we do now?"

DENNY SOMACH: Was there any thought of having Cozy [Powell of Black Sabbath, the Jeff Beck Group, et al.] take the place of John?

RP: No. I read a lot about it. I wonder who said it, but it was none of us! It was natural that there would be a lot of speculation, I think. But it's only right, now, that we put the speculation to rest.

DS: Okay . . . the Who didn't make that same choice.

RP: Well, it's each to their own, really. I was looking at the Who at Kampuchea [a benefit held in London for Cambodian victims of Pol Pot in 1979] on the TV in England the other night, and they're still great, but I mean, they have to make the decision themselves. What's good for one is not necessarily good for the other, you know?

DS: Speaking of Kampuchea, how did you get involved with that particular benefit?

RP: I went to the gig and Dave [Edmunds, the Welsh singer, guitarist, and producer] was on Swan Song [Led Zeppelin's label] at the time, so I went to see him in the dressing room. "Hi, Dave, good luck . . . " and that sort of thing, and he said, "Well, why don't you do a song?" I said, "Well, I . . . I . . . " splutter, splutter. . . . And I said, "Well, I don't really know all the words to any of your songs," you know? I can't do "Queen of Hearts" or anything like that because Dave is very popular, and I could hardly go on and do "Black Dog" or something like that. So we plumbed for "Little Sister" and we just found out what key we'd do it in and just went for it. That's why I fell apart at the very end! Which is the best part of it, really! When Nick Lowe keeps singing and everybody else stops! As we came offstage, you could tell by the film that I was a bit embarrassed. I wasn't ready for it. As we walked offstage, Elvis Costello turned around and said, "I never thought I'd see Rockpile [UK rock band featuring Nick Lowe and Dave Edmunds, which disbanded in 1981] do 'Stairway to Heaven!'" Sarcasm reigns in English rock.

DS: It was a great concert, though. What are the other guys in the band doing? What is Jimmy Page doing?

RP: Well, Jimmy worked on that film sound track, which I think he made an incredible job on, on the Charles Bronson movie [*Death Wish II*]. He was offered it, and I think he looked at it as being a challenge because it was taken away from a group format, you know. He was left to compose pieces of music that went around clips of film for maybe eight and a half seconds. The challenge was quite enormous. So after he did that, I think he's just sitting back now and thinking about exactly what to do.

DS: What about John Paul Jones?

RP: Well, I don't see John as much as I see Jimmy. I see Jimmy quite regularly, and the last time I saw John he

said that—you know how guys are with their projects . . . you know if you collect stamps you're after the ultimate stamp, or whatever it is. Well, he's working on something like that. He won't even tell anybody about it. It's one of those numbers where he's keeping it real quiet. I couldn't tell you. I haven't got a clue.

DS: When you were doing the solo album [*Pictures at Eleven*], was it ever tempting to go to the phone and call Jimmy and say, "Hey, why don't you do this on the album?"

RP: Not really. Because I think we both came to a conclusion where we had to go our separate ways for as long as it takes to draw on new stimuli, if you like, to bounce off other people, to just go, "You go that way. I'll go this way."

RP: Now, I guess a total alternative, something . . . I can't say "dreamy." That's not the right word. But it's always good to follow one thing with something that's totally different. "Moonlight in Samosa" sums that up.

DS: Perfect. "Pledge Pin."

RP: "Pledge Pin." Well, there was once, well, in fact there are many, many characters that you come across who are so full of their own attributes that they spend the whole night being looked upon by the masses; and they're in the position to take anyone anywhere that they want to go—I don't know, movies, lunch, anything you'd like. But in the end they're so choosy that they end up standing on their own. "Pledge Pin."

And we keep comparing notes—"How's it going, what are you doing?" That sort of thing. But there's a time for everything . . .

DS: Okay, I want to do something that we have a lot of success with, and it's a perfect way to introduce an album and I would like to do it. It's what we call a mini view, where we have an artist actually, essentially play disc jockey to his own record.

RP: Why? Having heard it so many times I'll probably get it all wrong! . . .

DS: Start it off, then we'll do track by track, you know, an introduction of each song. Could you start it off with the introduction?

RP: Well, I know what my name is. Okay. This is Robert Plant and this is my first solo album, called *Pictures at Eleven*, and it's quite hot.

DS: Tell us who is on the album.

RP: On the record, lead guitarist is Robbie Blunt, who helped me write two songs. Paul Martinez on bass and drums, two drummers—Phil Collins and Cozy Powell.

DS: So now you want to say the first track on the record is called "Burning Down One Side," then tell us something about the song.

RP: I can't tell you without getting into trouble. . . .

DS: Okay, the song plays and it's fading out and we're coming out of "Burning Down One Side" and we're going into "Moonlight in Samosa."

DS: Great. Perfect. Now, "Pledge Pin" is playing, and now it's fading out and the next one is "Slow Dancer." Make sure that you identify yourself.

RP: The closing cut on the first side of *Pictures at Eleven* is a track called "Slow Dancer." Been a lot of interest in this track already from the people who've listened to it. I spend a lot of time, as much as I can, listening to North African music. This is "Slow Dancer" and I'm Robert Plant.

DS: Great. Okay, we're in the middle of the record. . . .

RP: Yeah, very quickly: side two opens with "Worse Than Detroit." This is Robert Plant. . . . I guess it's a little bit tongue-in-cheek, this track. It relates to a man and a woman situation that's broken down. Nothing to read between the lines. The guy's in a motel and he's trying to court this lady and things are not going well. He's really upset, he couldn't be any worse off than he is, so he's worse than Detroit.

DS: I like that! "Fat Lip."

RP: Well, there's no story to "Fat Lip," really. It's the second cut on the second side. It's an interesting track because it's a track without a drum kit. It's the track that Cozy Powell kept saying, "Look, in the solo I can put in some great drums on there. You just fade the drum machine out and I'll do some real neat drumming, you know?" But it stands up without a drum kit. It's got some nice space in it . . .

DS: Great. Okay. "Fat Lip" is playing and it's fading, and the next song is "Like I've Never Been Gone."

RP: Yeah. What can I say about "Like I've Never Been Gone?" I guess it relates to some of the nice and more emotional moments from the past that are still quite present in my mind. It's just a simple love song.

DS: Great. And the last track, "Mystery Title."

RP: "Mystery Title" relates to the hunger for the road. You're gonna talk to me about touring, you know. I may or may not go on tour within the next twelve months, but I've always got my mind on moving. Even if it's only around the corner to look at somebody else. "Mystery Title."

DS: I still don't understand how "Mystery Title" . . .

RP: Oh, the title has absolutely nothing to do with the song at all. God, that would be too easy, wouldn't it?

DS: And now for something totally different! Okay, so the show is over, the show has ended, so you can close your show any way you'd like to. Because America has just spent an hour listening to the new album with you introducing it.

RP: Yeah, well that's about it. I mean, that's the first time around. It wasn't particularly hard work. It was great fun to do and I guess there's a lot of room to do a lot of other things in the not-too-distant future. We've already got five ideas for the next album. So it's just a good little workshop.

DS: Tell us who you are again and say good-bye.

RP: Well, I am and always will be Robert Plant. Good-bye.

DS: Let me ask you some questions about a group you used to be with. You were in a bunch of bands, weren't you? The last and probably the most famous before Led Zeppelin was Band of Joy. Tell me about the Band of Joy. What kind of group was that?

RP: Well, I think there wasn't a great deal of West Coast music in England. I had a great love for Moby Grape and Buffalo Springfield, Arthur Lee [of the seminal West Coast band Love], and people like that. There wasn't a platform to play all that music because England was on the tail end of sort of a Herman's Hermits–type thing, you know. A lot of bands played it safe by playing watered-down Beach Boys–type renditions and all that sort of thing. So John [Bonham] and myself had this band called the Band of Joy, and we suffered a lot. We couldn't play many places, but when we played we played real well. We used to pride ourselves on doing one gig a week and bringing the house down and then starving for the next six days!

Ioannis, Robert Plant: The Rain Song (detail), 2011.

> (The Band of Joy) was a good band. It was in those days when you might call music "progressive," but what that meant and what it was, I don't know. They were just good musicians and interesting music.

DS: Were there any other guys in that band, besides you and John, who went on to make names for themselves in bigger bands?

RP: Not really. The Band of Joy did reform at one point and they did a deal with Polydor or something like that, using the name, for which I chase them even now! When I see them, I quickly turn the car around and go tearing after them, going, "You fools! That's my name! Leave it alone!" [Note: Band of Joy formed again in 2010 with Robert Plant.]

DS: How did you meet up with Jimmy Page?

RP: Well, that's so long ago. I think when Jimmy was forming the band, he was working at the format that he wanted. He wanted [British singer-guitarist] Terry Reid to sing with him. I don't blame him because Terry's a great singer. He was being recorded by Mickie Most in London and he had a great deal of promise. He still has. He's still a great singer, but at the time Terry said, "No, I'm gonna do it by myself, but I know this bloke who lives up north of England who's real loony—he screams and sings and does whatever. Find him and try him." And that's exactly what happened—with great results.

DS: Yeah, I'll say. It was your idea to bring John into the band?

RP: Yeah, well, John and I had been playing for a long time together; the Band of Joy hit real rock bottom because in the end we didn't even do one gig a week! But I wasn't prepared to change the actual musical approach, so the band slid into nowhere. During that time, John was working with Tim Rose. Remember Tim Rose? Wrote some great songs.

DS: Sure!

RP: I thought "I Got a Loneliness" and "Morning Dew," stuff like that, was great. And John was really happy and he said, "You can have all your music till the cows come home, but I'm having a great time here and I'm getting paid, too!" Which was quite novel in those days. But I managed to seduce him. No, that's the wrong word, isn't it? I manage to lure him into coming along and just trying it out.

DS: Now, the band into which you were recruited wasn't Led Zeppelin. It was something else.

RP: Yeah, the New Yardbirds was what it started out as.

DS: How did you feel about being a member of the New Yardbirds? The Yardbirds were such a legend . . .

RP: We worked three days a week. It was paradise! I didn't care, really. My singing voice was so different from Keith's [Yardbirds singer Keith Relf] anyway. I found a platform for my voice. I was very young and really kind of super-impressed playing with Jimmy, you know, because everybody knew who he was, although we didn't see him much in England because he was always over here [in the United States] with the Yardbirds. So it was great to play with somebody that dramatic, that powerful.

DS: So did you become Led Zeppelin before the record deal with Atlantic?

RP: Yeah. Before.

DS: Tell me the story of how the band got its name.

RP: Well, I think there was gonna be a famous band that was gonna be comprised of loads and loads of famous folks. That [was] what you call "pub talk," I guess. You know, it was gonna happen and then it didn't happen. And the drummer was gonna be Keith Moon. Or he was talking about it, or promising his oath under certain circumstances. And he said, "Well, you should call the band Led Zeppelin because in America they have this term that when you tell a joke or a quip that isn't particularly well received, it goes down like a lead balloon." And what better way to start?

DS: So it was Keith Moon? I read that in some places they say it was Keith Moon and in other places they say it was John Entwistle.

RP: No, it was Moon. Keith Moon.

DS: The first album, I heard, was recorded in a week. Is that true?

RP: No, it was about eight days. I can't remember now, but it was a very short time. Most of the stuff was done live there and then in the studio. You can hear voices whizzing around the background that we couldn't wipe off, you know, because it was coming through on the drum track. But it was great. It was like that. Bang! And it was done.

DS: Led Zeppelin got a very big deal with Atlantic Records. I mean, it was a big contract for what was essentially a new band—even though Jimmy had had a sizable reputation with the Yardbirds.

RP: Well, I don't even remember too much of that. I was

at home all the time in England, thinking, "Well, who am I gonna join if this don't happen?" You know? Where am I gonna go next? I think that Ahmet [Ertegun] had heard the record and was greatly impressed. I mean, I never came to Atlantic, never met anybody or anything to begin with. But the record spoke for itself.

DS: Let's talk about some of the music. On the first album, would you tell me something either anecdotal or provide some explanation of the lyrics, or a story about some of the tunes—"Good Times Bad Times" . . .

RP: Well, you know, I was a little boy then! I mean, it's pretty simple, straightforward stuff—it just speaks for itself. I mean, when you sit down to write a song you just think of something like that . . .

> I mean, "Good Times Bad Times" is just—there's nothing to it, really. Not a great deal at all. I mean, it's just a nice song. The lyrics were very straightforward. It was like, "la de da da da . . ." Nothing particularly to be proud of.

DS: But that was the introduction . . .

RP: Yeah, but that track was great. I'm saying that my lyrics weren't that much . . . but the track itself was stupendous. And Jimmy's solo on the fade, that sort of Leslie [West] sound. It was great! Like all new and very powerful—great! I'd like to do that again.

DS: Do you ever think of doing that?

RP: No.

DS: "Dazed and Confused." Is there a story?

RP: Well, there isn't a story. But it's just that, in rehearsals, when we were working, we were just seeing how good we could get it, which was virtually similar to what I've been doing recently with *Pictures at Eleven* in rehearsals. It was amazing the kind of mood Jimmy would create with a violin bow. Then there was no particular instant drama—I mean, you were working in a small, tiny little room in London and the only thing that you were knocked out on was everybody's ability to play, you know? The musicianship, and the fact that already, there was a sort of . . . we were melting together and Jimmy and I, it was remarkable to see and really that was just a beginning of what extended on stage with "Dazed and

Confused." So in the end, I mean, some nights it was undescribable. The kind of affinity . . . the closeness we had. I mean, Jimmy would be pitching and we'd both come out with the same note at the same time. I mean, woo! And we'd both look at each other and we'd go, "Ah, that's very nice!"

DS: That's amazing. I guess that's why it worked.

RP: I guess that must have been it. If you can knock yourself out, knock each other out, genuinely, rather than doing it just for the sake of it, you know? Saying, this is working so we must look as if we're having a good time—well, that was never the case.

Ioannis, Robert Plant: The Rain Song *(detail), 2011.*

DS: I read in an interview with Jimmy somewhere, he said that the idea behind Led Zeppelin was to be able to fuse acoustic music with heavy metal and come out with something that had texture.

RP: Yeah, quite light-and-shade. It goes back to drama . . . the dramatics of it. Unfortunately, it would seem that the acoustic material almost was overwhelmed by the more aggressive, the more electric stuff. I find, especially in Europe, we're always attributed as being this sort of a heavy metal band, and it's most aggravating because any heaviness that we had was the first name of our group. You know, "Led"—that was about it. Anything else was light-and-shade. "Babe I'm Gonna Leave You" is so beautiful. You know, for what it is. I mean, it's great. But it isn't thunder and lightning, and it isn't a constant riff that bores you to tears after the fourth listening.

DS: It's the up-and-down. And the epitome of that philosophy was "Stairway to Heaven." Probably one of the most requested songs on radio today.

RP: Why didn't everybody request "Kashmir?"

DS: I don't know. It's "Stairway to Heaven." But it's the perfect blending of that up-and-down. Tell me about "Stairway to Heaven."

RP: I'll tell you. It was one of those on-off situations where we sat down. . . . See, we'd done the third album. We'd made a purposeful attempt to move away, or to try very, very hard to show people that we had more than one string to our bow. So we went up to the Welsh mountains and started writing. And we came out with the third album, which was prominently acoustic on the one side, and that atmosphere, that blend, obviously, had been with us through "Ramble On" and "Your Time Is Gonna Come" and that sort of thing. Naturally, it was gonna go right through whatever we did. So when we sat around the fire again [to write songs for Led Zeppelin's fourth album] and "Stairway" began, there was the introduction thing and I just started musing around something that would be simple and sweet, very positive and to the point and over in a flash.

You know, like a four-minute track. But I mean, what happened was it just kept extending, Jimmy just kept extending with the bridge work on the guitar that would move it on to the next section. . . . And there were still no drums and we were going, "Wait a minute. We can't do this. It's gotta come in somewhere," and then it went into that sort of third section, you know, and the drums came in. And then it had to go somewhere. I mean, how do you say how you write a song? It's like shelling out peas and yet it's not, you know? You either do it or you don't. There's no particular secret. By the time ["Stairway to Heaven"] got its musical format, half of the lyrics were more or less in shape, once the actual format of the beginning and at the end was established and everything in the middle. I don't know, within a day and a half it was done.

DS: Songs aren't really written in a vacuum, are they? I mean, very rare, I would imagine, that you would sit down and write a song complete and that's the way it turns out on the record.

RP: Exactly. I mean, "Trampled Under Foot": the lyrics I managed to do while they were laying the track down. I just ran upstairs, got the first line, "Greasy slicked-down body, groovy leather trim, like the way you hold the road . . . " you know, that sort of thing. So once I got the meter of it, I just ran away, locked myself in a room, and wrote a whole lot in about half an hour. But I got three-quarters of the way through it, and the door smashed open, because the rest of the guys thought I was up to no good, you know? I was writing feverishly, sprawled on a bed. So "Stairway to Heaven" was just "Here we go. Let's see what happens here."

DS: "Whole Lotta Love" is a Muddy Waters song, isn't it? Originally? Or very similar to a Muddy Waters song— "You Need Love?"

RP: It's very similar to a lot of songs. I mean, with a lot of blues records, you get people copping, "I wrote this or I did that," and [with] the Chicago blues in the '50s and the Chess [Records] recordings, you get a tendency to get one record that crops up here that you've already got at home by somebody else. But the title's different. And then you look back further, maybe 1934, Tommy McClennan did it in Chicago. Back to Chicago again, and in 1929 maybe Memphis Minnie did it in Tennessee and so the whole thing has a passage during time. It changes its name a million times, so "Dust My Blues," the Elmore James classic, when I was a kid I thought, "That's great! That guy is such an innovator," you know, and what a great riff! The introduction to "Dust My Blues" and the solo has been used by everybody. And then they issued a Robert Johnson LP, *The King of the Delta Blues,* and he wrote "Dust My Broom" in 1934 and played it, too, so it kind of goes, it's spread out so everybody pulls a little bit from here and a little bit from there.

DS: It's like passing along a story. It changes as it goes.

RP: Really, yeah, more or less. I think so. I mean, you could probably go back to, I don't know, when they first started recording the blues, Papa Charlie Jackson in 1923 played blues with a banjo. And he was American, too. But I mean, there were field hollers and chants that were sort of syncopated, work songs and all that sort of thing. I mean, who knows where everything begins? I've heard the Small Faces do a version of it. I've heard loads of people do a version of it.

DS: Did Jeff Beck ever do a version of it?

RP: I don't think so.

DS: No? "Dazed and Confused" was recorded by the Yardbirds, wasn't it?

RP: I believe. Yeah.

DS: I'm confused.

RP: I'm confused! You see? That's what happens! I've heard similar things to "Immigrant Song" by a very famous group from Salt Lake City. I've heard . . . I mean, I've heard bits and pieces of our stuff coming out all over the place.

DS: What was the name of the song—it's on the flip side of the "Immigrant Song" on the single—that was never put on an album?

RP: "Hey Hey What Can I Do?"

DS: Right. Why was that never included on a record?

RP: Well, you can only cut so many tracks on an album before time is a problem, as far as pressing the record goes. And we just got tracks left over.

DS: How many other tracks are left over, sitting in a vault somewhere?

RP: Loads.

DS: Really? Are we gonna see more Led Zeppelin albums?

RP: I don't know, really. To be perfectly honest, I've been that immersed in what I'm doing I personally haven't given it a great deal of immediate thought. . . . Some good stuff, though.

DS: Oh, people want more!

RP: Hmm. Don't we all?

DS: You also did a song way back, by Alexis Korner, called "Operator." Was that your first recording?

RP: No, I did three tracks for Columbia. One was issued in America on Columbia and the first track was called "You Better Run." It was a Young Rascals song. It was a great song, actually. I remember the company who recorded it, who were recording me, was owned by Eddie Kassner and Danny Kessler. They owned the wonderful and marvelous record, even if I never expected anything from it and I never got anything from it. Except for one free copy!

DS: You got what you expected, then?

RP: Yeah, I guess so. I never got the masters, though. So yeah, "You Better Run" came out. It came out in America, too. Then I did a track, a song . . . an Italian ballad with English lyrics called "Our Song." Which Jack Jones did, finally. Can you believe it?

DS: Really. You and Jack Jones covered the same song!

RP: Yeah, yeah, oh, dear. The last record was called "Long Time Coming." And that was not much better, either. They weren't that good. But they're fun. I mean, the ballad, especially, is great.

DS: Fun to look back at that stuff. Let me ask you about a few other tunes. Tell me about "What Is and What Should Never Be."

RP: Well, in a strange way, that's connected with "Moonlight in Samosa" from my album. It's just a kind of emotional theme that's on a slant over there that's been going on for a while in me. It's just a sort of an attitude that I've got to a certain area of my life that doesn't have any beginning or any end, you know? It's a nice song. It's a bit dreamy nowadays, though. "To a castle I will take you." Howard Johnson's is more like it!

DS: Great lyrics, though. Why does the song "Houses of the Holy" appear on *Physical Graffiti* and not on *Houses of the Holy*?

RP: Being silly, isn't it? I mean, I could go into some great profound reasoning, but . . . I can't even remember why. I think we thought, "Well, hold onto that and we'll do something [with it]." It was just having a laugh.

DS: Gets people talking! Radio interviewers get curious about it, so it was worth it.

RP: It's good fun, you know. It's nice to sort of . . . I mean, it makes people smile a lot and then they go, "They're at it again. Now what have they done?"

DS: Explain for me "D'yer Mak'er."

RP: Well, Jamaica. And you know the feel of the song is like a reggae thing. It's kind of lighthearted. . . . Because there's a joke in England and it goes something like this: There's two guys talking and one guy says to the other one, "Your wife went on holiday this year?" And the guy

Ioannis, Robert Plant: The Rain Song *(detail)*, 2011.

says, "Yeah." The guy says, "Jamaica?" And he says, "No. She went on her own accord." Did ya make her? No, she went on her own accord. Really corny, you know? Cornball. We have a sense of humor, or we had a sense of humor we tried to kind of put across.

You couldn't really go around cracking jokes and being silly with everybody who was gonna buy the record, but you could at least let everybody know that you enjoyed having a laugh.

DS: Yeah.

RP: I've never really [talked about] my own record before. It's most embarrassing! "Now, the second track is really meaty, and it contains every sort of facet of my emotional . . . " Wow! I mean, I can't talk like that. It sounds a bit like Liberace. I love him and he can do it. But I can't! But that's the thing about writing. You don't really want to do that. You want to leave it to . . .

DS: The music is the way that you've communicated that emotion. Yeah, I understand.

RP: It drips from the record or it doesn't work.

DS: The people will want to hear you. They just want to hear you talk about it. So that's my job!

RP: Yeah, you're doing it well.

DS: Let me ask you. You were in an auto accident in '75 in Greece. You were in a wheelchair for a while, weren't you?

RP: Uh-huh.

DS: I read that you actually recorded the vocals to the *Presence* album from a wheelchair. Is that true?

RP: Well, I got up on crutches and hopped into the recording booth, sat on a stool, then hopped back and got in the wheelchair. It was very cold. We did it in Munich. It involved about one-quarter of a mile walk from the car to the studio. It was like an underground place—in ze bunker! It was horrible because it was freezing cold and the end of me toes obviously took a bit of a belting, and it was then that "Achilles Last Stand" got its name because on one of my many journeys from the control room back to the stool, where I was singing, to do another take, I slipped and hit the floor with my bad foot, and I mean it was like murderous pain, and I went wang! Right on my bad foot! Jimmy came tearing out of the control room and carried me, and I mean, he's not as big as me by any means, but has superhuman strength—and he laid me down and I thought, "Oh, no, I've really ruined it, it's

gone forever." Because I had to be ever so careful, but I wasn't. No problem at all.

DS: What are your thoughts about the album *Presence*?

RP: Well, I thought it was really good. I was really pleased with it. And naturally now, I play the records a good deal more than I did when I was right on top of the situation. I was . . . I had to remove myself from the original way of doing it when I got on stage. I could give it a different . . . turn it a bit, you know? But now I play them a lot and I think it's great. I mean, I know that sounds a bit mundane. "I think it's great." But "Tea for One"—the way that track begins and the way it slips into the feel, and Jimmy's playing on "Tea for One," his solo is really beautiful, really pretty.

DS: I only ask because for some reason, I can't tell you why, but it was probably the—

RP: Least popular—

DS: —the least popular of the Led Zeppelin records, and I don't know why.

RP: And then tracks like "For Your Life"—I think that's great. I mean, it's really like a sneering track, trying to tell everybody, "Now, you've got to look after yourself," for what difference it makes, I don't know. "Hots On for Nowhere" . . . I mean, when I was stuck in the wheelchair, I was really kind of frustrated. I wanted to get up, do things, move about, and it obviously affected my personality to the degree that I was writing. I was quite embittered, you know. So, on those two tracks especially, it was evident.

DS: When you were making *In Through the Out Door*, you didn't realize at that time that that was gonna be your final album, obviously. Looking back, are you pleased that this is the final work, the last chapter in the Led Zeppelin story? Is this a fitting end?

RP: Well, if it had only been *Led Zeppelin I* it would have been a fitting end. Anything that you do that you're proud of, you stand by it. *In Through the Out Door*, we just moved along through so many facets of our own capability that by the time we got to *In Through the Out Door*, we were quite smooth, hah-hah-hah. You know? "All of My Love" was especially good. And "Carouselambra" still carried on that kind of epic proportions of "Achilles Last Stand" and "Stairway"—that sort of thing. By the time we got to those numbers they were . . . we were all really pleased with them. And of course recording at the Abbey [Road] Studio, the quality of the recording and the facility were much better than we'd been used to, that we were all going for the ultimate sounds. I mean, Jimmy's work on the vocal sound on "I'm Gonna Crawl," the vocal sound is amazing. I mean, because there was all the equipment, Abbey Road stocked their studio with the most amazing gadgets, which I'm a bit prone to get into.

DS: Do you have a lot of live material in the can?

RP: Well, this "can" word. It's quite an amazing thing. I mean, there's no vault. There's, like, a wooden shack somewhere in the country full of tapes that are going moldy!

DS: A lot of stuff in the shack?

RP: There's loads of stuff from all over the place. Some of it good, some of it was bad—or the recordings were bad, or, you know—and some of it's really good.

DS: XYZ: what was that? [Note: XYZ—short for ex–Yes and Zeppelin—was a short-lived group comprising Jimmy Page and ex-Yes members Chris Squire and Alan White.]

RP: It was a pen I received in the post.

DS: What?

RP: A ballpoint pen that somebody sent me from America. That was my full knowledge of XYZ. Somebody said [post–Led Zeppelin], "Hey, man, like your new band," and I said I knew nothing about this. "Well, I'll send you a pen." So I got this ballpoint pen in the post, which said, "Alan White, Chris Squire, Jimmy Page, John Paul Jones, and Robert Plant: the XYZ Band." It's run out of ink.

DS: That's beautiful!

RP: It doesn't work.

DS: It doesn't work, huh? Are you serious? There was no . . .

RP: I'm serious, yeah. There must have been some merchandising. Who did that?

DS: That was certainly the rumor, I mean, from people who were in a position to tell.

RP: I've heard so many rumors about the band, about Zeppelin, and . . . it's all such baloney, you know?

DS: How did Swan Song get started?

RP: Well . . . we'd all come from bands where the luck hadn't been so good. We'd been surrounded, each of us, with people who perhaps weren't as discerning as we would have liked. You know, management, agencies, and stuff, in the past. So we tried most notably to create the situation . . . understanding that where we could give the artist who we liked and who we thought would have a crack at it a little more understanding and a little more straight talking. So we took on the Pretty Things and

I mean, they recorded two great albums for us, *Silk Torpedo* and *Savage Eye*, great albums, you know? And the intention was to keep in touch because as artists we knew what it was like to get blown out, to be on the edge, not to have anybody to talk to and stuff. [But] I don't know whether it's always a good idea. It's great to have lovely motives and principles but it's really hard at four in the morning and somebody calls you up and says, "My album isn't in the shops," or "There's no window display in Warrington" or something.

DS: I was under the impression that Bad Company was the first act on the label.

RP: They were. But Pretty Things is an example of actually taking that principle and trying to make it work. Working alongside a band. You really gotta break it, you know?

DS: I don't know how you feel about this, but would you make one comment for me about the death of John Bonham? The circumstances surrounding his death, or your feelings?

RP: Well, I'm just really sad to have lost my pal. That's all.

DS: Okay, so Led Zeppelin never appeared on television, did they?

RP: Yeah. I can't remember when. It was just after Jim Morrison had dropped his pants—round 1969, '70. I remember it well. But I can't remember ever seeing it. I think they showed it after we left town or something. We did bits and pieces [television appearances] here and there, but we realized the folly. We had a really hefty sound and you really couldn't get that through a little speaker on the side of a television set in a Holiday Inn. Who wants to watch the television when you're in the Holiday Inn, anyway?

DS: Well, are you gonna be touring with this album?

RP: I'd like to, but I don't think I have enough material, really. I've got . . . this album's about forty-five minutes long, and that doesn't constitute stepping out.

DS: You wouldn't consider playing Led Zeppelin material?

RP: No. No, I mean the principles are strong for everybody. You know, there's no point. I might as well go to Vegas. Hadn't I?

DS: The Sands. Robert Plant at the Casino Hotel . . .

RP: Yeah. It's not for any of us to do that. You know, it was great. It was beautiful. And it's not there now. So it should be left alone.

Ioannis, Robert Plant: The Rain Song, *2011.*

John Bonham

JOHN BONHAM, ACCORDING TO MANY TOP DRUMMERS, OTHER MUSICIANS, AND ROCK AND ROLL JOURNALISTS, WAS ONE OF THE GREATEST DRUMMERS IN THE HISTORY OF ROCK. MORE THAN THREE DECADES AFTER HIS DEATH, BONHAM CONTINUES TO GARNER AWARDS, INCLUDING FIRST PLACE IN *ROLLING STONE* MAGAZINE'S 2011 READERS' SURVEY OF BEST DRUMMERS OF ALL TIME.

BONHAM, BORN IN THE TOWN OF REDDITCH IN WORCESTERSHIRE, BEGAN DRUMMING AT THE AGE OF FIVE, IMITATING HIS IDOLS GENE KRUPA AND BUDDY RICH, ALBEIT ON COFFEE CANS. HE RECEIVED HIS FIRST DRUM KIT AT AGE FOURTEEN. SHORTLY THEREAFTER, BONHAM JOINED HIS FIRST LOCAL BANDS.

AFTER LEAVING SCHOOL IN 1964, BONHAM WORKED AS AN APPRENTICE CARPENTER FOR HIS FATHER AND CONTINUED DRUMMING FOR VARIOUS LOCAL BANDS. THAT SAME YEAR, BONHAM JOINED HIS FIRST SEMIPROFESSIONAL BAND, TERRY WEBB AND THE SPIDERS. HE ALSO PLAYED IN OTHER BIRMINGHAM-AREA BANDS, SUCH AS THE NICKY JAMES MOVEMENT AND THE SENATORS, WHO HAD MINOR SUCCESS WITH THE SINGLE "SHE'S A MOD." BONHAM WAS SIXTEEN WHEN HE TOOK UP DRUMMING FULL-TIME. IN 1966, HE JOINED A BLUES GROUP CALLED CRAWLING KING SNAKES, WHOSE LEAD SINGER WAS A YOUTHFUL ROBERT PLANT.

WHEN PLANT DECIDED TO FORM BAND OF JOY, HIS FIRST CHOICE AS DRUMMER WAS BONHAM. IN 1968, AMERICAN SINGER TIM ROSE (WHO RECORDED "HEY JOE" AND "MORNING DEW") TOURED BRITAIN AND INVITED BAND OF JOY TO OPEN FOR HIM. UPON ROSE'S RETURN MONTHS LATER FOR ANOTHER TOUR, BONHAM WAS ASKED TO BE HIS PERMANENT DRUMMER.

AFTER THE BREAKUP OF THE YARDBIRDS, GUITARIST JIMMY PAGE WAS FORMING A NEW BAND AND RECRUITED ROBERT PLANT, WHO IN TURN SUGGESTED BONHAM. IN THIS RARE INTERVIEW, RECORDED IN 1972, BONHAM IS ASKED TO NAME THE POINT WHEN HIS CAREER AS A MUSICIAN BEGAN.

JOHN BONHAM: When I was fourteen years old, I think. Something like that. When I was at school. That was about the beginning of it. Played in a school pantomime [school show]. And it just sort of materialized from there, you know. Left school, then we formed small groups and things like that, played locally and everything.

DENNY SOMACH: What musicians can you remember being impressed with when you were in school?

JB: Oh, crikey. It's easier to say groups. I mean, in those days it was sort of, like, Johnny Kidd and the Pirates, and Liverpool groups like the Hollies, and things like that were a strong influence there. But particular musicians? It's hard. Graham Bond [UK musician and founding father of the British R&B movement in the early '60s] was one of those then, wasn't he? [His group, the Graham Bond Organisation,] included [Cream's] Jack Bruce and Ginger Baker. . . .

DS: Did you get straight into music when you left school?

JB: No. I used to play, you know, but I used to have a job as well. I used to be working all the time. . . . When I first left school, I was working with my father in the building trade. We used to be good builders there.

DS: When did you first become a full-time musician?

JB: When I was sixteen, I went full-time for a while. We had off and on periods. You'd, like, have an attempt to make a success of a professional group, and then it wouldn't go the way you'd planned it out to go, and you'd have to go back to work to get a little bit of money to carry on, you know, to sort of live with, really. And that's how it used to go, really; you know, you'd have a time, going out on the road, and everything would be roses, and then all of a sudden, no more gigs, no more money, you'd get back to where you started. And that's how it went on, really, right up until—just before Zeppelin started.

DS: What sort of music were you playing then?

JB: Going back as far as most of those groups, we used to just sort of play other people's stuff, you know. It was like you'd play anything from the latest hit by the Hollies to just sort of, you know, something by a blues artist. It was that sort of thing you had to do to survive, really, to play locally, anyway. And that was about it then—because we didn't do any writing or anything in those days.

DS: Did you have any particular tastes in music developed at the time?

JB: No, I don't think so, not really. Then, I used to buy all sort of completely different records. Even now, I still do. You might like the poppiest record ever. You might just like it for some reason, you know? I don't think I've ever really been set on something.

DS: How did you first come to join Led Zeppelin?

JB: Oh, well, I've known Robert for a number of years, 'cause we were in two groups previously. I was in a group with Robert when we were about sixteen. . . . And then we also got back together only about a year before Zeppelin formed. . . .

John Bonham with Led Zeppelin at the Forum, in Inglewood, California, June 3, 1973.

DS: Describe for us in minute detail what it was like the first time the four of you got together.

JB: Pretty strange, really. The first time the four of us got together . . . a day was arranged at Jimmy's house at Pangbourne for us all to meet. And apart from myself knowing Robert, I didn't know anybody else. It was the first time I met Jimmy—no, sorry, I met Jimmy when Robert and Jimmy came to see me play in London one night. But it was only for a few minutes, really, and then they went. It was quite strange, really, meeting John Paul [Jones] and Jimmy, coming from where I'd come from, you know.

DS: What was it like the first time you all got together and played?

JB: Well, I was pretty shy, you know. I was sort of, I just sort of—you know, the best thing I liked to do when you're in that situation is not to say much and just to soldier along and suss it all out. And we had a good play that day, and it went quite well, you know. But it wasn't—it got together very quickly because there was, at this stage, already sort of a tour that had to be done by the Yardbirds, which was a few dates in Scandinavia, you see. And we actually went there as the Yardbirds— well, of course it got billed as the New Yardbirds and all this sort of thing. And then it went so well, really, that the group became strong enough for it to start fresh, rather than to keep the Yardbirds name. It was a decision that we'd change the name. And we made the first album straight after coming back from Scandinavia.

> You play in local groups and . . . [then] there's a chance of becoming one of the Yardbirds; it was a gift from heaven, wasn't it?

[The first session] went well, you know, and there was a lot of ideas that came out of it, and it was really good. The playing was really good. Even the first time we played together, you know. There's a feeling, you know, when you play in a group, whether it's gonna be any good or whether it's not, you know, and it was good. It was very good indeed. And it sort of went on from there, really.

And in no time it sort of grows, you know. You suddenly find yourself sitting back, you know, and the next album came out and we went to America, but it seems . . . it was the middle of '69 before [there was] any reaction in Britain as far as compared to anywhere else. We went to the States, you know, which we had to because nobody would touch the group in England. You'd say you wanted to take some dates as Led Zeppelin and all this sort of thing, and people wouldn't even book you. Then you'd come back from America after the first album and all this, being sort of the number one album and everything, and then of course everybody wanted to book the group. Then it was like a change of tune. And that's really why a lot of people said, "They go on about going to America" and abandonment, really, and all this, you know—"Why don't you play for us?" But at that time, you bloody well couldn't! Nobody'd book the band, you know, you couldn't play there! So you'd actually sort of have to go to America to play, you know.

I always liked playing in Britain, probably more than anywhere else. It's a funny thing. If we're ever playing gigs in Britain, I look forward to it. And then you get to America and—I don't know. It's so much easier to play in England. You can get the motor out of the garage and tottle off and you're so at ease all the time, you know, whereas if you're in America, you're all day in a hotel somewhere, having arguments with bloody rednecks and turdheads and everything. And then you gotta go to the gig, you know, where all the kids are gonna think you should be doing your best and playing and feeling good about it, but it does affect you, what's happened previously in a day. Whereas in England, you're in your own atmosphere all the time. You're in your own homes and everything. You get to a gig and you feel bloody great because you've gone through nothing to get there. You understand what I mean? That's the difference, really.

DS: What are your feelings on where the individual Beatles are at now [in 1972]?

JB: Mmm. The individual Beatles? I don't know. They seem to be very different at the moment. You can like each one of them for what they're doing. It's been a terrific change, especially if you lived in England all the time, you're actually seeing it in front of your eyes. If you listened to Beatles albums, you know, the songs got much more individual towards the end. Like, McCartney would do a song and Lennon would do a song, and a lot of all-together singing songs gradually filtered out from *A Hard Day's Night* and stuff, which was more like multiple singing all the time, you know. And it got much more individual, didn't it, on later albums, and I think they just got different. I mean, let's face it, how many years were they together? You know, it's a long time. But I would have liked to [see] them stay together. I really would. It's quite a shame to see a group like that suddenly break up. I think everybody, really . . . from, like, two years old to a hundred years old, everybody seems to like the Beatles. It was just amazing, wasn't it? You can go around with us and there'll be loads who say, "No, I don't like Zeppelin," but

with the Beatles it was just ridiculous. Everybody seemed to like them, you know. Like a fever!

DS: What was your favorite thing that stood out from the Beatles' time?

JB: One thing I always loved to see of theirs was the film when they played at Shea Stadium, you know. I don't know whether you've seen that film yourself. . . . It's one of the most amazing pieces of film you've ever seen, if you want to see sort of absolute—girls just collapsing at the sight of them, and it was just absolutely stunning. Ridiculous! Getting them into the gig in an armored car, you know! They were being ripped to pieces, you know! But in actual fact, you look back at that film, and that concert went incredibly well. If you'd have looked at the police force they had at that concert compared [to] if you tried to do that concert again now, you'd find it completely different. Because they had more or less a skeleton police force, you know. It was just unheard of that there'd be any trouble. You know, they had enough to keep the crowd sort of back, sort of thing. . . . If you did that concert now, you'd probably find yourself with wagons full of riot police outside waiting for any trouble. . . .

DS: What significance does Led Zeppelin's fourth album hold for you?

JB: I don't know. I suppose the fourth album, really—one little thing that it was for me, that I found a drum sound. The sound that I got on a couple of tracks was a sound I sort of stumbled on, and yet looked for, for three years, if you know what I mean. Apart from that, no more than any other album. You know, 'cause I can still listen to, say, *I* and *II* and *III*, and still get as much from them as I would from listening to *IV*. I don't think the fourth is any better than the other albums. It's just the fourth album and doing stuff that happened at the time, with what we were doing then. You'll find each member of the group, if you asked their favorite tracks, they're probably a lot different. Everybody's got their little favorites on each album, and yet there's no album I like more. . . . You just find yourself liking [some] songs perhaps more than others, but that will change as well. You often start out when an album comes out, you'll probably like so and so a bit better than the others, but then it will change and in a year's time you might play it and then decide, "Oh, no, this [track] is [better]." But on the fourth, at the moment, I like them all. If I play it, I don't take any tracks out at all.

Ioannis, Zeppelin IV: The Hermit, *2011.*

At that time, I don't think I had any idea that the group was gonna achieve what it has. You could tell it was going to be a good group, you know, not being sort of flash about it. But I am! But I didn't give it much thought, really.

John Paul Jones

JOHN PAUL JONES—LED ZEPPELIN'S BASSIST, MANDOLINIST, AND KEYBOARDIST—IS ALSO A COMPOSER, ARRANGER, AND RECORD PRODUCER. PRIOR TO LED ZEPPELIN, HE WAS AN IN-DEMAND SESSION MUSICIAN. SINCE THE BAND'S BREAKUP, JONES HAS ENJOYED A SOLO CAREER AND HAS GAINED EVEN MORE RESPECT AS BOTH A MUSICIAN AND A PRODUCER.

KNOWN AS A VERSATILE MUSICIAN, HE ALSO PLAYS GUITAR, KOTO, LAP STEEL GUITARS, AUTOHARP, VIOLIN, UKULELE, SITAR, CELLO, AND MORE. JONES CURRENTLY PLAYS BASS, PIANO, AND OTHER INSTRUMENTS IN THE SUPERGROUP THEM CROOKED VULTURES WITH JOSH HOMME (QUEENS OF THE STONE AGE) AND DAVE GROHL (NIRVANA AND THE FOO FIGHTERS). THEY RELEASED THEIR EPONYMOUS DEBUT ALBUM IN NOVEMBER 2009.

IN THIS INTERVIEW, WHICH HE GAVE IN SUPPORT OF HIS 1999 DEBUT SOLO EFFORT, *ZOOMA*, JONES IS ASKED WHAT KEEPS HIM MOTIVATED TO CONTINUE TO MAKE MUSIC—THE UNDYING URGE JUST TO CREATE?

JOHN PAUL JONES: Yeah, I guess so. I can't really do anything else, to be honest. [Laughs] I've never done anything else. There's so much in music to be curious about. There's just so many areas, there's just a ton of music out there, and [looking around inside the studio] a ton of music in here, too.

DENNY SOMACH: A lot of people that don't know about the period after Zeppelin disbanded might have thought, "Oh, he took almost a twenty-year hiatus from doing things," but that's actually not true. You're involved with so many diverse people—R.E.M., Butthole Surfers, Diamanda Galás [American avant-garde composer, vocalist, and performance artist]. . .

JPJ: And that's just the records. I did a lot of composition and a lot of stuff that wasn't recorded. I even taught for a bit. Composition. Electronic composition.

DS: What was that like?

JPJ: That was all right. Just had a few students. It was at a college in the south of England, just for a bit, you know. But all at the same time. I didn't do this for a bit and that for a bit. I tend to do everything all at once. It just keeps going.

DS: You were thinking for a long time about doing a solo record. What made you take the jump to finally get in there and do it?

JPJ: I was never sure what to do, and the thing that focused my mind was touring with Diamanda Galás about five years ago. We had an album called *The Sporting Life*, and we took that out on the road, and I realized then I'd neglected playing live. . . .

DS: Did you miss it?

JPJ: Yeah! Yeah, and I realized that I simply hadn't done it, and so I started really wondering how I was going to go about getting onstage again. It occurred to me that if I did the solo album I probably had in the back of my mind forever, I would then have something to play onstage. It'd be my own music; then I'd take it out on the road and promote it. There'd be a reason to play it, and I'd be doing all my own stuff.

> It's difficult in my position to actually play live. You've gotta just turn up with some band and say, "Ah, I'm gonna play with you tonight," and they go, "Oh, no."

DS: Now, with Diamanda, you played some fairly small arenas as well, and on this tour you're playing some intimate places, which is a total far cry from what you were used to. What's it like having that real eye contact with everyone in the audience?

JPJ: It's much better. It's how I started as a musician. It's how Zeppelin started. By the time we got to the stadiums, we really didn't see much point. I mean, it was kind of an event, and it was nice and everybody'd enjoy themselves being at the event, but you couldn't—wasn't too much in the way of music going on at some of those. Couldn't really be that subtle.

John Paul Jones performs as a guest with Seasick Steve at the Leeds Festival, Bramham Park, Leeds, UK, August 28, 2011.

DS: What was your idea in putting together the solo record? Obviously, it's mainly drums and bass, and there are some other instruments, but primarily that's the focus.

JPJ: And steel guitar. The bass lap steel.

DS: Could you talk about the concept of choosing that format to work within and also choosing not to have a singer or for you to sing?

JPJ: Well, I don't sing and I don't write lyrics myself, so I didn't feel it was part of what I do. And also, as a producer, if I had a singer-songwriter, my instinct would be to produce him or her, and so it still wouldn't be my record. So instrumental is what I do. Again, it was informed by what I needed to do with it. I needed to play live, and so I sat down with, "Oh, what do I like doing live?" And in fact, it's blues-based rock.

DS: Your record has Eastern elements and different sounds on it.

JPJ: Right, well, that still comes out of sort of my store of music, I suppose. Everything that's in there. I mean, there was a time that I could have, in the '80s, I think, maybe I should do a more experimental album or electronic album or acoustic album or—there was quite a lot of things I could have done. And really, it was needing something to actually perform onstage that informed how it was going to be.

DS: You mentioned blues, and Jimmy and Robert were really immersed in the blues, [but] you had much wider influences.

JPJ: Right. Yeah, I didn't know much about the blues. I mean, most of my blues comes through jazz and some blues artists. My father was an all-music enthusiast as well, and he turned me on to Sonny Boy [influential blues musician, singer, and songwriter Willie "Sonny Boy" Williamson]. . . .

DS: Was he a player?

JPJ: He was a pianist.

DS: Did he teach you?

JPJ: No. [Laughs] It's like your mom teaching you to drive. I mean, it doesn't happen, really. But both my parents were vaudeville, so I used to tour out with them and basically absorb all the music of all the other acts because it was all—in Europe, everything's pretty international . . . and I'd just hear all this music every night.

DS: How comfortable are you being the center of attention? Obviously, in Zeppelin, you didn't have to do as many interviews and things, and you weren't the focal point, but with this, do you feel comfortable with that? How are you handling that?

JPJ: Yeah, I mean, I did more interviews with Diamanda because I had to stop her doing interviews. She was doing interviews all day and then trying to sing all night, and I said, "I'll talk. You sing." And so yes, I'm pretty used to it.

DS: It's always good to have something that people can recognize you by, which brings more people into the mix that wouldn't be there otherwise. Do you view your past as more of a positive, the "of Led Zeppelin" type of fame?

JPJ: Sure! I mean, obviously, it's very newsworthy and people want to know about the stuff and, you know, they have to listen to my stuff in order to get to the other stuff.

DS: Does it amaze you that it's been almost twenty years since the band disbanded and people still care so passionately about the band?

JPJ: Yeah, I mean, it was a good band, the greatest band in the world, I thought at the time. So maybe it doesn't surprise me, but there's been no precedent for any band, really, of this length. We're kind of all first-generation rock 'n' roll, really, so nobody knows how long the music would last, never mind [how long] a band would last. It's all quite new, but it was a good band, and it was a very different band, very unique band, and I think that probably has something to do with its longevity.

DS: A lot of people feel the foundation of any band is really the interplay between bassist and drummer. And obviously this record reflects that. I was really surprised—I'm a big Elvis Costello fan, and you worked with [longtime Elvis Costello drummer] Pete Thomas on a few.

JPJ: Well, [Pete Thomas] was on the Diamanda album as well.

DS: Was he?

JPJ: That'll surprise even more people. He likes working on my stuff. But basically, I write all the lower drum parts, all the bones of the drums, the kick drum, the snare drum, in order to fit in, to lock in with the bass, and obviously it's informed by the work that John Bonham and I did. . . . I learned a lot of things when we were working together. . . .

> **We couldn't be anywhere else. That's the way we played rock 'n' roll, and that's the way I like to do it.**

DS: So you clicked immediately with Bonzo when you guys first played?

JPJ: Yeah. Yeah. Immediately. Drummers and bass players kind of recognize each other because there are certainly awful ones around. When you—any new situation you're in, you say, "What's the drummer like?" Because the drummer is gonna be the one you're going to have to deal with all the time, really closely, and if they're no good, I want out. I don't want to deal with this at all. But we recognized each other immediately as compatible musicians.

DS: You play many, many different musical instruments: keyboards, guitar, mandolin, bass—a lot of different things. If you could talk about your approach, as a writer, to this record: did you write a lot of the songs on bass or did you write them on guitar or different instruments and translate them to bass?

JPJ: No, I write in my head. I'll go out for a walk and take a little manuscript book and—

DS: Without an instrument!

JPJ: Well, it frees you. The only thing I did write on an instrument [for this record] was "The Smile of Your Shadow" because it was a particular picking thing, and I just fooled around and came up with a nice, slightly rolling style. . . .

DS: "Black Dog." I heard you wrote the riff for that.

JPJ: That's right. I wrote that on a train coming back from rehearsal, yeah. There was a song on *Electric Mud*, a Muddy Waters album, which I can't remember what it was called. [Note: The track in question is "Smokestack Lightning," not from *Electric Mud* by Muddy Waters but from an untitled album by Howlin' Wolf released around the same time.] But the main thing I remember about it is it was this rolling riff that kept kind of turning back on itself, and I just liked the idea of a riff that you think was going to go somewhere and didn't. It came back round and went round again, and so I wrote "Black Dog" because I wanted to do something like that myself.

DS: It's a tricky riff. I mean, there are a couple of time-signature changes in there that you really have to concentrate on.

JPJ: It was originally written slightly different, but we changed the accents because it was easier to play that way.

DS: "Nosumi Blues" definitely has a Zeppelin feel, and the riff quotes almost from a Zeppelin song.

JPJ: Does it?

DS: [Hums "Nobody's Fault but Mine"]

Ioannis, John Paul Jones: No Quarter *(detail), 2011.*

JPJ: "Nobody's Fault but Mine"? No, I don't think there's a quote in there.

DS: Yeah, it seems like there's a little bit. It has that—

JPJ: I can't change it now. [Laughs]

DS: It has that atmosphere, I guess. You were in the band, so you can't take that away. . . . Any memories of "Moby Dick"?

JPJ: It was a Page riff, that one. It started off slightly different, as a different riff, and we sort of changed it as it went. But yes, that was written as a vehicle for John. I forget where the riff really came from. It just popped.

DS: How about "Snake Eyes"?

JPJ: "Snake Eyes," again, I wanted to use the steel guitar and I wanted something real slow and I had this sort of feeling of a swamp, real down-South, but then I wanted really slinky strings on it, a string section. And then I'd written quite a large string part, and I thought, well, I'm booking the London Symphony Orchestra on this. I couldn't quite figure out how to end it. Normally, it would just fade. . . . I thought, well, it would be much more interesting to fade the track, keep the strings going, and then write them something quite meaty at the end.

DS: "Trampled Under Foot" had a funk groove. Any memories of that? You're listed as the first writer of that song.

JPJ: Yes, it's mine, it's my track. Again, written instrument–inspired.

DS: In your head again?

JPJ: No, I think that might have been written at the Clavinet, which was just an electric clavichord. It's got that percussive attack.

DS: Stevie Wonder's the master.

JPJ: Yeah. Yeah, influenced by Stevie Wonder. I think I was listening to a lot of—what was it?—*Innervisions* then. Yeah, around that time I was going to rehearsals, listening to Stevie Wonder.

DS: That's pretty interesting. Don't tell anyone.

JPJ: Well, no, I know, it's a shame you can't tell anyone because they might go, "Ah, I should check out *Innervisions* by Stevie Wonder." A lot of people would really like it that probably wouldn't listen to Stevie Wonder.

DS: Are there some songs that you've written or cowritten over the years that you might hear again and you'll say, "Wow, that song stands up more today than it did then," or "Now I know what that song was about"? Obviously, you mention that you don't write lyrics, but musically, have there been any surprises that you've heard on a record that you hadn't heard for a while and you said, "Wow, that's better than I remember. I forgot about that"?

JPJ: There was an organ intro to—was it the intro to "Thank You"? Was there a big sort of churchy organ intro to that? [Note: The song is "Your Time Is Gonna Come."] When I heard the *Remasters* [a box set issued in 1990], it came in a different place and I really wasn't expecting it. I didn't recognize it at first. Because I didn't listen to it after I recorded it.

DS: The one thing that did take me by surprise was on the *BBC Sessions*. It was a song that you guys never did [live], "The Girl I Love (She Got Long Black Wavy Hair)."

JPJ: Ah. Maybe that's where the "Moby Dick" riff came from. That's a Page riff.

DS: Were you happy with that BBC session?

JPJ: Yeah, well, it was very interesting for me because it was actually a chance for me to listen to Bonzo in a live situation but where we're recorded. Normally I'm either standing next to him, in which case the perception is different, or it's a bootleg and you can't really hear. And so it was good to—I used to say to my friends, "Look, that's what I was telling you about, that he does all the time." That little stuff that makes it all the more interesting.

DS: In America, people don't recognize the importance of radio to anyone. They never really had the *Saturday Club* or the *Top Gear* or those—

JPJ: No, but on the other hand, in America, [there was] FM underground radio, which was just in its youth in those days. . . . They were a tremendous help to us because they used to put the whole album on and then back-announce it at the end, which you can't do anymore. That was enormously helpful to us.

DS: You did beautiful work with R.E.M.'s record [*Automatic for the People*]. What was that experience like, and did it take you by surprise that a group like that—

JPJ: No, not really, I mean, all sorts of people call me up. I had a handwritten letter from Michael Stipe that was really nice and it said that he really liked my stuff and these are the tunes; they sent me a tape and they'd like it if the strings came in halfway through, the normal sort of instructions you get for an arrangement. And I just did the arrangements and just turned up in Atlanta and we recorded it in a day or so and hung out for a couple of days, and it was very pleasant, really nice. Professional people. I really like those sort of jobs.

DS: They were really blown away by what you did with that. It really elevated—

JPJ: They were good songs. It's easy to arrange good songs.

DS: We just turned our daughter onto Donovan about six months ago. She's a big Zeppelin fan and I told her, "Hey, John Paul Jones did a lot of work with Donovan." What do you remember about working with him?

JPJ: I remember "Mellow Yellow" because I had that sort of brass arrangement [starts humming the melody]. We came into the control room afterward and they hated it. [Laughs] They really hated it; there were all these long faces going, "Oh, the session's finished. That's it." They were wondering what to do, and then Paul McCartney walked into the session and he heard the track and went, "Wow, that's really great, that's really fantastic," and everybody was going, "Oh, yeah, isn't it?" [Laughs] And so we were saved by Paul.

DS: I was going to bring up Paul because you had some experience working with him a couple times— "Rockestra" [a 1978 McCartney song recorded for Wings by an all-star lineup of musicians], and then the movie *Give My Regards to Broad Street*. You played on "Ballroom Dancing," and you were in the movie.

We used to turn up, we used to go round to loads of radio stations and talk to people and they'd play the whole album.

JPJ: Yeah, with [noted session guitarist] Chris Spedding and Dave Edmunds, yeah.

DS: What are your recollections of "Rockestra," which was a really interesting session? Bonham was there also.

JPJ: Yes. I can remember that Dave Gilmour had all these pedals, hundreds of pedals everywhere. And Pete Townshend just kind of wandered in, and he saw all these pedals and he just started dancing on them. [Laughs] There was this horrible noise happening around us.

DS: What was it like to work with Paul, a fellow bassist?

JPJ: Yeah, again, nice man, very easy to work with. Professional people, you know, they always know what they want, no attitudes, and it was good.

DS: What was your opinion of him as a bass player?

JPJ: I always liked his bass playing. It was very melodic. He had a sort of quirky view of things as well. He'd put the unexpected notes in, but everything was right. Everything was in the right place, and he never did too much. No, he was a fine bass player.

DS: Was it fun to appear in his movie? It's a good scene, the "Ballroom Dancing" scene.

JPJ: Yeah, it was long, it took forever to do that scene, like a whole week to do the scene.

DS: Do you remember recording the track?

JPJ: Well, yeah, because the—when we were onstage, actually, it probably took so long because there was all these musicians onstage waiting around doing nothing; of course, we just went through endless rock 'n' roll songs and all sorts of stuff, and everyone was saying, "Uh, can we—you know, we wanna do the take now." "No, no, we're having too much fun." [Laughs]

DS: And everyone had the pompadours.

JPJ: That's right, yeah. Every morning, you had to go and get all the hair done.

DS: I heard that when you met Elvis, he took to you pretty well. I think he gave you rings or something?

JPJ: We swapped watches. I have a beautiful Baume et Mercier lavish luxury watch that he gave me, and somewhere in his estate he's got a Mickey Mouse watch on an Indian bracelet. So people would go around asking, "What?" [Laughs]

DS: When did you meet him, in the '70s?

Ioannis, John Paul Jones: No Quarter *(detail), 2011.*

JPJ: Yeah, I went—me and [Zeppelin tour manager] Richard Cole went around to his—see, I was never a big fan of Elvis, funny enough. Boys often weren't—'cause girls often were—although my father was. I think maybe that did it as well, because he said he had this great voice, real rhythmical voice, and I went, "Oh, yeah, yeah, I like Jerry Lee Lewis myself." [Laughs] Or Ray Charles. But no, we got on real well, probably because I wasn't a fan, and you know, we were insulting Capricorns. "Oh, we're all Capricorns here, mate." [Laughs] And all that sort of stuff, so it was good fun. Because he's Capricorn, and so am I, and so is Richard. And so we'd say, "Oh, those bloody Capricorns." "Hey, watch what you say!" . . .

DS: And how did he give you the watch?

JPJ: We just started exchanging clothing and stuff like that [laughs] because he'd say, "Oh, I like that." "Here, have this T-shirt." "Oh, okay, I'll give you this T-shirt." "Wow, nice watch." "Oh, I'll have that watch." We got into that.

DS: Do you think he ever heard the band?

JPJ: I think he did, yeah. He was curious to see what was out there, and he ended up in that awful scene where he was working forever and ever and ever in Vegas.

DS: What's funny is McCartney told me the story when they met Elvis, and it actually seems like his get-together with them was pretty tense but it seems like his get-together with you, and when he got together with the band, was pretty loose.

JPJ: Yeah, pretty much. [Laughs] Well, see, I wasn't in awe of him, so it was kind of easy, and I think he was happy to see somebody who wasn't going, "Ooh . . ."

DS: What did you think of a band like Kiss putting on a show with the makeup?

JPJ: Ah, they do a great show with the makeup. Musically, they didn't interest me.

DS: Yeah, but does it interest you that people like that could be interested in something that you were doing, or is it just because—

JPJ: No, it's a show, it's an event, I mean it's the same; that's what the stadiums were all about. It's a show. It's an event where people go for a good time. They pay their money. [Laughs] They do what they want to do, you know; different people want to do different things.

DS: What's happening now at the shows you're doing now? What kind of people are you seeing in the audience? Probably a lot of young and old fans.

JPJ: Well, yeah. A good cross-section of ages, actually, which is very nice. I mean, we weren't really sure who was going to turn up. Obviously, there's a lot of Zeppelin

fans. They're obviously listening to all the other stuff and they seem interested in what I'm doing.

DS: Do you do the whole record?

JPJ: Yeah.

DS: And do you add any other songs?

JPJ: Yeah, there's three or four, but it's no surprise with the Internet, everybody knows. I do "No Quarter" on keyboard, I do "Levee Breaks" on steel guitar—which is made for steel guitar, sounds incredible when you do it—"Trampled," and I'll leave one as a surprise.

DS: What song on *Zooma* best crystallizes how you heard it would sound in your head?

JPJ: Well [pauses] . . . probably "Zooma" and "Snake Eyes." I quite like the epic. I liked "Kashmir," and "Stairway" was fairly epic. And so "Snake Eyes" is kind of that. It starts here, and then it goes through there where the organ comes in, and then the strings come in, and it takes you on this journey. . . .

DS: Do you have good memories and feelings of the Led Zeppelin reunion for Live Aid, in Philadelphia? It was a pivotal show.

JPJ: Yeah, I mean, it was a good thing to do. It was for a good cause. It was kind of—it was the first thing we had done together for a long time. Generally, I have good memories. I mean, again, I had to kind of muscle my way in. I think Plant was asked first and he said he'd do it with Page, and then they were going to do Zeppelin numbers, and I kind of heard about it and I said, "Well, if you're going to do Zeppelin numbers, then maybe I should be there."

DS: If you hadn't muscled your way in, it probably would have been what the Page and Plant project turned out to be ten years later?

JPJ: Who knows, who knows? It wouldn't have been what it was, I didn't think. Everybody would've called it Led Zeppelin. And even then, Plant insisted on having his bass player there.

DS: You may not want to answer this, but I have to ask it out of just being honest. [Pauses, then laughs] I can tell by that face . . . why do you think you weren't asked to be involved with the project that they did?

JPJ: Um, well, it was their project, I mean, uh . . .

DS: Do you think that if you were involved, it would have put the big mantle, it would have put too much pressure on it, and people would have to call it Led Zeppelin?

JPJ: Well, that's what Robert says, yeah. But then I saw their set lists and, you know, that was pretty much like Led Zeppelin to me.

DS: And a lot of your songs, too.

JPJ: Yeah, and then they called the album *No Quarter*. I never found out why they did that.

DS: [Laughing] Another of your songs!

JPJ: Yeah. But, you know, hey, um, I'd have liked to have been informed about it. It was hard reading it in the papers and then having journalists ask me. Because I was on tour with Diamanda and I walked into a room full of journalists and they went, "Hey, why weren't you asked?" And I said, "I don't know." But ultimately, they'd done me a favor.

DS: I was at the Rock and Roll Hall of Fame when you were inducted. I talked to you then, too. I was happy with your comment, "Glad they remembered my number."

JPJ: [Laughing] Well, yeah, yeah. I felt I had to say something. . . .

Ioannis, John Paul Jones: No Quarter, *2011.*

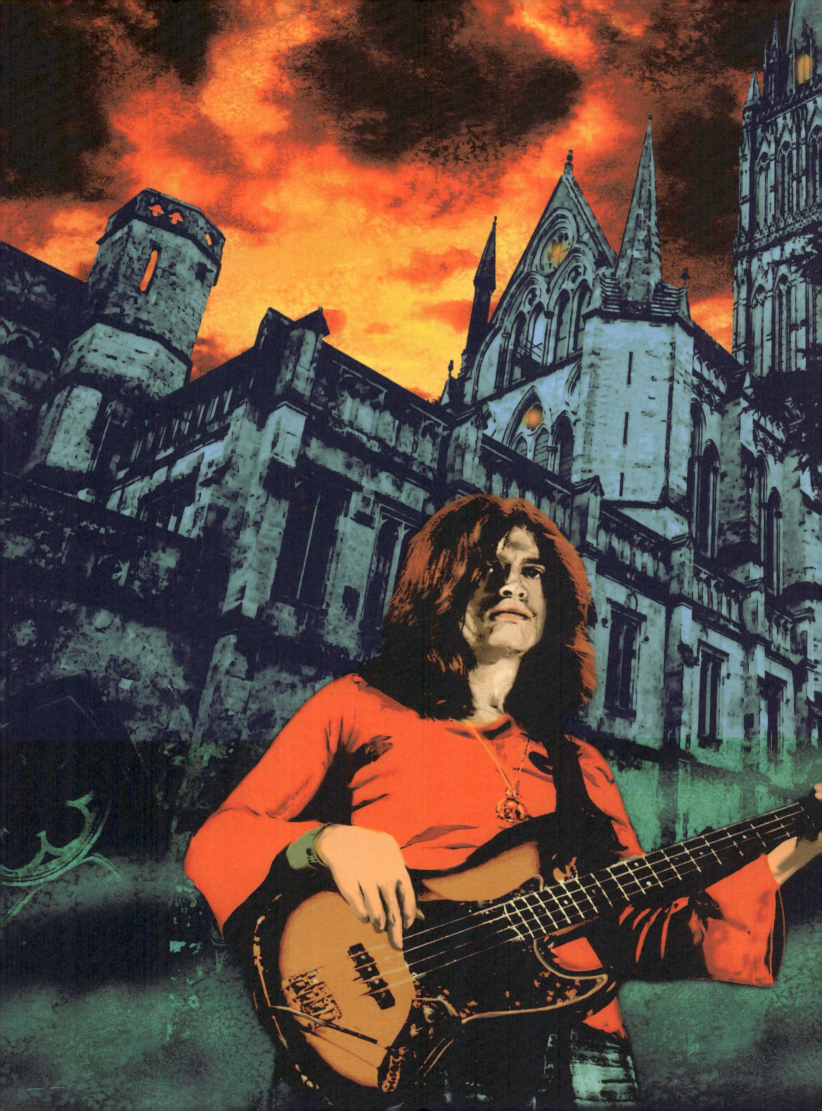

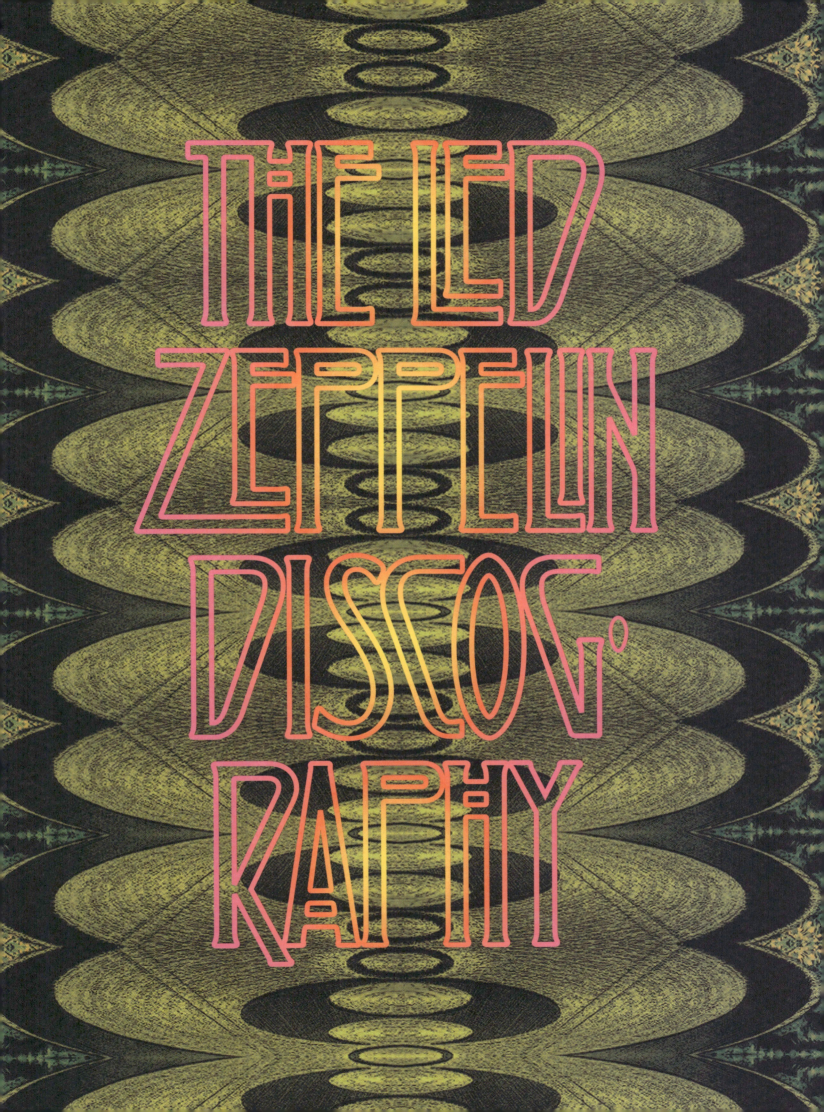

❧ *REFLECTIONS OF A DJ* ❧

IN NOVEMBER OF 1971, when Led Zeppelin's fourth album was released, I was working as a DJ at WSAN in Allentown, Pennsylvania. Typically, when a DJ receives a promotional copy of a new album, it comes with suggested tracks for radio play. Ironically, "Stairway to Heaven," which was to become the most requested song on the radio, was not included among the suggestions. Who knew that "Stairway" would have the life it's enjoyed? Perhaps master producer Jimmy Page. After all, this was the fourth track on the four-man band's fourth album. Could there have been a mystical component to the omission? An otherworldly significance?

And what of the much-hinted-at backward masking on the song—the cryptic messages embedded in the track when played backward? While we may leave these esoteric questions to musical mystics, there is still much to marvel at— musically, technologically, and businesswise—when considering the band's catalog of ten albums, a few official live releases, hours of essential viewing, and numerous compilations. For example, knowing that radio stations were averse to playing long-format songs, Page listed "How Many More Times," the final track on *Led Zeppelin*, as coming in at a radio-friendly three minutes, thirty seconds on the album sleeve. The track, however, actually runs about eight minutes. Equally maddening to some DJs, "Heartbreaker"

and "Living Loving Maid (She's Just a Woman)," the fifth and sixth tracks on *Led Zeppelin II*, are fused together by a famous, nearly seamless segue, making it quite a challenge to play only one of the songs on the radio.

Over the years, music aficionados, academics, journalists, and rock 'n' roll cabalists have interpreted and reinterpreted the Led Zeppelin canon—with no end in sight. The conceptual nature of Led Zeppelin's untitled fourth album, with all its hidden meanings, has brought fans back to the sound time and again. After forty-plus years, there might not be a consensus on the meaning of every song. But the works have remained fresh, relevant, and inspiring to new generations of music lovers. —Denny Somach

PAGE 228: *Ioannis,* Houses of the Holy, *2011.*

LEFT: *Ioannis,* Zeppelin IV: The Hermit *(detail), 2011.*

Led Zeppelin

JANUARY 12, 1969; REMASTERED 1994

According to Jimmy Page, Led Zeppelin's first album was essentially the same as the band's live act at the time. One can feel the raw energy in the room at Olympic Sound Studios in the London suburb of Barnes, where engineer Glyn Johns had no idea what to expect. But Jimmy Page, twenty-four years old, knew. It was exactly what he'd had in mind when he brought all the other band members together.

He knew that John Paul Jones had a solid and steady bass, and that he and Jones could follow each other with ease. He knew the same was true of Robert Plant and John Bonham. Going into it, each band member stood out as individuals in their previous projects.

"Virtuoso" was the way Atlantic Records boss Jerry Wexler had described Page before even hearing a note from the guitarist's new band. Peter Grant's description and praise of Led Zeppelin must have been so compelling that Wexler made a leap of faith and signed the band to what was, at the time, the greatest record deal in rock history.

The moment the four musicians gathered in a room, they picked a song with a blues chord progression in the key of E but also with a heavy rock riff. Page briefly showed the others and counted it off. The song, "Train Kept A-Rollin'," had been a Yardbirds staple before and during Page's tenure with the band. By all accounts, Page, Plant, Jones, and Bonham didn't just play a spot-on rendition of the song. They annihilated it. The room exploded.

Yet before too long, recording that song wasn't even a consideration anymore. When they brought their live act to the studio in Barnes for thirty-six hours of recording over a few days in October of 1968, the new lineup blended "Train Kept A-Rollin'," "Smokestack Lightnin'," and all the rest into something so different from the Yardbirds that the new band needed a whole new name. These weren't your older brother's Yardbirds. These weren't even *New* Yardbirds.

Led Zeppelin quickly pulled together a brand-new repertoire, including "Good Times Bad Times," not the first song Led Zeppelin ever recorded in a studio but the first one ever heard by fans—track one on album one. It's the song with which Led Zeppelin kicked off an enduring legacy.

Thunderously, Led Zeppelin's instrumentalists pound out their opening power chord of E, and John Bonham replies with some percussive fills that, over the years, have become sonically iconic. When a drummer pulls these precise fills off, you know he's schooled in the right sounds. Robert Plant, barely twenty years old, enters with lyrics about being a man and leaving his childhood behind. This is a guy who doesn't seem to care when his woman leaves home for a brown-eyed man!

By March of 1969, when "Good Times Bad Times" was released as a single in the United States, Zeppelin was no longer playing it in concert. As the single climbed the *Billboard* chart to No. 80, "Communication Breakdown," on the flip side, helped the band gain notoriety at home in England. But there was no single released in England, nor would there be for the next thirty years. Bands who released singles were compelled to appear on the BBC's *Top of the Pops*—and Peter Grant's strategy was to keep Led Zeppelin off television altogether because he didn't think the power of the band could be properly presented through the medium.

The earliest tracks cut by Led Zeppelin in the studio are blues jams on which Robert Plant sang some of his favorite lyrics. Jimmy Page was still on his Yardbirds kick, turning musical elements of Howlin' Wolf's 1956 hit "Smokestack Lightnin'," which the Yardbirds liked to cover, into "How Many More Times," which incorporated Plant's favorite lyrics from another Howlin' Wolf tune, "How Many More Years." There was no shame in quoting from these songs. They were transforming them and adding astonishing new sounds.

The backward-echo studio effect placed on the electric guitar on "You Shook Me" was something Jimmy Page knew could be done. He'd done it before. Engineer Glyn Johns doubted him. Page proved himself right, and it was done—yielding a unique sound that Robert Plant could duplicate effectively and convincingly as the song ends.

As that song ends, the band switches gears completely, turning out yet another song—"Dazed and Confused"—using E as the root note. While it may not have been the most original of ideas—Page had previously played the song with the Yardbirds after he picked it up from an opening act in 1967—it was transformed by the way Page and the others approached it. Jake Holmes (the original author of "Dazed and Confused") never had a drummer in his group. His guitarist never used a violin bow. Entire original passages resulted from Led Zeppelin's studio sessions. The "Dazed and Confused" that emerged from London was a far different creature from the track that influenced it. Yet as has been documented in this book and elsewhere, Jake Holmes was not acknowledged as the original songwriter.

"Babe I'm Gonna Leave You" was a highlight on the album—something completely unexpected yet natural for Page and Plant to bond over while they were discussing common influences and ambitions. They tackled the song with finesse: the acoustic parts were light and airy, with Plant never ceasing to hint at trouble through his voice. The electric parts were heavy and solid, shifting drastically from section to section. It kept the band on their toes, listening to one another, which is what makes it such an entertaining piece of music more than four decades later.

Led Zeppelin's first album comprises nine tracks, most of which were staples of their live act in 1968 and 1969. Only "Your Time Is Gonna Come" is not known to have been performed live during that period, probably because it requires an organ, an instrument to which John Paul Jones did not have access during concerts until later. Jason Bonham has said that the song's bright and cathedral-like organ prelude—which he heard on a record player at his house as a child—was one of his earliest memories, and made him curious about music before he finally understood that it was his father's profession. Here, Plant croons a vengeful lyric over a pastoral riff played mainly on acoustic guitar with occasional add-ins from Page on electric lap steel, an instrument he might have been fiddling with for the very first time. Page was, after all, a guy who'd joined the Yardbirds not as a guitarist but as a bassist—and he'd never played bass before, either!

No portion of the lyrics to "Your Time Is Gonna Come" has been traced to any previous sources, but if Plant was the lyricist, the writing credits don't reflect it. "You Shook Me" and "I Can't Quit You Baby" were straight blues covers credited to songwriter Willie Dixon (additionally credited to J. B. Lenoir, in the case of "You Shook Me"). These were the only times that songs on any of Led Zeppelin's original studio albums were credited solely to outside authors. Muddy Waters was the first blues singer to record "You Shook Me," and Otis Rush holds that distinction for "I Can't Quit You Baby."

"Black Mountain Side," which Page had recorded during another session prior to the formation of Led Zeppelin, does not feature any other members of the group. On this track, Kenya-born Indian musician Viram Jasani is credited with playing the tabla; Jasani stands as the only outside musician credited with playing on any of the first three Led Zeppelin albums.

Unfortunately, as mentioned, the authorship of some songs on the album was subject to dispute. Page's instrumental on "Black Mountain Side" was credited solely to him, although one could point to the similarly titled Irish folk song "Black Water Side" as more than a source of inspiration. Just as undeniable—from the fact that Page and Plant admitted listening to a live version of the song by Joan Baez—is the inappropriate labeling of "Babe I'm Gonna Leave You" as something originally created only by Jimmy Page, not as something created by him and songwriter Anne Bredon. This has been revised in the official credits.

One track whose authorship has yet to be revised fully is "Dazed and Confused." So far, its only revision on record was a shift from crediting Jimmy Page alone to crediting Jimmy Page and Robert Plant. Then, in 2010, Jake Holmes filed a claim seeking royalties as a songwriter; Holmes's claim was dismissed by a judge in January of 2012.

"How Many More Times" was originally credited only to members of Led Zeppelin but has since been revised to include Howlin' Wolf under his legal name, Chester Burnett. The song also includes uncredited lyrical snippets of "Kisses Sweeter Than Wine" by the Weavers and "The Hunter" by Albert King. The Yardbirds' adaptation of "Smokestack Lightnin'" by Howlin' Wolf is not the only song from which "How Many More Times" draws musically; there's also a nod to "Beck's Bolero" by Jeff Beck, whose original studio recording in 1966 also featured Jimmy Page and John Paul Jones.

Incidentally, comparisons between this album and Jeff Beck's album *Truth* were rampant at the time of release, partly because both former Yardbirds guitarists chose to include their versions of "You Shook Me"—coincidentally featuring John Paul Jones on keyboard in both versions—and partly because the high-pitched stylings of vocalists Rod Stewart and Robert Plant were similar. In fact, Stewart has accused Page of pilfering more than just that from the Jeff Beck Group.

Similarities between "Communication Breakdown" and the Eddie Cochran song "Nervous Breakdown," although often noticed, are not strong enough to warrant any claim in court.

As with all Led Zeppelin releases, Jimmy Page is listed as producer and Peter Grant is listed as executive producer. Glyn Johns was the engineer and mixer for this album, recorded and mixed early in October of 1968. Separate mastering by Barry Diament resulted in the original CD release. George Marino remastered the album.

Led Zeppelin II

OCTOBER 22, 1969; REMASTERED 1994

It kicks off with a laugh and launches immediately into Jimmy Page's now legendary riff. "Whole Lotta Love" was a revelation. Its release on *Led Zeppelin II* was a revolution. Robert Plant tells us what we need and what he's gonna do about it. And then he goes and does it. During an instrumental section quite unlike any before it, producer Jimmy Page and engineer Eddie Kramer improve on the recorded layers of theremin and sound effects by twisting studio knobs to send these sounds to the left and right channels. They did this to take advantage of stereo sound systems, which were still relatively new in the homes of fans and even in the homes of members of the band. All the while, John Bonham holds down the upbeat pulse with his hi-hats, cymbals, and bongos. Following in the footsteps of "You Shook Me" and "How Many More Times" from the first album, Led Zeppelin's experiment in psychedelic blues was finally complete. And it was a resounding success.

"Whole Lotta Love" was the only track from *Led Zeppelin II* to be released as a single in the United States. On the *Billboard* chart, it reached No. 4—a position that would make it Led Zeppelin's highest-ranking single ever—and remained immensely popular for a year. At home in the UK, the band intervened at the last minute to prevent its release as a single. There was no need for a single anyway; the album sold like hotcakes in its first year. Because "Whole Lotta Love" had so much momentum in 1970, even its B side ("Living Loving Maid (She's Just a Woman)") saw some separate chart action, rising to No. 65 in the States. It was the only B side of Led Zeppelin's ever to chart.

"Whole Lotta Love" was originally credited only to the four members of the band, but Willie Dixon has been added because he is the author of the Muddy Waters song "You Need Love," from which the song is drawn. A remake of "You Need Love" by the Small Faces, entitled "You Need Lovin'," also served as musical inspiration for the members of Led Zeppelin, including Robert Plant, whose vocal delivery was inspired by that of Small Faces singer Steve Marriott.

The album features Plant's first deliberate attempts at songwriting with Led Zeppelin: "Thank You" and "Ramble On." The former opens with lyrics inspired by "If 6 Was 9" by Jimi Hendrix. As Plant was a *Lord of the Rings* fan, the latter references author J. R. R. Tolkien's character Gollum and the book's setting of Mordor. All the while, Led Zeppelin tightened as a unit —from the slinky bass lines on "Ramble On" and "What Is and What Should Never Be" to Jimmy Page's layered acoustic and electric guitar tracks on "Thank You" and his solos on "Heartbreaker" and "The Lemon Song."

Incidentally, "The Lemon Song" was originally credited to members of Led Zeppelin, although it is now also credited to Howlin' Wolf as Chester Burnett, since the song is based mainly on his "Killing Floor." (Live versions of the tune as performed by Led Zeppelin in 1969 also incorporated the riff from Howlin' Wolf's remake of "Smokestack Lightnin'" on his album for Chess Records released that year. This riff would also serve as a source of inspiration to John Paul Jones two albums later, on "Black Dog.") Musically, "Cross-Cut Saw" by Albert King influenced Page's playing. As for Plant's other contributions, the most memorable lyrics in "The Lemon Song" come from "Traveling Riverside Blues" by Robert Johnson.

Credit to Willie Dixon was added not only to "Whole Lotta Love" but also to "Bring It On Home." However, in this case, Dixon's song (originally sung by Sonny Boy Williamson) is referenced only in the beginning and ending portions of the Zeppelin song. Lawyers eventually paved the way for the main chunk of the song to be considered a separate composition, entitled "Bring It On Back." This is now legally recognized and credited to members of Led Zeppelin, with only the beginning and ending portions referred to as "Bring It On Home," written by Willie Dixon.

"Bring It On Home" was also a prime example of how the second Led Zeppelin album was pieced together from recording sessions held throughout the United States, Canada, and England; the hectic recording itinerary allowed them to get their second album done while also touring to promote their first album. Some songs, including "Bring It On Home," were recorded in more than one studio. Sources differ on the full recording schedule of this track, but one theory suggests that recording was completed in four separate locations in 1969: at Olympic Sound Studios in Barnes, London, with engineer George Chkiantz; at Mystic Studios, Los Angeles; at Atlantic Studios, New York, with engineer Eddie Kramer (for vocal overdubs); at the Hut in Vancouver (for harmonica overdubs); and finally at A&R Studios in New York on August 29–30, 1969, with Kramer (for mixing).

Jimmy Page is listed as producer and Peter Grant is listed as executive producer. Eddie Kramer is credited with engineering and mixing the album, and Bob Ludwig is credited with engineering and mastering. Other engineers are mentioned for certain tracks: George Chkiantz for "Whole Lotta Love" and "What Is and What Should Never Be"; Chris Huston for "The Lemon Song" and "Moby Dick"; and Andy Johns for "Thank You." Separate mastering by Barry Diament resulted in the original CD release. George Marino remastered the album.

Led Zeppelin III

OCTOBER 5, 1970; REMASTERED 1994

Led Zeppelin III is drastically different from the group's previous two releases in that it features a higher proportion of songs on which the guitars are primarily acoustic. The opening track, however—which was also the A side of the single released in the United States—is an exception. "Immigrant Song," immortalized by Robert Plant's wail and Jimmy Page's hammering riff, became an instant Led Zeppelin classic. Plant recalled his lyrical inspiration for the song in a radio interview: "We went to Iceland and it made you think of Vikings and big ships . . . and John Bonham's stomach . . . and bang, there it was . . . 'Immigrant Song'!" During the making of the song, Plant penned the phrase "hammer of the gods," with which Led Zeppelin is often associated. The tune spent thirteen weeks on the *Billboard* pop chart, finally peaking at No. 16 in January 1971. The RIAA certified *Led Zeppelin III* a gold album the week of its release, and it reached No. 1 on the U.S. and UK charts.

"Immigrant Song," with its driving rhythms and heavy metal edge, stood in sharp contrast to the abundance of acoustic material found elsewhere on the album—and even on the single itself. The 45 featured a nonalbum track as the B side—"Hey Hey What Can I Do"—a song saturated with acoustic guitar, mandolin, and four-part vocal harmonies. This shift in tone on Led Zeppelin's records confused critics and fans alike. However, it was a sign of Led Zeppelin's expansion into uncharted territories—an expansion that would continue on all the band's subsequent studio efforts. On stage, this transition emerged as dedicated acoustic sets featured in the middle of their shows.

The track "Friends" delivered in a way that no previous Led Zeppelin song did. It features an array of violins played by unnamed guest musicians and, for the second time on a Led Zeppelin record, a tabla played by Viram Jasani. "Friends" segues into "Celebration Day" by way of a synthesizer connecting the two. The rhythm track at the start of "Celebration Day" was accidentally erased by an engineer, so the synthesizer from the end of "Friends" leads into "Celebration Day" until the rhythm track catches up. John Paul Jones plays lap steel throughout the track.

"Since I've Been Loving You" is an example of Led Zeppelin reinventing the blues, adapting the traditional I–IV–V chord progression in a minor key with some unusual changes and riffs added for color. Lyrical comparisons to the Moby Grape track "Never" abound; Plant, who acknowledges he is a fan of that West Coast group, probably used the opening line as a kickoff point in tribute to the group rather than as an offense warranting a legal claim. (The Led Zeppelin line is "Working from seven to eleven every night," whereas the Moby Grape version is "Working from eleven to seven every night.") Jones, this time on organ, complements Page's electric guitar, particularly during the solo, which is one of the most emotional Page ever set to wax.

"Gallows Pole" is listed as a traditional song arranged by Jimmy Page and Robert Plant; numerous artists preceded Led Zeppelin in recording versions of the song under a plethora of titles, although Page has acknowledged using the version released in the 1950s on the album *Gallows Pole and Other Folk Songs* by Fred Gerlach and 12-String Guitar.

"Hats Off to (Roy) Harper" is listed as a traditional song arranged by Charles Obscure, a pseudonym for Jimmy Page; some of its lyrics are based on "Shake 'Em on Down" by Delta blues guitarist and singer Bukka White, although it is uncredited as such.

"Tangerine" is credited solely to Jimmy Page, although Renaissance singer Jane Relf has claimed lyrics authorship that should have gone to her late brother, Keith Relf of

the Yardbirds. Indeed, an unreleased 1968 outtake called "Knowing That I'm Losing You," recorded by the Yardbirds (when Jimmy Page was a member), was poised for release on the album of outtakes called *Cumular Limit* in 2000 until Page's legal threats prevented the song's appearance on that album.

The lyrics on the subtle "That's the Way" exhibit Robert Plant's maturity without divulging the precise subject to which he may be alluding; the song could be about class or race segregation imposed by a child's parents, leading to a separation between childhood friends. Plant astutely leaves the question unresolved, leaving the song ambiguous and open to interpretation, a tool he would use to even better effect on the centerpiece of the next album.

As always, Jimmy Page is listed as producer and Peter Grant as executive producer. Eddie Kramer, Terry Manning, and Andy Johns are credited as mixing engineers on the album, with Johns also credited as recording engineer and Manning also credited as mastering engineer. Paul Richmond is also credited for mastering. Separate mastering by Barry Diament resulted in the original CD release. George Marino remastered the album.

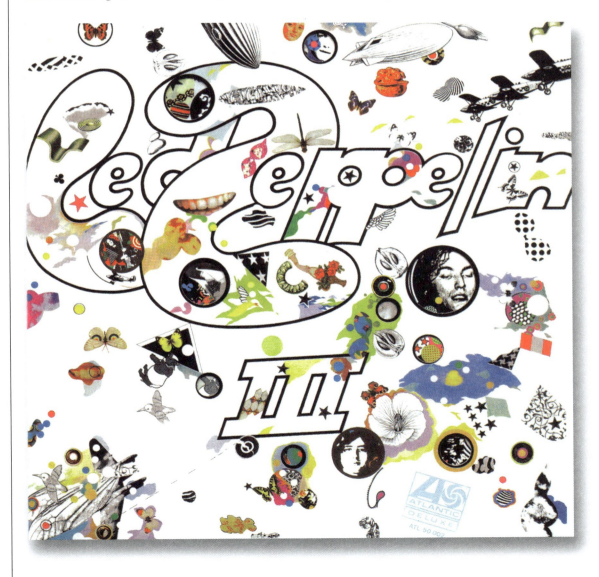

Led Zeppelin's Untitled Fourth Album

NOVEMBER 8, 1971; REMASTERED 1994

In a move that frightened the executives at Atlantic Records, Led Zeppelin's untitled fourth album was released without any written information on the outside packaging and without any title whatsoever. Despite these perceived disadvantages, the album went on to become not only Led Zeppelin's biggest seller but also one of the best-selling albums by any artist, ever.

Right off the bat, the band kicks things off with the chaotic "Black Dog," which has become instantly recognizable. When the band was recording this song at Headley Grange, where the spacious rooms allowed them to experiment with alternative microphone placements, they noticed an old but sexually energized black Labrador retriever that was hanging around the neighborhood—hence the title.

"Rock and Roll" was the result of an in-studio jam with guest pianist Ian Stewart of Rolling Stones fame. John Bonham's drum introduction closely resembles that of Little Richard's 1957 cover of "Keep A-Knockin'." By the time Little Richard covered the song, it was already thirty years old, which may be one of the reasons that this similarity would not warrant any legal action from its songwriter or songwriters, whose identities are disputed anyway.

Another guest was brought on for "The Battle of Evermore"—singer Sandy Denny, who was beloved in England for her work with folk-rock band Fairport Convention before she formed her own group, called Fotheringay. Her call-and-response delivery is the perfect complement to Plant's voice.

The first side of the LP closes with "Stairway to Heaven," which was rock radio's most requested track for decades running—and with good reason. This fourth song on the fourth album by the four guys offers everything the ultimate Led Zeppelin track should offer:

namely, the formula of light and shade delivered through dynamic shifts in volume, instrumentation, and tempo. The lyrics were ambiguous enough to lend themselves to myriad interpretations "'cause you know sometimes words have two meanings." And Page's electric guitar solo offers its own melody and brilliance.

The biggest surprise to fans is that the opening guitar line resembles "Taurus," a song by the band Spirit, recorded in 1967 and released in 1968. No claim reached court, although "Taurus" songwriter Randy California said in an interview in 1997, shortly before his death, that he would have appreciated either some acknowledgment or compensation, or both, from the members of Led Zeppelin.

"When the Levee Breaks" is another exploration in psychedelic blues, this time with a whirling riff backed by a steady drumbeat. The track credits not only members of Led Zeppelin but also Memphis Minnie, who released a song by the same name in 1929; however, her version was cowritten and recorded with her husband, Kansas Joe McCoy, who is not credited on Led Zeppelin's version. Musically, the two tracks are worlds apart.

More than one single resulted from this album—unprecedented at that point in Led Zeppelin's career. The first was "Black Dog," backed with "Misty Mountain Hop." This single reached No. 15 in the United States. Its follow-up, "Rock and Roll," was released in 1972, with "Four Sticks" on the B side; that single reached No. 47.

Jimmy Page is listed as producer and Peter Grant as executive producer. Andy Johns is credited with engineering and mixing. George Chkiantz is credited with mixing as well. Separate mastering by Joe Sidore resulted in the original CD release. George Marino remastered the album.

Houses of the Holy

MARCH 28, 1973; REMASTERED 1994

According to Atlantic Records executive Phil Carson, although this disc was not the pinnacle of Led Zeppelin's commercial success, it may well have been be the pinnacle of its artistic success. Ingeniously varied, the album opens with "The Song Remains the Same," which is graced with an instrumental overture and instrumental interludes between powerful sets of lyrics and high-pitched vocals. Next is a ballad, "The Rain Song," with high points interspersed around quiet, pastoral passages and lyrics dealing with the seasons. Only an album like *Houses of the Holy* could perfectly juxtapose the jolly feel of "D'yer Mak'er" with the jocular James Brown twist of "The Crunge." Flower power, explored on the previous album's "Misty Mountain Hop," returns on "Dancing

Days." "No Quarter" is a highlight that was held over from the fourth album. This album yielded two singles in the United States. The first was "Over the Hills and Far Away," reaching No. 51. Its B side was "Dancing Days." The follow-up was "D'yer Mak'er," which reached No. 20, with "The Crunge" on the B side.

Jimmy Page is listed as producer and Peter Grant as executive producer. Andy Johns was the engineer and responsible for the mix. The rest of the engineering and mixing credits are split between Eddie Kramer and Keith Harwood. Bob Ludwig is credited with mastering. Separate mastering by Barry Diament resulted in the original CD release. George Marino remastered the album.

Physical Graffiti

FEBRUARY 24, 1975; REMASTERED 1994

Halfway through the decade, with tastes in music shifting, Led Zeppelin continued to deliver albums that mattered. *Physical Graffiti* has twice the amount of material of previous Zeppelin albums; the double album contains numerous tracks that could have been released on earlier albums but weren't, including "Houses of the Holy," which did not appear on its namesake album. If there is a centerpiece to *Physical Graffiti*, it may be "Kashmir," which employed the brass and strings of an orchestra in the studio to fill out the sound. John Paul Jones was responsible for the Eastern-tinged orchestration, and his powers also shone on the long and equally non-Western introduction to "In the Light." Jimmy Page's layered acoustic and electric guitars on "Ten Years Gone" provide a "guitar army" that here represents subtlety while Robert Plant pouts over a relationship lost a decade earlier. The country-tinged "Down by the Seaside" is folk-rock inspired by Neil Young. The solo instrumental "Bron-Yr-Aur" contains some of Page's prettiest acoustic guitar work. "In My Time of Dying" is another one of the band's experimentations in blues-rock. Good old-fashioned straightforward rock tracks like "Sick Again" and "The Rover" are here, too, rounding out the album.

"Custard Pie" is the second song in Led Zeppelin's catalog—after "Hats Off to (Roy) Harper"—to use Bukka White's "Shake 'Em on Down" as a lyrical basis. The song lyrics also quote "Drop Down Mama" by Sleepy John Estes and "I Want Some of Your Pie" by Blind Boy Fuller. None of these songs is credited in Led Zeppelin's version.

"In My Time of Dying" is credited only to the members of Led Zeppelin. The same title had been used in 1945 by guitarist Josh White, who'd also recorded it as "Jesus Gonna Make Up My Dying Bed" in 1933. Blind Willie Johnson is thought to have been the first person to record the song, which he did in 1927 under the title "Jesus Make Up My Dying Bed." Bob Dylan covered the song as a "traditional" tune in 1962, and John Sebastian recorded it under the title "Well, Well, Well" in 1971.

"Boogie with Stu" became the subject of a lawsuit concerning authorship, as it is basically a cover of "Ooh My Head" by Richie Valens. The band credited all four Led Zeppelin members on the song, plus Ian Stewart as guest pianist, with a sixth writing credit going to "Mrs. Valens," Richie's mother. This was a gesture intended to earn the woman some royalties, because she did not ordinarily earn any income from her late son's songs. However, as Jimmy Page revealed in an interview published in 1997, Led Zeppelin's gesture backfired when the publisher of Richie Valens's music sued Zeppelin for not properly crediting Valens himself. The suit reportedly resulted in an out-of-court settlement.

Physical Graffiti yielded only one U.S. single, "Trampled Under Foot," inspired partly by Stevie Wonder and partly by Robert Johnson. Its B side was "Black Country Woman." The single reached No. 38.

Jimmy Page is listed as producer and Peter Grant is executive producer. Because the album draws together new sessions and outtakes from previous albums, several engineers are credited: George Chkiantz, Keith Harwood, Andy Johns, Eddie Kramer, and Ron Nevison. Harwood and Kramer are also credited with mixing. Mastering by Barry Diament resulted in the original CD release. George Marino remastered the album.

Presence

MARCH 31, 1976; REMASTERED 1994

Often cited as Jimmy Page's favorite Led Zeppelin album, *Presence* marked a return to the energy that carried the band through their early days. The songs were written quickly at rehearsals. Robert Plant had escaped death in an automobile accident, but was in pretty bad shape, sitting around in a wheelchair.

The lyrics on *Presence* are some of Plant's most candid, blunt, and barefaced, all the while matching the mood of Page's guitar lines. On "Tea for One," the singer deals with abject boredom and isolation, while Page's brooding guitar solo lingers unconstrained. Plant acidly mocks the lifestyle choices of drug users in "For Your Life," and expresses frustration with his situation in "Hots on for Nowhere"; Page's music appropriately bounces around the lyrics in response. Page and Plant were the perfect foil for each other, and *Presence* shows the extent to which that was true.

When Plant decided to cover the subject of his own mortality in song, he met the challenge by devising lyrics of mythical proportions. In "Achilles Last Stand," the words "mighty arms of Atlas, hold the heavens from the

earth" refer to the Atlas mountain range, which he and Page had visited in Morocco, home to the nomadic Berber tribes, as well as to the Greek deity Atlas, who supported the heavens on his shoulders. The worldliness and humanity of the lyrics are matched by the pulsations of the rhythm section and by a veritable "guitar army" in the person of Jimmy Page. "Achilles Last Stand" ended up becoming one of Led Zeppelin's most popular songs of all time.

Despite these triumphs in the studio, *Presence* is actually one of the least commercially successful entries in Led Zeppelin's discography, judging from the sales figures. But its reputation has improved over the years. It's not only Jimmy Page's favorite album, but it's also the favorite of many a Led Zeppelin fan.

The drawback is that it contains only seven songs total, fewer than on any other Led Zeppelin studio LP. On the plus side, *Presence* is just as long as the other single-disc releases in the group's catalog; its opening and closing numbers hover around ten minutes each.

"Nobody's Fault but Mine" is credited to Jimmy Page and Robert Plant. Lyrically, it is based on a traditional gospel song of the same name recorded by Blind Willie Johnson at some point between 1927 and 1930. Nina Simone released a version of it on her 1969 album *Nina Simone and Piano*, and an earlier version of hers was included as a bonus track on a 1991 reissue of her 1967 album *Nina Simone Sings the Blues*. "Nobody's Fault but Mine" is sometimes listed on her releases as traditional and is sometimes credited to Simone. On Led Zeppelin's version, Page and Plant are the only authors listed.

The single released from this album, "Candy Store Rock," was Led Zeppelin's only U.S. single not to chart. The B side was "Royal Orleans." These two songs, and three others on this album, never made it into Led Zeppelin's live sets in their remaining years. Only "Nobody's Fault but Mine" and "Achilles Last Stand" hold this honor, and they quickly became perennial favorites, so much so that Page and Plant were still playing "Achilles" briefly during their performances in the 1990s, and "Nobody's Fault" was an obvious choice for the two-hour Led Zeppelin reunion concert in 2007.

Jimmy Page is listed as producer of *Presence* and Peter Grant is listed as executive producer. Keith Harwood is credited with engineering and mixing. Mastering by Barry Diament resulted in the original CD release. George Marino remastered the album.

The Song Remains the Same

SEPTEMBER 28, 1976; RERELEASED 2007

Led Zeppelin's movie was unique when it was released because there were so few other films like it at the time. Its reputation may have diminished over the years, but it will always be regarded as a classic. Consider, for example, the onscreen effects during Jimmy Page's solos, especially in the twenty-six-minute version of "Dazed and Confused." *Woodstock* had its trademark split-screen effects. *The Song Remains the Same* had its mirrored images and its revolving camera angles.

The movie also features Peter Grant and Richard Cole as trigger-happy gangsters. There was John Paul Jones reading "Jack and the Beanstalk" to his three daughters and then hesitantly reading a hot-off-the-presses touring itinerary that begins "Tomorrow, tomorrow, tomorrow . . . " Later, he's playing a cathedral's pipe organ and masquerading on horseback away from home. Robert Plant has his own share of iconic scenes: enjoying his time with his wife and children; wielding a sword to defend a fair maiden's honor. There's John Bonham shooting pool and racing vehicles. And finally, there's Jimmy Page cranking away on a hurdy-gurdy on Autumn Lake, and later climbing a snow-capped mountain to meet his older self, who's waving a polychromatic wand the way Page handled his violin bows onstage.

The movie's sound track was underwhelming. The limitations of the LP format in 1976 prevented the double-album sound track from containing all fourteen songs. In fact, six were missing: "Black Dog," "Over the Hills and Far Away," "Misty Mountain Hop," "Since I've Been Loving You," "The Ocean," and "Heartbreaker."

Even as the Led Zeppelin back catalog was being remastered in 1990, the live cuts from this movie and its sound track went untouched. Warner Home Video issued a VHS cassette of the film in the 1980s, and it eventually came to DVD when that format was rolled out, but with no significant upgrades and some lackluster bonus features.

It wasn't until the film's thirty-first anniversary that this situation was remedied. "We have revisited *The Song Remains the Same* and can now offer the complete set as played at Madison Square Garden," Jimmy Page said in a statement issued on July 27, 2007, the same date as the first of the New York '73 shows included on the film.

All fourteen of the concert performances included in the film but not on the original sound track would now be on the revised sound track, and the content of both would match up better than ever before. The sound was intended to be state of the art for 2007, designed to support Dolby Digital 5.1 surround sound, with one deluxe edition in high-definition DVD and another edition in Blu-ray.

Bonus features included complete versions of songs featured only partially in the film's original theatrical

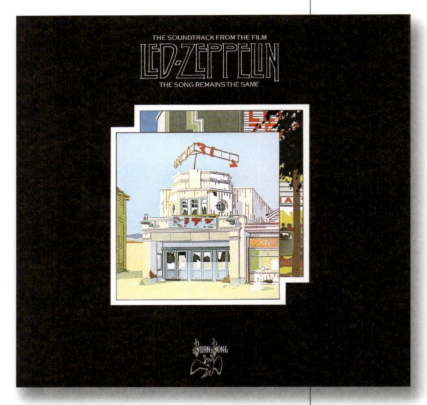

release, as well as clips from television interviews. The package included liner notes by Cameron Crowe. The first run also included a radio show Crowe had hosted in the late 1970s.

Although the film's visuals remained the same between 1976 and 2007, the new edition's sounds were vastly improved. "It would have been a whole can of worms with directors, and legal hassles, and whatnot, if you started editing the movie," sound engineer Kevin Shirley explained at the time, in an interview for *Modern Guitars* magazine conducted in October of 2007. Matching the sixteen-track audio recordings from each of the three Madison Square Garden concerts to fit the visuals was the task at hand for him. "We started from scratch," said Shirley. "Everything was reassembled from the ground up."

The end result: a movie that takes full advantage of the DVD format's sonic capabilities. Said Shirley, "There's the subway train that comes in the middle of the movie right before 'No Quarter'—the train comes from right behind you and through the middle of your head, which is pretty cool, actually. It's a surround experience, no doubt."

Just as on the Led Zeppelin albums, Jimmy Page is listed as the film's producer and Peter Grant is listed as executive producer. Eddie Kramer is credited with engineering and mixing. Separate mastering by Barry Diament resulted in the original CD release. Kevin Shirley is credited with remixing for the 2007 release, and Bob Ludwig is credited with remastering for the 2007 release as well.

IN THE EVENING
SOUTH BOUND SAUREZ
FOOL IN THE RAIN
HOT DOG
CAROUSELAMBRA
ALL MY LOVE
I'M GONNA CRAWL

SWAN SONG INC., 444 MADISON AVENUE, N.Y., N.Y. 10022. DISTRIBUTED BY ATLANTIC RECORDING CORP. 75 ROCKEFELLER PLAZA, N.Y. N.Y. 10019 ℗ © 1979 ATLANTIC RECORDING CORP. PRINTED IN JAPAN. WARNING: UNAUTHORIZED REPRODUCTION OF THIS RECORDING IS PROHIBITED BY FEDERAL LAW AND SUBJECT TO CRIMINAL PROSECUTION.

AMCY-2441

In Through the Out Door

Agust 15, 1979; remastered 1994

In Through the Out Door features an ambitious opening track for any album, but this isn't just any album. It's the album that was Led Zeppelin's first new effort since 1976. "In the Evening" comes on full-blast, but only after a 56-second intro consisting of Jimmy Page's guitar played with a violin bow over a drone in Led Zeppelin's favorite key, E. John Bonham's timpani rumbles confidently. Robert Plant croons dramatically. Then, at the magic moment, the full band comes in—and they're on. Jimmy Page's guitar solo is like none ever recorded before it. Hear how he smacks the side of his guitar! Hear how John Paul Jones layers synthesizers and how Page adds a separate guitar track to support himself for the last set of bars. This complex music lasts just under seven minutes.

Harking back to the fourth album, which bears no title, no band name, and no written information on the outer wrapper, *In Through the Our Door* was the subject of another of the group's outlandish packaging demands: they wanted to sell the record in a paper sack! Indeed, they got their wish: a brown paper bag with a label on it would house the LP on store shelves.

Because music critics had taken to trashing Led Zeppelin so heavily by 1979, the band took the metaphor to a literal level, hiding their so-called trash inside a paper bag with an arrogant self-assurance that the product would sell regardless: *Oh, yeah? Well, if our record is trash, then we'll sell it in a brown paper bag and see who all buys it!* And it sold.

The unconventional brown paper bag wasn't the only anomaly about the packaging of *In Through the Out Door*. Technically, it didn't have just one cover image, but twelve separate cover images, two per each variation.

You couldn't see which variation you were going to purchase because of the outer bag, and you wouldn't even know that there were five other variations unless you heard about them by word of mouth.

Also, there was a watercolor section inside. It went completely unannounced at the time, but if you touched that section with a wet paintbrush, or accidentally spilled some water on the side of the paper record sleeve that had the black-and-white artwork on it, color would appear. A special type of invisible ink was used to produce this effect.

In any event, *In Through the Out Door* was collectible because of the packaging as well as because of the music. Some people felt the need to own all six variations, so they kept on buying new copies until they'd obtained them all! This definitely didn't hurt sales.

Unfortunately—possibly owing to the many challenges of packaging the album—*In Through the Out Door* came out later than originally scheduled. At first, the album's release was to coincide with the band's twin appearances at the Knebworth Festival in August of 1979, where the band was supposed to perform a nonalbum track, "Wearing and Tearing." This didn't happen, but Jimmy Page and Robert Plant tried to make up for that by performing the song in its entirety at the same setting more than a decade later, on June 30, 1990.

The Led Zeppelin single that did come out in 1979—in the States, not the UK—was the jazz- and Latin-inspired "Fool in the Rain," backed with the country-fried "Hot Dog." The A side, for which John Bonham and John Paul Jones transformed themselves into a Latin rhythm section in the middle interlude, reached No. 21. The track was also notable for Bonham's take on the "Purdie Shuffle" (named for the strict musical timekeeping of American session drummer Bernard "Pretty" Purdie) and Page's strict adherence to the C major scale during his modal electric guitar solo. Jones also found himself to be an expert whistle player!

For all its cheekiness, "Hot Dog" had an awful lot of nice rollicking piano, courtesy of Jones, particularly in the opening sixteen bars. Page might have envisioned something out of the Scotty Moore or James Burton catalog when he prepared to lay down his solo. Plant may have even been thinking of delivering his vocal in the

style of the singer who was accompanied by both Moore and Burton: Elvis Presley. They definitely went for an American vibe on this track, even if it was, in reality, about as authentically American as, say, the Rolling Stones' "Far Away Eyes."

"Carouselambra" is a multifaceted song, sharing some structural attributes with "Kashmir." Apart from the lyrics, Plant sings the syllable "Oh" or "Ah" over certain lines and lets the instrumentation take center stage. For some of the time, the instrumentation is a relentless rock rhythm with loud drums, guitars, and synthesizers. At a dramatic point in the song, the music drops to a half-time laze, followed by a heavily keyboard-laden section. This is arguably the most complicated song structure in the Led Zeppelin catalog. And it outlasted "In My Time of Dying" (until then the longest Zeppelin track) by a good twenty seconds, to fade out around the ten-and-a-half-minute mark.

"I'm Gonna Crawl," the album closer, features a lush intro from John Paul Jones on the synth strings, then a slow 6/8 ballad beat from John Bonham, and tasteful tremolo guitar touches throughout each bar. The tension builds up several times during the song and is resolved temporarily between the first and second verses. After this, the pinnacle of the track is Page's anguished solo.

Once the solo is over, this roller-coaster ride of a song continues upward, with Plant leading the charge. He even elicits a mournful screech that is among the very highest upper-range notes the singer had ever belted out on an LP. And it's all within the last minute of the last Led Zeppelin song released in the 1970s! Who ever said he'd lost it?

What he had lost was his son, and "All My Love" speaks to the new birth in his family, that of another son. Unfortunately for Plant and the others in Led Zeppelin, they were about to lose somebody else very important to them. John Bonham's death on September 25, 1980, would prove to be the end of Led Zeppelin, making *In Through the Out Door* their permanent swan song.

As with all Led Zeppelin releases, Jimmy Page is listed as producer and Peter Grant as executive producer. Leif Mases is credited as an engineer, with Lennart Östlund credited as an assistant engineer. Mastering by Barry Diament resulted in the original CD release. George Marino remastered the album.

Coda

NOVEMBER 19, 1982; REMASTERED 1994

When John Bonham died and Led Zeppelin ceased to exist, their unreleased recordings lived on; recordings that had been put on hold but hadn't yet been heard. *Coda* was a clearing of the vaults, so to speak. It was Jimmy Page cleaning out the Zeppelin closet and putting out a complete collection of finished products from different eras and of varying quality.

There was "Bonzo's Montreux," an experiment in which Page was placed in charge of adding electronic effects to Bonham's drum and percussion solo. It was released in tribute to Page's departed friend and bandmate. For only the second time in Led Zeppelin's recorded history, the track presented Bonham as the sole point of focus.

Although no singles were released from *Coda*, three songs from the album appeared on *Billboard*'s listing of Top Tracks (today called Mainstream Rock Tracks). Of these, the most successful was "Darlene," which reached No. 4. It was very much a '50s-style doo-wop track with standout piano from John Paul Jones, recorded during the keys-heavy era of the *In Through the Out Door* sessions.

"Ozone Baby" was also from 1978, charting at No. 14. "Poor Tom" reached back even farther, to 1970, when Led Zeppelin was experimenting with acoustic music. It features the energetic chug of a Robert Plant harmonica solo and a military-style backbeat from John Bonham.

On this album, "I Can't Quit You Baby" receives another airing, this time in the form of a live version from the London stage, performed on Jimmy Page's twenty-fifth birthday. His guitar solo is temporarily muted at one point before catering to our inner demons, serving as a prime example of the dynamic shifts of which Led Zeppelin was capable.

The unlikely closer is "Wearing and Tearing," a Page and Plant original they had intended to release in 1979 as Led Zeppelin's first-ever single in England. It would have been a knockout of a choice, again redefining their sound at a time when many in the UK had suggested that Led Zeppelin's relevance had dwindled and that they had taken a backseat to punk music. "Wearing and Tearing" was Led Zeppelin's response to punk. They didn't despise punk; they actually fed off its energy. Just as "Train Kept A-Rollin'" had informed the original songs "Good Times Bad Times" and "Communication Breakdown" in 1968, punk informed the original "Wearing and Tearing" ten years later. It's an astounding track.

Jimmy Page is listed as producer and Peter Grant is listed as executive producer. Stuart Epps, Vic Maile, and John Timperley are credited as engineers for the first time on any Led Zeppelin album. Because the collection includes outtakes from previous albums, other engineers are credited: Andy Johns, Eddie Kramer, and Leif Mases. Mastering by Barry Diament resulted in the original CD release. George Marino remastered the album.

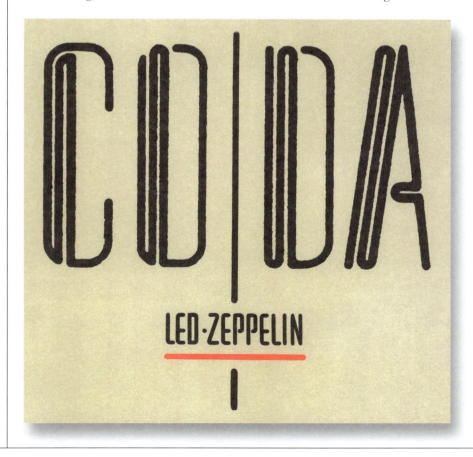

Led Zeppelin

SEPTEMBER 7, 1990

The main purpose of this box set was ostensibly to improve the sound quality of the Led Zeppelin back catalog for the CD format. As the original Led Zeppelin studio albums were put on compact disc in the late 1980s, little care went into capturing the sound from the original masters. Jimmy Page was chief among those complaining about the sound, so as the producer sought to remedy the situation by bringing George Marino on for a remastering project.

As it turned out, two-thirds of Led Zeppelin's studio output easily fit onto four compact discs. Each of the four discs loosely concentrated on a general time period in the group's studio output, although strict adherence to that rule was abandoned in favor of a flow between songs. Jimmy Page said the running order presented the old picture in a new frame—the second goal of the box set—and was something fans would come to appreciate.

As examples of this secondary goal, no longer did "Heartbreaker" segue directly into "Living Loving Maid (She's Just a Woman)"; instead, it kept the rock beat alive with "Communication Breakdown." The *Led Zeppelin III* pairing of the inseparable "Friends" and "Celebration Day" remained in place, but now the songs fell in between a pair of previously unreleased rarities: Led Zeppelin's one-off 1969 BBC recording of "Travelling Riverside Blues" (their first new single in more than a decade) and the 1970 B side "Hey Hey What Can I Do."

The U.S. CD single of "Travelling Riverside Blues" reached No. 7 on *Billboard*'s Album Rock Tracks chart. The remastered version of "Over the Hills and Far Away" was also released as a CD single.

The discs representing the chronological second half of Led Zeppelin's career packed several punches, in a few instances featuring four or more consecutive songs from different albums. Disc 3 sees "When the Levee Breaks" from the fourth album leading into "Achilles Last Stand" from five years later, on *Presence*, then into "The Song Remains the Same" from *Houses of the Holy*, and finally to a pair of *Physical Graffiti* tracks in "Ten Years Gone" and "In My Time of Dying."

Disc 4 includes another representative assortment of songs from various sources. "In the Evening" kicks things off, just as it did on *In Through the Out Door*, but it eases into the underappreciated *Presence* single "Candy Store Rock." Next up is "The Ocean" from *Houses of the Holy*, followed by "Ozone Baby" from *Coda*, which gives way to "Houses of the Holy."

This is followed up with another one-two-three-four punch: the *Coda* duo of "Wearing and Tearing" and "Poor Tom" (actually recorded eight years apart from each other), followed by "Nobody's Fault but Mine" from *Presence*, "Fool in the Rain" from *In Through the*

Out Door, and a back-to-back *Physical Graffiti* contribution of "In the Light" and "The Wanton Song."

Before the pair of synth-driven *In Through the Out Door* songs, "I'm Gonna Crawl" and "All My Love"—which complete the disc in reverse order from the original—one final new cut appears: a studio combination of both John Bonham tribute tracks. Appropriately, "Moby Dick/Bonzo's Montreux" was released within weeks of the tenth anniversary of Bonham's death.

Another strong point of this repackaging was that the selected tracks were drawn not only from the original nine studio albums but also from *Coda*. The image of a mesmerizing and mysterious crop circle was emblazoned on the LP-size cover, and the set's liner notes incorporated a history of the band, including the accounts of journalists who supported the group throughout its career. All in all, the four-CD *Led Zeppelin* set was for many reasons the most vital assortment of the group's studio work released up until that point.

As with every Led Zeppelin release, Jimmy Page is listed as producer and Peter Grant is listed as executive producer. George Marino is credited with the remastering. In addition to the engineers whose names appeared as they had on the original releases, the set also credits Bruce Buchanan, John Mahoney, and Tony Wilson. Yves Beauvais and Jeff Griffin are listed as producers.

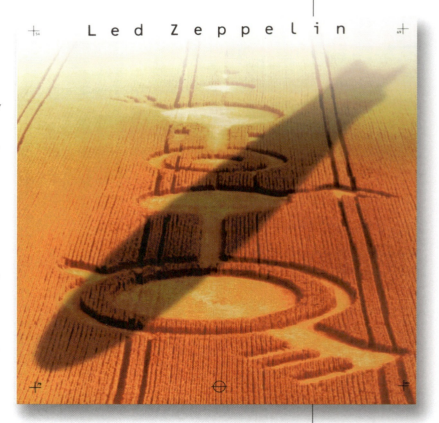

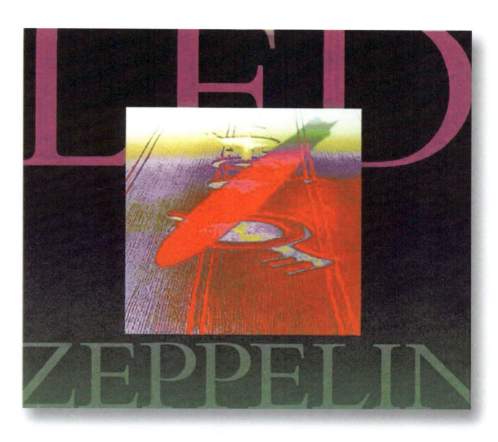

Boxed Set 2

SEPTEMBER 21, 1993

This supplement to the 1990 Led Zeppelin box set was released in 1993 under the name *Boxed Set 2*. Encased in a small package, and featuring art based on the same crop-circles concept, it contained only those studio tracks that were excluded from the four-CD set. Some people have said that this tiny, two-CD collection showcases "the rest of the best."

This set yielded one U.S. single: "Baby Come On Home." It was the only track that was unique to this box set. Previously unreleased, and apparently forgotten, the song was an outtake from the first album sessions in 1968. Like few other Led Zeppelin tracks, "Baby Come On Home" employed four-part harmony from the band as well as John Paul Jones on gospel organ. Jimmy Page used a tremolo-heavy electric guitar effect while Robert Plant reached for the soul sound in his vocals, a sound that could be heard on mid-1960s sides produced by Bert Berns, who receives partial writing credit on the song. The whole time, John Bonham reinvents rock drumming in a 6/8 meter. Twenty-five years after the song was recorded, the CD single reached No. 4 on *Billboard*'s Album Rock Tracks chart, tying the peak chart position previously achieved by the band's "Darlene" in 1982.

As with all Led Zeppelin releases, Jimmy Page is listed as producer and Peter Grant is listed as executive producer. George Marino is credited with the remastering. As with the *Led Zeppelin* box set, Bruce Buchanan, John Mahoney, and Tony Wilson are credited, along with the original albums' engineers. Yves Beauvais and Jeff Griffin are listed as producers.

On a side note, the definitive collection of the group's studio work exists as *Complete Studio Recordings*, an exhaustive ten-CD box set also issued in 1993. It contained all nine studio albums, plus *Coda*, in their entirety, with their original running orders intact. The set's *Coda* disc, which would have otherwise contained the shortest running time of all, was also expanded to include the few tracks that had been previously unavailable on CD prior to the box sets. Even with its high price tag, *Complete Studio Recordings* was a critical grab for many ardent Led Zeppelin fans.

The year after *Boxed Set 2* and *Complete Studio Recordings* were released, the individual studio albums of Led Zeppelin's back catalog were reissued in their remastered form for the first time.

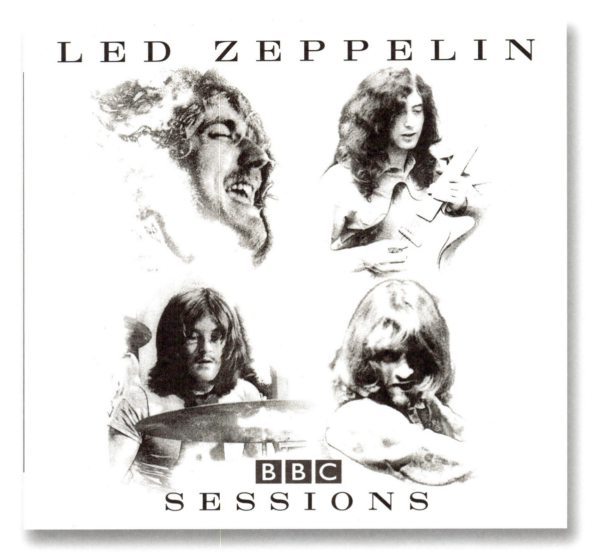

BBC Sessions

NOVEMBER 11, 1997

Throughout the 1990s, many of the popular bands that had recorded special sessions for the British Broadcasting Corporation so that they could receive airplay in England (per legal requirements for "needle time" with the musicians' union) began seeking out the BBC's master tapes and asking permission to release them as albums. It became a trend for bands to use these special takes as a retrospective. In Led Zeppelin's case, studio takes from 1969 and live takes from 1969 and 1971 were candidates for release. Producer Jimmy Page sifted through the master tapes, made edits wherever he deemed them necessary, and prepared the set for release.

As always, Jimmy Page is listed as producer and Peter Grant is listed—posthumously, in this case—as executive producer. Numerous engineers and producers are credited on this album, which is a compilation of sessions with various personnel. The main participants, organized by session date, are: *Top Gear* session, recorded March 3, 1969—Bernie Andrews, producer/Pete Ritzema, engineer/Bob Conduct, tape operator/John Peel, host; *Rhythm and Blues* session, recorded March 19, 1969—Jeff Griffin, producer/Alexis Korner, host; *Tasty Pop Sundae* session, recorded June 16, 1969—Paul Williams, producer/Chris Grant, host; *Top Gear* session, recorded June 24, 1969—John Walters, producer/Tony Wilson, engineer; *In Concert* session, recorded April 1, 1971—Jeff Griffin, producer/Tony Wilson, engineer/John Peel, host.

The album yielded one U.S. CD single: "The Girl I Love (She Got Long Black Wavy Hair)," released with "Whole Lotta Love (Medley)" as the disc's second track. It reached No. 4 on *Billboard*'s Mainstream Rock Tracks chart.

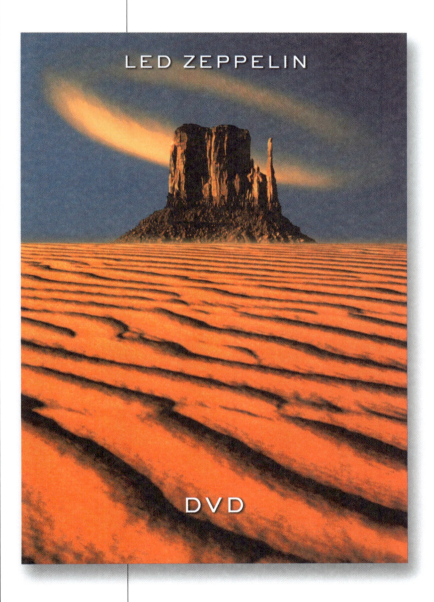

Led Zeppelin DVD

MAY 27, 2003

Beginning in 1977, Jimmy Page often hinted that someday he'd like to compile a chronological set of Led Zeppelin's live output. This is that set, in video form—probably something Page had not envisioned a quarter of a century earlier, when the project was only a gleam in his eye. This is the definitive official release, highlighting the best of Led Zeppelin's in-concert output available on video. Because the band rarely authorized video to be taken of their performances, there is little footage at all to be had, which makes the five or so hours' worth of material on this two-disc set of DVDs so special. No wonder this went on to become one of the biggest-selling music DVDs of all time!

The chronology includes some of the earliest filmed moments of 1969, from lip-synching "Communication Breakdown" for a promotional video shot in black-and-white to performing in front of a circle of contented Danish kids sitting cross-legged on the floor around them to performing in a large hall for a bunch of stoic Parisian marching band members and one fidgety bellhop. Also from the early years is footage from the Royal Albert Hall show in 1970, including "Whole Lotta Love" and "Dazed and Confused."

Some footage from the 1973 Madison Square Garden concerts was included, as well as six songs from the 1975 performances at Earls Court. Fan-shot footage from the Forum show in L.A. in 1977 helped fill a gap in official Led Zeppelin recordings. The triumphant 1979 Knebworth concerts conclude the entertainment package, which also assembles, as bonus features, most of the promotional music videos the band released, plus a few interviews. The set truly stands as an exhaustive collection of entertaining and historic features presented chronologically.

Jimmy Page is listed as producer and Peter Grant is listed, posthumously, as executive producer. Dick Carruthers is credited as both producer and creative director. Kevin Shirley is credited with sound engineering.

How the West Was Won

MAY 27, 2003

Released the same day as *Led Zeppelin DVD*, this three-CD set reaches back to California in the year 1972. It presents roughly a complete Led Zeppelin concert, assembling the best bits from a pair of shows on that year's tour. Heard here are inserts of then-unreleased studio jams like "The Crunge" and "Walter's Walk," both played during a marathon version of "Dazed and Confused." There's an acoustic set with "Bron-Y-Aur Stomp," which offers a change of pace from all the loud electric firepower. There's a drum solo in "Moby Dick" that reminds listeners why John Bonham was the right man for the job. Fortunately, we do get an early preview of "Dancing Days," but the timing of this 1972 concert ensures we won't yet hear tracks like "Kashmir" or "Achilles Last Stand," which are essentials on the second disc of the DVD set. This CD set, because it does feature early-to mid-career gems such as "Immigrant Song," "What Is and What Should Never Be," "That's the Way," "The Ocean," and "Stairway to Heaven," makes up for the songs that couldn't yet be part of the compilation.

Jimmy Page is listed as producer and Peter Grant is listed, posthumously, as executive producer. Eddie Kramer is credited with engineering. Kevin Shirley was credited with additional engineering and mixing. Drew Griffiths was credited as a sound assistant.

Mothership

NOVEMBER 12, 2007

Prior to *Mothership*'s release, a promotional statement described the new Led Zeppelin set as "a 24-track, two-CD comprehensive collection that spans their illustrious career." Its songs drew mainly from the same pool as the earlier four-CD set, with the notable exception that the two-CD 1990 box set *Remasters* altogether ignored Zep's 1982 release, *Coda*. The set also boasted new liner notes from rock music journalist David Fricke and modernized iconic images in the cover art from the avant-garde artist Shepard Fairey.

At the time of this collection's release, Led Zeppelin made their albums and individual tracks available for download for the first time. Consequently, four digital tracks charted in the U.S., and five charted in the UK. In both regions, the one to chart the highest was "Stairway to Heaven"; it reached No. 30 in the U.S. and No. 37 in the UK. It was also the most successful digital download of Led Zeppelin's in Canada, where a total of seven tracks charted.

"The [original] box set was [about] fifteen years ago," Page said in a radio appearance promoting *Mothership*. Referring to Led Zeppelin's "Best of" compilations, released in 1999 and 2000, he continued, "Along the way, we had a piece of product that was going to be in two sections—one called *Early Days* and [one called] *Latter Days*. And then of course in true sort of marketing spirit, they were sort of shunted together as *Early Days & Latter Days*, two CDs, now. And personally, I felt that there was quite a deterioration with the quality—not the music, of course, but with the quality of the packaging; I just thought that it felt worse and worse and worse. When you compared it to any of the other Led Zeppelin product, it just didn't have that stamp of authority about it, you know?"

Page continued: "There'd been a sort of proposal on the cards for ages about putting one out. . . . A collection, we'll call it. You could also call it a sampler because it's an access route through to the albums. . . . The biggest question is how do you actually choose the numbers for, you know, a 'Best of'? It's impossible, and that's the answer." John Paul Jones agreed, "It's really difficult."

In the end, the tracks they selected were not very different at all from the two previous two-CD collections.

As with all Led Zeppelin releases, Jimmy Page is listed as producer and Peter Grant is listed, posthumously in this case, as executive producer. In addition to the original engineers and producers, John C. F. Davis is credited with the remastering.

Live at the O₂

RECORDED IN 2007; UNRELEASED

At its famous one-time reunion, the band performed sixteen songs—including two encores—covering its entire career (except for *In Through the Out Door*). The set list includes "Good Times Bad Times," "Ramble On," "Black Dog," "In My Time of Dying"/"Honey Bee," "For Your Life," "Trampled Under Foot," "Nobody's Fault but Mine," "No Quarter," "Since I've Been Loving You," "Dazed and Confused," "Stairway to Heaven," "The Song Remains the Same," "Misty Mountain Hop," and "Kashmir."

The first encore included "Whole Lotta Love" and the second featured "Rock and Roll."

"Big" Mick Hughes (Metallica's live audio engineer) mixed the sound; the entire concert was filmed for a possible DVD release. In a March 2008 interview, Page said, "It was recorded, but we didn't go in with the express purpose of making a DVD to come out at Christmas, or whatever. We haven't seen the images or investigated the multitracks. It's feasible that it might come out at some distant point, but it'll be a massive job to embark on."

In January of 2010, when asked whether a DVD of the O₂ reunion gig was expected, Page responded: "Not in the foreseeable future. I can't give you an answer on that."

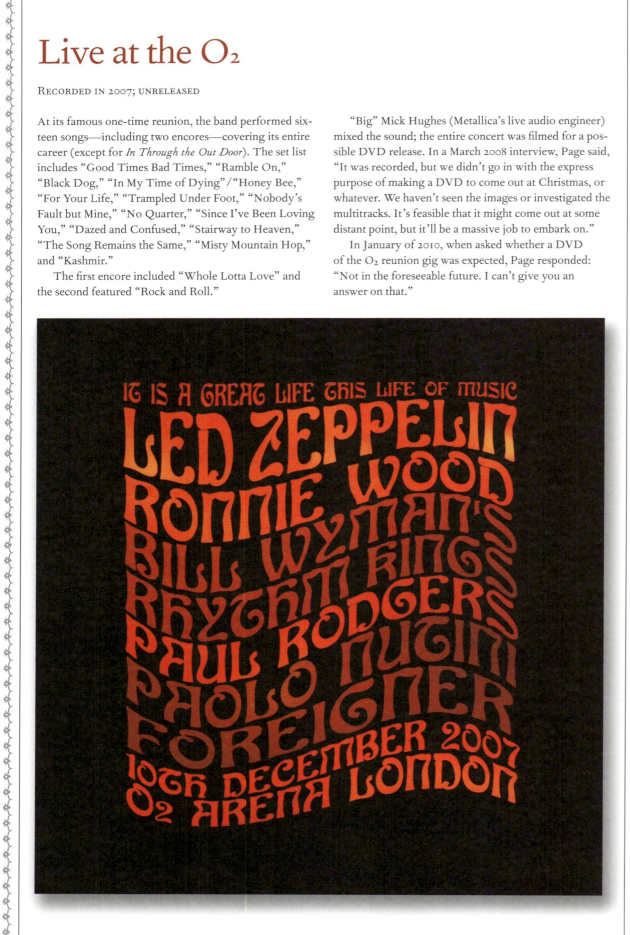

❦ *ACKNOWLEDGMENTS* ❦

THIS BOOK IS THE COMBINED WORK of many and I would like to thank them for their help.

First of all, thanks to Steve "the Lemon" Sauer, who has to be one of the leading fans and authorities on Led Zeppelin. No one is more knowledgeable on the topic. His enthusiasm and determination have been amazing.

Thanks to Louis Greenstein, who helped make sense of it all so you can hold this book in your hands and enjoy it.

Thanks to Joe Cristiano, the line producer for the radio show, whose great ears and fingers make the show magic each week.

Brian Knapp gets a very special thanks for supplying much of the memorabilia displayed in the book. Brian has one of the largest collections of Zeppelin-related items known to man as well as the real stories to go with it. Special thanks to Ioannis for his art, input, and friendship. You helped get the ball rolling and I am very grateful to you.

I also want to mention Eric Wellman of WAXQ, who green-lighted the original pilot. Thanks also to the many staff members at Q104.3 past and present who have been very helpful along the way, including Jim Kerr and his staff, Jonathan Clarke, and Bob Buchmann.

At United Stations Radio Networks, thanks go to Andy Denemark, Charlie Colombo, James M. Higgins, and the big boss, Nick Verbitsky. A special tip of the hat goes to Julian Woolsey for his expertise and tireless help.

Extra large thanks to my editor, Barbara Berger at Sterling Publishing, whose enthusiasm for the project was amazing and also got the attention of the vice president and editorial director, Michael Fragnito. She is a big fan and one of the most creative people I have ever worked with. Special thanks also to packager Barbara Clark, designer Russell Hassell, Sterling cover art director Elizabeth Mihaltse, and cover art designer *The*BookDesigners.

Thanks for help with transcriptions are due to Emily Somach, Kari Barlow Miller, and Cyndy Drue.

I also want to thank Tim Sabean, Jon Hein, and Gary Dell'Abate at Sirius for bringing my Zeppelin expertise to the attention of Howard Stern. My appearance on his show helped fuel the *Get the Led Out* radio show. Thanks to Larry Kane for his encouragement and Richard Somach for the legal help.

My sincere thanks go out to the numerous guests of the radio show, many of whom are quoted in this book.

Most of all, I want to thank Carol Miller, who "gets the Led out" better than anyone and has been doing so for more than thirty years. Carol makes this whole thing work every week and has allowed me to share her love of Zeppelin with the rest of the world.

Finally, I want to thank the most important people in my life—Theodore, Emily, and Reilly Somach. They are all twenty-first-century Zep fans.

❀ INDEX ❀

Note: Page numbers in *italics* include picture captions. Page numbers in **bold** indicate featured interviews and accompanying pictures. LZ refers to Led Zeppelin.

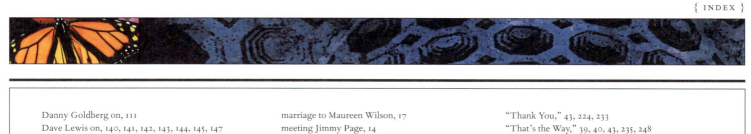

PICTURE CREDITS

Every effort has been made to secure permission and provide appropriate credit for photographic maerial. Any omissions are deeply regretted. All omissions called to the author's attention will be rectified in subsequent editions.

© *Ioannis/Zografou Media LLC:* Page borders throughout, 1, 2, 3, 10, 11, 25, 41, 49, 56, 58, 63, 69, 72, 76, 83, 92, 93, 117, 123, 161, 177, 197, 202, 203, 205, 209, 211, 212, 215, 219, 223, 225, 227, 228, 229, 230

Courtesy Brian Knapp Archives (photography by Laurence L. Levin): 4, 5, 7, 17, 20, 21, 22, 23, 28, 29, 30, 31 (top), 32, 33, 35, 39, 40, 42, 43, 45, 46, 48, 52, 53, 54, 55, 59, 62, 64–65, 66, 68, 70, 84, 85, 86, 87, 89, 90–91, 99, 105, 109, 111, 120, 125, 131, 132, 136, 140, 146, 160, 164, 169, 171, 250

Courtesy Carol Miller: 6

Courtesy Denny Somach: 31 (bottom), 113, 126

Getty Images
Getty Images: 14–15, 81, 157, 173, 198–99
Getty Images (Michael Ochs Archives): 36, 50–51, 71, 191
Redferns: 8–9, 12, 13, 18–19, 26–27, 38, 60–61, 74–75, 78–79, 94, 182
WireImage: 107, 153, 162, 181, 186, 189, 217

Newscom
Neal Preston/Dreamworks/ZUMA Press/Newscom: 156
Daniel Gluskoter/Icon SMI 464/Daniel Gluskoter/ICON SMI/ Newscom: 207
Mike Gray/LFI/Photoshot/Newscom: 221

Rex USA: Brian Rasic/Rex/Rex USA: 201

Shutterstock vector illustrations
© Shutterstock/Eric Lifton: 6, 37, 77, 96, 116, 134–35, 172, 184–85, 187, 200, 226, 242; © Shutterstock/Vector Ninja: 85, 142–43, 234; © Shutterstock/Ondreybo: 88, 101, 147, 192

Wikimedia Commons/U.S. Navy: Hindenberg, 154–55

Other: Mick Wall: 118; Dave Lewis: 138; Ron Nevison: 148; *Courtesy Global Plus/photo by Marek Hofman:* 167; *Courtesy Doreen D'Agostino Media:* 178; *Courtesy Peters Management Syndicate, Inc./photo by Norman Seeff:* 194–95

Courtesy Rhino Records: 231, 235, 236, 237, 238, 239, 240, 241, 243, 244, 245, 246, 248, 249

Warner Music Group: 247